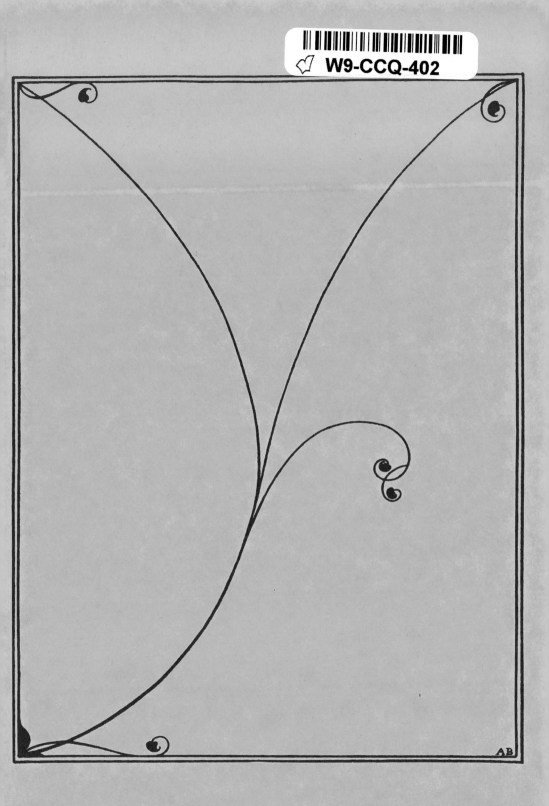

Aubrey Beardsley

Aubrey Beardsley

A BIOGRAPHY

MATTHEW STURGIS

THE OVERLOOK PRESS
WOODSTOCK • NEW YORK

To Rebecca

First published in the United States in 1999 by
The Overlook Press, Peter Mayer Publishers, Inc.
Lewis Hollow Road
Woodstock, New York 12498

Library of Congress Catalog-in-Publication Data

Sturgis, Matthew
  Aubrey Beardsley : a biography / Matthew Sturgis
    p. cm.
  Includes bibliographical references and index.
  1. Beardsley, Aubrey 1872-1898.   2. Artists--England--Biography.
  3. Erotic drawing--England.   I. Beardsley, Aubrey, 1872-1898
  II. Title.
  NC242.B3S78   1999
  760'.092--dc21   98-48817
  [B]

Manufactured in The United States of America

Originally published in the United Kingdom by HarperCollins Publishers

ISBN: 0-87951-910-X

9 8 7 6 5 4 3 2 1

Contents

ILLUSTRATIONS		vii
ACKNOWLEDGEMENTS		ix
INTRODUCTION		I
I	'A Delicate Child'	3
II	'A Good School Time'	25
III	'An Art Training'	53
IV	'A New Style'	91
V	'Oof and Fame'	125
VI	'The Beardsley Boom'	169
VII	'A Declaration of War'	233
VIII	'The Hardworking Solitaire'	273
IX	'An Invalid's Delay'	313
X	'The Death of Pierrot'	341
	EPILOGUE	353
	BIBLIOGRAPHICAL NOTE	363
	NOTES	367
	INDEX	389

Illustrations

Beardsley's birthplace: 12 Buckingham Road, Brighton.

Beardsley's maternal grandfather, Surgeon-Major William Pitt. (*Reading University Library*)

Surgeon-Major Pitt's wife, Susan (née Lamb). (*Reading University Library*)

Vincent Beardsley, Aubrey's father. (*Reading University Library*)

Ellen Pitt at the time of her marriage to Vincent Beardsley. (*Reading University Library*)

Aubrey and Mabel as children.

Aubrey aged seven, with his toy engine.

An embroidered bookmark made by Aubrey for his father. (*Princeton University Library*)

A decorated menu-holder made by Beardsley at the age of ten. (*Princeton University Library*)

21 Lower Rock Gardens, Brighton, where Aubrey and Mabel lived with Beardsley's great-aunt Sarah Pitt in 1884.

Father Alfred Gurney, Vicar of St Barnabas.

Frederick Evans. (*Courtesy of The Royal Photographic Society, Bath*)

Beardsley's self-caricature. (*Pinceton University Library*)

Beardsley's sketch-portrait of Edward Burne-Jones. (*Princeton University Library*)

Robbie Ross and Reggie Turner.

Beardsley's 'Annovale della Morte di Beatrice'.

'Hamlet Patris Manem Sequitur'. (*Photograph © The British Museum*)

114 Cambridge Street, Pimlico.

Gleeson White, first editor of *The Studio*. (*Courtesy of the National Portrait Gallery, London*)

Max Beerbohm's 'Some Persons of "The Nineties"'. (*Courtesy of Mrs Reichmann. Photograph © Ashmolean Museum, Oxford*)

Beardsley's portrait of Mrs Patrick Campbell.

Ada Leverson. (*Courtesy of Francis Wyndham*)

Brandon Thomas. (*Courtesy of Donald Dearnley*)

Edmund Gosse. (*Courtesy of Mary Evans Picture Library*)

Oscar Wilde and Lord Alfred Douglas. (*Photograph © Hulton Getty*)

John Lane. (*Reading University Library*)

Mabel Beardsley as Mrs Maydew in *The Queen's Proctor*. (*From the Enthoven Collection. Photograph © The Board of Trustees of the Victoria and Albert Museum*)

Beardsley photographed by Frederick Hollyer. (*Photograph © Hulton Getty*)

Leonard Smithers with C.A.E. Ranger-Gull and Hannaford Bennett.

Marc André Raffalovich: portrait by Sydney Starr.

John Gray.

A Beardsley sketch in the MS of *The Story of Venus and Tannhauser*. (*Rosenbach Museum and Library, Philadelphia*)

H.C. (Jerome) Pollitt as 'Diane de Rougy'.

Bournemouth in the late 1890s. (*Photograph © Hulton Getty*)

Father David Bearne, S.J. (*From* Letters and Notices, *Vol. XXXV. Courtesy of The British Province of the Society of Jesus*)

Menton, on the French Riviera. (*Photograph © Hulton Getty*)

The last photograph of Beardsley, in his room at the Hotel Cosmopolitan in Menton. (*Courtesy of the National Portrait Gallery, London*)

Acknowledgements

I OWE A GREAT DEBT to the staffs of many libraries and institutions in both the United States and the UK for their courtesy and assistance. Among the collections I consulted were: the three great gatherings of Beardsley's drawings, at the Victoria and Albert Museum, London, The Fogg Art Gallery, Harvard, and the University Library, Princeton; the A. E. Gallatin, Harlin O'Connell and R. A. Walker manuscript collections, also at Princeton; the Houghton Library, Harvard; Boston Public Library, the Athenaeum, Boston; the Rosenbach Museum and Library, Philadelphia; Library of Congress, Washington DC; Columbia University Library, New York; Arizona State University; British Library; India Office Library; Guildhall Library; Public Record Office; Somerset House; St Catherine's House; the V&A Library; Islington Public Library; the Witt Library (Courtauld Institute); the Eighteen Nineties Society; the Bodleian Library, Oxford; Cambridge University Library; Scottish National Record Office; National Library of Scotland; Blackfriars, Edinburgh; Glasgow University Library; Reading University Library; Sussex County Record Office; Brighton, Hove and Bournemouth Public Libraries.

I would like to thank Mrs Eva Reichmann for permission to quote from the works of Max Beerbohm; Merlin Holland and the Oxford University Press for permission to quote from the letters of Oscar Wilde; Brian Reade M. A. (Oxon.) for permission to quote from the works of Arthur Symons; and the Houghton Library, Harvard University for permission to quote from their William Rothenstein archive.

David White has been an invaluable guide to the exciting mysteries of genealogical research, and my account of Beardsley's family would lack much of its detail but for his skilful and diligent aid. Linda

ix

Zatlin, who is working on a Catalogue Raisonné of Beardsley's work, has generously shared her knowledge and enthusiasm.

During the course of my researches I have received much other useful assistance, and want to record specific acts of kindness from: Fr Bede Bailey; Jodie Barratt; William and Susan Bealby-Wright; Robert Booth; Stephen Calloway; Sheila Colman; Donald Dearnley; Ted and Kitty Dreyer; Rodney Engen; Clive Fisher; Josephine Grever; Steven Halliwell; Donald Hossack; Barry Humphries; Dr G. K. Krishnamurti; Mark Samuels Lasner; Don Mead; Joan Nordell; Gregor Murray; Jan and Marjorie Perkins; Julian Potter; Michael Seeney; John Smithies; Chris Snodgrass; John Stratford; Tim and Jean Sturgis; Alice Wood; Ann Wyman.

Introduction

AUBREY BEARDSLEY had a very brief life. As Oscar Wilde remarked, with more poetic truth than botanical accuracy, he died 'at the age of a flower'. He was, however, a flower which achieved full bloom. His life was in many ways complete. He won recognition as the most original draughtsman of his generation, and created a body of work of extraordinary originality and depth. Tainted by tuberculosis even from childhood, he knew that his time was circumscribed. The knowledge did not paralyse him or fill him with resentment: it drove him forward. He burnt with a peculiar brilliance and energy.

His genius developed almost at a stroke, and was sustained. The pattern of his career – from early promise, first achievement and full assurance to conscious elaboration, commercial neglect and rich late work – echoes that of many artists who had three times his span. All was encompassed in less than six years of professional life.

Beardsley's chosen medium was pen-and-ink. And if his best work was in black and white, reactions to it were similarly stark in contrasts. He received lavish praise and vehement opprobrium. And not only for his work; it extended to his person. Gaunt, dandified, racked by disease, Beardsley mirrored the perverse yet elegant distortions of his art. It was a striking connection, promoted by the press and embraced

OPPOSITE 'Self-portrait', 1896.

I

by the public, which assured him a level of personal fame – or
notoriety – more usually accorded to stars of the popular stage. For
a brief moment at the middle of the 1890s Beardsley seemed to
embody the very spirit of the fin de siècle.

Although he first achieved a reputation for his black-and-white
work, his genius was not confined. He was among the first British
artists to recognize and extend the possibilities of poster design, he
wrote three mature poems which deserve their place in anthologies
of late-Victorian verse, and through the baroque playfulness of his
unfinished novel, *Under the Hill*, he sounded a new note in English
prose.

Not the least of his creations, however, was himself. He was a
master of pose, a striker of attitudes; artificiality was natural to him.
A record of his life must acknowledge and discriminate these phases,
and acknowledge that Beardsley adopted his masks not to obscure
his personality but to express it. He was in all things an artist.

MATTHEW STURGIS

CHAPTER I

'A Delicate Child'

AUBREY BEARDSLEY was born in Brighton on 21 August 1872. It was later claimed that his horoscope revealed 'a strange configuration of the moon, the dominant of the imagination, and Herschel, the planet of eccentricity', but at the time this celestial arrangement passed unnoticed. No portents of greatness heralded his arrival: his mother immediately fell ill with puerperal fever, and the new-born infant was given over to the care of the household.[1]

The household was extensive, for Aubrey's parents – Vincent and Ellen Beardsley, with his one-year-old sister, Mabel – were living in Ellen's familial home at 12 Buckingham Road. The three-storey house on its corner site was well appointed and substantial. It was presided over by Ellen's father, Surgeon-Major William Pitt, who, although retired, was only in his mid-fifties. There were also Ellen's mother, Susan, and Ellen's two unmarried sisters, Mary and Florence, who at twenty-nine and twenty-one were respectively three years older and four and a half years younger than Ellen. There was a live-in maid of all work and probably additional help for the ailing mother and her child.[2]

Surrounded by solicitous females, bolstered by the assured presence of the medically trained Surgeon-Major and the practical benefits of resident domestic service, Aubrey spent his first weeks as comfortably as the adverse health of his mother allowed. Quite what place Vincent

3

Beardsley, the proud father, held in this attentive throng is difficult to gauge. The history of his relationship with the Pitt family was troubled.

The Pitts were a well-established and respected Brighton family. William's father, Thomas Best Pitt (c. 1784–1844) had been a fashionable doctor in the town when the Prince Regent made it famous as a resort. William, with at least one of his four sisters, was born in Brighton; his name was selected to emphasize a supposed connection with the late, great and eponymous statesman.[3]

Like his father, William chose medicine as a profession. In 1838, at the age of twenty-two, he was elected a member of the Royal College of Surgeons, and received his Assistant Surgeon's certificate the following year. Soon afterwards, he departed for India, having joined the Indian Medical Service.

The empire offered opportunities both professional and personal. In July 1841 at St Thomas's, Dacca (Dhaka, now capital of Bangladesh), William Pitt married Susan Lamb, teenage daughter of a Scottish indigo planter. The match was propitious. The Lambs were a powerful and closely knit expatriate family: Susan's sister, Georgiana, had married her cousin, George Henry Lamb, at the same church in 1838; and George Henry's father (George senior), already a Senior Surgeon, was on the way to becoming president of the Indian Medical Service. He gave his approval to the union of his young niece with William Pitt, and was a witness at the ceremony. He would be a useful ally for the twenty-four-year-old Assistant Surgeon.

Children followed: Mary in 1843, and a second daughter on 28 August 1846. The indigo planter suggested that this new granddaughter be called after him, but as the name Alexander Imlach Lamb did not commend itself as suitable for a young girl, a compromise was decided upon. The addition to the Pitt family was christened Ellen Agnus Pitt, 'Agnus' being the Latin for lamb. It is impossible to tell at this distance what prompted this over-ingenious solution; most official documents ignore the pun, and give her name as Ellen Agnes.[4]

Only the dimmest outline of the Pitt family's peripatetic life is traceable. In June 1849 the family returned to Europe on extended leave. They spent time in France – where a third daughter, Florence, was born in December 1850 – and also probably in England. When the furlough ended in March 1853, William, together with his family, returned to the East. Immediately on his arrival in India, he was dispatched to serve in the Burmese campaign, was present at the capture of Rangoon, and was promoted full surgeon at the end of the conflict. It is unlikely that Susan Pitt and her three daughters would have followed William and his regiment on this expedition; perhaps they spent their time on the Lamb family plantations at Berhampore, in north-west Bengal.[5]

After another period of respite, and a further two years' leave in the Cape, the Pitts were back in India in 1857 for the cataclysm of the Mutiny. William was involved in the desperate defence of the residency at Lucknow, and received a medal for his part. His wife was with him during this ordeal, as was one child, though Ellen's silence upon the subject suggests that it was not her. Perhaps the experiences of the Mutiny made William reconsider his course in life. He left India in March 1858, ostensibly on 'leave to Australia and the Cape'. He never returned. In February 1859, in his absence, he was raised to the rank of Surgeon-Major, but retired from the service in May. He received a pension of £147 per annum (net).

The Pitts returned to Europe, spending the first years of their new-found leisure in the Anglo-French atmosphere of Jersey. By 1864, however, they had come 'home' to Brighton. The retired Surgeon-Major, his wife and three growing daughters settled first at 2 Lansdowne Square, close to William's elder and unmarried sister, Sarah, who lived at No. 4. In 1867, they moved to No. 9 Clifton Place and three years later took up residence at 12 Buckingham Road.[6]

If the Pitt girls were an adornment to Brighton social life, it was generally agreed that Ellen sparkled most brightly. She was tall, slender, and attractive in a slightly equine fashion; her conspicuous points were vivacity, vanity and a well-cultivated gift for self-dramatization: she would make a late entrance into the drawing-room alone, after her sisters had obeyed a parental summons. Such tactics were evidently effective. At social gatherings men would often turn to the sprightly Ellen while more conventionally 'beautiful' women were neglected. She had a reputation for daring and even for mischief. On one occasion she pretended to be a deaf-mute in order to secure a reserved pew at the front of a crowded church.

She was talented, especially at music, and played the piano with 'more than ordinary amateur skill'. Her other great enthusiasm was religion. She was, in the parlance of the time, a 'sermon taster', going to any church where the preaching was supposed to be good; for a dilettante churchgoer Brighton was then an exciting place to be. The town was one of the centres of the Anglo-Catholic revival throughout the second half of the nineteenth century.

The pre-eminent local figure in this movement was the Reverend Arthur Douglas Wagner, a second-generation Brighton prelate. He poured his substantial private wealth into the cause, building five churches and gathering around him bright and able young men from the universities as his curates and emissaries. He sought to revive the ancient usages, adopting eucharistic vestments, the cult of the Blessed Virgin Mary, sacramental confession and daily celebration of the mass. He strove, too, to reassert the cultural power of the church, employing innovative architects such as G. F. Bodley and Edmund Scott for his building projects, and commissioning windows and altarpieces from Edward Burne-Jones, William Morris and other Pre-Raphaelite artists.

Such innovations inevitably prompted the wrath of the 'Protestant Party', which mistook them for a step on the primrose path towards Roman Catholicism and the pope. There were assaults on members of the clergy; altars were stripped, and hostile notices proclaiming 'Daily Opera' went up around churches which offered a sung eucharist. Wagner was summoned before a Royal Commission set up to inquire into the principles and practices of the so-called Ritualists. Such dramas are likely to have heightened Ellen Pitt's enthusiasm for churchgoing. She frequently attended St Paul's, West Street, the church where Father Wagner presided, and the priest and several of his curates became friends of the family.[7]

Ellen was confident of her family's social status. There was much in the family background of which she could be proud: service in the empire, a career in the professions, an easy familiarity with France, an illustrious name, a sense of place, an appreciation of culture. It was, in the middle years of Queen Victoria's reign, a powerful legacy. In the case of the Pitts, however, these achievements did not only proclaim social worth, they concealed social flaws. On Susan Pitt's baptismal registration, signed in 1825 in Dacca, she is listed only as the illegitimate daughter of Alexander Lamb; no mother is mentioned. In such instances (far from uncommon in mid-nineteenth-century India) the unnamed mother was almost invariably a native servant. It is all but certain that Susan Pitt was not only illegitimate but half-caste.[8]

William Pitt would probably have known and accepted his wife's history; such things were common on the sub-continent and, besides, the professional benefits of marrying a Lamb more than compensated for any notional flaw. It is doubtful, however, that the couple's children would have been told of this perceived double stain: Ellen would not have known that she was a quarter-blood, and so, by extension, it is unlikely that Aubrey would have guessed the intriguing probability that he was a Bengali octaroon.

The other besetting shame of the Pitts was less easily concealed: the Surgeon-Major's debts. He was hopeless with money. Certainly he borrowed heavily from both George Lamb and George's son, George Henry. When the former died, in 1862, his will contained the telling provision that 'any sum in which Mr William Pitt, Surgeon late of the Bengal Establishment may be indebted to me' shall be got from him and given for 'the sole and separate use and benefit of his present wife Susan Pitt (who is a niece of mine) so that the amount may not be subject to the debts or engagements of her said husband'. The death duty register shows the amount to have been over £1000.

Moreover, in 1865, when the Surgeon-Major became entitled to an increased pension from the Bengal Medical Retiring Fund, he was obliged to assign this medical annuity of £300 per annum to George Henry Lamb. It is impossible to unravel the exact reasons for these manoeuvres, but, although there is no evidence that the Surgeon-Major went bankrupt, he does seem to have existed in a state of protracted financial crisis.[9]

There is nothing like the spectre of hidden disgrace to make an English middle-class family stand upon its gentle status. The Surgeon-Major, concealing both the taint of his wife's 'bad blood' and the awkwardness of his financial constraint, had made the family duly and proudly aware of their position in the world.

They were also aware of Vincent Beardsley's position. They were aware, at least, that it was ambiguous. In later years, Ellen Beardsley liked to represent the match as a *mésalliance* – a doomed pairing of cultivated Professions and uneducated Trade – but in the summer of 1870 such a divide was, it seems, willingly overlooked. When Vincent Beardsley met Ellen Pitt, his principal claims to attention were a luxuriant moustache and a private income. These gave him the air, and indeed the airs, of a gentleman, even if behind the pose there was little of enduring substance.

Vincent Beardsley's father *had* been in trade. A manufacturing goldsmith in Clerkenwell, he had died of consumption in 1845, when Vincent, his only child, was five years old. Vincent's mother, Sarah Ann, married again two years later, a young surgeon named William Lait, and they soon had a family of their own. Next to nothing is known of Vincent's childhood, though he was apparently a weak boy and was not, therefore, put into any trade.* There was enough money to support such a course of action. Vincent's maternal grandfather, David Beynon, a Welsh-born property developer from north London, made handsome provision for him in his will. When Beynon died in 1859 he left his grandson, then nineteen, £350, a quarter share of his estate (valued at over £12,000), and the rights to a house in Bernard Street, Russell Square. The bequest was made on the curious, but not unheard of, condition that Vincent should not 'intermeddle in the affairs' of his late father's estate. The clause was clearly intended to prevent litigious wrangling, although there is no further evidence of a quarrelsome side to Vincent's character or a strained relationship with his mother (one of the other three main beneficiaries).†

* In the 1851 Census, eleven-year-old Vincent was not listed as living with either his mother and Dr Lait, or with his grandfather, David Beynon. It is possible that he was at school in the country for his health.
† David Beynon rose steadily in the world. On his marriage certificate he is listed as a publican; in the 1851 Census he is a property speculator; by the time he made his will in 1855 he had become a gentleman. The will was proved on 1 May 1858. The Bernard Street house is mentioned in a codicil. Although the probate value of the estate is given as less than £3,000 (and quoted as such by Walker and others), the Death Duty Register shows the full value of the estate, including property, to have been over £12,000.

The sums in Beynon's will were healthy enough; the combination of property and money would have yielded Vincent a fair income, although not so large that the temptation to erode the capital was not present. Whether Vincent succumbed to this temptation after he came into his inheritance at twenty-one is not known. Indeed, he disappears entirely from view for over a decade, and it is difficult to suppress the scarcely rational desire to take this want of any historical record as a reflection of want of character on Vincent's part. In 1870 Vincent reappears. He was visiting Brighton, for pleasure probably and perhaps for health. There, on the old Chain Pier, he saw Ellen Pitt, slender, vivacious and twenty-four. And he spoke to her.[10]

Within the constraints of Victorian social etiquette, to strike up an acquaintance in a public place without a formal introduction was a sovereign impropriety. Vincent Beardsley, however, had the practised charm of thirty-one years and a metropolitan upbringing; while Ellen Pitt boasted that streak of daring and perverseness which had already earned her a reputation for unconventionality (it was even suggested in some quarters that Vincent Beardsley might not have been the *premier venu*). The first encounter led to others, and they took to meeting clandestinely in the trim gardens of the Pavilion.

Brighton was a small place, devoted to idleness and gossip. Ellen Pitt was well enough known in Brighton society for her assignations to be talked of and, soon after, relayed to 12 Buckingham Road. It is not therefore surprising that Vincent Beardsley's first introduction at Ellen's parental home was fraught. It is a tribute to something in his manner that, from this disadvantageous position, he 'won over' the Surgeon-Major and convinced him of his good faith towards Ellen and of his suitability as a son-in-law. Perhaps the medical background of his stepfather stood him in good stead; perhaps it was the lure of his undefined private income.

In due course an engagement was announced, and the wedding of Ellen Agnus Pitt and Vincent Paul Beardsley took place at the old Brighton parish church of St Nicholas on 12 October 1870. The day was so wild, with a storm blowing in from the Channel, that the wedding party was unable to enter the church through the south portal, and had to use the sheltered vestry door at the other end of the building. The scope for metaphor is tempting, but the misfortunes that beset the Beardsley marriage were bathetic rather than tempestuous. The first setback arrived promptly.

Even before the honeymoon was over Vincent Beardsley was sued by the widow of a clergyman for 'breach of promise'. She claimed he had undertaken to marry her. Such cases were all too common in the late nineteenth century, and were open to unscrupulous opportunism – but they were no less distressing for that. Scandal and embarrassment loomed. The Surgeon-Major insisted that his son-in-law settle the matter before it came into the glare of open court.

It is hard to imagine a less propitious start to a marriage: in a single blow Vincent forfeited the trust of his wife, the respect of her family, and the means of his own support. He was obliged to sell some property he possessed on the Euston Road to pay off the widow.[11] The solution had dire consequences. Deprived of financial security, he was thrown back upon Ellen's family, and the newly-weds, unable to set up home on their own, were obliged to live under the parental roof at Buckingham Road. It can be imagined with what sentiments the Pitts welcomed their son-in-law, and with what arguments he sought to explain his behaviour.[12]

There were moments of respite: the birth of a daughter – Mabel – on 24 August 1871; and a sparkling appearance in February 1872 at Brighton's premier social event, the Fancy Dress Ball, at the Pavilion, when Ellen's costume – a blue velvet tunic with white silk skirt and trousers, and matching cap – drew general admiration. The man from the *Brighton Gazette* was moved to verse, proclaiming '. . . then Mrs Beardsley – may her honours increase,/Looked quite picturesque as a native of Greece'. Vincent did not attempt fancy-dress for himself, but Ellen recalled his whirling her through the 'adorable suite of rooms' with pleasure and pride. Despite such giddy intervals, the overall tenor of Vincent Beardsley's existence must have been dispiriting.

It is to be supposed that at the outset he contributed to the household expenses, but even this practicality soon proved beyond him. In the weeks immediately after Aubrey's birth in August 1872 some new reverse overtook him, and he lost the remainder of his fortune. This grim news greeted Ellen when, after the passing of her fever, she left her room to be re-united with her infant son.[13]

Whatever the emotional strain between Aubrey's parents, or

between his father and the Pitts, 12 Buckingham Road was still a 'family home'. The financial structure which supported it might be precarious, but it provided the semblance of stability and the reality of material comfort. It was a household 'devoted' to Art, in the conventional, feminine and domestic sense favoured by middle-class Victorians. The Surgeon-Major was a man of limited imagination, but his family showed more aptitude. Susan Pitt's clever silhouettes of flowers, landscapes and figures adorned the walls of the drawing-room, several modest watercolours by Ellen and her elder sister were included in a family album; and of course there was music.

Ellen was always keen to display her accomplishments as a pianist. And Aubrey, it soon became apparent, was an accomplished and appreciative listener. Even before his first birthday he would crawl to the piano and settle himself beside it when his mother was about to play. She recalled many years later, with a maternal pride which may require some discount, that Aubrey would beat perfect time with his toy to her playing, and that when, in an effort to fox him, she changed from four- to six-time, Aubrey too changed tempo.[14]

The altering tempo of life at Buckingham Road proved less easy to adjust to. Vincent, shorn of his inheritance, needed to work, and for work he needed to be in London. Employment opportunities were limited for an untrained thirty-something-year-old with no previous experience and delicate health. Nevertheless, at the beginning of 1874 he got some secretarial work with the West India & Panama Telegraph Company, and a few months later a more satisfactory post as a clerk at the New Westminster Brewery, in Horseferry Road. He brought Ellen, Mabel and Aubrey up to London, where the Beards-leys took lodgings with Henry Russell, a retired music-hall star, and his young family, at 90 Lancaster Road, Notting Hill.*[15]

* Brigid Brophy in her excellent book *Beardsley and his World* (London, 1976) castigates Ellen Beardsley as socially pretentious for saying that she lodged with 'the parents of Landon Ronald' (Ronald became a famous pianist and a knight, under what Brophy assumed was a stage name). Ellen's description, however, was exact. Henry Russell and Emma Ronald were not married. Landon's birth certificate (7 June 1873) gives his full name as Landon Ronald and records his mother only as a parent. The certificate gives the address of the Ronald/Russell household as 19 Lancaster Road, although Kelly's London Directory shows it to have been number 90.

Living in other people's houses: for the next twenty years this would be their lot, with its sense of compromise, lack of permanence, and want of privacy. For Ellen and Vincent there was always the knowledge of what had been, and the rebuke of what was now; for Mabel and Aubrey there was only unease and instability. Although they had left behind the familiar comforts of Buckingham Road and Brighton, the Beardsleys were not quite adrift in London. At Lancaster Road they were close to Ellen's cousins, the Lambs. By the 1870s George Henry Lamb and his wife Georgiana (Susan Pitt's sister) were back in England, living at 11 Colville Gardens, no more than four hundred yards from Lancaster Road, with five of their grown or growing offspring. One of the sons, Henry Alexander, worked in the liquor trade and it is possible that he assisted in finding Vincent his job at Westminster Brewery. Also nearby, at 1 Addison Villas, were Ellen's well-connected half-uncle, David Wight Lamb, and his wife.

Barely a year after the Beardsleys' exodus, the Pitts also left Brighton. What provoked this upheaval – financial reverse or advance? familial solicitude? desire for change? – is unknown. The Surgeon-Major seems to have taken up residence in Westbourne Road, Islington, between 1875 and 1880, and then to have left the country. Meanwhile, Ellen's younger sister, Florence, was living in Denbigh Street, Pimlico in March 1876 when she married Moritz Schenkel – who appears to have been a neighbour, a 'gentleman' and the son of a Viennese hotel proprietor. Mary Pitt, the eldest sister, was probably living with her, and was a witness to the marriage. The other signatory was David Imlach Lamb, George Henry's fourth son.*

The Beardsleys accommodated themselves to their new surroundings and circumstances. For Vincent the move to London must have been something of a relief. He was back on home ground in his native city, free of the disapproving Pitt household, and he had a job. Although he scarcely emerges from the shadows, it is perhaps

* The Pitts' departure from Brighton is indicated by the Brighton Directories for 1874– 5. A William Pitt appears in the London Directory at Westbourne Road from 1875 to 1880 but it is impossible to confirm whether this was the Surgeon-Major. In the 1881 Census he was recorded as a 'visitor' in Bedfordshire, staying with friends, without his wife or unmarried eldest daughter.

possible to make out his attempt to play the part of the Victorian *paterfamilias* in Ellen's assertion that he beat both children when they were naughty.

The disappointments of married life, meanwhile, were amplifying Ellen's histrionic traits. As reality became increasingly harsh and dull, she strove to project herself beyond it. She clung to her High Tory sentiments and to the prerogatives of gentle birth and began to construct a picture of herself as a martyr to an ill-considered marriage; the picture would become bolder in outline and detail over the years. She retreated into Art and Sentiment. And she sought escape through her children, imbuing them with her aspirations, enthusiasms, prejudices and pretensions: she wanted them to shine.[16]

Despite material constraints, Ellen fostered a continuing awareness that the life of the spirit counted. The household at 90 Lancaster Road was steeped in music: Henry Russell had enjoyed a brilliant career as a music-hall performer, and had written hundreds of popular songs, including 'Cheer, Boys, Cheer' and 'Life on the Ocean Wave'. His common-law wife, Emma Ronald, was a wonderful pianist, and their eldest child, Landon (born in June 1873), became a concert performer. Ellen must have relished such an environment, and Aubrey seems to have responded to it with real feeling. When the family attended a 'Symphony Concert' at the Crystal Palace, four-year-old Aubrey 'listened intently' and with obvious enjoyment to the music. He received piano lessons from his mother and he was soon able to play Chopin quite 'as charmingly as anyone could wish'. Mabel learnt too. Ellen used to perform six pieces every evening for the family, making up a little book of programmes so that 'they did not hear the same thing too often, and learnt to know and appreciate the best music. I would not', she added, 'let them hear rubbish.'

The same disdain for 'rubbish' guided her children's reading. Mabel read prodigiously, taking up Dickens and Scott at a 'very early age', though at six she felt obliged to 'draw the line at Carlyle'. Aubrey showed an early enthusiasm for books, learning to read (according to family legend) by some strange osmosis without effort or tuition. What his first reading was remains unknown. Ellen would certainly have pushed him towards Dickens – if not Carlyle – as fast as possible.

There was, however, time for the more conventional pleasures of childhood, and here Aubrey was fortunate: the last third of the nineteenth century was a great age for illustrated children's books. The combination of new technologies, enterprising publishers, aesthetic doctrines, and rare talents resulted in exciting work: the nursery rhymes of Randolph Caldecott, the annuals of Kate Greenaway, the *Toy Books* of Walter Crane. Aubrey was exposed to, and enraptured by, the magical world of clear lines and bold tones. Nevertheless he was not encouraged to experiment in that direction. It was through music and literature that Ellen sought to expand her children's horizons; visual art did not seem to interest her particularly.

Despite this limitation, she did much to foster her children's (particularly Aubrey's) sense of specialness and self-worth. Family lore preserves several anecdotes on this count. When, as a child of six, he was taken by his parents to a service at Westminster Abbey, he was much intrigued by the numerous monuments to National Greatness. He asked for an explanation of the imposing bust of Brunel near their seat, and of the commemorative stained glass window opposite. Coming away after the service, he demanded with touching solemnity whether he should have 'a bust or a stainglass window' when *he* died. 'For', he is supposed to have added, 'I may be a great man some day.' When his mother asked what memorial he would like, he is said to have pondered the question before deciding upon a bust – 'because I am rather good looking'.[17]

The excursion to Westminster Abbey, though memorable, marked only a small part of the family's churchgoing regime. Ellen had lost none of her enthusiasm for 'sermon tasting', and London offered considerable scope for her discerning palate. For a while she abandoned her High Church sympathies and fell under the sway of the Revd Thain Davidson, of the Presbyterian church in Colebrook Row, Islington. Indeed it seems likely that during the mid-1870s the Beardsleys moved to Islington (which would have made sense if the Surgeon-Major lived in Westbourne Road). Certainly the minister of Colebrook Row was for a while Ellen's 'chief advisor' in spiritual, if not in practical matters. Davidson, a formidable Scot, was one of the great preachers of the age. He regularly filled not only his own church but also the Agricultural Hall on Upper Street with his direct, humorous preaching style. His particular theme was the dangerous attractions that the Modern City held for 'young men'.

Aubrey, however, was too young to take an interest in this subject, though he was beginning to exercise his parents' concern in other ways. He had developed into a delicate child, frail and pallid; his mother likened him to a 'little piece of Dresden china'. She recalled how once, like a miniature aged man, he helped himself up a flight of steps with a twig – an incident which seems to reflect the infant's propensity for self-dramatization quite as much as his actual frailty. From a young age he fell under the care of his barely older but more robust sister. The two children were thrown increasingly together. Ellen was obliged to work to help support the family. She taught privately, giving piano lessons (to the children of the German ambassador among others), and French tuition to students trying for the Civil Service Examination. Although, in her free moments at the end of the day, she lavished attention upon Mabel and Aubrey, giving them lessons of their own, and although it seems unlikely that the children were left absolutely alone at so young an age, Ellen characterized their existence during these years as 'a lonely life in lodgings'.[18]

This isolation from children of their own age fostered that quaint and distinctive precocity of manner common among children brought up in mainly adult company; while the early shared loneliness bound the siblings together, forging mutual reliance and stimulating their escape into the realms of imagination. The imagination, however, could only offer so much. It was no real proof against an existence of boredom, loneliness, cramped conditions and irregular hours. In the summer of 1879, soon after his seventh birthday, Aubrey fell ill; he went off his food, developed a cough and became feverish. The doctor, applying his stethoscope to the boy's puny chest, detected the faint yet ominous whisper of infected lung tissue. He diagnosed tuberculosis.

The verdict was grim, but not yet an irrevocable death sentence. The disease was common in late Victorian England, but it touched more people than it killed. Rest, fresh air and the body's own resources could, in time, heal any minor lesion in the lungs. The cause of the disease – the tuberculosis bacterium – was not identified

until 1882, and even then acceptance and understanding of the discovery and its ramifications were painfully slow; the popular belief
remained that the disease was hereditary. (The diagnosis of Aubrey's
condition would, one suspects, have further damaged Vincent's
standing with Ellen and her family, as it would swiftly have been
recalled that his father had died from the disease. Poor stock was
revealing itself two generations on.) The doctor, who already harboured doubts about the healthiness of Aubrey's London life, urged
his removal to the country, and it was decided to send him to
Hamilton Lodge, a small boarding preparatory school at Hurstpierpoint, about eight miles out of Brighton. There seems to have been
some existing connection with the school; Ellen appears to have
known Miss Barnett (who ran the school with her aunt, Miss Wise)
– perhaps from her Brighton days.

It is not known who paid Aubrey's fees, but by 1879 the Beardsleys
had been confirmed in the sad role of 'poor relations': the recipients
of ingeniously disguised charity from parents, uncles, aunts, cousins,
and even family friends. Lady Henrietta Pelham, the elderly unmarried
sister of west Sussex's principal grandee, the Earl of Chichester, took
an interest in the family. She had met them in Brighton and maintained the connection in London, where she had a house in Chester
Square. She paid for Aubrey's piano lessons at Hurstpierpoint.[19]

Transported from his 'lonely life' in London to the company of
boisterous contemporaries and the backdrop of the Sussex Downs,
Aubrey rallied. Anxiety that he might be teased on account of his
Christian name proved unfounded and on the evidence of his letters
home Hamilton Lodge was a happy place. He does not appear to
have suffered from homesickness, although the suspicion that this
might have been due to the unsatisfactory nature of his 'home' life
seems belied by the tone and content of his letters; he makes frequent
and solicitous inquiries after not only Mabel and his mother but also
his father. Indeed, Vincent's continuing place at the centre of family
life is illustrated by a decorated bookmark Aubrey sent him, inscribed
with the word 'Affection' ('because', as he explained in an accompanying note, 'I love you'), and by a Valentine card which Vincent
sent his son.

There were about twenty-five boarders (aged between seven and twelve) at the school and the regime was relaxed. Academic work did not, it seems, play a prominent part. The only books Aubrey mentions are Captain Cook's *Voyages* and a volume on French and English ships from which Miss Wise would read to them. Outings were frequent and imaginative: to the circus, to Hurstpierpoint 'Exhibition' (a glorified bazaar), to Danny Park, the local Elizabethan manor house, to Wolstonbury Hill, to the nearby 'Chinese Gardens', and to Brighton. Aubrey's delicate health, although known, seems to have been unremarked and unremarkable. He threw himself into the school's activities, enjoying the 'drilling practice' on the lawn, the daily walks with 'Fido' the school dog, the games and excursions. He seems not to have been accorded, or to have required, special treatment.

The piano studies progressed slowly. Despite Ellen's insistence upon his 'great feeling' for music, Aubrey confessed to driving Miss Barnett 'nearly bald' teaching him. But with continued support, if not pressure, from home he improved and by the end of his first year was planning to play a duet in the school end-of-term concert.

From the evidence of his correspondence, Aubrey was an engaging if unremarkable seven-year-old. His stated interests – cake, circus elephants, fireworks, nautical adventures, pocket money, and the condition of his toy engine – though largely conventional, give perhaps some hints of aesthetic and dramatic sensibility. Ellen described his childhood character as 'gentle, affectionate and whimsical', and these traits are present in his solicitude for his sister and his delight in the circus elephants. But Ellen also noted sharper forces at work, recognizing her own fault of 'vanity', the desire to 'shine', to impress whatever company one was in. At school this force began to inspire contradictory impulses: what impressed teachers (and parents) was often different from what impressed classmates. Aubrey desired to shine on both fronts. His enthusiastic participation in the life of the school secured the approval of the staff, but he also took care to gain a reputation among his peers for mischief and stoicism. When Miss Barnett was obliged to beat him for some infraction, he defied her best efforts and refused to cry.[20]

From an early age Aubrey developed this ambiguous relationship to authority. He recognized authority, and frequently sought its approval, but he also delighted in subverting it. He was much beaten for wilful naughtiness during his childhood, not just by his teacher but by his parents; and certain family friends, who were delighted to invite Mabel to lunch, wouldn't have Aubrey because 'they thought he would be troublesome'. Yet he knew well how to please and impress when he wanted. As yet, however, his range of effects was limited. Any precocity he displayed was more apparent than real and relied upon his mother's connivance. For example, she sent him a sonata to play when Miss Barnett was offering a piece with the unsophisticated title, 'Fading Away'.

At Hamilton Lodge Aubrey began to show an interest in drawing. His first efforts were 'copies of Cathedrals', but he then turned to his imagination and produced work which, curiously, prefigured many of the enduring themes of his adult art. One of his first successes was a picture of 'a Carnival' – a 'long series of grotesque figures' which he presented to his grandfather.

He stayed at Hamilton Lodge for only four terms. Perhaps the cheerful tone of the letters and the frequent assurances of his well-being concealed a worsening condition, or perhaps the fees were proving too heavy a burden for whoever was paying them. In either case, Ellen, in her own phrase, was 'obliged to have him home again'. Home by 1880 was Pimlico. The Beardsleys lodged at 57 Denbigh Street (the same dull thoroughfare from which Florence had married Moritz Schenkel).* It was an area they were never entirely to escape.[21]

Pimlico was then, as it is now, an unlovely district of London, between the characterful worlds of Westminster and Chelsea. In the 1880s it had neither the colour of historical association nor the glamour of newness. It had been developed in the 1840s and 1850s by London's prolific speculative builder, Thomas Cubitt, on the marshlands abutting the Thames, as a middle-class suburb, a bourgeois equivalent to his earlier 'aristocratic' development of Belgravia.

* The 1881 Census, taken in April, records 57 Denbigh Street as a lodging house kept by Joshua Hanniball and his family. Besides the Beardsleys there was one other couple, Mr and Mrs Edward Linging.

While Belgravia derives charm from its architectural variety – the grand squares and terraces broken up by little service courts and mews – Pimlico was designed without thought for carriages and large establishments. There is an appalling uniformity of standard tropes and stucco fronts; the streets are of tedious length, and the regular height of the houses (all four or five storeys) combined with the flatness of the site shuts off any vista of the city or the river, resulting in an enclosed, oppressive air. In addition, Cubitt's demographic ambitions were only partially successful. By the 1870s the area could boast a few enclaves of respectable affluence and even – in its tree-lined squares – modest grandeur, but among the long, unbroken files of stucco terracing a strained and straitened respectability marked the inhabitants: Pimlico had become a land of lodging houses.[22]

Ellen Beardsley struggled against this fate on Aubrey's account. His health was still delicate and the London smogs were oppressive. Early in 1882, she decided to 'give up her work' and take the two children to Epsom. They lodged there, for two years, with a Mrs Ann Clark, at 2 Ashley Villas. Vincent, it is to be supposed, went with them and commuted the fifteen miles to his work in town (the Epsom train service stopped at Vauxhall, where he was now the manager of the London branch of Crowley's Brewery), or remained in town and travelled out at weekends.* Vincent was already drifting to the margins of family life, and the decampment to Epsom isolated him further from his children, who were placed in a yet closer relationship with their mother.

Ellen filled her children's lives. She took them walking every day on the Downs; in Aubrey's case, 'to get strong'. She also gave them regular lessons, and beyond such schoolwork there was, of course, the great ocean of culture: the piano lessons, the evening programme of suitable pieces, the directed reading, the drawing and copying.[19] Given that Ellen's artistic gifts were interpretive rather than creative, it is unsurprising that she viewed art in terms of public projection rather than private enjoyment. It was not enough that Mabel should read Dickens, she must learn to recite him. Ellen tutored her

* Crowley & Co. Ltd were based at Alton in Hampshire. Walker accidentally refers to the firm as 'Crawley & Co.'

ten-year-old daughter in this most Victorian of skills, though their
lessons were often interrupted as teacher and pupil dissolved in tears
over a pathetic passage from the master of dramatic sentiment.[23]

Mabel's party-piece, however, was comic rather than pathetic;
Ellen tells us that she performed the skating scene from *Pickwick* 'too
wonderfully', and could recite from the same work for 'two hours
on end'. The choice of *Pickwick Papers* was, of course, a convention,
but is it perhaps possible to trace the influence of Ellen's will behind
it? The dramatic hinge of the novel is Mr Pickwick's arraignment
on a breach-of-promise charge brought by his widowed landlady; it
is easy to imagine Vincent's discomfort, and Ellen's bitter satisfaction,
as they sat listening to their daughter recounting the grim court case
and Mr Pickwick's principled, if foolish, line of defence.

Aubrey's response to Dickens was pictorial. He was showing
marked fondness, if only limited ability, for drawing. He made careful
illustrations of both the 'Maypole Inn' and the 'Boot Inn' from
Barnaby Rudge. He occasionally worked from his own imagination,
but seems to have had the impatience with his technical shortcomings
which often characterizes the imaginative temperament. He wanted
the gratification of finished achievement and found that he could
obtain more satisfactory results by copying from books than by conjuring stiff-limbed little figures from his own imagination. One reason
why he was anxious to produce finished work, even at the age of
nine, was that he was already working to commission. Although this
public projection of his talent had Ellen's approval, it was more an
accident of family circumstances than a tribute to her son's talent.

The financial plight of the Beardsleys was a matter of continuing
concern to their relatives and friends, especially since Ellen had given
up work to look after the children; there seems to have been a benign
conspiracy to provide covert charity for the family by commissioning
drawings from Aubrey. Lady Henrietta Pelham bought some; a set
of place-cards, illustrating characters from Dickens, was ordered for
a family wedding, and other requests were made. Aubrey earned
about £30 during the year: a considerable sum.

However derivative these juvenile efforts are, they have a certain
charm (largely lost in reproduction) and display care and facility: an
attention to detail was not surprising in a boy whose grandfathers

were a goldsmith and a surgeon.* More importantly, these drawings represented a first success, which brought the intoxicating rewards of approbation and cash, and they presented Aubrey to himself and to a limited public in the role of 'draughtsman'. Satisfaction in this achievement must have gratified him often during his childhood. But drawing was never regarded as Aubrey's main accomplishment. Music, Ellen had decided, was his forte. Under her tuition, both Aubrey and Mabel had become able pianists; they played duets and nocturnes, and Aubrey had begun to compose.[24]

After two years of Epsom air and maternal solicitude, Aubrey's strength returned; the isolated lesions of his lungs healed over, and he regained the semblance of health. In 1883 the Beardsleys returned to London. Their friends, anxious to support them, soon took to inviting the talented children to perform at private parties. Ellen dramatized this as an entry into 'public and social life', while Aubrey, who had quite as much histrionic flair as his mother, later amazed his friends by oblique references to his early years as a musical prodigy. In fact, his career as a child wonder was extremely limited. Ellen Beardsley, writing in the 1920s, remembered Mabel playing and reciting often, but could recall only two occasions on which Aubrey played 'in public': once at Lady Derby's, where he played solos and duets with Mabel, and at a fashionable church concert. The location of this concert is not recorded, but it may well have been St Paul's, Knightsbridge. Ellen's enthusiasm for good sermons and genteel surroundings would have been satisfied by the chic high-church establishment in Wilton Place, and one of the curates there – Robert Eyton – made a particular friend of Aubrey at about this time.[25]

In recalling these two occasions, Ellen always claimed that Aubrey was very shy and hated being asked out: nine is indeed a self-conscious age. Having a more assured elder sister can make it more so, but there may also have been a touch of fastidiousness in Aubrey's reluctance to perform. It is possible that he felt the hint of well-meaning condescension at those gatherings in St James's Square and Belgravia. The same note could have been detectable behind the place-card

* The critic Roger Fry likened Beardsley's capacity for taking pains to 'the patience of an Indian craftsman', an allusion which takes on unexpected resonance in view of his possible Indian connections.

commissions, but drawing is work where the artist can be protected from his audience.

Despite the 'public and social' successes of the Beardsley children, the stability of family life in London was impossible to maintain. Vincent lost his job at Crowley's in 1884 when 'one of the younger partners took his post'; he received excellent references, but at the age of forty-four new jobs were hard to come by. Ellen fell ill and had to enter a nursing home. In the face of this double crisis the extended family rallied round: Aubrey and Mabel were sent to a great-aunt at Brighton.

Sarah Pitt was the Surgeon-Major's elder, and unmarried, sister. Unlike her brother, she seems to have had a firm grasp of money and its management. She had over £3000 of debenture stock at 4 per cent, and lived carefully off the interest. In the summer of 1884 she was approaching seventy, and had recently moved from Lansdowne Square to a three-storey house close to the sea-front, at 21 Lower Rock Gardens. It was here that Mabel and Aubrey were to live.[26]

CHAPTER II

'A Good School Time'

RESENTFUL PERHAPS THAT ANYONE ELSE could offer succour to her offspring, Ellen Beardsley came to characterize Miss Pitt as 'a strange old aunt', and was critical of her 'peculiar notions about children', notions which included a general contempt for toys and a firm belief in the benefits of early-to-bed-early-to-rise. There was, moreover, Ellen complained, scarcely a book in the house.

It is, however, unsurprising that the household of a septuagenarian spinster was not geared for juvenile excitement; nor is it to be wondered at that Sarah Pitt could not compete with the 'accomplished' Ellen Beardsley in providing cultural stimulation and instruction. Her strengths appear to have lain elsewhere. From the evidence of her will at least, she was a generous, thoughtful, independent spirit with a disdain for show or pretension. She left separate legacies to her married nieces, independently of their husbands; and she wished to be buried at a cost of not more than £30 in a common grave at whichever graveyard was nearest at her death.

Now 'show' and 'pretension' were two of Ellen's conspicuous weaknesses, and this may have led to some tension between the two women. Certainly Sarah Pitt was not impressed by Ellen's fevered

OPPOSITE 'La chymist', a caricature of E. J. Marshall, Beardsley's headmaster, c. 1887.

tales of the children's advanced abilities. To her way of thinking, they were 'too precocious', and she took a mischievous pleasure in pointing up their educational shortcomings, if only to their mother. She was clearly fond of her charges and they, it seems, were fond of her. Lower Rock Gardens, after the lodging houses of Pimlico and Epsom, offered Aubrey and Mabel a lost world of stability and accepted comfort, and took them back to Brighton, with its heady combination of Regency extravagance and bracing sea air.[1]

The tensions of home life were absent, and the house regime made existence simple. They did not, at first, go to school; if they studied, they studied at home. There was time to explore, not only Brighton but the expanding realms of the imagination. Aubrey plunged into the pages of J. R. Green's *A Short History of the English People* (the one book in the house, according to Ellen) and, as ever fired by the desire to turn everything to account, began to compile a chronicle of the Spanish Armada. He wrote ballads, composed nocturnes, drew pictures. There was, it seems, access to books other than Green's *History*, for it was probably at Lower Rock Gardens that Aubrey produced his first recorded (but now lost) set of illustrations: a series of drawings for the Revd R. H. Barham's gothick fantasy, 'The Jackdaw of Rheims'. Surrounded by so many happy opportunities, there seems no reason to doubt Miss Pitt's view that Aubrey and his sister were 'happy as birds' during their time with her.[2]

One of the children's principal pleasures, and one of which Ellen would have approved wholeheartedly, was churchgoing; both lived intense 'spiritual' lives even then. Aubrey always claimed that as a child he had woken one night to a vision of 'a great crucifix with a bleeding Christ, falling off the wall' over the mantelpiece. The image lived on vividly in his thoughts.

Ignoring the claims of nearer establishments, Aubrey and Mabel chose to worship at the Church of the Annunciation, Washington Street, high on the Downs, almost a mile from Lower Rock Gardens. It was a long trek to a simple church in a recently developed poor area of mean two-storey terraces. Founded as an evangelical outpost in 1864 by the indefatigable Revd Arthur Wagner, the Annunciation did not achieve the status of parish church until 1888. In 1884 it still had the fervent glamour of a mission cell. Its structure, though recently remodelled to accommodate an ever-growing congregation, remained decidedly simple: brick-trimmed and flint-faced outside and criss-crossed with open beam work within, it resembled a medieval barn. Throughout the open interior there were touches of devotional decoration, side chapels, paintings of religious scenes, and – above the altar – three stained-glass windows. The central panel was designed by Dante Gabriel Rossetti, those flanking represented the Annunciation and were by Burne-Jones.

Whatever the simplicity of the church fabric, or indeed of the local congregation, the rite (as might be expected from a Wagner foundation) was ornate. The priest in charge was Father George Chapman, a gaunt, keen-eyed man in his late thirties, who burned not only with the zeal of his vocation but with the fire of tuberculosis. Both these traits perhaps helped to forge the close bond established between the priest and Aubrey. Indeed Father Chapman became a quasi-parental figure. Given the absence – and perhaps the shortcomings – of his own father, it is not to be wondered that Aubrey sought out a surrogate; nor, given his mother's influence, that he should seek him in a church. Father Chapman's health, however, was breaking down rapidly under the burden of work and disease, and his ministry was interrupted by frequent periods of enforced convalescence. The work of the church nevertheless continued under his curates. And Aubrey, with his sister, continued to make the arduous ascent to Washington Street with undiminished regularity.

The church had energy: Father Chapman's sympathetic yet earnest personality drew many people, but his extreme ritualism and love of 'romish' details (he wore a biretta) provoked antagonism among the town's low-church faction. In the popular imagination, Anglo-Catholic ritualism was only one step from Roman Catholicism. This – at least in theory – was far from the case. The Anglo-Catholic movement professed to uphold the Anglican church's claims to Apostolic Succession, separate from Rome; the ritualist wing sought merely to restore appreciation of England's old liturgical traditions. Inevitably, though, the Anglo-Catholic ritualists and the Roman Catholics held many outward forms in common, and it is well to register – in view of later events – that Aubrey's early life was filled with the scent of incense, that he found an easy and rewarding companionship with biretta-topped priests, was accustomed to making confession, and was brought up with a reverence for the Blessed Virgin Mary.[3]

It is doubtful whether Sarah Pitt, with her no-nonsense views on funeral arrangements, would have shared the Beardsley children's enthusiasm for the Church of the Annunciation, but she does not seem to have discouraged their visits. If she was concerned about anything, it was the loneliness of her wards, their separation from the company of their peers, the patchiness of their education, and their tendency, through isolation, to eccentricity. The facts are obscure, but it seems that when Ellen recovered sufficiently to have her children back, Miss Pitt recommended that Aubrey should stay on in Brighton and be found a proper school; she would pay the fees.

Brighton was honeycombed with educational establishments. They were so numerous that it had earned the soubriquet 'School Town'. The two pre-eminent foundations were Brighton College and Brighton Grammar School. The former, it was claimed, catered for the sons of gentlemen, the latter for the sons of trade. This distinction, however (although it was unlikely to have influenced Miss Pitt) had, by the 1880s, already been eroded. The Grammar School, moreover, was under the direction of a truly impressive educationalist – E. J. Marshall. And it was to Mr Marshall that Sarah Pitt applied.

From surviving photographs Ebenezer Marshall might seem the incarnation of the mythic Victorian pedagogue: profusely bushed eyebrows, shaved, almost simian, upper lip, and the spreading fan of an Old Testament beard. But this severe aspect concealed an imaginative and generous spirit, as well as proclaiming a driving will. It was Marshall's dynamism that established the reputation of Brighton Grammar School. He was headmaster for thirty-nine years, and died within weeks of his retirement in 1899. His staff found it hard to keep pace with him. Amongst some of the teachers he had the reputation of a 'slave driver'. He refused to countenance the establishment of a 'staff room', considering that his teachers should be out among their pupils, not skulking in a den consuming tea and digestive biscuits.

Marshall was an original and successful teacher, with an enthusiasm for inculcating facts through rhyme. An early advocate of science as a school subject, he placed it prominently on the syllabus, and gave illustrated lectures on interesting natural phenomena. His real originality, however, lay in his grasp of the importance of extra-curricular activities in the communal life of the school. Nature excursions, sketching parties, school plays and concerts, visiting lecturers, informal exhibitions, and, of course, games: a constant round of stimulation, carried through with a sense of enjoyment and fun. On one school outing to the picturesque village of Glynde, the long walk from Lewes station was transformed into a carnival procession by the accompaniment of the school's drum-and-fife band. He had also instituted *Past and Present*, the first school magazine in England. Published monthly, it combined reports on school activities with news of the ever-widening diaspora of Old Boys across the empire, strengthening a sense of fellowship both within the school and beyond its walls.

In 1885 Marshall had been headmaster for twenty-four years and had seen the school grow and prosper. It had a handsome home in Buckingham Road (just down the hill from where Aubrey was born) and boasted almost 300 fee-paying boys between the ages of seven and eighteen. The great majority were day boys, but about forty were boarders who lodged either with the headmaster or 'in house'.[4]

There was much to recommend BGS as a school for twelve-year-old Aubrey. It had a good academic record and, perhaps more importantly, Marshall had a reputation for being good with problem children. And it seems that already Aubrey was considered, at least within his family, as something of a problem. When he was taken, in November, to meet his prospective headmaster, there remained some doubt whether he would be accepted. Marshall later recalled that he 'hesitated to receive a boy whose physique and nervous temperament and special intellectual bent might not profit by the routine of class work and discipline of a large public school'. But the Pitt influence in Brighton was exerted and, at 'the special request of a valued friend' (perhaps the Hon. T. H. W. Pelham, Lady Henrietta's cousin, and a vice-president of the school) Marshall accepted the challenge of Aubrey's schooling. It was decided that he should go to the school as a boarder, but with the Christmas term already drawing to a close he did not start until January 1885.*

To be taken from the quiet life of Lower Rock Gardens and thrown into the rough-and-tumble of a large school would have been an alarming experience for anyone, the more so for a delicate boy with a foolish Christian name, an idiosyncratic haircut and an outmoded pair of juvenile knickerbockers.† Moreover, although Aubrey would probably have attracted notice in any gathering of boys, he arrived at his new school not as part of a vast influx but partway through the academic year.

A contemporary recalled him on his first day, sitting in a corner of the 'day room' looking 'a picture of misery and showing very evident signs of homesickness'. His figure, straight and slender, gave an impression of a 'sprightly well-groomed boy', while the 'curious red-brown colour' of his hair claimed instant notice (no two memorialists agree upon the exact hue). Beardsley wore it 'brushed smoothly and flatly on his forehead and over part of his immensely high and narrow brow'; the effect was charitably deemed 'eccentric'.

Among the boarders, there existed a system of 'fagging': each junior was supposed to act almost as a servant to an assigned senior – brewing up his tea, making toast, cleaning his football boots, and running his errands. Beardsley's fag-master was W. W. Hind-Smith. At the general inquisition of the new boys on the first evening Hind-Smith quizzed Beardsley about his usefulness: 'Are you any good at cooking?' Beardsley admitted that he was 'not much good at cooking'. When Hind-Smith pressed, 'What can you do?' Beardsley answered with perfect assurance that it depended what Hind-Smith *wanted* him to do.

Hind-Smith remembered the developing exchange. 'I said, "Can you play?" and he replied directly, "Oh yes! What sort of music

---

* Robbie Ross recorded that Beardsley started at school as a day-boy in November on a month's probation. This is suggested by Beardsley's application, dated 25 November 1884. The BGS master A. W. King, however, asserted that Beardsley arrived in January 1885, as a boarder. Given his role in events, King's version is preferred.

† It is worth noting that in the more leisured days of the late nineteenth century Beardsley's christian name was pronounced with a long, open first syllable; to his contemporaries he was known as 'Ah-brey Beardsley'. (Information from Moresco Pearce, via Barry Humphries.)

would you like? Something classical, or a piece of my own composition?" Of course we said the latter. There was no piano in the
room but Beardsley went over to Mr King's [the housemaster] little
harmonium – in place of something better – and gave us "something
original". We then asked him if he could draw; and he replied, "Yes,
what shall I draw?" I said, "Draw me", which he proceeded to do,
and made a clever outline of my face . . . I then said, "What else
can you do? Are you a poet?" "I am very fond of Shakespeare," he
said, "but perhaps you would like me to give you something of my
own." So he immediately went to the other end of the room, stood
up and recited a piece called (I think) "The Pirate".' This was showing off and, in other circumstances, might have provoked ridicule
or rebuke. But Hind-Smith and his fellow inquisitors were in genial
mood, and besides, steeped in the puerilities of school life, they were
genuinely impressed by Beardsley's unboylike manner and accomplishments. His drawing may have been meagre; the poem (it survives) is unremarkable, and the musical piece probably no better, but
they projected a sense of achievement. They showed a precocious
understanding of the forms of the adult world, which inspired a
certain awe among his contemporaries.

Hind-Smith's instant verdict was to pronounce Beardsley 'a regular
Shakespeare' (one suspects Shakespeare was the only poet he had
heard of) and to proclaim that this would be his new fag's nickname.
This seems to have provoked a discussion of the poet's work and
when Mr King looked in on his charges he found 'this thin talkative
youngster . . . discussing the qualities of Shakespeare's plays, contrasting in grand style the histories, the comedies and the tragedies'.

By the time he went to bed on his first night at BGS, Beardsley
must have been conscious of a sense of triumph. He had been allowed
to shine on his best fronts; he had won something of a jester's licence,
as well as a scholar's reputation, and he had been liked. He knew
he was being talked about. A sharp fall, however, awaited him.

The next day, when the new boys were tested and classified into
forms, it was found that Beardsley, for all his knowledge of Shakespeare's *oeuvre*, was unversed in the mysteries of multiplication
tables. His cocky rejoinder that such an accomplishment was
'entirely unnecessary', as long as he could count money (and, more

importantly, had money to count), was not well-received. He was 'ruthlessly sent to the Lower School and told to stop chattering'.

He did not allow this setback to cow him, and after tea that evening he entertained his fellow-boarders to a 'graphic delineation of his experiences', protesting with mock horror at the absurdity of a 'man of his years and experience being put with babies to learn tables and spelling'. This one-man show was interrupted by the appearance of Mr King. The housemaster was amused by the performance but, feeling that a proper respect for discipline had to be maintained, sent Beardsley to his rooms, telling him to tidy the bookcase there while he waited. No chore could have been more agreeable to Aubrey. King returned to his sitting-room to discover the miscreant poring happily over the piled volumes. It was a first sign of shared interests and enthusiasm, and the beginning of a friendship which transformed Beardsley's three years at BGS.[5]

Arthur William King was barely thirty, but had been at BGS for nine years. He was a twinkling, animating spirit. A man of real culture and even intellectual power, he loved music and the beautiful in nature and art, and he enlivened everything he undertook with a keen sense of fun. He was renowned for performing impromptu Gilbert and Sullivan pastiches while accompanying himself on his 'aged and wheezy' harmonium. His role as 'House Master in charge of boarders' left him with only the most perfunctory and general teaching duties; it was his brief to organize the out-of-school activities. This he did with 'extraordinary energy and enthusiasm', fulfilling, if not surpassing, Mr Marshall's ambitions in that direction.

King very quickly divined Beardsley's talents and limitations. There was much about school life to which Beardsley was unsuited. He was physically timid and broomstick thin, so the great realm of 'games' was beyond him, though he did pretend to a spectator's interest in football and a scorer's involvement in cricket. As a 'fag' he was, in the conventional sense, a grave disappointment; Hind-Smith recalled an unhappy history of burnt toast and spoiled teas. More surprisingly, he does not seem to have excelled at lessons. Although the punitive sojourn in the Lower School was brief and he was soon raised to the Second Remove, his progress was slow, his interest never fully engaged. He spent much of his time drawing caricatures of the masters or drifting into a dream world. If he did involve himself, it was often in the cause of mischief. On one occasion he delighted his classmates by stuffing the tails of Mr Marshall's gown into an inkwell. The unsuspecting, and rather deaf, headmaster set off across the room, taking the inkpot with him in a shower of permanent black.

His natural cleverness allowed him to keep up with the class – but little more. In the one external exam he took – the College Preceptors Examination, Second Class, which he sat in December 1886 – he achieved a disappointing 'Third Class' pass. According to the report, he obtained sufficient marks to put him in Second Class, but was placed in Third 'through weakness in some special subject'. Perhaps his maths were still stalled at monetary addition.[6]

Despite his inattention in class and weakness as an examinee, he managed to preserve and foster his reputation as an intellectual. For much of the time he hid in a world of his own. The habits of self-sufficiency he had developed during his childhood with Mabel were not readily abandoned: he retreated into books. One of Beardsley's contemporaries recalled the extraordinary power literature had over him: 'He had a delightful and engaging smile for everybody, but once he took up a book you could see the intelligence retreat and retreat' from his large dark eyes, 'until his mind deserted them for adventure in space and eternity'. There he would sit 'with his long hands drawn up on one side of his face like the paws of a squirrel'. (This rodent-like attitude seems to have been noted by others; one of his several nicknames was 'Weasel'.)

His reading was eclectic. He began to explore the 'English classics', but he was already drawing away from set texts and towards proscribed authors. He grew 'bored' with Dickens, whom he would praise (and dismiss) as 'our Cockney Shakespeare'. He turned instead to Chatterton, Byron and Swift. He read the *Decameron*, *Gil Blas** and 'most of the tales and verse of Edgar Allan Poe'. The

---

* Alain Le Sage's *Gil Blas*, which Scotson-Clark described as 'not exactly a book for boys', was William Pitt's favourite novel. Beardsley cherished his supposed connection with the great statesman, and he regarded the cartoon of Pitt being introduced into Hell as 'a family portrait'.

unexpurgated reprints of the Mermaid Series (which began in 1887) opened up the realms of Elizabethan and Jacobean drama and the gay world of Restoration wit and libertinage. He became a devotee of Congreve and Wycherley. Mabel had drawn the line at Carlyle, but Aubrey stepped over it and read *The French Revolution*. Even among the conventional canon of boyhood literature he had an instinct for the outré. He read Hawthorne's *Wonder Book* and *Twice Told Tales*, and A. B. Mitford's *Tales of Old Japan*. He particularly enjoyed Lewis Carroll's *Alice* books and William Thackeray's *The Rose and the Ring* – books also distinguished by their idiosyncratic illustrations. And he surprised some of his heartier contemporaries by his love of fairy stories.[7]

It was a constant challenge to feed so voracious an appetite. Beardsley was fortunate in having the run of King's bookshelves; he bought each volume of the Mermaid Series as it appeared; and on a visit to a schoolfriend's house came away with a haul of borrowed booty from the family library. This last incident suggests that Beardsley's reading was not entirely a force for isolation. While it did on occasion take him away from his contemporaries, emphasizing his self-sufficiency, it also drew him into contact with them. His desire to shine ensured that he turned what he read to account: he amused his friends with twice-told tales of his own, with pictures of imagined genii in a fairy tale; a book on the *Lives of All the Notorious Pirates* provided a rich vocabulary, and inspired a series of pirate games with his friends. Beardsley's speech became thick with piratical argot: some boys he considered 'ill-looked dogs', while to others he hissed, 'Harkee ye rogue, you will be hanged because ye have a damn'd hanging look.'

Nevertheless, King recognized that Beardsley's eccentricity might leave him on the margins of school life. His 'contradictory and humorously sarcastic cast of mind', though a source of amusement to some, might – when coupled with his lack of interest in work and games – become a force for considerable disruption. King's achievement was to harness Beardsley's energies and draw them into the fuller life of the school. He encouraged his histrionic bent. At the 'Boarders' Evening At Home', towards the end of Beardsley's first term, King got his new protégé to recite his pirate poem, 'The

Valiant', once again. It was well received: the school reviewer called it 'a really creditable little poem', and the following term it was published in full in *Past and Present*, Aubrey's first appearance in print.

Interestingly, after his first-day success with the piano piece of his 'own composition', Beardsley abandoned musical performances. He still occasionally improvised on the wheezy harmonium for his own amusement, but stopped if anyone came into the room. His skill soon rusted. In part, this retreat from music was due to the new distractions of school life: there was no time to practise. But there was also perhaps a desire to mitigate the influence of his mother.

He continued, however, to draw. Although the school offered technical drawing classes, art was not a central part of the syllabus. Beardsley's sketching and doodling were largely a matter of private pleasure, but he would occasionally take his drawings to 'Johnny' Godfrey, the semi-retired technical drawing master, for 'criticism'.

In the summer term of 1886 he met at these after-school 'crits' around Mr Godfrey's desk another boy with artistic aspirations: George Scotson-Clark. Although the same age as Beardsley, he was in the year below, making good the deficiencies of an interrupted early schooling. His late father, the Revd Frederick Scotson-Clark, had been a noted organist and composer, and the family had led an itinerant life. They had recently settled in Brighton, and the previous year George had begun attending the grammar school as a day-boy. Like Beardsley, young Scotson-Clark was an unschoolboy-like character, and it was not surprising that they should have gravitated towards each other. One contemporary remembered Scotson-Clark as a 'strange impressive youth' with pronounced views on music, literature, art and even food (in later life he wrote several cookery books). He was the great-grandson of the painter George Chinnery and, though his interests ran to acting and music, his great love was art.[8]

He and Beardsley became firm friends and at the end of the year, when Scotson-Clark was moved up into the fourth year, they sat together at the back of the form. There they warmed themselves over the hot-water pipes, doodled and generally distracted each other until they were separated after handing in very bad, but all too similar,

test papers. Their friendship was not affected. They signed up for
painting classes given by Henry Earpe, 'an excellent water-colourist
and a charming old gentleman of the old school'. They were, however, too 'full of spirit' and would not 'take instruction seriously'.
After a very short while they were told 'firmly but kindly' that they
were wasting their time, that they had no 'talent for drawing' and
would be best advised to give up. They returned, unchastened, to
independent study, using H. R. Robertson's *Handbook on Pendrawing*
as their principal guide. They showed their work not only to Godfrey
but to King and to their fourth-form master, Mr Payne. They also
submitted it to the even more critical jury of their peers.

Indeed most of Beardsley's adolescent pictures were clearly made
for the amusement of his schoolfellows; the predominant note was
humour. The caricatures, cartoons and sketches, the cod-illustrations
for schoolbooks, all reveal a desire to entertain and to subvert the
authority of a closed world. Artistically, they are of little merit –
unfinished and ephemeral, their most obvious debts are to Gilbert
A'Beckett's illustrations for *The Comic History of England*, and to the
Punch cartoons of Keene and Doyle. Aubrey was 'enthusiastic' over
the drawings of Fred Barnard, especially his caricatures of Henry
Irving. He poured out drawings of 'Irving à la Fred Barnard', rather
as Tommy Traddles in *David Copperfield* used to draw skeletons – as
a means of expressing his emotions.

The caricatures of the headmaster, however, and the comic scenes
of school life, though worked up from his imagination, were founded
upon direct and close observation.* King tried to encourage this side
of Beardsley's talent (while lessening the offence it might cause) by
getting him to do lightning portrait sketches at the house 'open days'.
Some rough drawings also exist which reveal Beardsley struggling –
apparently from a model – to master the outline of a violin in
perspective, but such instances of working from life were few.[9]

Brighton itself made little showing in Beardsley's juvenile art,
though he got to know the town well during his schooldays; he
developed a particular fondness for the Old Chain Pier and would

---

* The accuracy and acuity of his observation are also suggested by the fact that he had
a remarkable, though rarely exercised, 'talent for mimicking' (Robert Ross, *Aubrey
Beardsley*, p. 30).

wander there whenever he had lines to learn. The eccentricity of the piers, the elegance of the Regency terraces, the rococo excesses of the Pavilion, the tawdry glamour of the sea-front: all these came to play a part in his art, but their influence took time to percolate. There is only an unfinished crayon drawing of the viaduct which cuts across the road out of Brighton to suggest that he ever attempted *plein air* work in the town. No sketch of the countryside survives. Although he later affected an elaborate disdain for nature, as a boy he 'relished' the regular school 'excursions' into the Sussex hinterland. He developed a love for the local Downs' scenery, describing it as 'at once emotional and artistic – a very rare combination in nature'. He also said it was 'inexpressibly beautiful'; this perhaps deterred him from trying to express it.

Beardsley found his readiest inspiration in books. In the same way that school life and schoolmasters supplied a shared world that could be sent up, so schoolbooks offered another readily understood basis for humour. Beardsley duly enlivened his history lessons with such facetiae as King John smiling at the signing of Magna Carta and 'The Pope weigh[ing] heavily on the Church'. During the Michaelmas term of 1886, when Beardsley, together with the rest of the fourth form, was studying the *Aeneid* Book II, he was fired to new heights of creative endeavour. He was inspired to produce not only the beginnings of a full verse translation in heroic couplets and an irreverent ditty about Aeneas attempting a balloon-assisted flight but a sequence of nineteen comic drawings illustrating Aeneas's escape from Troy. The popularity of these pictures was such that he was obliged to create a second (smaller) set for Mr Payne. Once again, it seems, Beardsley was able simultaneously to undermine authority and win its approval.[10]

The strong link between art and literature in his work is seen in the liberally decorated margins of many of the books he bought at this time. He illuminated his copy of Swift's *Prose Writings* with two elaborate portraits of the author and numerous incidental illustrations; he adorned Christopher Marlowe's plays with pictures of their heroes; other volumes in the Mermaid Series received similar treatment. In these private performances he broadened his stylistic range, attempting, for instance – in a portrait of Francis Beaumont – to reproduce the effect of a steel-engraved frontispiece in pen and ink. There is little evidence, however, of wider artistic experiment or influence; he does not seem to have studied the work of great artists, either past or present. Hind-Smith had four 'copies of etchings' by Beardsley in his study, but it is probable that they were conventional topographic scenes, like the carefully copied drawing of Egham church he produced in 1886. The great achievements of the 1860s book illustrators, though readily available, do not seem to have touched him. There is certainly no trace of Pre-Raphaelitism or Aestheticism in his work at this stage, no hint that he knew the *Moxon Tennyson* or Millais' *Parables*. Even the Japanese lanterns and fans he saw in the windows of 'Aesthetic' Brighton shops excited only admiration and not, as yet, emulation. The appealing and familiar grotesqueries of Tenniel and Thackeray (and of Arthur Boyd Houghton) made no obvious showing in his juvenile work. His schoolboy drawings give little hint of what was to come. They were adjuncts to his interest in literature and drama, and they were a means of showing off.[11]

The stage also offered him a means of self-expression and self-advertisement. After some modest contributions to the boarders' 'At Homes' he began to discover a wider audience.

One of the high points of the BGS year was the Christmas Entertainment, held not on the premises at Buckingham Road but in the Dome (the Prince Regent's former riding stables next to the Pavilion), which had been converted into a theatre-cum-concert-hall for the town. Almost the whole school was involved in some capacity in these spectaculars. Mr Marshall initiated proceedings in October, settling on some theme – Robin Hood perhaps, or Christopher Columbus, or King Arthur; Messrs Fred Edmonds and C. T. West – 'the Gilbert and Sullivan of the Grammar' – then composed a comic opera on this theme. Mr King contributed a prologue in verse, while another master wrote music for the overture and procession. As a final refinement, the elements of the production made up the syllables of a charade. The boys provided the cast, chorus and band; with so many people involved, the performance could command an audience of 'three thousand not uncritical people'.

Beardsley was inevitably drawn into these events and in time took a prominent role. His contribution (if any) to the 1885 entertainment is not recorded, but by the end of his second year his talents were well enough known for him to be given a substantial part as the narrator of King's prologue. As 'Schoolboy' he was responsible for several hundred lines of rhymed pentameters giving an overview of the year and introducing the other characters in the piece: colonial types from around the empire. His name appeared first on the cast list, and an illustration of him by F. J. Stride, a junior master, was included in the programme. Here was a taste of celebrity.[12]

At the beginning of the following term his thespian interests received another boost. A new boy arrived in his year, a 'merry-faced youngster' named Charles Cochran, later a famous theatrical impresario. At fourteen, Cochran had already served notice of his love of spectacle: he had been expelled from his previous school for sloping off to see the Guy Fawkes fireworks display in the town. Beardsley exerted himself to welcome this infamous new arrival; he sat next to him at dinner the first evening. Cochran recalled Beardsley's bearing: 'He was a particularly quick talker, used his hands to gesticulate and altogether had an un-English air about him.' Their conversation soon revealed a shared interest – the stage. Beardsley greatly impressed Cochran with his recherché knowledge and tastes, and they became friends.

Mr King was delighted to have another drama enthusiast 'in house', and encouraged Beardsley and Cochran to organize a house-concert together. It was the first of several. Together with Scotson-Clark, who as a day-boy was not officially supposed to take part, they organized frequent small-scale theatrical entertainments, made up of 'a farce, songs and recitations'. Each boy had his own speciality: Beardsley, borrowing from Mabel's repertoire, performed the skating scene from Pickwick with amazing brio – and perhaps even on rollerskates; he also recited Thomas Hood's Victorian stock favourites 'The Dream of Eugene Aram' and 'Mary's Ghost'. Together, the three mounted productions of one-act staples such as Box and Cox, Ici on Parle Français and The Spitalfields Weaver, productions which (according to Cochran) were distinguished not only by Beardsley's 'remarkable' characterizations but also by the striking 'facial makeups' which he effected 'with a box of water-colours and brushes'.

These enterprises-in-common bound the three friends together, and inspired them to the usual round of schoolboy mischief. They concocted ingenious schemes to raise funds for their clandestine trips to matinées at the Brighton Theatre, and became aficionados, passing 'many a youthful judgement' upon the actresses they saw. They also carried their dramatic activities beyond the stage. On one occasion (if Cochran is to be believed), when Brighton Grammar School was playing a cricket match in Eastbourne against the college from which Cochran had been expelled, Beardsley and Cochran accompanied the team in the nominal capacity of 'scorers'. Arriving at Eastbourne, Beardsley disguised himself as an old man, with a false beard and wig, and called on the host school's headmaster. He presented himself as 'Jasper Rayner', claiming to be recently returned from the Californian goldfields, and asked whether he might take his two nephews out for tea. The headmaster, apparently taken in by the deception, agreed; Beardsley was able to whisk the two Rayner boys off to the Albion Hotel, where they met Cochran and had crumpets for tea.[13]

All three friends were in the following year's Jubilee spectacular. Beardsley again took the narrator's role in the prologue: he embodied the Spirit of Progress and was dressed as Minerva (the school crest) in one of matron's nightdresses, a flaxen wig, and a Roman gladiator's helmet from a theatrical costumier. He introduced a succession of historical figures, including Henry II, played by Scotson-Clark, and Henry VII, played by Cochran. The clarity of Beardsley's diction and the effectiveness of his make-up earned 'special praise' from the *Past and Present* reviewer.

His status at the school was growing. King asked him to contribute some cartoons to *Past and Present*. His 'Jubilee Cricket Analysis' – a series of pictorial puns on cricketing terms – was published in the June 1887 issue, and marked Beardsley's first appearance in print as an artist. He had been obliged to re-draw the pictures for reproduction in the 'less manageable medium' of lithographer's ink, and

OPPOSITE 'The Jubilee Cricket Analysis': Beardsley's first published drawing, printed in *Past and Present*, June 1887.

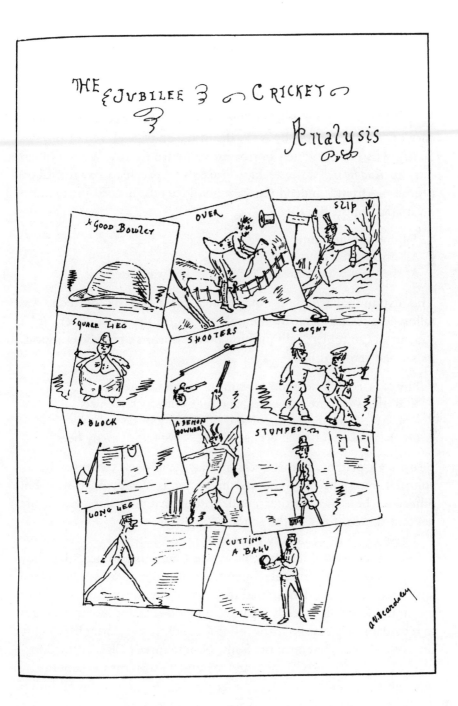

they appeared with a caption explaining this and apologizing for any loss of clarity. There was advance, too, on the literary front. After the satisfaction of seeing 'The Valiant' set in type, Beardsley had raised his literary sights. Soon 'prolific in original verse', he began submitting his efforts to a local weekly. The same month that saw the publication of the 'Jubilee Cricket Analysis' witnessed the appearance of 'Two-To-One' by A. V. Beardsley on page eleven of *Brighton Society*. His poem, which borrowed its metre from a W. S. Gilbert ditty in *Ruddigore*, was a feckless gadabout's paean to pawn-brokers ('those old friends indeed who are good friends in need'); its chorus a variation upon the theme,

> Till my fortunes amend
> All my chattels must end
> At the shop where three balls o'er the doorway extend.

This extramural triumph, considerable for a boy of fourteen, was followed a month later by the publication, in the same paper, of 'A Ride in an Omnibus', a disquisition on the horrors of public transport. Its second stanza runs:

> First you get a little huddled with the odorous unélite
> And unless you are a Socialist, and love with such to meet,
> You have most distracting visions of an army of disease
> Or the tortures of an insect, which are – well not exactly bees . . .

Beardsley's delight on this occasion may have been tempered by an editorial oversight that rendered his name as W. V. Beardsley, but otherwise here was further confirmation that his talent had a life beyond the confines of the school.[14]

These two bits of literary puerilia are too slight and too derivative to bear much exposition. It is, however, interesting to note that they both reflect with wry detachment the travails of a fastidious and aristocratic temperament forced into contact with the imperatives of vulgar life. Beardsley clearly regarded himself – had indeed been taught to regard himself – as above the 'odorous unélite'; no matter how many of his chattels might end at the house 'where three balls o'er the doorway extend', he proclaimed and extended this innate superiority through the exercise of art. Though his achievements gained him a reputation, they did not dominate the life of the school. One master, when pressed in later years for reminiscences of Beardsley's time at BGS, excused himself as unable to remember anything, remarking peevishly, 'Who was to know he would be great?'

Some, however, seem to have recognized at least the possibility. Beardsley had several supporters among the staff. There were those, like Payne, who saw something in his 'quaint personality' that raised him 'above the level of other boys of his own age'. Indeed his easy familiarity with the masters, as well as the senior boys, provoked comment, and sometimes resentment, from his contemporaries. It was not that he toadied to his elders; almost the reverse. He was not awed; unlike most schoolboys, he treated the masters without alarm or, indeed, deference: Payne recalled how Beardsley was wont to use his 'peculiar dry wit' at his 'academic preceptor's expense'. Another contemporary's suggestion, that the masters sought Beardsley's favour because they feared his caricatures, seems to misread the equation.

Although he was on friendly terms with many of the masters -- Mr Marshall, Mr Lampson, 'Mr Sam' Marshall, Mr 'Fred' Carr, and particularly Mr Payne – his greatest ally remained Mr King. He was 'a great favourite' with the housemaster, taking long walks with him and spending many happy evenings in his room discussing books, plays, art, the aesthetic effects of candlelight and the intoxicating possibilities of life beyond school.[15]

To many of his contemporaries, however, he remained something of an enigma. Among the school's 'more lively spirits of adventure' (as one schoolfellow put it) he was 'looked upon as a very quiet boy': 'We used to think he cared a little too much for himself. He always looked very white – and often in manner seemed very sad. If you were a sportsman you could not chum up to him a bit.' (Something of his attractiveness is suggested by the hint that these sportsmen *wanted* to 'chum up to him'.)

His predilection for day-dreaming and solitude caused bewilderment, if not exasperation, in some quarters. To Hind-Smith, Beardsley was always 'mooning around'. Another classmate, when asked for a recollection, answered tersely that all he could recall of him was that he 'sketched in school hours instead of working, that he was very cadaverous looking, and astonishingly greedy and was not one of my pals'. A marked individuality seemed to stamp everything he did: a third contemporary preserved the memory of him 'sliding down the banisters beneath the morosely ticking old clock' with 'a peculiarly lithe movement, not like other boys'.

He could always, when he chose, draw a crowd for one of his extemporized flights of fancy; he was not unpopular: his propensity for getting into 'mild scrapes' endeared him to the majority of his fellows. Nevertheless, his real 'pals' were few; of the circle of 'three or four intimate schoolmates' the closest remained Cochran (who became his study companion) and Scotson-Clark. With them he formed the strongest ties and, bound by their joint endeavours, they made a triumvirate. To the other two, Beardsley was known by a meaningless but affectionate nickname: Beale.[16]

He cultivated his reputation and personality with some care; certain affectations of expression were already becoming apparent. He enthused over aesthetic details with the convoluted exclamation, 'Is not that very good indeed', delivered in a peculiar 'restless, persistent way'. To enhance his reputation for obscure learning, he began 'of his own accord' to study Greek; although any achievement of his in this direction was largely a myth. In dress, while yet to gain the reputation of a dandy, he had, after his first term, exchanged the embarrassing knickerbockers for long trousers and an Eton jacket, but was hampered in his attempts at sartorial elegance by the speed with which he was growing. Early each term his trousers parted company with his Eton jacket; and though he stooped slightly to hide the gap at the front, this merely exposed an expanse of shirt at the back. His socks appeared in the ever-widening margin between the bottom of his trousers and the top of his boots, and his long thin hands dangled 'some four or five inches below his cuffs'.

At some time, probably during the summer of 1887, Beardsley's flair for self-dramatization found a new outlet – in romance. There was a small privately run girls' school around the corner from Buckingham Road in Alexandra Villas, and Beardsley conceived a passion

OPPOSITE C. B. Cochran and G. F. Scotson-Clark as Mr and Mrs Spriggins, in T. J. Williams's farce, *Ici On Parle Français*, performed at BGS on 23 February 1888 (and revived 9 March). Beardsley took the part of the Frenchman, Victor.

for one of its pupils – though passion is perhaps too strong a word. The two letters that survive from him to his 'own love', Miss Felton, are so facetious, so hedged with irony and mock excess, so copiously decorated with self-caricatures, as to suggest that his love was as mythical as his knowledge of Greek. It is doubtful that there was any basis to this relationship; he was merely playing at love, exercising his wit and discovering the dandiacal convention whereby an emotion can be avoided by exaggerating it to the point of absurdity. His one essay at love poetry was:

> For thee I am dying,
> For thee I am sighing
> For thee I am bursting, like fine ginger pop,
> Whilst this letter is flying
> With rapture I'm crying

(PS) Don't show this, I beg you, to dear Betsy Topp.
[Headmistress of Miss Felton's school]*

That the episode was a self-regarding performance seems confirmed by Beardsley's slip of the pen in his opening sentence: 'Imagine my *delight*, rapture, joy, *delight*, pleasure, happiness on opening & reading my [sic] letter.' The offending 'my' is lightly scored through and replaced with 'your'; hardly the sign of an anxious lover. An echo of this sealed emotional stance is found on the flyleaf of Beardsley's copy of Marlowe's plays, purchased on 4 May 1887; he inscribed it to 'A. V. Beardsley from his loving self'.[17]

Despite the social and cultural distractions of school life, he tried to maintain his association with the Church of the Annunciation. One of the masters accompanied him several times to evensong there, and indeed was under the impression that Father Chapman was Beardsley's guardian. The gulf between the cheerful profanities of schoolboy existence and the earnest sobriety of Washington Street must have been great. Although there is some suggestion that Beardsley did try to bridge the gap between his artistic and his religious

---

* Miss Felton's identity is a mystery. There was a Felton family living near Buckingham Road at 7 Hova Villas. The 1891 Census shows that Mr Felton was a dentist and that he had a daughter Gladys, aged eleven. It is, however, unlikely that Aubrey was writing mock love letters in 1887 to an eight-year-old girl.

interests by illustrating the *Psalms* and the *Song of Solomon* (and it is known that Charles Thornton, an assistant curate, was an admirer of Beardsley's early drawings), for the most part the two worlds remained separate. Father Chapman did not approve of the theatre, so that whole new side of Beardsley's interest remained closed off. The ability to compartmentalize his life and his friends – an ability which became such a marked feature in later years – was already apparent in his dealings with his schoolboy world.

Another division to be negotiated was between family and school. Although Aubrey continued to visit his great-aunt at Lower Rock Gardens throughout his schooldays, Mabel had, it seems, left Brighton for the parental home in London soon after Aubrey started at BGS. What her schooling was remains unknown, although her aptitude for academic work clearly exceeded her brother's. She walked off 'with every prize for which she competed' (a fact which further disinclined Aubrey to scholastic exertion). In the holidays he returned to Pimlico, where home life was limited and drab. His grandfather, the Surgeon-Major, died suddenly on 27 October 1887, in a Bloomsbury guesthouse, but his death brought no windfall to the Beardsleys. He left only his meagre army pension for the support of his widow; and she was obliged to take shelter with her sister, Georgiana Lamb (also recently widowed), in Holland Road. Ellen and Vincent still had to seek work wherever they could find it. Although, on one occasion, Aubrey was taken to the theatre to see his hero, Irving, such treats were rare. There was little real possibility for his enjoying the opportunities London afforded.[18]

In the face of this pinched constraint, he strove to prolong the excitements of his school world and to communicate them to Mabel. Left alone together for most of the day, Aubrey could relive the experiences of the term for his sister's benefit, refining his understanding of events in the process. Together they read the plays of the Mermaid Series. And it was during the school holidays that they began the tradition of putting on little theatrical performances in the family drawing-room. 'My husband and I', Ellen Beardsley later recalled, 'were the only spectators and as we were busy people then, these performances were got up to brighten our evenings.' She remembered one 'wonderful' three-hour (!) performance of Goethe's

Faust, with Mabel in the title role and Aubrey (with 'long straw plaits fastened on each side of his head') as Margaret. To increase the scope of their repertoire they even made a model theatre; Aubrey painted the scenery, while Mabel and Ellen dressed the puppet performers.

Spurred by the success of the concerts he was putting on at school with Cochran and Scotson-Clark, Aubrey deserted the classics. He and Mabel began to stage similar shows of songs, recitations, and short sketches. The scale of their performances grew: they produced elaborate hand-drawn programmes, playbills and even tickets; it is to be supposed that the audiences were swelled by a few family friends.[19]

The Michaelmas term of 1888 was Beardsley's last at Brighton Grammar School. It was garlanded with triumphs both artistic and theatrical. The headmaster had spent the summer holidays travelling in British Columbia, visiting many of the Old Boys who had settled there. Marshall decided to give a lecture to the school on his experiences, and commissioned Beardsley (whose caricatures of him were well known) to draw a series of humorous pictures which could be used as lantern slides. The pictures were simple and stylized, constrained by the limitations of the medium, but the commission shows Marshall's imagination and magnanimity as a schoolmaster; it also highlights, once again, Beardsley's ambiguous position as both supporter and subverter of the established order.

With the coming of November plans for the Christmas 'Dome' were formulated. Mr King would, once again, contribute a prologue, and 'The Pied Piper of Hamelin' would provide the story for the operatic charade. By chance – if we are to believe his testimony – Scotson-Clark had already done some illustrations for Browning's poem, and he submitted these to Marshall in the hope that they might be used to publicize the opera. The pictures, however, were deemed unsuitable, and Marshall asked Beardsley, who was seeing him on some other matter, to return them. Beardsley, his curiosity piqued, examined the pictures and decided to attempt his own sequence.

Although it is difficult to establish an exact chronology of Beardsley's surviving BGS drawings, he appears to have made some advance in technique and ambition during 1888; portraits of Paganini and Sarah Bernhardt and an illustration for Congreve's *Double Dealer* display a more confident handling of line, a richer sense of detail and the reawakening of his interest in the grotesque. The drawings he did for the 'Pied Piper' give a fuller account of this progress. They were executed in faint brown ink, and there is an expressive fluidity in the fine lines which is not to be found in his earlier work. The grotesque aspect of the story – well illustrated in the bold design of the rats gathered on the truckle cheese – is, however, undercut by the return of another of Beardsley's early influences: Kate Greenaway. Greenaway's drawings for the 'Pied Piper' were not made until 1889, but it is her spirit which infuses the gambolling children in Beardsley's illustrations.

He submitted these efforts to Mr Marshall. The headmaster was impressed by their strength of conception and design and, after consultation with some of the school's arbiters of style, decided to accept them for inclusion in the Dome programme. Scotson-Clark, while admitting the superiority of Beardsley's pictures, was understandably shocked at the duplicity and ruthlessness of his friend, and a short-lived *froideur* ensued between them.

The performance of *The Pay of the Pied Piper* was held on 19 December; it was an evening of sustained triumph for Beardsley such as few schoolboys can hope to experience. Eleven of his pictures appeared in the programme; the glory of the moment was slightly undercut by an appended notice apologizing that, 'lacking experience in the preparation of drawings for the photo-engraver', the reproductions should fall so far short of the original sketches. This was a second reminder, after the struggle with the lithographer's ink for the 'Jubilee Cricket Analysis', of the gap that could open between original artwork and printed reproduction. Although the grace and detail of his figures were indeed lost in the crude published versions, some fractured charm remained. And the audience, without the originals before them, accepted and admired the printed pictures.

Beardsley, as ever, took a prominent part in the evening's dramatic proceedings. Once again he had the leading role in the rhymed prologue, and his performance and 'get-up' as Mercury, the messenger of the gods, drew general praise. In the comic opera he contented himself with the minor part of Herr Kirschwasser, alongside Cochran, but even here he made an impression. One impartial observer recalled him as a 'lanky youth of sixteen' who brought an adult spirit to the performance hardly less convincing than that of Mr (E. H.) Payne (as the Pied Piper) himself.

Beardsley made his exit from the stage of the Dome, and from the happy world of Brighton Grammar School, as a published poet, a reproduced artist, an acclaimed performer: a boy very much 'in conceit with himself'.*[19]

Illustration to *The Pay of the Pied Piper*, 1888.

* At the end-of-term 'Prize Distribution' Beardsley was one of eleven boys awarded a 'Good Conduct' medal; the medal is preserved at the Brighton Museum and Art Gallery. Ross states that Beardsley left school in July 1888, and this dating has been followed by others, but a letter from A. W. King to H. A. Payne (4 December 1920) in the BGS archive makes it clear that Beardsley 'left at Xmas 1888'.

CHAPTER III

'An Art Training'

BEARDSLEY LEFT SCHOOL in December 1888 and trailed his clouds of glory back to 32 Cambridge Street, the modest Pimlico lodging house where the family was currently settled. Returning to the small domestic circle and the imminent prospect of conventional employment, Aubrey tried to prolong the moment, and the momentum, of his recent triumph. On 31 December he and Mabel staged a grand Christmas Entertainment, transforming the first-floor drawing-room into the 'Cambridge Theatre of Varieties'. They offered a programme of songs, monologues and, as a finale, the one-act farce *Box and Cox*, for which Ellen Beardsley was drafted in to take the part of Mrs Bouncer, the landlady – her 'first appearance', as Aubrey's hand-drawn playbill proclaimed. It is certainly to be hoped that Vincent was not the only audience on this occasion, not least because one of the main plot devices of the playlet was a threatened breach-of-promise action, which, in an exclusively familial setting, would have twisted the blade in the wound of his embarrassment and remorse.

Drawing-room theatricals, however, offered only a limited respite. The decision to take Aubrey out of school seems to have been prompted by practical considerations; reality had to be faced, and reality meant paid employment. Vincent, apart from occasional

OPPOSITE 'Self-portrait', *c.* 1891.

clerical work from wine merchants, had no job, and Ellen's teaching was piecemeal and erratic. Mabel, conspicuously bright academically, was allowed to continue her schooling, but this concession had its practical aspect: Ellen knew that teaching, one of the few respectable job opportunities then open to women, depended upon a sound education.

For Aubrey, whatever his interests and talents, there was no question of an artistic career; he was destined for the City. A family connection of the Pitts was exerting influence to secure him a clerkship at the Guardian Fire and Life Assurance Company in Lombard Street. Such things, however, took time, and in the meanwhile he was found a place as a clerk in the district surveyor's office of Clerkenwell and Islington at 8 Wilmington Square. He began work on the first day of the new year, and although he came to represent his time there as an apprenticeship in an architect's office, giving it a professional and artistic aspect, his real duties were dull and narrowly clerical. If he did any drawing it was in the margins of his ledger. Certainly he could muster little enthusiasm for his new position, though he admitted to King in a letter that he did not 'exactly dislike' the job and that the work was 'not hard'.

Throughout 1889 Beardsley made the daily cross-town trip from Pimlico to Islington, travelling on foot or by horse-drawn omnibus, one of the great army of office workers who headed east each morning to sit on high stools at sloping desks scratching away with steel-nibbed pens for the meagre reward of 'thirty bob a week'. Beardsley would have started on even less than this. Nevertheless, the fact of a first pay packet is exciting, and although he was expected to contribute substantially to the family expenses there was something left over for pleasure. During that first year of salaried metropolitan existence he eked out his free money and time on music, books and – particularly – the theatre. The London stage offered a range of possibilities far beyond Brighton. Among the highlights, Beardsley records Henry Irving's 'splendid' *Macbeth* with Ellen Terry as Lady Macbeth, and music ('a great disappointment') by Arthur Sullivan.[1]

He continued to read voraciously, consciously building up his knowledge of the canonical authors. Besides collecting the Mermaid books, he bought a handsome edition of *Shakespeare's Poems*, decorating its title page with a delicate pencil portrait of the poet, and marking its margins with numerous annotations. Beyond some conventional comments upon Shakespeare's enduring genius, his main concern (to judge from the marginalia) was to establish not so much the identity as the sex of the recipient of the Sonnets. Other books he acquired at this time were Scott's *Poems* (an unlikely choice, but it appears to have been part of his school prize), Fielding's *Tom Jones* and an English translation of Goethe's *Faust*.

He began to frequent Holywell Street, the long-vanished maze of alleys and courts thick with second-hand bookshops that used to exist where the Aldwych now stands. It had a Dickensian (if not Hogarthian) charm, and though it was a haven for the capital's bibliophiles it also had a reputation for scandal. There were frequent raids on the under-the-counter pedlars of obscene literature and art. It was a place and an atmosphere that appealed to Beardsley; he captured both in a small, impressionistic wash drawing he did at the time.

He presented this little picture to Cochran, for, though the close and artistically stimulating world of the grammar school had fragmented, Beardsley maintained a connection. He attended the meetings of the London branch of the BGS Old Boys' Association and, more importantly, kept in touch with his old friends in Brighton. Mr King was still at the school, as were Mr Marshall and Mr Payne; while Scotson-Clark and Cochran were both working in the town, the former for a wine-merchant; the latter, like Beardsley, was in the district surveyor's office. The train service from Victoria was swift and frequent, and so was the penny post. Cochran and Scotson-Clark were both fretting at the drudgery of clerical work and refusing to abandon their dreams of careers in the service of art; Cochran longed for the stage, while Scotson-Clark's aspirations flitted from painting to acting to music. The sense of shared hope and ambition bound the three young friends in mutual support and encouragement.[2]

Encouragement was necessary. Despite the excitement of occasional visits to Brighton and fitful correspondence, despite also the companionship of Mabel and the diversions of theatre trips, concerts and book browsing, the limits of Beardsley's London life remained

frustratingly narrow. The one regular escape from the pinched reali-
ties of existence was afforded by religion. At this period the Beardsleys
were attending St Barnabas, Pimlico, which, despite its designation,
was some distance from Cambridge Street across Ebury Bridge,
almost on the fringes of Belgravia. Hailed soon after its completion
in 1850 as the 'most sumptuous and correctly fitted church erected
in England since the Reformation', in the late 1880s it was still among
the 'highest' Anglo-Catholic churches in London. It had a small
attached choir school and, under a series of musicological choir-
masters, had developed a reputation for ecclesiastical music and plain-
song 'unsurpassed and unsurpassable'.

The priest in charge was the Revd Alfred Gurney, a wealthy
ecclesiastic of aesthetic aspect and inclinations, whose enthusiasms
extended from art and literature to riding and opera. He had known
the Beardsleys in Brighton when, as a junior cleric, he had been a
curate at the parish church. He was also a close friend of Father
Chapman, the priest at the Annunciation, which may have persuaded
Mabel to seek him out when she returned to London. There exists
a copy of his volume of devotional verse, *A Christmas Faggot*, inscribed
to 'Mabel Beardsley, Christmas 1885' from the author. Father Gurney
lived in the clergy house adjacent to the church, where old furniture,
Pre-Raphaelite pictures and liveried servants carried over the sense
of aesthetic splendour from the church into the priest's domestic life.
The Beardsleys had access to this charmed home, and were occasionally invited to stay to lunch after the Sunday morning service. The
ambience of the Gurney dining-room offered a cultured affluence far
removed from the drab semi-respectability of Mr Gardner's lodging
house. It gave Aubrey sight of an adult world governed by love of
the beautiful and appreciation of the fine.

There were often other guests: the priest's brothers – Edmund,
an author of books on psychical research, and Willie, who had a
reputation as the black sheep of the family – and their widowed
aunt, Mrs Russell Gurney, who was spending her fortune on the
decoration of the Chapel of the Ascension in the Bayswater Road.
Lord and Lady Halifax came sometimes. The church's erstwhile
organist, G. H. Palmer, editor of a celebrated collection of office
hymns and (like Father Gurney) a Wagner enthusiast, was a frequent

guest; as, of course, were the assistant clergy. Among Father Gurney's curates was one with the conspicuous name Oscar Wilde*. Another was Gerald Sampson; he met the Beardsleys often at lunch, perhaps sometimes together with his dilettante brother, Julian. Often children were of the party, and Aubrey – a shy sixteen-year-old removed from the scenes of his schoolboy success – gravitated to them. He befriended Edmund Gurney's seven-year-old daughter Helen and drew pictures to illustrate her homeric poems; when he was drawn into the circle of the grown-ups it seems to have been his love of music rather than any precocity at drawing which distinguished him. Father Gurney looked on him kindly, and Palmer was delighted to find in Aubrey another spirit keenly responsive to German opera.†[3]

In the late summer of 1889, Beardsley met Mr King, who was passing through London on his way back from a holiday in France. Mr King had recently been appointed secretary of the Blackburn Technical Institute and was due to take up his post in September; Beardsley was about to begin his probationary period at the Guardian Insurance office. Nevertheless, the principal topic of conversation was contemporary French culture. King had been dazzled by what he had seen of French art and literature, and was eager to communicate his excitement. He primed his encomium with the remark that there was something peculiarly akin to the gallic spirit in Beardsley's make-up. This perceptive observation, backed by King's enthusiasm, stirred new impulses in Aubrey; his previous cultural explorations had been confined to England; French literature was a novel and enticing vista. The chance to explore it arrived more promptly than he expected, and more dramatically than he would have wished.

As the autumn of 1889 advanced, his health, for so long in a state of illusory equilibrium, declined sharply. The primary tuberculosis

* Revd Oscar Wade Wilde, BA Oxon. (1858–1945) served as a curate at St Barnabas between 1885 and 1893. He subsequently became a rural dean in the diocese of Ely. There is no record that he ever met his illustrious namesake.

† Beardsley's love of music in general and Wagner's operas in particular impressed itself on all who knew him. One friend recalled sitting behind him at a performance of *Tristan und Isolde* and watching his 'transparent hands clutching the rail in front, and thrilling with the emotion of the music'. (Gleeson White, 'Aubrey Beardsley In Memoriam', *The Studio*, 1898, p. 260.)

infection, dormant for almost a decade, reawakened with new force. The strain and pace of London life, the stressful prospect of a new job, the unhealthy conditions of the airless office and the crowded omnibus, the physical changes of adolescence: all probably contributed to this grim development. As ulcerated cavities began to form themselves on his lung tissue, he succumbed to exhaustion. His nights burnt with fever, his days were racked with frightful coughing, and he became used to inspecting his sputum for the telltale flecks of red. Then, before the year was out, he suffered his first alarming haemoptysis: a sudden and ineluctable flow of blood from the mouth.

Work, of course, became impossible. A specialist had to be consulted. Aubrey was taken to Cavendish Square to see Dr Edmund Symes-Thompson, a second-generation expert on the subject of tuberculosis, who had written extensively on the suitability of different climates for consumptives. Confronted by Beardsley's case, he pronounced himself shocked at the overall state of his patient's health and amazed that he could have continued so long before falling victim to the present crisis. He could, however, offer no practical solution beyond complete rest. And indeed if, at this point, Aubrey could have had total rest, together with fresh air, he might have recovered; but, rather than embracing the regime of mountain air and enforced stillness which a sanatorium would have offered, he was merely put to bed at 32 Cambridge Street with the window open and left to his own devices.

His own understanding of his condition, and its seriousness, seems at first to have been limited. Although doubtless frightened by the 'blood spitting' episodes, he wrote to King soon after the consultation that the real problem was his 'heart' and that his lungs were 'not diseased at all'. This seems almost certainly to have been a misinterpretation of Symes-Thompson's remarks, and it is uncertain how long Aubrey persisted in it. Perhaps the specialist had deliberately sought to allay his patient's anxieties by directing attention away from the seat of the disease; perhaps Beardsley had merely misunderstood him. Nevertheless, the debilitating exhaustion which was the illness's most constant symptom could not be ignored. Rest was not only prescribed; it was all that was possible.[4]

Forced to idleness, he sought relief from the tedium in books. He made a study of medical encyclopaedias in an attempt to learn something of his disease; he read the Romantic poets, and, following King's prompting, turned to the literature of France. Though he read Racine with real pleasure, the main force of his reading was directed towards the French novel: *Manon Lescaut*, *Madame Bovary*, *La Dame aux Camélias*, the works of Daudet, Dumas and Zola, and – most importantly – of their great predecessor, Balzac. It was at this time that he laid the groundwork for his reputation as the man who had read the whole of the *Comédie humaine*. Although some of the titles were available in translation, Beardsley read most in the original. His schoolboy grasp of the language improved to a point where he was able to boast that he could read French 'almost as easily as English'.

The impact of this reading was enormous. From the medical text books he learned something of his illness, but rather more about the curiosities of nature: the weird forms of unborn embryos and twisted cripples. In the career of Keats and the story of *La Dame aux Camélias* Beardsley encountered the two most powerful contemporary myths of the consumptive as a figure of doomed genius and infinite fascination, and began to assimilate them to his vision of himself and his alarming condition.

Dumas' book, together with the other French novels, opened a wider horizon: sex. Flaubert, Prévost, Balzac and others put sex at the centre of human experience. They treated it with a frankness and cynicism quite alien to English novelists; it is not going too far to say that the harlot was the presiding genius of the genre. This trait was, of course, present in the Restoration dramas which Beardsley knew and loved, but in the French novel it found settings all but contemporary and situations immediately plausible.

Beardsley's excitement at this new world struggled to find an outlet in self-expression. He began a series of small ink-and-wash sketches illustrating some of his favourite scenes and characters: Emma Bovary, Manon, Cousin Pons, and the *Dame aux Camélias* herself. Reading also inspired him to write. He attempted an elliptical and humorous short story. Although the tale – a first-person account of a lover's fall from grace after his fiancée discovers his mock declaration of love for another in a friend's 'Confession Album' – shows little obvious influence of French 'Realism', it must have derived from his rising sense of the possibilities of literature. Moreover, the narrator's castigation of those painfully conventional individuals 'who claim Shakespeare for their favourite poet, Beethoven for their favourite composer and Raphael for their favourite artist' suggests that Beardsley's explorations in French literature had given a boost of confidence to his heretical enthusiasms. Elsewhere in the story, an allusion to the narrator's fortunate escape from a breach-of-promise suit perhaps marks Aubrey's growing impatience with, and independence from, his father.

If the story hinted at a new vision of independence, it also suggested a means of achieving it. Beardsley sent 'The Story of a Confession Album' to the popular periodical *Tit-bits* and was immediately crowned with success; the story was accepted.

Although he kept to his bed, or to a large armchair in the family sitting-room, the exertions of writing and drawing, even of reading without a bookrest, were more than had been intended by the prescribed 'complete rest'. The haemorrhages continued. Aubrey, in his own rueful phrase, spent the Christmas of 1889 'on slops and over basins'. The new year, however, was brightened by the appearance of his short story, published on 4 January. He received a cheque for thirty shillings. After the limited and parochial literary triumphs of *Past and Present* and *Brighton Society*, this was national exposure, though not, alas, national fame: contributions were unsigned. The fee, however, was a tangible measure of success; it represented more than a week's wages for a junior clerk.[5]

The afterglow of this achievement spread over the early months of 1890 and doubtless hastened his slow return of strength. The equation between a week's wages and one very short short story perhaps occurred to him. Certainly he was proudly conscious that people were prepared to pay for his writing, and this awareness gradually resolved into a decision. If he were to escape the treadmill of office life and make a career in art it must be with words rather than with pictures. He resolved to 'crush' the 'drawing faculty' out of himself.

At the beginning of May, in what appears to have been a deliberate act of closure, he gathered up the best of his recent pen-and-wash pictures and mounted them in a half-roan-bound album, which he solemnly inscribed with his name and the date. Henceforth he would be a writer. Given his great love of the theatre and the constant demands of the Victorian stage, it was not surprising that he decided to write a play. He embarked, rather too ambitiously, on a three-act drama, and could not get beyond the first act. He had more success with a monologue entitled, perhaps revealingly, 'The Race for Wealth'; at least he finished it.[6]

By July, time was running out. After the false beginning of the previous year, Aubrey was due to start in earnest at the Guardian Assurance office at the end of the month; the horizons were closing in once more. Mabel contributed to this mood. Having won a prize at the Higher Local Cambridge Examination, she had been offered a scholarship at Newnham College, Cambridge, but had been obliged to decline it. Instead, she had accepted a post as a high school teacher; term would begin in September.*

In mid-July Cochran came up to Pimlico from Brighton, and the three of them spent a happy day in town. They went to a 'memorable' matinée performance of *As You Like It* at the Lyceum, with the great American actress Ada Rehan as Rosalind. Cochran's love of the theatre was undiminished, and he was still scheming how he might escape from his office job to a life on the stage. His infectious energy and optimism must have sustained Aubrey at such a time; it would have touched Mabel too, for she was stage-struck and would have loved to have been starting in the theatre rather than the schoolroom.

It was perhaps on this day that Cochran asked Beardsley to write a play for him. He wanted something to perform at that year's BGS Old Boys' 'Conversazione' in November, and thought that his literary friend might be able to provide it. Beardsley was delighted at the prospect and set to work to produce a one-act farce revolving around the comic confusions of two neighbours called Charles Brown.†

* Mabel's exam successes are attested to by Aubrey's letter to E. J. Marshall (autumn 1892), but the exact dates are difficult to pinpoint and remain conjectural.
† In the Minute Book of the BGS Old Boys' Association, 1879–1900, the proposed play is mentioned at a meeting held on 14 October 1890. Its title was given as *Neighbours*, but was subsequently changed to *A Brown Study*.

On 30 July he went to Lombard Street for his first day at the
Guardian Fire and Life Assurance office, as a 'temporary junior clerk'
in the Home Fire Department at a salary of £50 per annum. The
work was tedious; as he sat on his high stool making out insurance
policies, his attention drifted. In King's phrase, 'his sketches were
numerous and so were his mistakes'.

Although the firm prided itself on its aristocratic connections and
sober tenor, there was a certain camaraderie among the junior clerks,
and anything that offered diversion from the drudgery of work was
readily accepted. When Beardsley arrived, there was still excitement
about a young clerk with a gift for mimicry who had enlivened long
afternoons with impromptu performances and had now become a
professional actor. Beardsley took note: escape was possible, and
artistic expression was tolerated. His caricatures had won him popularity at school and he tried the same ploy in the office. One friend
who visited Lombard Street recalled Beardsley showing him 'a piece
of paper from his blotting pad, on which he had sketched the portraits
of many of his companions, and some exceedingly able portraits
of . . . senior officials of the office, all of them slightly tinged with
caricature'. One of these was so 'amazingly clever' that Aubrey
retreated to a darker corner of the office before he would show it;
from that position, his friend had a clear view of the official in
question inside a glass enclosure, and was able to appreciate the
skill of the caricature. Such 'dangerous work' was enough to secure
Beardsley a reputation among his fellows. Caricaturing sharpened
Beardsley's vision: it required close observation from life. His depth of
concentration and almost compulsive delight in drawing were revealed
when, overcome by a 'sudden impulse to sketch portraits of two curious countrymen' who came into the office, he 'entirely spoiled an
important document he was copying by drawing upon it'.[7]

His interest in art drew him into particular friendship with A. G.
Pargeter, a young clerk with artistic yearnings, who sat on the next
stool to him. They took to exploring the City's bookshops and
printsellers during their lunch hours, and at weekends they visited
the British Museum and the public art galleries. They even found a
few points of artistic interest in the office: not only were there some
impressive portraits of past chairmen, but the current directors had

commissioned a painting of the company emblem ('Minerva in her Temple') from Sir Edward Poynter, RA. This highly stylized 'classical' picture had been converted into a 'notable and richly coloured' poster, a copy of which hung above their desks. And though Beardsley joked that it added fresh horror to office hours, the image must have offered a tantalizing reminder of an artistic world pulsing beyond Lombard Street.

This pulse could be felt more strongly in the bookshop of Jones & Evans in Queen Street, off Cheapside. The place was a City institution. Due to its wide-ranging stock and happy tolerance of browsers, it was known as the 'University of the City clerk'. Beardsley became a keen student. He was a conspicuous figure each lunch hour: pale, angular, 'dipping into eighteenth century books', he soon aroused the curiosity of Frederick Evans, the joint proprietor. Evans was a diminutive red-haired Cambrian in his late thirties, a man of fragile health but febrile energy and sensitivity. He was a pioneer photographer, erudite bibliophile and discriminating print collector; a music lover for whom (according to his friend Bernard Shaw) 'an exciting performance of a Beethoven symphony was as disastrous as a railway collision to an ordinary philistine'; he was both a passionate Wagnerian and one of the first people 'to perceive and publicly uphold . . . the subtler possibilities of the pianola'. It is not surprising that, when he engaged the diffident Beardsley in conversation, he struck some answering chords.[8]

Beardsley's enthusiasm during the last quarter of 1890 was Italy. His reading – after the concentrated French study during his illness and convalescence – had swooped on Florence and the Middle Ages; under the influence of Pargeter he discovered Dante, and affected to read him in the original. This shift towards the medieval, and the Italian, was also precipitated by a discovery on another front: Dante Gabriel Rossetti. It seems that Scotson-Clark introduced Beardsley to the work of the great Pre-Raphaelite. Rossetti was not exactly a contemporary figure; he had died in 1882 after many years of chloral addiction. The Brighton wine merchant, however, for whom Scotson-Clark worked was something of a connoisseur and owned several of his pictures. Scotson-Clark was much struck by their distinctive blend of intense mysticism and eroticism and 'lost no time in acquainting his friend' with this 'new outlook'.

It was an 'outlook' that chimed exactly with Beardsley's current literary enthusiasm. Dante Gabriel Rossetti had been fascinated by his Florentine namesake; he had made translations of Dante's verse and illustrated incidents from his works and his life. Memorials of Rossetti were close at hand: Beardsley could hear anecdotes of the artist's later years around the lunch table at the Gurneys; he could search out reproductions of his work in the printshops and at Jones & Evans. He 'began to collect everything [he] could' about Rossetti and other Pre-Raphaelites.

The great excitement and access of energy occasioned by this 'discovery' of Rossetti – coupled with his compulsive caricaturing at the office – suggested to Beardsley that he had perhaps wilfully mistaken his vocation. He must, he realized, 'submit to the inevitable': he began to draw again in earnest. In emulation of his new hero, he turned to Dante for his subject matter: the *Divine Comedy* provided him with ready material; a wonderfully vivid drawing of 'The Glutton in Hell' and a lush Rossettian pencil portrait of Francesca da Rimini survive.[9]

The conscious – and momentous – decision to return to drawing was softened and blurred by the fact that Rossetti had triumphed as both poet and painter. Perhaps Beardsley could emulate this twin achievement. The intention stands squarely behind the illustrated, flame-lettered sonnet, 'Dante in Exile', which he produced at this time. The theme of the poem and the sensuous treatment of the drawing proclaim the influence of Rossetti, although there is a suggestion that Beardsley's interest in Dante had led him to discover the work of another of the poet's illustrators, William Blake. Frederick Evans was a great admirer of Blake, and had made photographic reproductions of his work; it is probable that he would have effected the introduction. He might well have cheered Beardsley with the additional information that Blake's friend, the artist and critic George Cumberland, had also been a clerk at the Guardian Assurance office. Certainly Beardsley was soon reading Blake's poetry, and attempting to illustrate it.

Neither Rossetti nor Blake had ever written a play, but at the beginning of November Beardsley enjoyed the satisfaction of having his one-act farce performed before a large and appreciative audience at the Brighton Pavilion, with Cochran and Scotson-Clark in the cast. The play (punningly titled *A Brown Study*) was part of an evening's entertainment laid on by and for the BGS Old Boys, and it more than held its own against another one-act drama, *In Honour Bound*, a band concert and 'Mr W. T. Burgess, with his bubbles'. Beardsley was unable to witness his triumph but would have drawn pleasure from the notices he received. The *Brighton & Sussex Telegraph* called the play 'charming' and recorded that it was 'received with a good deal of favour'. The *Past and Present* reviewer found it 'full of clever hits', allowing that 'if the situations were sometimes impossible, well – it was a farce'.[10]

Despite this gratifying literary success, the claims of drawing continued to assert themselves. In mid-November Father Chapman, in an advanced state of his illness, came up from Brighton to see a London specialist and stayed for two weeks at the St Barnabas clergy house. Beardsley's schoolboy reputation for drawing had been well known at the Church of the Annunciation, and it seems possible that Chapman brought his friend, Father Gurney, to a fuller appreciation of his potential as an artist, a potential which was then reasserting its claims. Certainly it was at this time that Beardsley made his first Christmas card for Father Gurney.

The new year of 1891 offered its customary promises of fresh starts and novel resolutions. It also provided the Beardsleys with a new home. Even though Vincent was still without regular employment, the family's material position had improved. Mabel had her teaching job; Aubrey's position on the staff at the Guardian had been confirmed as permanent, and his salary increased to £70 per annum. Buoyed by these modest ameliorations the family was able to exchange the cramped conditions of Cambridge Street for less-constricted accommodation at 59 Charlwood Street, just around the corner. They shared the new house, in its only too familiar stucco-decked four-storey Pimlico terrace, with just one other family – a Neapolitan chef and his wife. To the eager young student of Dante this Italian connection was perhaps exciting, the scent of Mr Attolini's frying garlic stirring up visions of the elusive South. There was also a sense of returning respectability: at Charlwood Street the Beardsleys, for the first time in many years, had the space – and the money – for a live-in housemaid.*[11]

For Aubrey, 1891 was the year of his artistic education, a period of close study, unwavering commitment and real advance. He visited galleries and exhibitions; he returned again and again to the British Museum and the National Gallery, coming to know their collections with 'extraordinary thoroughness'; he collected prints and illustrated volumes; he read, he thought, and he drew.

The artistic world he set out to explore, and hoped to enter, was exciting. Over the course of his short life, the visual arts in England had risen to unprecedented prominence. The wealth of industrial and imperial Britain could support a thriving art market, and commercial galleries became a feature of London life. Periodicals devoted to art sprang up and flourished: the *Artist, Atalanta, Magazine of Art, Art Journal*. Art societies burgeoned; artists became respectable; art became fashionable. At the beginning of the 1890s, the vital forces of British art, separate from accepted academic orthodoxy, were divided between two schools, one established, the other just emerging. The older school was made up of the heirs of the Pre-Raphaelite movement, gathered beneath the banners of William Morris and Edward Burne-Jones. The new school (and it was determinedly 'New') was represented by the young men of the New English Art Club. They looked for their inspiration to Whistler and to France, to the examples and experiments of the *soi-disant* Realists, Naturalists and Impressionists.

The bifurcation was characterized in various ways by contemporary commentators. The reactionary Royal Academician, William Powell Frith, writing on 'Crazes in Art: "Pre-Raphaelitism" and "Impressionism"', found the two schools equally 'offensive' and misguided, but – obliged to make a distinction – supposed that the Pre-Raphaelites offered 'over-wrought details', the Impressionists 'no details at all'. Among the protagonists and their partisan followers the distinction was more carefully delineated and more jealously

* Attolini and his English wife lived in four rooms, the rest were taken up by the Beardsleys. Their servant was Sylvia Hogg; she was twenty-one and, like Ellen, had been born in India. On the 1891 census form Vincent listed his occupation as Gentleman.

fostered. It was classified variously as a division between Imagination (backed by close observation from Nature) and Nature (refined by the artistic imagination); an opposition between significant subject matter and pure form; a rift between ennobling beauty and degraded ugliness; a choice between literary medievalism and metropolitan modernity. Very different philosophies underpinned the two schools. The second-generation Pre-Raphaelites continued to draw on the tradition of Ruskin, the great directing critic of the Victorian age. Ruskin proclaimed not only the beauty of art but its moral and social purpose. He believed that the artist, through beauty, could and should reform society. The concept was nebulous but attractive. It achieved concrete expression in William Morris's revival of the 'applied arts', which aimed to bring art and beauty into every aspect of daily life. Beautiful books, beautiful joinery, even beautiful soft furnishings would, it was thought, make people better. Burne-Jones subscribed to the theory in a more mystical but no less real way. 'Only this is true,' he wrote, 'that Beauty is very beautiful, and softens, and comforts, and inspires, and rouses, and lifts up and never fails.'

The English Impressionists looked to the ideas of Théophile Gautier and his disciples. Whistler gave a personal distillation of these in his 'Ten O'Clock Lecture'. For him the theoretical division between the two schools had been sharpened by personal spite: he had taken Ruskin to court in 1877 over a defamatory review. Burne-Jones, much against his will, had appeared as an expert witness for Ruskin. Whistler never forgave him, nor did his disciples. In his lecture (first delivered at Prince's Hall, London in 1886, and published as a pamphlet two years later), Whistler opposed Ruskin's philosophy with combative wit. He considered Ruskin's attempt to draw art into the moral and practical life of the nation a travesty. Art, he declared, is 'selfishly occupied with her own perfection only – having no desire to teach'. In place of moral duty, Whistler offered the idea of an artist free of didactic obligations to society, working only for his own pleasure – 'seeking and finding the beautiful in all conditions and in all times'.

He claimed that only practising artists knew about art. The pretensions of the cultured public and literary art critics were alike ridiculous. As an artist, he disparaged the Pre-Raphaelite school's slavish copying of local detail – an attempt to render the truth of nature by copying every blade of grass. (Likening Nature to a keyboard, he remarked, 'to say to the painter, that nature is to be taken as she is, is to say to the player that he must sit on the piano'.) It needed the artist's eye to select the telling tones and significant details from nature, to draw beauty from it.

Although it was a feature of both schools that they claimed 'beauty' as the aim of their art, each had different notions of where beauty lay. Though the early Pre-Raphaelites (particularly Rossetti) had been excoriated for introducing a new, fleshly and cruel beauty into art, by the beginning of the nineties this had refined itself into the sexless and idealized form of the 'Burne-Jones type', and the dense patterning of Morris's vegetable motifs. The English Impressionists delighted in taking up subjects ignored by conventional art as too ugly, too upsetting, or too rude, and rendering them (as they thought) beautifully: modern London and commercial sex were two of their favoured themes.[12]

Beardsley rapidly learned the terms of the debate but was ambivalent about taking sides. Artistically, his sympathies lay almost entirely with the Pre-Raphaelite tradition; he had come to revere Rossetti and to consider Burne-Jones the greatest living painter, and his intensely literary imagination found echoes in their pictures. Intellectually, however, the Impressionists were more exciting, with the potent attractions of novelty, controversy and publicity to recommend them. Faced with this dilemma, Beardsley ignored it. He embraced both movements; his curiosity and eclecticism were less concerned with drawing distinctions than in making connections.

During the late spring of 1891 Beardsley went to Brighton for two weeks' holiday from the office. He stayed with his great-aunt in Lower Rock Gardens, but spent much of the time with Scotson-Clark, who was living and working nearby. This was a 'glorious' fortnight for the two of them: fired by common purpose and shared enthusiasm, they became almost drunk with excitement. They drew, they sketched, they painted, they built 'castles in the air'. One fond scheme was to establish a shop in Bond Street off Piccadilly, selling 'little original drawings in black and white' and 'little impressionist landscapes'. As they sat through the night in the drawing-room at Lower Rock Gardens, mapping out bright futures and 'occasionally taking a draught from a flagon of Australian Burgundy à la Balzac', all things seemed wonderfully possible.

All styles too seemed within reach. For although Beardsley maintained his first loyalty to the Pre-Raphaelites, producing, among other works, a portrait of a femme fatale, christened 'La Belle Dame sans Merci' in homage to Keats, but known less formally as 'the Frog Lady', he also experimented with other modes. The two spent a Sunday sketching on the Downs; they worked together on a Whistleresque wash drawing of a Japanese girl. Beardsley created a bold 'Impressionist' representation of a dancer and entitled it 'Ballerina Dissoluta'. Scotson-Clark thought the picture was in the manner of Jules Cheret, the French poster designer, but the title suggests that the inspiration was Wilson Steer's painting 'Ballerina Assoluta', which had a scandalized critical reception at the New English Art Club's spring exhibition. The nexus between art, scandal and publicity was one which Beardsley recognized and relished even at this stage.

During the charmed fortnight he was introduced to oil paints by his friend. While Scotson-Clark slept off a night of talk and Australian burgundy in his lodgings, Beardsley, still burning with energy, painted a 'Burne-Jones head with a green face [and] blue hair against a purple sun'. The result perhaps spurred his conviction that colour was not his forte; his next experiments were with charcoal.

The desire to escape the yoke of office life for a career in art grew in intensity, but the possibility of escape seemed as remote as ever. As a practical first step, the two friends considered enrolling at an art school. Before leaving Brighton, Beardsley sought an interview with his former headmaster. Marshall, rather than dismissing the notion of art school out of hand, was encouraging and offered unspecified 'help' should it be required. Emboldened, Beardsley wrote to the secretary of the Herkomer School of Art at Bushey Park for an application form, but immediate action could safely be put off as (he was informed) the school's intake was full for the coming term. He was obliged to return to the tedious 9.30–5.30 of the insurance office. After dinner each evening, however, he settled himself to the real business of the day – or, rather, night – drawing, plundering Keats, Boccaccio and other conventional Pre-Raphaelite sources for his subject matter. Frederick Evans pointed him in the direction of interesting illustrated volumes and prints, and accepted his drawings in exchange for books.

Alfred Gurney, too, continued his support. It became the custom for Beardsley to take his latest drawings over to the clergy house for the vicar's inspection. Gurney was enthusiastic and bought several early works, which he displayed on his walls alongside pictures of the Pre-Raphaelite school. In the light of this gratifying approbation, Beardsley appears to have considered approaching him for assistance in his planned escape to the art school at Bushey Park. The request, however, was deferred.[13]

Meanwhile, on Sundays and half-holidays, he continued his artistic exploration of London. At some time, probably in early June, he and Mabel made an electrifying visit to 49 Princes Gate, the imposing town house of Frederick Leyland, the Liverpool shipbuilder and art patron who, in 1877, rather to his surprise, had found his dining-room transformed by the eccentric genius of Whistler into an iridescent chamber of golden birds and peacock blues. The enduring fame of the Peacock Room and Leyland's awkward position as its reluctant patron have rather obscured Leyland's contemporary reputation as a collector of other types of art. Princes Gate also housed what Beardsley described as a 'GLORIOUS' collection of Pre-Raphaelite and Renaissance works: a dozen Rossettis, eight Burne-Joneses, Millais' 'Eve of St Agnes', Ford Madox Brown's 'Chaucer at Court', works by Botticelli, Lippo Lippi, Giorgione, Memling, Luini, da Vinci, and Rubens. Indeed it was these paintings, and particularly the Pre-Raphaelite ones, which had the initial impact upon Beardsley. He listed the works with care in a letter to Scotson-Clark, highlighting his favourites with enthusiastic exclamation marks.

It was only towards the end of his reply to the next letter from Scotson-Clark that, after further enthusing over Ford Madox Brown, Rossetti and Burne-Jones, he finally turned to Whistler and his contribution to Leyland's house. He was immediately keen to claim Whistler as his property, and his letter was illustrated with Whistleresque peacocks and a copy of the portrait of the 'Princesse du Pays de la Porcelaine', which hung at one end of the dining-room. He also boasted of his recent acquisition of an early Whistler etching of Billingsgate, and enclosed a selection of 'Jap sketches' showing that he could, if he chose, adopt the master's oriental style.

Robert Ross, in his 1904 study of Beardsley, considered this exposure to Whistler as a healthful blast of the 'antithesis' to Burne-Jones and the Pre-Raphaelite school, a verdict which Whistler would have been delighted to endorse; but to Beardsley, in the summer of 1891, the antithesis was far from clear. The 'Jap' drawings were no more than a pose; they were 'official performances' (done, in other words, at the office) and did not deflect his art from its Pre-Raphaelite course. The Peacock Room, after all, revealed Whistler at his most lush and 'aesthetical'; its *japonisme* was a matter of stamped gold and paper fans rather than any radical new aesthetic. The Princesse du Pays de la Porcelaine, with her dark hair, exotic title and poor modelling, was not very far from a Rossetti princess, and Beardsley had discovered her after passing through rooms of Pre-Raphaelite (and pre-Raphael) pictures. Whatever his mind and his reading might tell him of the differences between Whistler and the Pre-Raphaelites, to his eyes everything at 49 Princes Gate was remarkably of a piece.[14]

On Sunday, 12 July, only a few weeks after the visit to Princes Gate, Aubrey and Mabel made another and even more significant artistic pilgrimage. They had been told – perhaps by Frederick Evans – that Burne-Jones kept an 'open studio' on Sunday afternoons, at which time the public were allowed to inspect his current work and perhaps even to meet the artist.

Beardsley conceived that it might be a chance to show his work to his hero, perhaps even to gain some small crumb of encouragement or advice. He laid his plans with some care, although the expedition was put off at least once. When, however, the appointed day arrived, he gathered up his latest designs in his portfolio with studied nonchalance. He could pretend that he was merely preparing them to show to the Gurneys after church, as usual. But after the Sunday morning service and the lunch that followed, Beardsley took care to take up the portfolio when he and Mabel set off for Burne-Jones's house in the North End Road.

The day was hot and the walk to West Kensington long. Burne-

Jones's house, The Grange, set back from the road behind its wall and iron gate, had a substantial eighteenth-century blockish look to it. (It had once been the home of Samuel Richardson, author of *Pamela*, which would have impressed Beardsley as much as the ball-surmounted gate-posts.) Any flutter of anticipatory nervousness that accompanied the ringing of the door bell was obliterated when the servant appeared and told them that the studio was no longer open except by special appointment. 'Somewhat disconsolate', they turned to go and had reached the street corner when they heard 'flying footsteps' behind them and were hailed, 'Pray come back, I couldn't think of letting you go away without seeing the pictures, after a journey on a hot day like this.' It was Burne-Jones himself in his loose-fitting jacket and wide-brimmed hat; he had seen them being turned away and, perhaps intrigued by Mabel's thick red hair, had hurried after them. He escorted the pair, now 'radiant with excitement', into the house.

Burne-Jones was then in his late fifties, yet, despite his silvered hair and a manner sometimes characterized as 'priestly', he had a Puckish sense of fun in his large grey-blue eyes. The impulsive generosity that had sent him dashing out to retrieve the weary Beardsleys was typical. Although he had recently moved his studio to a building at the bottom of the garden, he led his charges to it through the house. They would have glimpsed the dark, jewel-like interior, the 'tinted gloom' of the hall and, beyond it, the booklined drawing-room, along one wall of which ran reproductions of Mantegna's 'Triumph of Caesar'. The garden studio was a huge gymnasium of a place. One vast work-in-progress, 'Avalon', filled a side wall; another, 'The Car of Love', was set up at the end, and a set of full-size gouache studies for the Perseus series found space on the walls. All these Burne-Jones showed and explained to his young admirers. During the tour of inspection he could hardly escape noticing the portfolio Aubrey was clutching. He must have been approached often in similar fashion, but with true generosity he inquired if his visitor 'drew'. Aubrey needed no second chance; he proffered the folder, and asked if the master would look at his work and give an opinion.

'I can tell you,' Beardsley wrote to King the next day, 'it was an exciting moment when he first opened my portfolio and looked at the first drawings: "Saint Veronica on the Evening of Good Friday", "Dante at the Court of Can Grande della Scala".' His first comment – at least as recorded by Aubrey – was decisive and extraordinary, 'There is no doubt about your gift, one day you will most assuredly paint very great and beautiful pictures.' Then, after further consultation of the portfolio, ' "Nôtre dame de la Lune", "Dante designing an Angel", "Insomnia", "Post Mortem", "Ladye Hero", etc etc), he said, "All are *full* of thought, poetry and imagination. Nature has given you every gift to become a great artist. I *seldom* or *never* advise anyone to take up art as a profession, but in *your* case I *can do nothing else*." '

For Beardsley this was an incredible moment. He had the support and encouragement of friends, even discerning friends, but this was different: the enthusiastic verdict of the man he considered 'the greatest living artist in Europe', and the promise of a glittering future in art. Burne-Jones's perspicacity was as impressive as his generosity. Only one of the pictures Beardsley showed him that afternoon is now known, but it is difficult to trace in its wooden figures and tentative sub-Rossettian tones the glorious future so confidently predicted.*

The practical difficulties in the way of this glorious future were explained to Burne-Jones as he led Aubrey and Mabel on to the lawn, where Mrs Burne-Jones was serving tea to a small party which included Oscar Wilde's wife, Constance, and her two young children. The painter, however, was not to be deflected. Over tea he discussed plans for his new protégé's training. He would inquire as to the best art schools; he thought 'two hours daily study would be quite sufficient', thus allowing Aubrey to continue at the Guardian office for the time being; there was no rush. He himself had not begun to study until he was twenty-three. Beardsley should visit him regularly,

* Aubrey sometimes redrew the same subjects several times, so his early drawings are difficult to date. Although he mentions showing Burne-Jones 'The Litany of Mary Magdalen', the existing drawing of that title seems to belong to the intensive Mantegna period which followed his visit to The Grange. 'Dante designing an Angel' would seem to be the same picture as 'Annovale Della Morte Di Beatrice', which he subsequently gave to Pargeter, clearly based on Rossetti's 'Dante drawing an Angel on the first anniversary of the death of Beatrice'. The word 'Annovale' does not exist in Italian, but suggests an attempt at rendering 'anniversary' in the language of Dante.

bringing his drawings for criticism. Burne-Jones stressed the importance of drawing: 'Design as much as you can,' he urged. But he
considered such work as an aid to, and preparation for, the principal
business of art – the making of 'beautiful paintings'. At this stage
Beardsley seems to have accepted this as the natural progression. As
a novice, however, he would concentrate on his draughtsmanship;
the beautiful paintings could follow.

There was mild amazement around the tea-trolley. Burne-Jones,
it was explained, was 'a very severe critic', and such enthusiastic and
practical approbation was rare indeed. Beardsley's glow deepened. 'I
left,' he later recalled, 'feeling, in the words of Rossetti, "a different
crit'ter".' The climactic significance of the visit was apparent: it set
ajar a door into a world which had seemed tantalizingly close yet
impossible of access. Beardsley at once set about mythologizing the
'great adventure'. He drew a picture of Burne-Jones and dated it;
he wrote a detailed account of his triumph not only to Scotson-Clark
but also to King (his first letter to his friend for over a year). To
King he shamelessly suggested that he had taken his drawings with
him only 'by the merest chance', and quoted long verbatim passages
of Burne-Jones's criticism. The letter bubbles with excitement,
touched in places by anxiety about how much had still to be
achieved.[15]

Aubrey carefully fixed the moment as a new beginning, and marked
out his place within it. 'I am now eighteen,' he wrote (he would be
nineteen five weeks later), 'with a vile constitution, a sallow face,
sunken eyes, long red hair, a shuffling gait and a stoop.' And yet,
through Burne-Jones's recognition of his powers, he already felt 'a
different crit'ter'; the withered stock might 'one day . . . bear real
good fruit'. In cod-heroic words he described his pursuit of art as a
submission to 'the inevitable', and hoped only that King would wish
him 'all success in years to come'.

In his desire to enhance the significance of the occasion, and his
importance at the centre of it, Beardsley casually fused Constance
Wilde and her toddlers into 'the Oscar Wildes'; indeed he did it
twice. The terminology was legitimate, but it created the false impression that Oscar – the Aesthetic *arbiter elegantium* – had been there,

adding his voice to the chorus of approval.* The irony of Beardsley seeking a connection with Wilde when none existed would return to haunt him, but in the summer of 1891 he was eager to attach himself to established fame, anxious to project his name into the charmed circle of art.

After making inquiries, Burne-Jones wrote to Beardsley ('a charming epistle (4 pages)') recommending two possibilities: the National Art Training Schools at South Kensington and the Westminster School of Art. He reiterated that 'two hours' daily work' would be sufficient for Beardsley 'to learn the grammar' of his art and cheered him with the assertion, 'I know you will not fear work, nor let disheartenment *langour* you because the necessary discipline of the school seems to lie so far from your natural interest and sympathy.'

Being committed to only two hours a day would allow Beardsley to continue at Lombard Street and attend night classes. He sent off for application papers, but was able to delay making any definite decision: August was approaching, and London was breaking up for the holidays. Burne-Jones departed for his annual sojourn on the south coast; Aubrey's mother and sister decamped to Woking; Aubrey, however, had used up his two weeks' holiday in Brighton, and was obliged to remain in town with his 'pater', having a 'horribly dull' time of it. Although the long hot days at the sparsely attended office were wearisome, and the evening meals with his father at Charlwood Street no better, Beardsley found an escape in art. It was a summer of intense experiment and development. He affected a certain Romantic melancholy, dramatizing his predicament in a poem which begins,

> The lights are shining dimly round about,
> The Path is dark, I cannot see ahead;
> And so I go as one perplexed with doubt
> Nor guessing where my footsteps may be led

and in a fine drawing of 'Hamlet following the ghost of his father'

* Ellen Beardsley, in her brief account of Aubrey's career, states that only Constance, Cyril and Vyvyan were present. She was doubtless anxious to disassociate Aubrey from Oscar Wilde, but there is no reason to doubt her veracity on this occasion. It is doubtful that she would have known of Aubrey's letter with its ambiguous reference to 'the Oscar Wildes'.

through a dark and hostile wood, but he was unable to sustain the pose. The general tenor of the almost weekly letters he wrote to Scotson-Clark is of irrepressible excitement and waxing confidence. He cheerily refers to himself and to Scotson-Clark as 'embryonic genii' (meaning, it is to be hoped, 'embryonic geniuses') and assesses his current work as 'A1'.[16]

The course of his artistic progress was directed by the example of Burne-Jones. Indeed, at one level, his lonely August in town was a protracted homage of imitation. His historical and literary cast of mind led him to a careful study of Burne-Jones's influences and inspirations: the Italian masters of the quattrocento, and the literary classics of medieval England and ancient Greece. Botticelli and Mantegna were the acknowledged progenitors of Burne-Jones's style and Aubrey set out to absorb their lessons. He had already admired the Botticelli pictures in Leyland's collection, and at the National Gallery in Trafalgar Square he was able to study more, as well as paintings by Mantegna. Further afield, at Hampton Court, he found the originals of Mantegna's great sequence, 'The Triumph of Caesar'. They were, he wrote excitedly to Scotson-Clark, an 'art training in themselves'.

Although the paintings were stimulating and suggestive, Burne-Jones had directed him to drawing, and it is likely that Beardsley sought out Botticelli's and Mantegna's graphic work at the British Museum or in books and early prints. The work of the two artists differs much in flavour: where Botticelli is gracile, sensuous and ornamental, Mantegna is severe, restrained, almost classical. Yet their drawing shares a distinctive flat, linear style. Both eschewed modelling and relied on the contours of pure outline. Burne-Jones employed the same technique in some of his drawings, and Beardsley would have recognized a similar approach in the work of Blake. But such a style required great skill and confidence and, though attracted to the effect, he edged towards it only in fits and starts. He attempted it in three drawings executed under the influence of Mantegna: 'The Virgin and the Lily', 'The Litany of Mary Magdalen' and 'The Procession of Joan of Arc', and in an illustrated poem, 'The Court of Love'.

For his subject matter he roved through literature and history.

Shelley, Blake, Shakespeare and Aeschylus provided him with models. 'The Court of Love' derived from Chaucer, one of several Chaucerian illustrations Beardsley did in emulation of Burne-Jones, who was even then embarking on the task of illustrating William Morris's Kelmscott Press edition of the poet. Beardsley read Morris's *Earthly Paradise* and found it 'simply enchanting'. He turned his attention also to the key text of the Pre-Raphaelites – Malory's *Morte D'Arthur* – and conceived a cycle of pictures based on the life of the 'wonder worker, Merlin'.

Such was his Arthurian enthusiasm that he encouraged Scotson-Clark to compose a cantata on the same theme, and it is possible that the two friends met in London to discuss the project. Certainly the solitariness of Beardsley's existence was relieved by happy distractions. Cochran visited him; he spent an evening with Mr King, who was passing through London. King was impressed by the progress that Beardsley had made, and agreed that his young friend should attend art school and 'take up drawing from life'; he also offered to try to sell some of Beardsley's drawings to aficionados in Blackburn. He took away with him several pictures, including the Hamlet (now resonantly entitled in Latin) and the Chaucerian illustrated poem.

The weekend of his nineteenth birthday, his 'pater' being out of town, Beardsley spent with Father Gurney at the clergy house, and it was probably through the Saint Barnabas connection that he enjoyed some 'grand nights at the opera . . . box and stall tickets hav[ing] fallen [his] way somewhat'. Another possible source of opera tickets was the music-loving Evans. Beardsley's friendship with the bookseller grew over the summer, and Evans even began making platinotype reproductions of some of his latest designs. There was considerable variety in Beardsley's production; despite the concerted course of Burne-Jones emulation, a natural eclecticism constantly suggested new and heretical lines of inquiry. At the very moment when he was striving to turn himself into the last of the Pre-Raphaelites, fresh vistas leading away from Burne-Jones's *hortus conclusus* kept presenting themselves.[17]

Interest in Whistler, awakened in the Peacock Room, could not be denied, and Beardsley was certainly appreciative of Whistler's art. He blew fifteen shillings, almost a week's wages, on a print by the artist, and even attempted several drawings in the manner of Whistler etchings – complete with distinctive 'butterfly' signature.* But it was the artist's personality which seems to have engaged his real attention: Whistler was the most controversial artist of the age, famously eccentric, caustically witty and extravagantly overdressed – a master of self-advertisement. Beardsley had probably been aware of this aspect of his reputation while still at school. Shortly before Aubrey became a pupil, Whistler had visited the grammar school to see an American boy, and Mr Marshall had introduced him to a local resident – a prosperous Bond Street tailor – who wished to commission a portrait. When Whistler returned to Brighton to deliver the picture, the tailor and his family were out. They returned home to find Whistler asleep on their sofa, and all their pictures turned to face the wall, except for the new portrait. So, at least, the legend ran.

By 1891 Beardsley could study Whistler's eccentricities in detail, and the ideas behind them; at the end of the previous year the artist had published *The Gentle Art of Making Enemies*, a compendium of his past battles, barbs and aperçus. Beardsley read it closely: the transcript of the Ruskin trial; the verbal sparring with Oscar Wilde; the waspish letters to the press, and – most significantly – the full text of the 'Ten O'Clock Lecture'. He became aware of Whistler's elevated claims for the artist as a privileged figure standing alone, free of the influence of critics, writers, moralists, reformers and society at large, part of a charmed confraternity bound only by a common quest for pictorial beauty. The theory would have intrigued Beardsley on its own, but three other books appeared during 1891 which played variations upon the theme and focused his attention yet more upon it: Oscar Wilde's two volumes, *Intentions* and *The Picture of Dorian Gray*, and George Moore's collection, *Impressions and Opinions*.[18]

Wilde's views on art were not consistent. In the early 1880s he had lectured in America and England on 'House Decoration' and

* At Princeton there is an early Beardsley pastiche of a *Punch* cartoon. Titled 'A Disappointment', it shows a young boy presenting a toy elephant to his mother. Mama: 'What Tommy! don't you like the elephant Uncle John gave you?' Tommy (tearfully): 'No-o-oo, Mama, I c-can't b-b-break it.' The drawing is in the manner of Linley Sambourne, though the mother has a Pre-Raphaelite air; a narrow picture on the screen behind her is distinguished by a butterfly signature, as is another picture on the wall.

'The English Renaissance of Art', adopting an essentially Ruskinian view of art's place in society. But his exposure to French *décadent* ideas, to Pater's philosophy, and to Whistler's company had led him to adopt a more radical line. It runs, with occasional contradictions, through the story of Dorian Gray and the four essays in *Intentions*, finding its fullest expression in 'The Decay of Lying'. 'Art never expresses anything but itself'; 'Life imitates art far more than art imitates life'; 'All art is quite useless'; 'All art is immoral'; 'The proper school to learn art is not Life but Art'; 'The artist is the creator of beautiful things' – these were the beguiling articles of Wilde's artistic faith in the early nineties.

Wilde extended Gautier's notions about the autonomy and amorality of art into something darker. Art, he suggested, was not merely separate from nature but opposed and superior to it; so too was the artist: the perverse and grotesque should be sought because, being anti-natural, they were necessarily artistic. Dorian Gray was not himself an artist, but he accepted these dicta and carried them into life. He devoted his diabolically charmed existence to a quest for strange sensations and perverted pleasures. His life became a work of art. These ideas were not of Wilde's creation; they had been percolating French intellectual life for some time, and had found an early advocate in the dandified anti-naturalism of Charles Baudelaire, but by the end of the 1880s they had coalesced into something approaching a cultural movement. Its proponents were dubbed *décadents*. The term was vague but evocative, conjuring failing empires sunk in luxury and neurotic languor, of exquisite sensibilities content to tickle the jaded palate with bizarre, yet minutely discriminated, sensations.

Wilde was familiar with the tradition. He had met the practitioners in Paris, he had read their works – Huysmans' *À Rebours*, the *contes* of Catulle Mendès and Jean Lorain, the novels of Rachilde, the poems of Verlaine – and had distilled their flavour after his own fashion. It was an intoxicating brew to someone of Beardsley's temper. At a practical level, Beardsley would have been interested to note that Wilde continued to prefer the work of the Pre-Raphaelites to that of the new English Impressionists ('a class that welcomes the incompetent with sympathetic eagerness, and that confuses the bizarre with the beautiful, and vulgarity with truth'). 'Art', Wilde declared in 'The Decay of Lying', 'begins with ... purely imaginative and pleasurable work dealing with what is unreal and non-existent.' But this golden stage gives way as 'life becomes fascinated with this new wonder and asks to be admitted to the charmed circle.' At this point, art is still able to 'transform' life through 'style', but a third stage soon succeeds, when 'life gets the upper hand, and drives art out into the wilderness'. Wilde considered this phase the 'true decadence' of art, and the coming state: a stage of misguided 'Realism' charac-terized by a slavish regard for nature, modernity of subject matter, and 'modernity of form'.

Beardsley appreciated the ideas and admired the style in which they were couched. He began to mimic elements of Wilde's epigram-matic and paradoxical voice; where Wilde likened Holbein to Balzac as an artist who 'created life' rather than copying it, Beardsley described the 'naturalistic' Neapolitan painter, Jusepe de Ribera, as 'a regular Zola in art'.

Moore's book was less stylistically assured, and less programmatic, than Wilde's or Whistler's, but offered Beardsley 'just the things one wanted to know about'. Moore saw himself as the leading con-temporary commentator on French culture. He had lived in Paris during the 1870s and early 1880s, as an art student then as a writer, and, through a combination of Irish charm and brazen insensitivity, had penetrated to the heart of the city's artistic life. He liked to boast that he received his education over the marble-topped tables at the Nouvelle Athène. He became the intimate of Manet and Degas, the friend of Zola, Mallarmé, Huysmans and Verlaine, and wrote about them and their work with colourful immediacy. *Impressions and Opinions* included essays on Zola, Verlaine, Laforgue, Rimbaud and Balzac. To Beardsley, marooned in Pimlico, it offered the intoxi-cation of Paris by proxy.[19]

He was, however, able to gain a little of the French experience at first-hand. One of the highlights of the 1891 London theatre season was a production of *L'Enfant Prodigue* at the Prince of Wales. A transfer from the Théâtre de Funambules, it was a play with music but without words: in the phrase of *The Times* critic, 'the story of the prodigal son, with a *fin de siècle* complexion'. The errant son and his intransigent father were represented as 'pierrots' with whitened faces; the rest of the cast wore conventional dress.

The play ran throughout the summer; Beardsley went often. He saw it three times with Cochran, who, even in the midst of his own excitement, was struck by his friend's intense 'interest and enthusiasm over the beautiful music and simple wordless story'. The revival of Pierrot as a figure of interest in the 1890s was noted at the time, and has been well-chronicled since. The sad bergamasque clown of the seventeenth-century Commedia dell'arte tradition became in the hands of the late nineteenth-century poets and dramatists a symbol of the alienated artist, consigned to life's margins and consoling himself with doomed love and art. This development, of which *L'Enfant Prodigue* was a conspicuous example, had been a French phenomenon. The transfer of the play to London, and its success, introduced the idea to the English public, and the image to the mind of Beardsley. While some balked at the unexplained incongruity of combining traditional pierrots with conventionally dressed contemporary characters, he relished the disorientating juxtaposition.

Indeed, he was developing a particular fondness for anachronism. One of his happiest discoveries of the summer was the recently completed Holy Trinity Church at the bottom of Sloane Street. Among the works of art decorating this great Aesthetic barn, an altar frontal by Reynolds Stephens claimed his attention. He sketched it for Scotson-Clark's amusement; it represented, he said, 'the infant saviour being worshipped by all sorts and conditions of men, in modern costume'.[20]

The varied elements of Beardsley's interest – Burne-Jones and Whistler, Mantegna and Pierrot, medieval romances and French novels, church furnishings and opera boxes – struggled to adjust themselves. As yet they remained disparate. He sampled them in turn, but lacked the artistic personality and the technical ability to synthesize them into something new and personal.

Burne-Jones recognized this tendency and its danger, when Beardsley once more presented his portfolio at the end of the summer. The master counselled that his young friend had already 'learnt too much from the old masters' and must urgently address the question of which art school he was to attend. Beardsley returned home and drew a caricature of himself being kicked down the steps of the National Gallery by Raphael, Titian and Mantegna, 'whilst Michael Angelo dealt a blow on his head with a hammer'. Having been banished from the National Gallery, where should he go?

Burne-Jones favoured South Kensington, if only because he thought it more prosaic in its approach. King urged Westminster. Scotson-Clark came up from Brighton to help Beardsley reach a decision, and together with Mabel they went to call on G. F. Watts, to whom Scotson-Clark had an introduction. After a tour of the studio, Beardsley saw a sketch of Burne-Jones's 'Wheel of Fortune' and spoke of his acquaintance with the artist. From there the matter of art schools arose. Watts proved unhelpful, urging 'emphatically' the virtues of 'self-culture'. In so far as he would give an opinion, he was against South Kensington.

Beardsley too had his doubts about the place, largely because its formal entrance procedure required him to draw 'scrolls and circles and spirals' and he doubted his ability. At the Westminster School of Art, things were simpler: 'You only ha[d] to pay the fees.' The school, moreover, offered the attractions of a radical and cosmopolitan edge. It was known as the 'Impressionist Academy', and its head, Fred Brown, was 'a young man with all the traditions of the Parisian studios' at his command. The school was located only a short distance from the Beardsley house in Pimlico (on the route home from work); these were not insignificant considerations for a delicate youth taking on the extra burden of night classes. In the event, he chose Westminster. He does not seem to have considered the choice as a rejection of Burne-Jones, who indeed supported his application, writing a letter of recommendation to Brown. Nevertheless, entry into the school brought Beardsley into closer contact with the impressionist current of contemporary art.[21]

The contact was perhaps more personal than practical, for although Fred Brown, as a founder-member of the New English Art Club and a painter of muddied landscapes, was regarded as a 'wild Impressionist', the drawing method he prescribed had much in common with the Renaissance tradition which Beardsley had been struggling to learn from Mantegna, Botticelli and Burne-Jones.

Brown was an inspirational teacher. After conventional beginnings in England, his training had been enriched by a stay in Paris at the *ateliers* of Bouguereau and Robert-Fleury, and he had brought back to England a keen appreciation of French methods and practice. At a time when English drawing, as taught at the Royal Academy and the National Art Training Schools, was obsessed with accuracy of detail and the representation of form through careful shading, Brown proclaimed the importance of simple virtues: firm outline and overall construction. He had taken over the teaching at Westminster in 1877, running night classes for working men, and the success of his methods and his gifts as a teacher had seen the school expand and prosper. By the beginning of the 1890s it was the largest in England exclusively devoted to the study of figure drawing and painting, and its studios were crowded with all sorts and ages of students, women as well as men.

Its premises were in the old Architectural Museum, a fantastical Venetian-Gothick building on the corner of Tufton Street, in an unfashionable and run-down quarter of Westminister. It was a pictur-esque setting: the museum was crammed with architectural models, plaster casts and medieval fragments (most of which are now in the V&A). A contemporary observer recalled, 'Angels and chimeras from half the temples of Europe looked down on the re-instated divinity whose turn it was to be copied in charcoal by the gaily pinafored art students . . . a skeleton, with the name of his bones on a blackboard beside him, dangled in front of the history of the Creation and Redemption; and an idol from India squatted in meditation before an Assyrian relief.'

Against this 'fantastical background' Fred Brown cut a sober figure. In 1891 he had reached his fortieth year. Lean and spare, his 'rock-like', even severe exterior was barely softened by whiskers more military than bohemian in effect. He had nevertheless a wonderful 'sincerity and sympathy' which distinguished him as a teacher, and set its stamp upon the school. His teaching methods had the virtue of being 'extremely practical'. Although painting was taught, the main emphasis was on drawing, particularly figure drawing. The painter C. W. Furse, who studied under Brown, characterized his idiosyncratic approach succinctly, 'The line is always used in drawing,

and with great simplicity; the character of the model in structure and development, the movement of the pose and unity of the whole design are insisted upon by a searching criticism.' Instead of the quest for 'absolute tone' there was 'severe observation of contour'.

Students began by making a number of studies from 'the cast', working in charcoal on cheap Michelet paper, so that their work could be 'easily obliterated and recommenced', before graduating to the life-room where they drew from the nude model in the same fashion. Brown would stride amongst the easels and 'donkeys' giving the 'help and encouragement best adapted to the special requirements of the individual'. Although he never allowed a study to proceed when a 'radical point of drawing had been missed which would invalidate all that followed', he placed few other constraints upon his students. His comments were generally 'terse and to the point' and 'calculated to make the student think for himself'. Experiments were encouraged, but, as Furse recalled, they had to be 'genuine' or they were 'quickly snuffed out'. Brown's seriousness crushed 'that amateur element so usual in the English schools' and induced 'a keenness equal to that of Paris'. This sense of earnest endeavour and responsibility produced and stimulated a great variety of talent without imposing a particular stamp on the work of the students. Indeed Furse described Westminster as 'the only school I have been in' (and he had attended the Slade, the Royal Academy and the Parisian *ateliers*) 'where individuality was more respected than fashion'. The roll-call of alumni supports this assertion. Many leading artists of the period – particularly graphic artists – had attended Brown's: Leonard Ravenhill, Bernard Partridge, William Parkinson, Maurice Grieffenhagen and Dudley Hardy among them.[22]

It was a happy place for Beardsley to have discovered. The profuse eclecticism of the setting, with its myriad juxtapositions and incongruities, must have delighted him, and a course of study which emphasized 'observation of contour' and allowed individual stylistic expression was perfectly pitched to his peculiar interests and abilities.

With an immediate assertion of his individual taste, he began by working from the 'grotesque cast', doing quick drawings which had

OPPOSITE Professor Fred Brown, Beardsley's art tutor, 1892.

to be finished at a sitting. Brown seems to have taken a special interest in the curious 'boy' who 'drew just like Burne-Jones', and came with that artist's recommendation. Brown's flattering interest doubtless boosted Beardsley's self-confidence, while the companionship of other young students probably added an edge of competition. Certainly his progress was brisk. By the middle of October he was reporting excitedly to King that Brown 'seems to have great hopes for me . . . I certainly make decided headway and it will not be so very long before I get into the life class.'

One day, Beardsley showed Brown some of his 'home drawings' – romantic-historical pictures steeped in the Burne-Jones tradition. Other teachers might have disapproved and urged a return to life drawing; Brown offered approval and advice. He encouraged Beardsley to 'persevere in his own line' and 'develop his own natural talent'. Scotson-Clark, to whom Aubrey was writing 'almost daily' now, had no doubt that Brown's influence was decisive: 'Without quibble or question,' he wrote after Beardsley's death, 'Frederick Brown is the one man who is wholly and solely responsible for what Aubrey Beardsley has given to the world.' Although the phrasing rather ignores Beardsley's own contribution to this achievement, the statement is interesting.[23]

Burne-Jones, too, was impressed with Beardsley's progress under Brown, and, after an inspection of the current work in early November, reiterated his appreciation. Although none of his class-work survives, something of the headway he was making can be gleaned from a comparison of two drawings of Perseus he made at this time; both are dominated by the influence of Burne-Jones, but the second shows an advance in overall conception, a less obvious reliance on extraneous detail. It is, moreover, his first known nude drawing.

Beardsley had set himself a taxing schedule: a full day's work at the insurance office followed by a two-hour night class. He set up a little 'studio' room at Charlwood Street and, with a fine sense of self-dramatization, worked at a small table bearing two tall, tapering candlesticks; the walls of the room were coloured vermilion. Such exertion took its toll. With the approach of winter, his health began to fragment. His eyes became weak and inflamed, and the strain of drawing was impossible to sustain for any length of time. Another blow fell with the news that Scotson-Clark and Cochran were leaving for America in search of fame and fortune. They sailed at the beginning of December. Beardsley was left without the support of his closest friends, and with an uncomfortable awareness of his physical weakness. Nevertheless, even as the year threatened to subside into frustration and ill-health, a flurry of small triumphs and unexpected breaks gave promise of future brightness.[24]

On 3 December 1891, Sarah Pitt died in Brighton; she was seventy-six. In her will, made in 1881, she left legacies of £500 each to Ellen Beardsley, Mabel and Aubrey. Vincent received a separate sum of nineteen guineas, suggesting that he was held in some affection at least by his wife's 'strange old aunt'. Although Aubrey managed to affect a worldly cynicism when writing of the bequest to King – 'The old aunt I used to pay so many visits to when at school died about three weeks ago, only left me £500' – the sum, more than seven times his annual income, was considerable. He would not come into it until he was twenty-one, but the knowledge that it awaited him must have opened some interesting vistas for his day-dreams.

In the short term, it was the continuing support of King and the patronage of the Gurneys that bolstered his self-esteem. King had sold one of the drawings he had taken north and the Gurneys continued to promote his reputation, showing his work to, among others, the artist Frederic Shields (who 'expressed himself warmly . . . about the talent revealed'). Such was Aubrey's rising reputation within the Gurney circle that Father Gurney's literary cousin, Augustine Birrell, the author of a volume of lightweight essays, Obiter Dicta, said he wished to meet him. Father Gurney thought the connection worth making, but confessed a private fear that Birrell was 'too much of a philistine (a very nice one however) to suit' Aubrey.

With the approach of Christmas, Beardsley produced a second series of cards for the vicar of St Barnabas. For these, he fell back on his most Botticellian manner: the circular format suggests that he drew his inspiration directly from the two Botticelli tondi in Helen Zimern's article, 'Angels in Art', printed in the December issue of Atalanta, but there was a new boldness and economy in his handling of line, particularly noticeable in his treatment of the lilies which he introduced profusely (and gratuitously) into both pictures.

Aubrey's Christmas Day celebrations were enlivened by the arrival of the second number of Mr King's publication, *The Bee*. It contained as a frontispiece a lithographic reproduction of Beardsley's drawing of Hamlet, printed in sanguine. Accompanying the illustration was a notice by King praising its 'masterful' treatment and prophesying that 'if health and strength be granted him', the illustrator was 'destined to fill a large space in the domain of art when the twentieth century dawns'. Beardsley swelled with pleasure; he punningly informed King, 'On reading your "notice on the illustration", I scarcely knew whether I should purchase to myself a laurel wreath and order a statue to be erected immediately in Westminster Abbey; or whether I should bust myself.'[25]

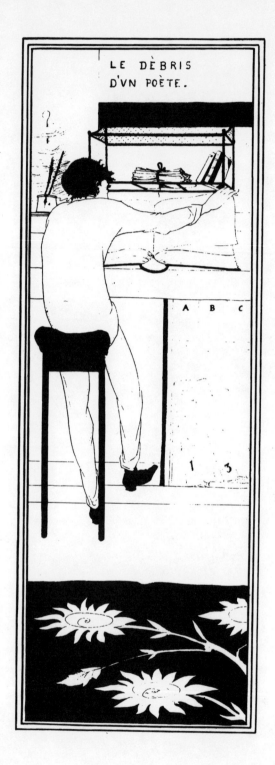

CHAPTER IV

'A New Style'

KING'S WARNING NOTE about Beardsley's 'health and strength' was apposite. Not for the first time, the Christmas holidays were spent in an invalid state, and when the new year began Aubrey was still unable to attend the office. Such was the anxiety of his employers that his annual increment (a further £10) was made 'subject to Dr Gower's report'.

The reality of his condition is not to be doubted, but sick-leave allowed him the illusion of freedom; though he should have rested, in his eagerness he strove to keep up his artistic work. He was full of plans: he immediately made another drawing for King's publication, but was uncertain how best to reproduce it. He experimented with several media: he did 'designs in transfer ink, lithographic ink and lithographic chalk', but these all proved unsatisfactory, and he eventually decided to 'etch' the picture. Even this solution, however, was not successful. No second picture appeared in *The Bee*.

Another scheme was for an article on 'lines and line drawing', Beardsley's current artistic preoccupation. He wrote rather pompously to King on his amazement at 'how little the importance of outline is understood even by some of the best *painters*. It is this feeling for harmony in *line* that sets the old masters at such an advantage to

OPPOSITE 'Le Dèbris [sic] d'un Poète', 1892.

the modern, who seem to think that harmony in colour is the only thing worth attaining.' However, the projected article was abandoned when Beardsley discovered, in a back number of the *Magazine of Art*, an article on line drawing by Walter Crane. It was, he assured King, 'too much like my own', assuming an easy equality with the man whom many considered the finest draughtsman of the age.[1]

In view of this similarity, it may be worth quoting some of Crane's dicta. 'I believe', he wrote, 'there is no greater test of the quality of an artist than his treatment and use of outline, and nowhere does his individuality and sense of style so clearly declare itself.' He cited, as masters of outline, Egyptian murals, modern Japanese drawings, Greek vases, and the work of the early Renaissance Italian and German masters. Crane contended that outline, properly used, was descriptive and expressive; it could convey not only the 'construction' but the 'character' of a subject. In rather mechanical fashion, he laid down some basic practical guidelines: 'The idea of repose', he declared, 'is associated in our minds with long and more or less level [horizontal] lines'; while to convey a sense of 'unrest', he advised the use of 'rugged lines, sharp angles and opposing curves'.

He placed a designer's emphasis on the need for careful composition while conceding that 'to the so-called modern realist or naturalist . . . one hardly ventures to breathe the word'. It was, nevertheless, through the use of outline that successful composition could be achieved. In two companion articles – one on 'Design', the other on 'Relief' – he made several telling points that would have alerted Beardsley's interest and directed his energies. While lamenting the 'divergency' that had sprung up between those 'two branches of the same tree' – the 'designer' and the 'painter' – Crane directed his remarks specifically to the former. The designer's aim, he suggested, was very simple: 'to fill certain spaces or panels with harmonious devices complete in themselves or related to other patterned panels or spaces'. For their subject matter they had 'the whole world, mythological and real' to choose from, though Crane acknowledged that 'good design . . . depends finally on the inventive fertility of the artist's mind.'

Crane once again set down some simple and useful rules. When designing for a circle, either the 'spiral' or the 'radiating form' principle should be adopted; when making a design in 'white on black', it 'will generally be advisable to increase the dimensions of the [white] masses . . . a little beyond the degree necessary if the same design were treated as black upon white': when shading an object, Crane favoured lines all flowing in the same direction rather than cross-hatching. At a time when Beardsley was working mainly in pencil, Crane advocated the pen: 'I should like to see it oftener in the hands of our students,' he wrote; 'with the pen we know about the worst to begin with. But', he added, with a flight of eloquence which stirred Beardsley's literary imagination and sense of ambition, 'the difficulties once mastered, it may prove a quill from the wing of Pegasus himself.'

Whatever Beardsley might claim about his own ideas on the importance of outline, Crane's practical suggestions and technical exhortations were new to him, and had a ready impact. It is tempting to trace their course in some of the drawings he produced at this time. He began working in pen, placing his figures in panels, designing in white on black. The wind-racked trees in the background of 'Withered Spring' or the swirling boughs in the 'Perseus' panel are essays in conveying a sense of 'unrest'.[2]

Progress was fitful. On many days he was overtaken by illness and 'had to stop drawing altogether', and it is doubtful that many of these pen works had been included in the portfolio when, early in the new year, Beardsley received a visit from a near-stranger named Aymer Vallance.

Vallance was ten years older than Beardsley, he wrote on interior decoration for the *Art Journal*, was a connoisseur of church architecture and a member of William Morris's circle. It was strange, though perhaps fortunate, that he had not met Aubrey before. Between 1886 and 1888 he had been one of Father Chapman's curates at the Church of the Annunciation, and might well have glimpsed Beardsley on his occasional evensong visits after school. But Vallance's two years at Brighton had been troubled and distracted by doubts. Early in 1889 he renounced his priesthood and was received into the Catholic Church. He learnt of Beardsley only after this apostasy, hearing of him from the Revd C. G. Thornton, another of the assistant clergy at Washington Street, who regaled Vallance with tales of Beardsley's talent in the summer of 1890. Vallance had not taken the clergyman's encomium as disinterested and had failed to follow up the lead for eighteen months. It was only in January 1892 that he sought out the young draughtsman.

Beardsley duly presented his portfolio at the visitor's request and then hovered for a moment in that perennial anxiety over the verdict. He did not have long to wait: Vallance's admiration was unfeigned, immediate and vocal. The pictures were 'nothing less than a revelation'; they displayed not only 'the most astounding imagination' but also an extraordinary ability. He admired the 'intimate acquaintance' with literature and 'fine appreciation of music' which the work revealed, and the conscientious workmanship which must have kept Beardsley up 'far into the night'. Aubrey's delight at these words of praise was 'child-like' in its openness. The terms of Vallance's enthusiasm (imagination, workmanship, literary influence) betray his Pre-Raphaelite sympathies. There is no doubt that he saw in Beardsley a new recruit to the ranks of the Kelmscott army. He urged Beardsley to give up his job at the insurance office and dedicate himself to art. The practical impossibility of this was explained; the income of £80 a year was indispensable to his family.

Beardsley did not reveal at this first interview that he was attending Fred Brown's night classes at the 'Impressionist Academy'. In part, this may have been out of deference to Vallance's pronounced Pre-Raphaelite sympathies, but it was also an early example of a recurring trait. Beardsley habitually concealed key facts about his artistic education and directed inquirers away from the true sources of his influence. Though his debts were many, he wished to escape easy classification and preferred to present himself as a solitary and exceptional figure, a self-taught prodigy toiling at a lonely drawing board, 'far into the night'. Though Vallance learnt to be suspicious of this pose, he was much impressed by Beardsley's 'extraordinary personality' as well as by his art, and resolved to help him. He would draw him, if possible, into the sphere of Morris's influence and introduce him to other discriminating spirits in the London art world who might be able to offer practical assistance.[3]

On 14 February 1892, Vallance hosted a small reception at his rooms in Wells Street, off Oxford Street, to present his new discovery to some of his 'most intimate friends'. Beardsley arrived to find the company assembled. Robert Ross was there, a short Pucklike man of twenty-two, just down from Cambridge and looking to make his name as an art critic; also at the gathering was More Adey, an older and more mysterious figure, with dark bushed eyebrows.

Beardsley was a little awed by the gathering and the air of expectation that greeted his arrival: Vallance had primed his friends about Aubrey's 'extraordinary personality'. But as the evening proceeded his shyness and self-consciousness fell away, and he became 'gay and more talkative'. His erudition and wit made the initial impact: his conversation was 'full of Molière and *Manon Lescaut*'; his knowledge of Balzac was astounding even to Adey, who had edited a volume of Balzac's short stories. To Ross he seemed 'an intellectual Marcellus suddenly matured'. He outflanked his literary and artistic listeners by introducing the subject of music, only to draw back, seemingly 'disappointed' that none of the company shared his passion. He displayed his familiarity with the British Museum and National Gallery collections, while once again distancing himself from conventional and contemporary influences: he told Ross that he had been only once to the New Gallery (which might have been true) and had never been to the Royal Academy (which was certainly not).

By the time the portfolio was produced, Ross found the drawings all but 'overshadowed . . . by the strange and fascinating originality' of their creator, but they soon asserted their claims to attention. Ross particularly admired the long Mantegna-inspired pencil drawing, 'The Procession of Joan of Arc'. So, too, did Beardsley, who refused to part with it, offering instead to make another version of the scene in his now preferred medium of pen-and-ink. Others had more luck. It was perhaps on this occasion that Adey bought 'The Litany of Mary Magdalen' and Vallance acquired 'Perseus and the Monstre'.

The gathering was Beardsley's first real exposure to the fashionable art-loving world of his generation, a step beyond the lunch parties at the clergy house. He determined to keep up the connection, and despite his recurrent ill-health he completed and delivered the new version of 'Joan of Arc'. Ross was also keen to maintain contact; he introduced Beardsley to another potential patron – and fellow Balzac enthusiast – Count Eric Stenbock. Stenbock was a thirty-year-old half-Estonian nobleman, amiable, witty, fantastically rich and richly fantastical. He had written several volumes of overwrought verse and a book of lycanthropic short stories. He loved music and indeed musicians: the latest object of his impassioned interest was a young music student, Norman O'Neill, whom he had met on the upper deck of an omnibus. He took to Beardsley at once.[4]

Others sensed the quickening tide of Beardsley's fortune. His friendship with Julian Sampson, the dilettante brother of the St Barnabas curate, seems to have developed at this time. The support of peers is different from the patronage of elders, and Beardsley delighted in sharing the interests of his coevals and responding to their enthusiasms. For the homosexual Sampson he produced an 'atmospheric' drawing of 'Hermaphroditus' (based stylistically on Burne-Jones's study of 'Love' for the *Chant d'Amour*). The twin-sexed hermaphrodite was a figure of particular fascination during the late nineteenth century. The famous classical statue of the sleeping hermaphrodite at the Louvre had inspired poems by both Gautier and Swinburne, its 'cursed beauty' a symbol of self-sufficiency, sexual confusion and the anti-natural. Beardsley was intrigued by these ideas, which related to current theories about the supremacy of art over nature and life. But he was interested too in the camp argot with which Sampson and his circle expressed these views. He was attracted to the homosexual milieu, with its extravagant phraseology, its self-deprecating wit, and its obsession with surface. Without committing himself sexually, he learnt the language and studied the pose. Although only one of his letters to Sampson survives, its camp paradoxical style and unsentimental wit were apparently characteristic of many others he sent.

Beardsley, perhaps inspired by such company, was becoming something of a dandy. It was part of the decadent pose, sanctioned by the examples of Wilde and Whistler and the writings of Baudelaire. In his essay on Constantin Guys, 'La Peintre de la vie moderne', Baudelaire had proclaimed the virtues of artificiality and distinction: '*le dandyisme*' represented 'the last gleam of heroism in times of decadence', an attempt to establish a new elite in a time of rising uniformity. The dandy, for Baudelaire, announced 'the aristocratic superiority of [his] mind' by the scrupulous distinction of his dress; he was fired by 'the burning need to create an originality for himself within the limits of decorum, to enjoy the pleasure of astounding and the proud satisfaction of never being astounded'. Dandyism was the 'cult of oneself'.

To a Victorian, and especially to one born in Brighton, the notion of dandyism conjured up the lost world of the Regency, so splendidly frivolous and so antipathetic to the contemporary creeds of practical utility and material progress. For Beardsley, trapped in an uncongenial job and an unsatisfactory body, the pose had clear attractions: it would allow him to outface his condition, both material and medical, and project him towards the desired world of art. His means were limited, but an effect could be achieved. The demands of the toilet were always scrupulously observed; one friend of Mabel's who met Aubrey at this time recorded, as his most distinguishing characteristic, that he was 'spotlessly *clean* & well-groomed – one was *impressed* by his cleanliness'. In dress he preserved a studied restraint, as Baudelaire recommended, rather than the foppish excess practised by Wilde and Whistler.

The dandy's pose and the camp banter of the homosexual fringe, though they amused Beardsley, did not find favour with all his friends. Certainly they would have appealed little to Vallance, who had a reputation as a harmless 'ladies' man' and was the butt of frequent jokes on this score. After the success of his soirée on 14 February, Vallance widened the scope of his operations: he tried to effect an introduction between Beardsley and Morris. He knew that Morris was finding it difficult to get suitable illustrators for his Kelmscott Press books, and was searching for someone to do the drawings for a proposed edition of Meinhold's *Sidonia the Sorceress* in a translation by Oscar Wilde's mother. Vallance persuaded Beardsley to draw, on spec, a picture of Sidonia. Beardsley read the book avidly, before producing a drawing of the sorceress with her demon cat, Chim. This was added to the portfolio when Vallance accompanied Beardsley to Morris's house at Hammersmith one Sunday afternoon. It was not quite a year since that other Sunday afternoon when Beardsley had called on Burne-Jones with such satisfactory results. He knew what advances he had made in his art since then, and must have been quietly confident.[5]

*   *   *

Morris was then in his late fifties but his energy was still phenomenal – he was actively engaged as a poet, designer, businessman, polemicist, socialist. Beardsley was a great admirer of his poetry (he had thought *The Earthly Paradise* 'simply enchanting') but he knew too his work in the applied arts. In 1890 Morris had launched the Kelmscott Press, a venture which aimed to reform and improve the standards of book design and production, rescuing them from mechanical standardization and unaesthetic vulgarity. He had installed the Press at Kelmscott House, his home on the river at Hammersmith.

With his 'usual courtesy', Morris looked at the pictures, but it was immediately clear – certainly to Vallance and probably to Beardsley – that 'they had failed to arouse . . . any particular interest'. He turned up the picture of Sidonia but failed to take the bait, finding the sorceress's face 'not pretty enough'. His only other pronouncement had the dismal ring of faint praise; 'I see you have a feeling for draperies,' he told his young visitor, 'and I advise you to cultivate it.'

Beardsley came away from Kelmscott House bitterly disappointed. He felt that he had been 'repulsed', but Vallance refused to give up hope. For a brief while he seems to have infected his friend with this spirit of perseverance, for Beardsley returned to his desk and tried to improve Sidonia's features. The attempt, however, was unsuccessful and Beardsley consigned the picture, and his aspirations of collaborating with Morris, to the bin.* The rejection rankled. It was a blow to his *amour propre*, but it also marked a first rift with the Pre-Raphaelite tradition which had, until then, seemed so welcoming and sustaining. However, he turned his disappointment into new channels. He reverted to the example of Whistler and Japan that he had first glimpsed in the Peacock Room the previous year but had not properly digested.[6]

The influence of Japan upon the European art of the late nineteenth century was great and various. In Britain it passed through several distinct phases. In the 1860s it had been a matter of individual collectors – Rossetti, Whistler and Leyland among them – searching out choice items of blue-and-white china; in the 1870s Japanese

---

* The picture, or its general scheme, was perhaps revived in Beardsley's japonesque drawing 'La Femme Incomprise', which shows a courtesan with her cat.

prints and furniture began to affect the work of artists and designers, such as Whistler and Godwin, with a new appreciation for simplicity, for flat colour, for asymmetry. By the 1880s, this artistic perception had deteriorated into a craze, a mania for oriental effects: paper fans and paper lanterns, kimonos and gilded screens; Japanese motifs appeared on everything from cheap trays to biscuit boxes.

Beardsley had grown up in the tawdry excesses of this third phase. The shop windows in Brighton had been full of 'jap' trumpery, which had amused him without suggesting anything to his art. The 'discovery' of Whistler's work, however, had begun to awaken him to the more interesting messages of Japanese style. These, of course, could not be picked up on a single visit to the Peacock Room, but there were opportunities for further study. In March 1892 a small retrospective exhibition of Whistler's work – including paintings and etchings; 'nocturnes, marines and chevalet pieces' – opened at Goupils in Waterloo Place. It was a splendid opportunity for Beardsley to absorb the full range of Whistler's work and the radical Japan-inspired aesthetic behind it, an aesthetic dominated by simplicity of form, asymmetry of design and flatness of tone.

He was also able to imbibe this lesson from other sources. He could study Japanese prints at first-hand at the British Museum and, more especially, at Jones & Evans, where Frederick Evans had a considerable collection. Evans also possessed several prints by Odilon Redon, an artist then barely known in Britain. Redon had adapted the tropes and forms of Japanese art in a very different way from Whistler, grafting the stark oriental style not to landscape or portraiture but to a bizarre symbolic world of the imagination. His art, viewed next to Whistler's, showed Beardsley that there were many ways of adapting Japanese art to a wholly personal style, a lesson which would have a decisive bearing on his stylistic development.[7]

As the spring advanced his health rallied and, after the frustrations of enforced idleness, he was able to return to drawing. He recommenced with a new sense of purpose, directing his energies away from the Pre-Raphaelite tradition and towards the example of Japan. He 'struck out', as he later told Mr Marshall, 'a new style and method of work which was founded on Japanese art but [was] quite original in the main'. Abandoning for the moment the broad linear technique of Pre-Raphaelite drawing, he mimicked the hairlines and flat tones of Japanese prints by using 'the finest possible outline with patches of "black blot" ', a method perfectly suited to his level of penmanship. The fine lines could be drawn with an 'etching pen', the 'blot' applied with a brush, and in 'certain points of technique' he was able to 'achieve something like perfection at once'.

The novelty of the technique was matched by a novelty of composition. He began dividing the picture plane with ruled lines, not into a conventional decorative panel, as he had done previously, but into an unexpected and asymmetrical arrangement of space. Though the drawings were 'severe in execution', their subjects were 'fantastic in conception'. Taking a holiday from the epic literary concerns of Burne-Jones and Morris, Beardsley conjured up a new world of his own invention. The stray discoveries of the previous year found an outlet in these 'mad and a little indecent' compositions, peopled with 'strange hermaphroditic creatures, wandering about in Pierrot costumes or modern dress'.

The pictures marked a great stride forward, a wilful decision to 'get out of the conventional – to do something that no other fellow had done, if I could'. But they achieved it without strain; for the first time the personal note in his art was heard above the clamour of his influences. He had taken the elements of Japanese design and fashioned them into something quite new, both in style and content. He was intoxicated by his new-found facility, and the drawings flew from his pen. In April and May, despite having returned to his insurance office, he produced almost twenty pictures in this style. Perhaps one of them was the sombre, sensual woman confronting a surly foetus with the text, 'Incipit Vita Nova'. Beardsley's new style held the promise of New Life. Though he was aware of the debt he owed to Japanese art, he was conscious too of his own originality, and did not wish his achievement to be too readily pigeonholed as just another example of contemporary Japonisme. While he was prepared to admit to Marshall the origin of his new style, to others he was less open. He convinced Ross that the resemblance between his new

OPPOSITE One of Beardsley's 'mad and a little indecent' figures; it was published in *Bon-Mots of Charles Lamb and Douglas Jerrold* in 1893.

method and oriental art was 'quite accidental', and that the source of his inspiration was the collection of Crivellis in the National Gallery.[8]

At this stage, Beardsley had no thought of repudiating the Pre-Raphaelite tradition entirely, but he began to show signs of dissent. It is significant that, in a letter to King, he characterized his new drawings as fantastic 'impressions'. The word was scarcely accurate because he drew from his imagination rather than his senses, but it served to align the work with the Impressionist camp of Whistler and his followers. One of his less fantastical 'japonesque' drawings, moreover, was a portrait of Raphael, the painter whose exclusion from the acceptable canons of influence gave the Pre-Raphaelites their name. Beardsley framed the drawing and cited it often as his first decisively individual statement. By turning Raphael into a personal icon Beardsley was surely suggesting impatience with the narrow limits of the Burne-Jones tradition.

Coupled with this impatience was a growing awareness that art was an expression of personality. The creation of a new style gave him confidence in this direction, but he noted it too in other more mundane ways. At the Westminster School he remarked with amusement how all the students reproduced their own 'personal types' in their drawings: whatever the shape of the models the stout men drew them as stout figures, the thin men drew them as thin. To amuse Vallance, whom he had told of this 'universal tendency', Beardsley constructed an imaginary portrait of Botticelli based on the recurring types that figure in his art. He must also have recognized the tendency in his own work towards thinness, angularity and the morbid.[9]

Life at the office continued to drag horribly, but there was good news even there. In April the holiday allocation for junior clerks was increased from two to three weeks. Beardsley determined to use this provision for a trip to Paris in May. The expedition seems to have been planned as a reconnaissance: he needed to learn Paris. He knew from reading George Moore and Wilde that a knowledge of the French capital, its art, its literature, its life, was vital to the pose of the *fin-de-siècle* artist. Not to have been there was a solecism. He inquired of Ross about a 'good cheap place to stay', but planned to travel with only his portfolio for company. No letters of his from

Paris survive but, while the details of his trip are conjectural, the overall picture is clear.

Paris was a feast of art: the wonderfully bold poster designs of Cheret, Grasset and Lautrec turned even the streets into a gallery. He, of course, visited and came to know the Louvre and its collection well. Mantegna's great allegorical painting of Minerva expelling the vices from the garden must have touched his interest; the artist had created his own fantastical, mad and indecent world.

Beyond the permanent sights, the two great exhibitions of the year – at the salons of the Champs Elysées and the Champ de Mars – were in progress. At their fringe, other shows had been mounted: 1892 was the first year of the Salon de la Rose + Croix, a gathering of work by the most modern of schools, the *Symbolistes*. Beardsley may not have grasped the Symbolists' quasi-mystical theories, but he would have recognized the debt their art owed to Rossetti and Burne-Jones. He would have noted, too, the irony that at a time when radical artists in England were looking to the French impressionist tradition, the most extreme artists in France were drawing inspiration from the British Pre-Raphaelite canon.

Beardsley's portfolio was an unofficial passport into this world. He took it with him when he went to call on Pierre Puvis de Chavannes, the president of the Salon of the Champ de Mars. (It is usually assumed that Beardsley had a letter of introduction from Burne-Jones but, in his self-dramatizing fashion, he always claimed that he had simply walked into Puvis's studio, inspired by some of the master's pictures.) Puvis received him kindly and examined the strange japonesque drawings with care, saying a few words 'in praise or blame' of particular pictures. Overall his verdict was enthusiastic. 'I never saw anyone so encouraging as he was,' reported Beardsley, who was emboldened to present him with a small drawing of some 'children decorating a terminal god'. Beardsley was introduced to another artist by Puvis as 'un jeune artiste anglais qui fait des choses étonnantes'. Astonishment might not be considered by some as the true aim of art, but Beardsley was delighted with the verdict and repeated it often; it was wonderful to hear himself described as 'un jeune artiste anglais' rather than an insurance clerk.[10]

*　　*　　*

At the end of his three weeks, though he returned to London 'not a little pleased with [his] success', he was obliged to resume his place as a square peg in a round hole at Lombard Street. His mind was less on his job than ever. He continued drawing in his 'new' style, refining it and making developments in technique. His technical advance and his growing frustrations came together in a magnificent autobiographical drawing of a clerk toiling at a high desk. He titled the picture 'Le Dèbris d'un Poète', borrowing the phrase though not the angle of the accent from a passage in *Madame Bovary*, where Flaubert suggests that within every notary lies the wreckage of a poet. The accomplishment of the drawing, however, defied the self-mocking image: the artist trapped within the insurance clerk, far from being wrecked, was bursting forth.

Beardsley's development was never linear; the discovery of a new style did not necessitate the abandonment of an old. Though his japonesque style was the dominating enthusiasm of the moment, he also continued to make drawings in the Pre-Raphaelite manner. He proliferated styles, adding them to his arsenal of effects, cross-fertilizing them.

There was a season of German opera in London that July, with performances of *Tannhäuser* and *Götterdämmerung* at Covent Garden. Beardsley, of course, attended, and, as a record of his enthusiasm, adapted his new style to produce pictures of the company's two stars, Max Alvary and Katharina Klafsky. The operas also inspired him to produce drawings in his Pre-Raphaelite decorative-panel style. He had created an extraordinary momentum. The setback of his rejection by Morris had been overcome, lost in the continuing approval of Burne-Jones and the 'surprise and enthusiasm' with which the French artists had greeted his work. He had the support of Ross and Vallance to add to that of Evans and Father Gurney; he had sold a picture to Count Stenbock. He felt the forelock of opportunity within his grasp.

But the decisive breakthrough, by which his potential could be transmuted into something palpable and golden, still had to be made if he was to escape from his high stool. Private sales were gratifying to his vanity, but – at between five and ten shillings a drawing –

OPPOSITE 'Raphael Sanzio', 1892.

they could not offer any real prospect of independence or escape. The 'next step' was clear: he had to 'besiege the publishers'. It was a large encampment to surround.[11]

The late Victorian age had seen a great increase in book production and, more particularly, in the illustrated periodical press. Improving education and increasing wealth had multiplied the publishers' potential audience many times. In tandem with this, there was the development of photo-mechanical reproduction. Until the end of the 1880s images could be reproduced only by engraving the original drawing by hand on to wood, steel or some other material: the process was time-consuming, expensive, and not entirely faithful, and the original drawing was destroyed during the procedure. During the late 1880s, a means was developed of transferring an image photographically to a zinc block from which it could be printed. A black-and-white drawing was photographed and a negative made; the negative was placed on a zinc plate treated with light-sensitive gelatine, and exposed under a strong light. Where the light passed through the negative image, the gelatine hardened. The unexposed, unhardened gelatine was then washed away leaving the black lines of the original standing in relief. This raised surface was strengthened by heat and chemical treatment to make a 'ground' strong enough to receive the ink.

The process was relatively cheap and quick and, within its limits, accurate. It could, however, only be used for black-and-white work. To reproduce intermediate grey tones, it was necessary to photograph a drawing through a glass screen with a cross-grid of fine lines. This broke the image into a series of tiny dots, larger or smaller depending on the strength of tone of the original, and a zinc plate was then made in the way described. Although only black ink was used, the microscopic array of dots on the plate created the illusion of halftones. These two related developments produced a revolution: illustrated papers, books and magazines proliferated – and so did illustrators. Black-and-white art during the opening years of the 1890s began to emerge as practically a recognized movement on its own. Such was the demand that increasing numbers of artists gave themselves up entirely to black-and-white illustration.

Nevertheless, Beardsley had to struggle to breach the defences.

He later claimed that this was due to 'stupid' publishers being 'frightened . . . of anything so new and daringly original' as his drawings. But he did little to help his own cause: when applying for a position on the staff of the newly-established *Daily Graphic*, he sent a sheaf of his Burne-Jones fantasies and Japanese grotesques, failing to acknowledge that the last thing a daily newspaper wanted of its artists was imagination. The drawings were returned.* The tribulations of his quest for work are shown even more clearly in another incident. He secured, probably through Ross, an appointment to see W. E. Henley, editor of the *National Observer*. On arriving at the magazine's Great College Street offices and climbing the two flights of stairs to Henley's room, he heard a terrible voice raised in anger, and, gaining the landing, saw through an open door a large red man haranguing an unfortunate, 'quaking' youth. Beardsley 'knew instinctively' that the irate figure was Henley; he turned and fled down the stairs, out into the street, past the Houses of Parliament, through the Horseguards and stopped only when he had gained the safety of the park. He did not return.

One publisher, however, did look kindly upon Beardsley's portfolio. Cassell's had built up a flourishing magazine business; their list included not only the *Family Magazine* and *Saturday Journal* but the *Magazine of Art* and *Woman's World*, the magazine which Oscar Wilde edited briefly in the late 1880s. There was a ceaseless demand for decorative initials and borders as well as for conventional illustrations, and it was probably work of the former sort that they offered Beardsley. Before he could undertake this first commission, however, a new excitement overtook him.[12]

Frederick Evans, as a bookseller, had close contacts with several publishers. He was particularly friendly with J. M. Dent, who had recently established a publishing house dedicated to bringing out well-designed but cheaply produced reprints of classic works. Evans learnt, through his book-trade contacts, that one of Dent's new projects was a lavishly illustrated partwork edition of Sir Thomas Malory's *Morte Darthur*, designed in imitation of Morris's mock-

* It was perhaps at this time that Beardsley approached the New Oxford Street bookseller Walter T. Spencer and offered to illustrate a book for him to publish. (W. T. Spencer, *Forty Years in My Bookshop*; London, 1923.)

medieval Kelmscott Press style but printed at a fraction of the price by using photo-mechanical reproduction processes for the illustrative material. Evans discovered that the publisher was still looking for an illustrator who could produce satisfactory 'mock medieval' illustrations. Evans, of course, immediately thought of Beardsley, the friend and imitator of Burne-Jones. He had some of Beardsley's pictures in the shop, so he sent word to Dent that he might have found an illustrator. With a fine sense of salesmanship, he urged haste, claiming that he could only hold on to the pictures for the day.

Dent, his curiosity piqued, hurried around to Queen Street. He looked over Beardsley's recent pictures but was not immediately convinced. He also studied, and perhaps with more conviction, an earlier picture, 'Hail Mary', which Evans owned and which owed much to Burne-Jones. And then, such is the force of serendipity (if we are to believe Evans's account) Beardsley stalked into the shop, bent on his lunch-hour browse. Evans pointed out the 'swift-moving, intent figure' to Dent, saying conspiratorially, 'There's your man'. Dent had only a moment to be struck by the curious appearance and gait of the young clerk, before Evans, catching Beardsley's eye, beckoned him over to the desk, and introductions were effected. Evans 'somewhat bewildered' Beardsley by presenting him as the ideal illustrator for *Morte Darthur*. Dent was probably alarmed: he thought Beardsley 'a strange boy', 'weird'. But he had faith in Evans's judgement, so the Malory project was duly explained.

Beardsley, who until then had been nursing his delight at having the minor decorative chores from Cassell's, was 't[aken] aback' at being offered the chance of such a huge and prestigious commission. He knew the book well and considered it 'glorious'; the previous year he had even thought of illustrating it for his own amusement. Nevertheless, he hesitated. Dent spoke encouragingly of Evans's high opinion of his work. The publisher's initial alarm at Beardsley's weirdness had waned as he realized that the young man was 'keen about his art'. It was agreed that Beardsley should make a 'drawing for approval'. Evans fetched a Kelmscott book from the shelves, perhaps William Morris's recently issued *A Dream of John Ball*, to give 'some idea of what was in Dent's mind'. Aubrey studied Morris's foliate borders and the woodcut frontispiece by Burne-Jones with an intensity born of excitement. Then, taking his leave, he hesitated at the shop door and, shaking Evans's hand, murmured earnestly, 'It's too good a chance. I'm sure I shan't be equal to it. I am not worthy of it.' Evans assured him that he had only to set himself to it and all would be well.

A breach had been opened, and Beardsley knew he must leap through it. He exerted all his powers to produce, within a few days, a stunning sample picture. He chose as his subject the climax of the book: 'The Achieving of the Sangreal'. He borrowed the support of tradition, taking some of the details of his picture from Crivelli and Pollaiuolo; the overall effect he derived from Burne-Jones. His labour was intense: three figures are placed in a minutely realized landscape, marked by myriad details and areas of subtle wash. Although the drawing marked a return to Beardsley's most derivative and italianate style, some traces of his recent japonesque enthusiasm intruded. There was the hairline work at the water's edge, the sinister flower sweeping across the foreground, and the curious three-line 'mark' he intro-duced as his signature.*

These neoteric details do not seem to have registered with the conservative Dent, who was impressed by the picture's conventional virtues. Any uncertainty he had entertained evaporated; he thought the picture a 'masterpiece'. He ignored Beardsley's failure to grasp that the drawing should have been made in stark black and white, without any grey wash, so that it should look like a woodcut and could be reproduced by the cheapest photo-mechanical process. Such technical niceties could be addressed later. The commission was agreed upon and by the third day of October a deal was struck, if not stamped. In its first form the contract offered '£50 for the 20 odd full page drawings, £25 for the 40 small drawings & designs and @ 5/- each for the initial letters', estimated at 'nearly 350'. There were to be two additional payments of £50 each, one on the sale of 'the second 2000 copies', the other 'in the event of having to

* This 'trade mark', which he used until mid-1894, though derived from Japanese pictoglyphs, has been variously deciphered: the *Boston Evening Transcript* thought it 'like the Crest of the Prince of Wales'. Beardsley once drew it explicitly, on a letter to Ross, as three candlesticks. Contemporary commentators have sought a sexual interpretation.

print a further 2000'. The book would be produced in twelve parts beginning early the following year.[13]

Beardsley was within the citadel. He had a commission giving him work for at least the next twelve months and guaranteeing him over £160, a sum more than twice his annual salary from the office job. Escape from Lombard Street was now possible. Mabel urged him to take the step; she had recently inherited her £500 from Sarah Pitt on reaching twenty-one, and could hold out the promise of support should it be necessary. And Aubrey would receive his own legacy within the year.

Emboldened, he handed in his resignation. Although he told King that he left 'to the great satisfaction of said office and myself', he gave 'ill health' as the official reason for his departure, not artistic commitment. He did not tell his parents of his decision until the break had been made. There were 'ructions' at first; Vincent was the most alarmed, but even Ellen, it seems, was not yet quite convinced of her son's potential as a freelance illustrator.

Aubrey, however, was not to be deflected. Released from the diurnal grind of the office he 'flung himself . . . with almost mad enthusiasm' into the *Morte Darthur* project. He was apprised of the technical constraints of the task and now knew that he had to work in stark black and white. He made an 'eager study of the Kelmscott tradition' and followed it to its roots in the early Renaissance woodcut. He bought a copy of Anton Springer's recently published work on Albrecht Dürer and studied the illustrations closely; perhaps he also returned to Walter Crane's article on pictorial design, to its practical advice on filling space and working in white on black.

His anxiety to succeed was apparent in these careful preparations and in the fact that, for some of his earliest designs, he plundered his own work. He adapted his drawing of 'Withered Spring' to make one chapter heading, and took the Medusa's head from his 'Perseus' panel for another. 'Soleil Couchant' was pressed into service, and even the Pied Piper reappeared, subtly transformed.* The tondo of

---

* Evans related the image of the piper to Beardsley's enthusiasm for Blake's 'Piping Down the Valleys Wild'.

Merlin, one of the first pictures he did, perhaps derived from his earlier drawing of the 'wonder worker'. Beardsley wanted, it seems, the assurance of existing achievement. His confidence, however, soon advanced and with it his imagination. Although the influence of Morris and Burne-Jones was strong in the first full-page illustrations and borders, it was leavened with a japonesque feeling for lightness and fluency of design, which he combined with the medieval elements to create something quite different from the dense olde worlde pastiches of the Kelmscott books. Although the subject matter of the full-page illustrations was dictated by the text, for the small chapter headings he allowed his fancy to wander.

He relied partly on conventional floral flourishes but also summoned up a strange world of satyrs and angels, knights and fauns. The juxtaposition was less jarring than might be supposed; the survival of the pagan tradition into the Christian era was a common theme in the late nineteenth century. The key text was Walter Pater's essay in *Studies in the History of the Renaissance* with its account of the Greek gods wandering in exile through the medieval world. It is tempting to read Beardsley's drawings as a commentary on this tradition.[14]

He kept in 'close touch' with Dent during the first months of the *Morte Darthur* commission. The publisher tried to interest his new friend in the activities of Toynbee Hall, the Universities' settlement in the East End which aimed to bring culture to the working man, and where Dent was secretary of the Shakespeare play-reading society. Beardsley seems to have evaded commitment on this front: the atmosphere of earnest non-denominational philanthropy at 'Toynbee' was not calculated to appeal to his fastidious temperament. On one occasion at least he pleaded ill-health: 'I soon knock up these days', he explained, 'so I have to be careful to avoid over exertion. Sad is it not to have to begin coddling oneself up at twenty.'

With the approach of winter, Beardsley's health was indeed taking its expected seasonal dip and he needed to conserve his energy for work. His first submissions were well received by Dent. Others too liked them. Burne-Jones generously accepted their tribute to his style as the sincerest form of flattery. Vallance was delighted by their careful workmanship; of the drawing 'Merlin and Nimue' he vouchsafed, 'Has anything superior to it been produced since the days of the fifteenth-century German woodcutters?' He thought the roundel of Merlin 'masterly', and in everything he found a 'conscientious elaboration of detail worthy of the very best Pre-Raphaelite work'. But, at the very moment when Beardsley seemed to be assuming his place at the Pre-Raphaelite round table, other forces were luring him away.

In part the force came from within. Beardsley's febrile, inquisitive nature became restless with sustained effort, seeking always the stimulation of novelty, the spice of variety. Dent seems to have recognized this trait, and the dangers it presented. At about this time he drew up a fresh and more formal contract for the Malory project, offering the incentive of a further £50 if the editions sold out but laying out in detail the exact numbers of pictures to be produced for each part and the dates by which they had to be delivered.

Dent also tried to make a virtue of his illustrator's restlessness. The memory lingered of the bizarre japonesque drawings Evans had shown him, and he conceived the idea of getting Beardsley to decorate a series of mini-anthologies of eighteenth-century wit that he was bringing out. The decorations were to be fanciful grotesques, little more than doodles but, on the principle that a change is as good as a rest, Dent thought they might offer relief from the serious work of the Arthurian legends. Beardsley seized this chance. The new challenge fired him with a blast of creative energy, and he shifted seamlessly from his medieval manner to his japonesque. Plundering his imagination, his memory, his library, his portfolio – or simply pushing ink around until something emerged – he created a gallery of hideous creatures: pierrots, hermaphrodites, foetuses, amputees, ballet dancers, geishas, costers, satyrs, whores and rakes. The distinctive figure of James McNeill Whistler even made an appearance. He produced sixty of these calligraphic grotesques in just ten days; the pen strokes that made up some of them could, he remarked, 'be counted on the fingers'. For these 'tiny little things' he received a cheque for £15. Beyond the diversion of these pictures for the *Bon-Mots* series, Dent held out the possibility of further commissions for Hawthorne's *Classic Tales*, Henry Mackenzie's *Man of*

OPPOSITE One of the early full-page illustrations for *Morte Darthur*.

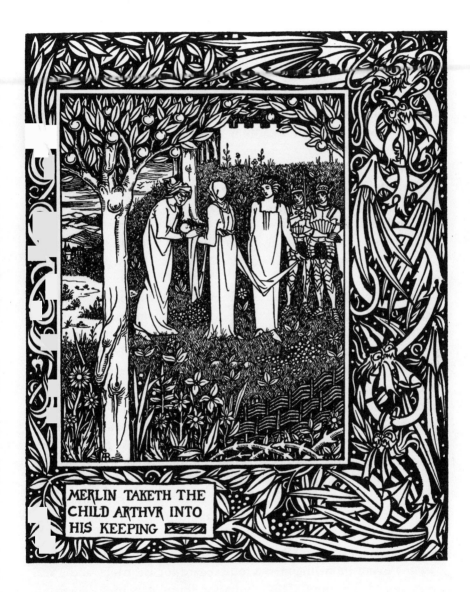

MERLIN TAKETH THE
CHILD ARTHVR INTO
HIS KEEPING

Feeling and Fanny Burney's *Evelina*. Beardsley was eager for everything.[15]

The family was amazed at his progress, and at his earnings. Mabel took great pride in his triumphs, and began to see in them the prospect of her own salvation from the drudgery of the Polytechnic School. Aubrey suggested that Dent might give her some 'literary work' for one of his reprint series; the suggestion came to nothing, but it served to draw Mabel into the orbit of her brother's new and exciting world. Vincent Beardsley began to pretend that he had always known Aubrey would make a success of his drawing; while Ellen, who *had* harboured great hopes for her son, was more than ever grateful that they were now being realized. She had fallen ill again with 'chronic sciatica', and was in too much pain to work; only 'perfect rest' would avail. In the face of her illness the care of the family thus fell increasingly on the two children and so, as Aubrey remarked, 'the money view' of his art had to be kept 'keenly in view'.

There was, however, he knew, more to art than money-making. He was reminded of the fact by a flattering communication from Fred Brown. With the onset of the *Morte* commission, Beardsley had given up his attendance at the Westminster School of Art. Indeed, he would henceforth pretend that he had scarcely attended there. He tried to convince Vallance that he had not been at the school 'more than half-a-dozen times altogether'. Brown had not noticed the desertion, for he had left the school to take up the Slade Professorship at University College London. It is possible that he may have felt some slight and indirect debt of gratitude to Beardsley for his appointment. Certainly he had shown the interviewing board the flattering letter he had received from Burne-Jones recommending Beardsley to his care; Brown had felt that Burne-Jones's name would carry weight and that the approbation of the nation's leading Pre-Raphaelite would soften his own reputation as a 'wild Impressionist'.

In any event he maintained a fond regard for Beardsley and a real admiration for his work. This admiration found generous expression towards the end of 1892 when Brown, in his capacity as a committee member of the New English Art Club, invited Beardsley to exhibit at the club's show the following spring. This was a great compliment. The NEAC had a tradition of showing some black-and-white work with the paintings, and Beardsley's inclusion assured him of a position on the contemporary scene as an 'artist' rather than as a mere hack illustrator. It would also give him a foothold in the impressionist camp, and confuse the expectations of those who viewed him as a disciple of the Pre-Raphaelites.

Although Beardsley did not, as he told Mr Marshall, 'forget to be thankful' for the good fortune piling up at his feet, his confidence was growing in bounds, and with it his sense of poise and pose. He was becoming conscious of his powers and his worth. Other publishers began to court him. He was approached by Otto Kyllmann, an editor at Constable & Co. R. & R. Clarke of Edinburgh made him a 'very good offer', though he felt obliged to decline it, and he began to conceive his own schemes.[16]

One of his plans was to illustrate that 'most glorious of books', George Meredith's oriental fantasy, *The Shaving of Shagpat*. The choice was decidedly Pre-Raphaelite: the book had been a great favourite of Rossetti's. It was admired too by Vallance and Evans. Although the novel had first appeared, in 1856, under the imprint of Chapman and Hall, Vallance told Beardsley that he knew of a young publisher with a passion for Meredith who might be ideal for the project.

In 1892, John Lane was at the beginning of his career. A clod-bound Devonian with literary yearnings but no formal education, Lane had come to London at fourteen to work as a clerk in the clearing house at Euston Station. His spare hours were spent over the secondhand bookstalls and he gradually assembled an 'extensive but peculiar' library in his rooms at Southwick Street. The peculiarity of his collection was the preponderance of works by George Meredith. Towards the end of the 1880s, Lane had the idea of turning his hobby into a business. He persuaded an Exeter-based antiquarian book-dealer, Elkin Mathews, that they should go into partnership and open a bookshop in London. They began trading in 1887 from tiny premises in Vigo Street off Regent Street, under the sign of the Bodley Head. At first, Lane continued to work at the clearing house, but the business grew; they launched from bookselling into publishing small attractively produced editions of poetry and *belles lettres*, including a volume on Meredith with a bibliography by John Lane.

At the beginning of 1892, Lane gave up his office job to become a full and open partner in the firm, and launched a drive to expand the publishing side of the business. He was on the lookout for new titles and would, Vallance thought, look kindly on anything connected with his beloved Meredith. Vallance arranged a meeting between Beardsley and Lane; the project was discussed excitedly among the three of them, and plans were laid. All, however, depended upon securing the rights from Chapman and Hall. They thought the idea so good that they wanted to cut Lane out of the equation and work with Beardsley themselves. Aubrey produced a drawing of the 'head of Shagpat' for Meredith's approval. Perhaps Meredith did not care for it; the project did not progress any further.[17]

Vallance was not discouraged by the setback. Other opportunities, he perceived, were opening up. He had learnt that a new art periodical was being planned. Financed by Charles Holme and edited by C. Lewis Hind, it was to be called *The Studio*; the first issue would come out early in 1893. Vallance knew Hind and resolved to try to interest him in Beardsley. Hind, however, was elusive. He had spent the previous months fending off acquaintances all eager to push the claims of their own undiscovered young geniuses, and had to be taken unawares. A plot seems to have been hatched.

Vallance discovered that Hind would be attending a Sunday afternoon gathering hosted by Wilfred and Alice Meynell at their new Aesthetic home in Palace Gate. The Meynells were very poetical and very Catholic, and were known as the discoverers and rescuers of Francis Thompson, an opium-addicted poet who had been down and out on the streets of London. Wilfred, the editor of a Catholic literary periodical, *Merry England*, had recognized Thompson's genius, published his poems, and helped him to regain a footing in society. Alice Meynell had a reputation as a poet herself. Tall and thin, with dark hair and melancholy eyes, she had the air and charm of 'a beautiful abbess'. Her flowing 'catafalque' robes contributed to the effect; her voice sank and rose 'like a Gregorian chant'. And even if the monastic calm of the home was frequently shattered by her six children, many came to listen. She delighted in gathering young writers and artists into her fashionably under-furnished drawing-room.

It was into this decorous setting of rattan dados, arts-and-crafts cabinets and bare boards that Beardsley, clutching his portfolio, was piloted by Vallance. A young man was at the piano singing a setting of Alice Meynell's poem 'Love of Narcissus'. Various guests were sitting in quiet absorption, listening to the music. Mrs Meynell was gazing poetically into the fire; her diminutive, genial husband was turning over the pages of a book. Hind was there, his back to the door. Vallance led Beardsley to a station behind the quarry's chair and when the music stopped, he pounced. 'Oh Hind', he cut in, 'I've brought a young artist here, Aubrey Beardsley. I wish you would look at his drawings; they're remarkable.'

Beardsley knew the part he had to play. He stepped forward with an air of quiet assurance, brought his heels together and presented the well-travelled portfolio. He said nothing. Hind, half-irritated by the intrusion, half-amused by the strange, silent youth, took the folder. Beardsley stepped back. The man at the piano began a new song.

Hind looked through the portfolio. The pictures he saw – japonesques, some early *Morte* illustrations, perhaps even some *Bon-Mots* grotesques – appealed to him instantly. It may be doubted that he really did say to himself, 'Either I'm crazy, or this is genius', but he undoubtedly recognized the work's novelty, daring and suitability for publication. He was looking for a 'sensational send-off article for the first number' of his magazine and thought that these pictures, which had never been published before, might make an arresting impact.* He wanted to take the portfolio to show his backer, Charles Holme, but Beardsley was not prepared to part with the pictures for even a single night. It was arranged that he would bring the portfolio to the *Studio* offices in Covent Garden the following day.

Holme was conditioned to appreciate Beardsley's drawings. A North Country textile magnate, he was an enthusiast for the arts-and-crafts movement and had recently bought William Morris's Red

---

* Hind's recollection of the pictures he saw seems to be faulty: he mentions 'three or four from Salome' which were certainly not there.

House at Bexleyheath. His abiding passion, however, was Japan. He had made his fortune in part through expanding his business into the East; privately he collected oriental artefacts; he had visited Japan; he was a founder member of the Japan Society. He had just retired from business at the age of forty-four, and intended to devote himself to promoting contemporary art and design: *The Studio* was his first venture. His manufacturing background had given him a quick understanding of technical innovation. At a time when the large-circulation British art periodicals – the *Art Journal* and *Magazine of Art* – were still reproducing pictures through wood-engraving, he recognized the economic and aesthetic advantages of embracing photo-engraving. It would be the principal medium for his new periodical.

Nevertheless, he was not a man to be stampeded by enthusiasm. He looked at the pictures carefully, assessing their suitability for the all-important first number. Finally, he said quietly but with conviction, 'These will do.' Then, displaying the business flair that had made his fortune, he added, 'I shall buy some of them.' It was, unsurprisingly, the Japanese element that had appealed to him. The works he acquired – 'Les Revenants de Musique', 'The Birthday of Madame Cigale' – were among the most concertedly japonesque.[18]

An article was needed to accompany the drawings. Holme suggested that Hind might write it, but the editor declined, declaring that Joseph Pennell would be the ideal choice. Pennell was an opinionated Philadelphian living in London. An illustrator and critic, he had established himself as an authority on pen-and-ink work and was a vociferous advocate of the democratic virtues and artistic possibilities of photo-engraving for reproducing it. In 1889 he had brought out a large book on *Pen Drawing and Pen Draughtsmen*, which combined examples of work from Europe and America with practical tips. It had gone some way towards establishing the credentials of the new art-form at a time when, as Pennell put it, it was treated in a 'very unsatisfactory manner' by the 'principal critics of the day'.

Pennell would indeed be a useful ally for a young illustrator at the start of his career. After consultations with Hind and Vallance, Robert Ross undertook to make the approach. He sought out the American and confided, 'I have found an artist. At least I think I have. Would you care to come to a dinner I am going to give in a few days and meet this artist ... Beardsley?' The bait was taken. Ross gathered an impressive group for the occasion. Besides Pennell, Hind was there, and Gleeson White, then working as art editor for the publishers George Bell & Sons; an elderly American, Justin McCarthy, was produced; and George Moore, art critic of the *Speaker*, had 'managed to get in somehow'.

Beardsley had learnt his mother's trick of arriving last, to make an entrance. He was on his way to becoming an accomplished performer. He had confidence that his dandified dress would impress; that the discrepancy between his youthful mien and worldly erudition would bemuse; and that the novelty of his drawings would startle. He certainly made a strong first impression on Pennell – though it was not altogether favourable. The American considered that the new arrival, in his elegant yet severely simple clothes, looked 'less an artist than a swell', and the portfolio too was over-smart for his taste: 'Not like an artist's portfolio, more like something a young lady would carry.' But, once the offending folder was opened, Pennell recognized that Beardsley was serious. He was particularly struck by an intricately worked headpiece of 'Men in Armour' which Beardsley had produced for the *Morte Darthur* title page. It combined, Pennell thought, 'in a remarkable manner the work of the Pre-Raphaelites and that of the modern designers', with 'a medieval feeling running through it'. Beardsley accepted the first wave of praise for his drawings before remarking nonchalantly that Burne-Jones liked them too. Pleased with the effect this achieved, he sallied beyond strict veracity by adding that William Morris liked them too, which really 'waked . . . up' his listeners.

However, Beardsley quickly set a distance between himself and the sage of Kelmscott by explaining that he and Dent would be reproducing the *Morte Darthur* drawings by process-engraving and not by laborious woodcutting, he had 'no use for Morris's hide-bound mannerisms'. These were sentiments close to Pennell's heart, and Beardsley flattered him further by asking advice on various matters of composition and technique. Nevertheless, there was a limit to Beardsley's candour: although Pennell had noted the stylized japonisme of some of the work, and suspected the influence of Whistler,

Beardsley dismissed the connection, and did not disclose that he had visited the Peacock Room. Beyond such manoeuvres, Beardsley seems to have warmed to something in Pennell; he liked him. Perhaps behind the simple attraction there was a trace of Aubrey's recurrent need to seek out father-figures to authenticate his achievements. Pennell, who was only thirty-two, was apparently flattered by the role; he agreed to write the article.[19]

Sadly, George Moore's impressions and opinions of the Beardsley portfolio are not recorded, but Ross was busy enlisting other critics to the cause. The young Scottish painter and journalist, D. S. Mac-Coll, who had already heard of Beardsley from Fred Brown, was brought under the banner. MacColl had recently written an article in which he had likened drawing to 'dancing upon paper', suggesting that 'the *verve* of the performance, not the closeness of the imitation' was the true mark of worth. There was indeed much more verve than closeness of imitation in Beardsley's art; MacColl recognized this and hailed Beardsley as a 'calligraphic acrobat'. He suggested that it was '*play*' to Beardsley to throw upon paper webs of spider lines – a 'gesture native and irresistible to him, as chasing its own tail is to a kitten'.

Beardsley's friendship with Pennell began to develop. Aubrey and Mabel began to attend the fashionably Bohemian gatherings which Pennell and his wife, Elizabeth, hosted on Thursday evenings in their rooms in Buckingham Street off the Strand. Another area of artistic London began to open up to him. Hind too was friendly, and the connection with the incipient *Studio* was progressing. There were discussions over which pictures should be selected for reproduction. The initial plan was to use four of the 'weird' drawings in the first number (scheduled for February 1893) and follow those with four or five more in the second.

The weirdness of Beardsley's style drew the attention of Lawrence & Bullen, the firm which was to publish *The Studio*. They thought it would be ideal for an illustrated edition of Lucian's fantastical *Comic Voyage* which they were bringing out as part of a series of 'exquisite' classical reprints. Beardsley accepted a commission from them to make thirty little drawings, 6 inches by 4: the fee was £100. For this new job, he struck a new style – a development of his japonesque manner. The bizarre story ('the original of *Gulliver*', he termed it) inspired his imagination. His illustrations, he considered, would be 'the most extraordinary things that have ever appeared in a book, [and] also the most indecent'.

He was now working simultaneously in at least four distinct styles: a mock medieval woodcut for the *Morte Darthur*, a calligraphic doodle for the *Bon-Mots* series, a severe, conventionally classical style for the title page of *Evelina*, and the developed hairline for Lucian. There were occasional borrowings of imagery – and even of technique – between the projects, but for the most part he kept them separate. Several sheets of paper survive with finished illustrations in one mode on the front and sketches in a different style on the back.[20]

Whatever the style, Beardsley's working method seems to have remained the same – and, indeed, endured through his entire career. Although W. B. Yeats claimed that Beardsley had told him, 'I make a blot on the paper, and I begin to shove the ink about and something comes,' in truth he seems almost never to have worked directly in ink. Rather, as Ross records and his extant pictures make clear, he sketched everything in pencil first. Even before setting pencil to paper, he would, according to Mabel, 'brood over an idea for days', evolving the composition in his mind's eye. This mental process having been completed, he would draw out a ruled border and then, within its frame, elaborate swirls and scrawls, constantly erasing details and blocking them in again 'until the whole surface became raddled from pencil, indiarubber and knife'.

Over this 'incoherent surface' he worked in black ink. He almost never had recourse to Chinese White, achieving his contrasts merely by leaving the white paper uncovered. Sometimes he would ignore the pencil lines he had set down for guidance, and would usually rub out extraneous marks after the ink work was completed. As a result, very few of Beardsley's pencil sketches survive: they were either converted into finished ink drawings: or, if they were abandoned, he would destroy them.[21]

Vallance always claimed that he had from the first noted the potential for 'evil' in Beardsley's work, and perhaps the first drawings for Lucian saw a threat of its being realized. He resolved to make a

second attempt to bring Beardsley under the healthful influence of
Morris, convinced that the careful workmanship and 'elaboration
of detail' in the *Morte* drawings had to find favour with the founder
of the Kelmscott Press. Beardsley welcomed the idea; he still wanted
Morris's approval. He assembled the best of his current *Morte* drawings – including 'The Lady of the Lake Telleth Arthur of the Sword
Excalibur' – and some early 'pulls' from the press. He could not,
however, be persuaded to accompany Vallance to Hammersmith.

Which was just as well. Morris was appalled by the pictures. He
considered them an 'act of usurpation': Beardsley had plagiarized
Burne-Jones's manner for the illustrations and his own for the
borders, and Dent was sedulously aping the outward form of the
Kelmscott style without regard for the principles of hand-
craftsmanship behind it. And they were perpetrating these crimes
upon the sacred text of Pre-Raphaelitism, Malory's *Morte D'Arthur*.
He swore a 'terrible oath' against Beardsley. 'A man', he fulminated,
'ought to do his own work.'

Beardsley was disappointed by this second rebuttal but had in the
space of seven months become less fragile. He soon transmuted the
blow into a mark of distinction, setting it down to Morris's jealousy.
'The truth is', he claimed, 'that, while *his* work is a mere imitation
of the old stuff, mine is fresh and original.' He took comfort in the
continued support and kindness of Burne-Jones, who indeed was
more supportive than even Beardsley knew; he had intervened to
dissuade Morris from writing an angry letter of complaint to Dent.
Beardsley, despite all his stylistic experiments, continued to believe
that he was following the 'best principles of the PRB'. At the end
of the year he called on Burne-Jones and presented him with a
magnificent drawing of 'Siegfried' which combined elements of his
diverse styles. Burne-Jones, to Beardsley's intense gratification, hung
it in his drawing-room.[22]

CHAPTER V

'Oof and Fame'

IN THE OPENING WEEKS of 1893, plans for the launch of *The Studio* were interrupted. Lewis Hind was offered the editorship of the *Pall Mall Budget*, a mass-circulation illustrated weekly recently acquired by Lord Astor. For Hind, a careerist, the lure of a 'nobler salary' (as he ignobly termed it) and the satisfaction of an established position were not to be gainsaid. Holme was understandably 'rather distressed' by this bombshell, but chose not to stand in Hind's way; as an earnest of his gratitude Hind offered to find his own replacement, and put forward the name of Gleeson White. ·

White was a good choice: a man in his early forties, he was art editor for George Bell & Sons; he contributed a regular column to the *Artist*, and even had some magazine experience, having worked in New York for a year as deputy editor of the *Art Amateur*. He jumped at the opportunity of working on *The Studio*, and Holme greeted him warmly.

Beardsley was unfazed by this development. He was confident of Holme's support and knew that his place in the contents list for the first issue was assured. Besides, he had met Gleeson White at Ross's dinner, and had liked him. White had admired his drawings, and

OPPOSITE Beardsley's satirical coin-design, showing Queen Victoria as a ballet dancer, 1893.

they had discovered a shared love of music. One of White's first editorial acts was to commission a cover design from his 'new illustrator', although he displayed his editorial independence by asking Beardsley to remove the piping faun he had introduced into his simple arcadian scene.

The other effect of Hind's move to the *Pall Mall Budget* was to open up an avenue for Beardsley in his wake. Arriving in his new job, Hind wanted to bring new men and distinctive talents with him, and he invited Aubrey to join his stable of illustrators – it was an impressive group. Beardsley found himself associated with some of the more radical spirits of contemporary art and illustration. His fellow pen draughtsmen on the *PMB* included the brightest young black-and-white illustrators – Leonard Ravenhill, Henry Sullivan and Phil May – and also London impressionists such as Walter Sickert and Philip Wilson Steer; Degas even contributed on occasion. Hind's adventurous policy was soon noted and praised: every drawing in the paper, it was remarked, was 'conceived in the spirit of a work of art, and not merely as an illustration for a periodical'.[1]

From late January Beardsley began a series of weekly assignments for the *PMB*, producing theatrical caricatures, comic takes on news items and celebrity portraits. The work provided a congenial change, taking him away from his room and the monotony of the Dent commissions; it required him to attend dress rehearsals, press viewings and first nights, and reminded him of the importance of close observation from life. The pay was good too: almost £10 each week. He wrote excitedly to Scotson-Clark in America, 'England . . . is the place for oof and fame.'* He became a regular at the paper's offices in the Charing Cross Road. One employee recalled his first appearance: 'Sauntering or lounging from one part of the room to another, he looked intently at various uninteresting objects, humming and hahing half inaudibly to himself in the manner of one accustomed to be looked on as a kind of curiosity, and somewhat sensitive on the subject.' The sensitivity would wear off quickly, but in January of 1893, though he felt fortune at his foot, Beardsley knew that he had

* Scotson-Clark had recently been appointed to an editorial position on *Art Amateur*, the New York magazine of which Gleeson White had been associate editor the previous year.

yet to make his mark with the public. An element of self-doubt persisted, which he tried to conceal behind a 'pose of affectation' and a manner which 'without seeming shy was by no means genial'.

With the delay of *The Studio*'s launch, Beardsley made his professional bow in the pages of the *Pall Mall Budget*. As ever when confronted by a new task, he strove to create a new style; indeed he was soon boasting that he had produced two: a 'wiry outline' for his caricatures and a freer wash-drawing technique for his portrait work. In truth, the challenge of reportage carried Beardsley back to the manner of his schoolboy sketches of masters, play productions and facetiae. Most of the drawings he produced for the *PMB*, though they look better on the printed page than reproduced separately, now appear feeble, conventional and uninteresting. It is only too easy to credit Beardsley's claim that he was able to knock them off on a Sunday evening.[2]

Some of the drawings do, however, have biographical interest. His first assignment was to make some spoof designs for the 'New Coinage'. Poynter and R. A. Brown had recently won an open competition to redesign the currency denominations; Beardsley went, with Hind, to the Royal Mint to inspect the plaster casts of the new dyes and then produced a series of 'designs not sent in for competition', imagining how various other artists might have interpreted the commission. The artists he chose to parody and the images he produced are an interesting barometer of his artistic attitudes and concerns at the start of 1893. He lampooned the work of Millais, Whistler, Burne-Jones and Walter Crane. In Beardsley's cartoons, Millais, one of the founding members of the Pre-Raphaelite Brotherhood, had transformed Britannia into a little girl sitting on a sandcastle; Burne-Jones had swathed her in improbable draperies and given her a bee-stung lip; the socialist Walter Crane abolished the head of the queen from the obverse and replaced it with an image of the worker and the legend 'Demos Rex'; while Whistler, such (Beardsley suggested) was the power of his personality and the strength of his conceit, had blithely replaced everything with his own butterfly signature.

With Beardsley, the line between homage and subversion was seldom clearly marked, and there was certainly an element of tribute

in these coins. He was fascinated by Whistler, he was 'the beloved
of Burne-Jones', he claimed still to cling to 'the best principles of
the PRB'. But there was a recognition of limitations and a desire to
escape them: to trump Whistler's egotism, to avoid the Pre-
Raphaelite obsession with drapery and tendency to sentimentality,
to break the strand of pious socialism that ran from Ruskin to Morris
to Crane. His designs were a tentative act of self-assertion.*

Despite its conventional style, he was pleased with his *Pall Mall
Budget* handiwork. Hind too seems to have been enthusiastic, commissioning Beardsley to do the cover-design (a picture of Henry
Irving as Becket) for the 9 February issue. The paper's news editor,
however, was less enamoured, and Mr Astor had to 'struggle . . .
to admire them'. Generally it is difficult to understand Beardsley's
enthusiastic report to Scotson-Clark that his *PMB* work was creating
'some astonishment' and had made the old 'black-and-white duffers
sit up'. Pennell, indeed, thought Beardsley's journalistic efforts not
worthy to be signed; Gleeson White's more temperate recollection
was that they did not arouse much curiosity.

The one exception was his picture of Emile Zola, also in the 9
February issue. It belonged stylistically to his series of japonesque
portraits, and was unlike anything else in the magazine. It made
people sit up, not only in England but in Paris, and was selected at
once for the *Pall Mall Gazette*'s round-up of 'Pictures of 1893'.
Beardsley was slow to grasp the reason for this success, but a dawning
awareness of it prompted him to try to introduce his personal
japonesque style into the pages of the *PMB* a second time.[3]

At the end of February John Lane and Elkin Mathews brought out
Oscar Wilde's symbolist drama, *Salome*. The play, written in French,
had become a *cause célèbre* the previous year, when the Lord Chamberlain had refused a licence for Sarah Bernhardt's proposed production
on the grounds that representation of biblical characters was forbidden
on the stage. Wilde had threatened to renounce his British citizenship
in protest at this crass censorship, but thought better of it. Instead

* The pictures did not it seems cause offence. Shortly after their publication Walter
Crane met Beardsley at one of Mrs Gleeson White's 'At homes', and – as White
informed Scotson-Clark – 'took to him greatly'.

he devoted himself to finding a publisher. The French firm of Paul Schmidt agreed to bring out an edition, and John Lane cannily offered to take up 350 copies for the English market if his firm's name appeared alongside Schmidt's on the title page. Its publication under Lane's provocative banner, 'The Play the Lord Chamberlain tried to ban', stirred up a fresh wave of publicity on which the *PMB*, and every other newspaper, was eager to surf.

Hind telegraphed Wilde suggesting he (Wilde) might like to write a review of his own play. Wilde demurred: 'I could not criticize perfection,' he replied, 'you must *hire* somebody to do that.' Hind also asked Beardsley to draw a picture based on the play itself or on Wilde. Compared to sketching unfunny cartoons of modern pilgrims and classical golfers, this was a task to exercise Beardsley's powers. He went straight to the climax of the play, and produced a picture of Salome, thick-lipped and sulphurous-eyed, kissing the mouth of John the Baptist's severed head. He employed his most japonesque conventions; the composition was daringly asymmetric and abstract, the action confined to the top half of the panel; the background was made up of overlapping circles; the borders bristled with 'hairs', a tracery of arabesques and peacock plumes swirled over the scene. The subject-matter was vividly repellent: Salome's features were harsh and lustful, and a flow of blood fell from the Baptist's truncated neck into the lily pond at the foot of the picture.*

It was much too much for Hind. When he saw the drawing he 'nearly had a fit', and told Beardsley that the magazine 'would lose its circulation if the picture was published'. The attempt to cause a sensation had been only too successful. Nor was it the first time the young illustrator had alarmed his editor. Among the spoof drawings for the new coinage, Beardsley had made several that had to be suppressed. One of these was a picture – after Degas – of Queen Victoria in the costume of a ballerina. The image of the monarch *en tutu* was considered too shocking for publication, but that Beardsley had chosen to ally himself to Degas, even in jest, was both timely

---

* The radical nature of Beardsley's composition is revealed by the difficulty many had in reading it. At least one contemporary commentator supposed that Salome (at the top of the composition) was leaping in the air in 'a paroxysm of ecstasy'. (*Saturday Review*, 24 March, 1894, p. 317.)

and telling.[4] Degas, the friend of Whistler, the admired of Sickert, was recognized as the most advanced member of the impressionist school. His position, in England at least, was dramatically confirmed in the early months of 1893.

Towards the end of February the newly furbished Grafton Gallery in Mayfair opened its doors with a daring exhibition of contemporary European and American painting. Among the works on view was a Degas, borrowed from a private collector, showing two people sitting at a café table. The picture had already been exhibited in France under the title 'Au café', but at the Grafton it was re-christened 'L'Absinthe', in token of the small glass of dark liquid on the marble-topped table. The new title was calculated to shock: absinthe was the very symbol of irresponsible bohemian life, a drink which, due to its flavouring with wormwood quite as much as its high alcohol content, acted powerfully upon the nerve centres of the brain to produce present oblivion and – it was said – future madness.

The picture became a lightning rod for artistic debate, reawakening with new force the simmering argument over the significance of subject matter in art. The exponents of the 'New Criticism' led by D. S. MacColl expatiated on the painting's merits. In his *Spectator* review, MacColl hailed it as a masterpiece. He boldly admitted that some might consider the subject ('two rather sodden people drinking in a café') 'repulsive'. But declared that Degas's complete understanding of the people, his avoidance of all 'blundering sentiment', his mastery of 'character, of form, of colour' had revealed the 'mysterious affecting note' of the scene and captured its essential beauty. This was anathema to the ultra-conservative critic from the *Westminster Gazette*; under his pseudonym, 'Philistine', he railed against MacColl's claims. He refused to look beyond the picture's subject matter, and expressed his horror that 'what the world has hitherto called repulsive' should now be set up as a new standard of beauty. He was, moreover, quite unimpressed by MacColl's claims for Degas's handling of this hideous subject. Impressionism in general he saw as no more than sloppy painting which failed to capture recognizable reality; 'circles and dots and noughts and crosses' would be just as convincing as impressionist 'cows and trees, and rivers and fields'.

Others hastened to join the fray. Harry Quilter, MacColl's predecessor at the *Spectator*, rallied to Philistine's banner and many followed. The picture was pronounced 'vulgar, boozy, sottish, loathsome, revolting, ugly, besotted, degraded, [and] repulsive'. Even some of those who sought to defend it did so on the score of conventional morality. The Royal Academician, W. B. Richmond, insisted that the painting was 'not a picture at all' but 'a treatise against drink'. This was the view that George Moore, for all his self-proclaimed avant-gardeism, inadvertently put forward as well. In vain the picture's owner tried to explain that the painting had been misnamed: the drink on the table was not absinthe but 'black coffee in a tumbler'.

The Degas controversy flared brightly throughout March. Although there was no conclusion or consensus, it gave Beardsley a clear idea of the furore that a picture could stir up in the philistine press. He noted the popular alarm at art that adopted conventionally 'repulsive' subjects, and the popular belief in the moral duties of painting. In the wake of the row he dashed off his own small homage to Degas's picture: a *Bon-Mots* grotesque of two figures at a café table; it was the first of several drawings that took up this supposedly 'vulgar, boozy, sottish' theme.[5]

For his 'repulsive' Salome drawing too Beardsley perhaps gained courage from Degas's example, and Hind perhaps was discouraged from publishing it in the charged atmosphere of artistic intolerance; others were bolder. *The Studio* was aiming at a different market and Gleeson White agreed to include Salome among the Beardsley illustrations in the first number – even then being prepared. For the *PMB* Beardsley was obliged to return to his conventional caricatures. Nevertheless, the Salome incident was not without immediate benefit: it provided Beardsley with a pretext for meeting Oscar Wilde. It was almost certainly Ross who effected the introduction. The playwright was in the midst of preparations for the opening of *A Woman of No Importance*, but he was delighted to learn of the tribute paid to his work. Both the picture and its creator impressed him, for he presented Beardsley with a copy of the French edition of *Salome* inscribed,

March '93, for Aubrey: for the only artist who, besides myself, knows what the dance of the seven veils is, and can see that invisible dance. Oscar.

The gift marked the beginning of a friendship. Wilde loved the company of youth (he was then in his late thirties) and Beardsley was fascinated to find himself close to the author of *Intentions* and *The Picture of Dorian Gray*. He began to study at Wilde's school of wit and learnt better how to adopt the dandy's mask. Wilde was not the only person impressed by the weird image of Salome; it seems to have awakened T. Dove Keighley, editor of the *Budget*'s sister publication, the *Pall Mall Magazine*, to Beardsley's potential as an illustrator of fiction. Beardsley left another of his japonesque drawings, 'La Femme Incomprise', at Keighley's office for consideration. Having heard nothing, however, by the end of March, he went to retrieve it, explaining with calculated nonchalance that he was submitting the picture for the New English Art Club spring show.

Fred Brown's offer had been genuine, and the retrieved picture was one of two accepted by the committee; the other was the Salome drawing. Beardsley found himself welcomed into the bosom of the club. MacColl invited him to dinner and introduced him to some fellow exhibitors, including a young painter, Alfred Thornton. The NEAC show opened at the Dudley Gallery in the second week of April. Beardsley's drawings were shown alongside works by Monet, Degas and Sargent, as well as those by his near-contemporaries – Charles Furse, Walter Sickert and Philip Wilson Steer. Even in this company he made an impression. Though not mentioned in every review, he drew considerable notice, and indeed praise. The *Magazine of Art* thought 'Mr Aubrey Beardsley's weird drawings . . . possessed a morbid attractiveness.' The *Artist* found his work 'delicately drawn' and quaint. MacColl, writing in the *Spectator*, closed his review with a mention of the 'one or two examples of the freakish talent of Mr Beardsley who has fancy and designing power, and technical resources in fine line and rich blacks'.[6]

The month brought other excitements: the prospectus for the *Morte Darthur* was issued – a folded leaf of paper with a Beardsley border design, chapter heading and initial letter and the intricate headpiece which had so impressed Pennell. It gave the public a first glimpse of Beardsley's prowess in this line and invited them to put themselves down for more.

Almost simultaneously the first number of *The Studio* was issued, with Beardsley's cover, his pictures (eight of them), and Pennell's article on 'A New Illustrator'. The article was short and, though the author later claimed that it was 'intensely hedging', Beardsley had reason to be delighted with it. Pennell's reservations were few and his praise was fulsome; he considered that Beardsley's drawings combined 'perfect execution' with 'remarkable . . . invention'. The young artist had founded his several styles upon 'every age and all schools': the fifteenth-century masters, the Japanese, the Pre-Raphaelites, without succumbing to the limitations of any. He admitted that the Burne-Jones influence in some of the *Morte Darthur* illustrations was perhaps over-insistent, but considered it was Beardsley's particular choice for a particular project, and pointed out that in his portraits and japonesques, not to mention his 'impressionist landscapes', there was no trace of Pre-Raphaelitism.

As might be expected, he reserved special praise for Beardsley's willingness to 'avail himself of mechanical reproduction for the publication of his drawings', thus allowing his actual handiwork to be seen, rather than 'the interpretation of it by somebody else'. He described the picture 'Merlin taketh the child Arthur', reproduced in the article, as 'one of the most marvellous pieces of mechanical engraving, if not the most marvellous, that I have ever seen'. When moved to define the particular quality of Beardsley's drawing, Pennell focused on his sinuous use of the 'single line' and 'interesting disposition of blocks of black'. He concluded with the lofty Whistlerian assertion that Beardsley had 'managed to appeal to artists (and what more could he want)'.

The first number of *The Studio* was not entirely taken up with Beardsley, however; there were articles by or on Sir Frederick Leighton, Frank Brangwyn, Lazenby Liberty, R. A. M. Stevenson, C. W. Furse, the Newlyn School of Painting and bookplate design. Nevertheless, Beardsley was prominent even among these contending distractions. With five full-page illustrations to his credit, he was better represented than the president of the Royal Academy.

A favourable article in the inaugural number of a special-interest art magazine is not a passport to instant and popular fame. The magazine received very limited notice in the press. The *Pall Mall Gazette* gave it a perfunctory puff; the *Artist* and *Academy* reviewed it kindly but did not mention Beardsley's contribution; *London Figaro* took note of the 'New Illustrator' but considered his pictures 'flat blasphemies against art . . . impotent imitations of Burne-Jones at his very worst, with pseudo-Japanese effects'. For the most part, however, the arrival of *The Studio* passed unheralded. It served only to raise Beardsley's reputation another notch, and disseminate examples of his work to a cultured public beyond the immediate circle of his friends and connections. The magazine, which had a limited international distribution, also allowed his name to be carried abroad – to America, to France, to Italy and to Germany.[7]

He was hankering to be abroad again himself. With the approach of spring he was planning to make a second trip to Paris, to visit the Salons. He conceived the scheme initially with his new friend Oscar Wilde; they planned to travel together. It was an intoxicating vision, the 'new illustrator' and the great aesthete arm in arm on the boulevards. Beardsley, tipsy with pleasure, hastened to inform King of the plan, but Wilde's commitments to the ever-demanding Alfred Douglas prevented his going.

Wilde, though married with two small children, had since the late 1880s been a practising homosexual. It is generally supposed that he was seduced into this new phase of experience by Robbie Ross. Certainly, since 1886 Wilde had pursued his clandestine and illicit passion with insouciant eagerness. One of his earliest infatuations had been for the young poet John Gray whose good looks and surname provided some of the inspiration for the hero of Wilde's only novel. In 1891, however, Wilde had been introduced to the beautiful Oxford undergraduate, Lord Alfred Douglas. Douglas adored Wilde's writings, while Wilde admired Douglas *tout court*. He had everything: looks, youth, a title and a reckless disregard for the feelings of others. Wilde seduced his young admirer.

By 1893, however, their relationship had changed in nature if not in intensity: it had become a joint exploration of the seamy world of London 'renters'. Emotionally Douglas (or Bosie as he liked to be called) had come to tyrannize over Wilde. Pettish and demanding, he would scarcely have approved a trip to Paris that did not include him. Wilde duly spent May in Oxford, while Beardsley decided to travel with Mabel and the Pennells.

Any disappointment he might have felt was sweetened by the prospect of collaborating with Wilde on his return from France. Wilde's advocacy, the coverage in *The Studio* and the success of the NEAC show had combined to convince John Lane that he should commission from Beardsley a series of ten full-page illustrations for the English-language version of *Salome*. No task could have been more exciting or so pregnant with possibility, and he accepted at once. He had learnt much from Wilde already: although Lane offered fifty pounds, Beardsley insisted on being paid in guineas, as the mark of a gentleman. Douglas was to provide the translation. Beardsley left for Paris before the details of the contract were complete, but the prospect of the work was an exciting thought to take with him.[8]

There was a scramble to clear away outstanding chores right up to the eve of his departure: his *Morte Darthur* contract with Dent required the delivery on 15 April of artwork for Chapters IV and V, which were to make up the second serial part of the publication. Meanwhile Keighley at the *Pall Mall Magazine*, perhaps prompted by the appearance of the *Studio* article and the success of Beardsley's drawings at the NEAC show, asked for an illustration to a macabre short story. Beardsley received his copy of the tale, 'The Kiss of Judas', in Brighton, where he was visiting his old school. King may have left, but Beardsley was fond of his *alma mater* and on close terms with Mr Payne and Mr Marshall, and he wanted their approval for his success. Although time was indeed short, there was an element of self-dramatization in his decision to do this drawing in France. It would give him a professional profile on the expedition; after all, the Pennells were taking work with them: Joseph was preparing a series of etchings of the gargoyles of Nôtre Dame, and Elizabeth was reviewing the Salons for the *Fortnightly Review*.

The quartet crossed the Channel at the beginning of May. In Paris they checked into the curiously named Hôtel de Portugal et l'Univers, a familiar haunt of the Pennells, close to the Louvre, in the rue Croix des Petits Champs. Beardsley, fastidious and retiring, was alarmed to find himself embraced and 'properly kissed' by the concierge, who appropriated all guests as part of her extended family. Paris was thick with anglophone artists and writers, all there to 'do' the Salons. Mac-Coll was covering them for the *Spectator* and *Revue Belge*; Charles Whibley, R. A. M. Stevenson, C. W. Furse, Robbie Ross, and the Glasgow painter James Guthrie were among the throng. Also in evidence were an engaging young American couple, Henry and Aline Harland.

Henry Harland was a writer with a flair for fancy and invention. Although only thirty-two, he had already invented himself several times over. He liked to claim that he had been born in St Petersburg, brought up in Rome and educated at the University of Paris. He hinted that he might be a bastard son of the Emperor Franz-Josef, and that he had studied briefly for the priesthood. He rarely admitted that he had in fact been born in New York, and that his first literary success had been a series of novels about metropolitan Jewish life written under the name Sidney Luska. In 1891 he had come with his young wife to Europe. Although they loved Paris, they had settled in London and Harland had begun to publish short stories in the English reviews. A first collection, *Mademoiselle Miss*, was brought out by Heinemann, and others followed. His natural gaiety and irrepressible sense of fun won him many friends; his semi-invalid condition – for he, like Beardsley, was a consumptive – brought him sympathetic solicitude. It is often stated that Beardsley met Harland by chance in the waiting-room of Dr Symes Thompson's surgery – a romantic myth both parties were prepared to endorse, but it now seems certain that it was Joseph Pennell who first brought them together, in the spring of 1893.[9]

There was a carnival atmosphere at the opening of the New Salon on the Champ de Mars. Whistler and Puvis were there; the crowd climbed on to chairs to see Zola and Carolus Duran pass by; eyes everywhere were seeking celebrity and distinction. A few people even looked at the pictures. Beardsley made a studied entrance on to this crowded scene. He had converted some of his earnings into a new outfit. While others veered between the poles of conventional decorum and hob-nailed bohemianism, Beardsley wore a carefully orchestrated symphony of muted shades: grey suit, grey gloves, and a golden tie; a light cane swung from his hand, a straw boater on his head. With his 'tripping step', strange physique and distinctive haircut he attracted a share of attention.

The pictures could be taken in at a glance. *Impressionisme, Pointillisme, Symbolisme*: all the schools of the moment were there, defined and recognizable. To the experienced Salonistes they were already 'old hat'. Burne-Jones had sent his 'Mermaid'; Carlos Schwarbe, an extreme Swiss *symboliste*, had contributed a bizarre image of death. MacColl enthused greatly over a series of small, dreamlike landscapes by Charles Conder, a young Australian working in Paris and exhibiting for the first time. There was much that was bad, and some that was very bad.

Away from the Salons Beardsley indulged himself with the illusion of work and the reality of leisure. He quickly completed his illustration for 'The Kiss of Judas', a wonderful drawing of sinister power and simplicity, and dispatched it to London. Ignoring the imprecations of his creaking lungs, he ascended more than once to the roof of Nôtre Dame to distract Pennell from his sketching, and on one of these visits made a drawing depicting Pennell as the 'Stryge', the most monstrous of the church's 'devils'.*

He also made the steep ascent of the narrow stairway to William Rothenstein's attic studio in Montmartre. Rothenstein was a diminutive dynamo in round glasses, and an exact contemporary of Beardsley. The son of a Bradford linen merchant, he had been studying painting in Paris for three years. With his bustling energy and unconquerable self-assurance, he had established himself at the centre of the Paris art student world. He was an intimate of Conder and Phil May. He had forged friendships with Toulouse-Lautrec and Verlaine. Whistler was fond of him and had nicknamed him 'Parson'. Two of his impressionistic pictures were appearing next to Beardsley's pair at the NEAC exhibition.

Beardsley, portfolio under his arm, exerted himself to win the friendship (and admiration) of this cosmopolitan figure. At first Rothenstein was sceptical. His informed eye was unimpressed by Beards-

* He also paid homage to the 'Stryge' in the strange single-horned creature with its head in its hands which appeared in the *Bon-Mots of Foot and Hook* (page 23); another of the Nôtre Dame 'devils' has a single horn.

ley's 'too smart clothes with thin hard-padded shoulders'; his Parisian sensibility was disturbed by Beardsley's 'staccato voice and jumpy restless manners'. He was even doubtful about his visitor's art, finding 'something hard and insensitive in his line, and something small and narrow in his design'. Nevertheless, it was an indication of Beardsley's new-found assurance and long-established courtesy that he soon overcame these reservations. He fell back on the infallible expedient of flattery. Rothenstein recorded with complacency: 'He seemed interested in my paintings'. The beginnings of a friendship had been kindled.[10]

Paris in the spring was the perfect stage for pleasure. And Beardsley, 'full of the pleasure of success and prospects for the future', was perfectly poised to enjoy it. He drank in the formal beauty of the Luxembourg Gardens and the informal jollity of the Latin Quarter. The whole London contingent, let loose in a foreign capital, felt an intoxicating liberation and sense of irresponsibility. There were japes and jests and pranks, and Beardsley, relishing being part of a group, joined in. He was part of the riotous lunch party which began at a table set up in the street outside the Palais Royal but ended, after complaints by the cabmen and the intervention of the police, in a nearby restaurant. He was involved in a dramatic accident one evening, when, coming back from a night in the bars of Montmartre, so many of the party crowded into a cab that the bottom fell out while it was in mid-career down the hill. Some tumbled into the road, others clung to the sides of the cab; drink and providence preserved them all from injury. The presence of Mabel, of Aline Harland and several other women gave the atmosphere a sexual tension, and there were, perhaps, moments of indiscretion. Joseph Pennell later recalled how 'extraordinary things happened' during that Maytime. 'Some', he added, 'can't even be told now.'

There was an excursion to Versailles. There, near the little lake opposite the Trianon, Aubrey, Mabel and the others succumbed to the seasonal languor. They lay on the grass under the flowering chestnut trees and, in Pennell's quaint phrase, 'invited their souls'.

OPPOSITE Sketch of Joseph Pennell as 'The Devil of Notre Dame', 1893.

When a troop of American tourists on a guided tour hove into view and threatened to disturb the peace, Charles Furse sprang up and announced that he was going swimming in the lake. Several of the women voiced their intention of joining him, and everyone began taking off their clothes. The tourist troop froze in amazement; although some of them produced their Kodaks, they were swiftly ushered away by the scandalized guide. Returning home at the end of the day the revellers made so much noise singing songs on the platform at Versailles station that they were shut in the waiting-room by the unamused stationmaster. The train, when it came, was 'a funny, double-deck', with seats on the roof. They sat on the upper deck and arrived back at the Gare Saint Lazare 'as black as real nigger minstrels'.

On another day they made a boat trip to St Cloud. Straw hats blew off in the wind, and several of the party tied handkerchiefs around their heads. In this improbable guise they joined a local wedding party, and then, wandering in the park of the demolished château, clambered on to the empty pedestals and posed as gods and goddesses. MacColl, who was working on the introduction to a book of Greek vase paintings, talked of classical art and mythology. Indeed, with all of the group sharing a common interest in art there was, over the course of the holiday, much debate upon the subject. Some of the themes aired and positions taken up can be gleaned from the review Elizabeth Pennell contributed to the *Fortnightly*. Although she feared it had been a poor year for painting and sculpture, she found words of praise for a few individual canvases, Conder among them. Her overview ended, however, with the assertion that 'it is really in the black and white work that the greatest activity and genuine originality is displayed'. The continuing development of photography, she noted, was pushing young draughtsmen 'to achieve results in which they can never be rivalled by the camera'. These were ideas to fire Beardsley's imagination and concentrate his vision. If the 'vitality of modern art [was] passing' into black-and-white work, as Mrs Pennell suggested, perhaps he need not look beyond it.

On their last evening, after the excursion to St Cloud, they had dinner by the river at a little restaurant where a parrot endlessly repeated the phrases, 'Après vous, Madame. Après vous, Monsieur'.

MacColl had with him 'the cast of a lovely drowned girl's head' which he had bought at the Paris morgue. He hung it from a tree near the dinner table and, in some bizarre ritual, Aubrey and Mabel 'worshipped' it.[11]

Aubrey had evidently become a personality in the party, but his growing confidence brought problems. His affectations and his deliberately extreme views on art did not please everyone. Some derogatory remarks he made about '*les vieux* and the stultifying observance of worn-out laws and principles' drew him into a 'violent discourse' with Stevenson and Guthrie. Stevenson (who had contributed an article to the first *Studio* decrying some of the trends in 'Recent Art') adopted a patronizing air, ponderously enumerating the virtues of convention, and frequently using the phrase 'at my age' to set a distance between himself and 'young' Aubrey. Beardsley was irritated but unchastened.

Far more distressing was his first encounter with Whistler. One evening he and Pennell went to a performance of *Tristan and Isolde* at the Paris Opera. Coming away from the theatre, they saw Whistler sitting on the terrace of the Grand Café with a friend. Pennell greeted him and introduced Beardsley, but Whistler was not to be drawn. He 'noticed' Beardsley, but that was all. All, anyway, that he was prepared to acknowledge openly. Usually so generous to the young, he could perhaps scent the danger of rivalry behind Beardsley's eager admiration. He seems to have taken the trouble to learn something of Beardsley's drawing, probably from the first number of *The Studio*. The next morning, when Whistler saw Pennell, he asked in a combative tone, 'What do you make of that young thing?', before promptly giving his own verdict: 'He has hairs on his head, hairs on his hands, in his ears, all over.' This mischievous charge, which does not seem to have had any basis in physical fact, may have derived from Beardsley's quirk, in his japonesque drawings, of adding a hairy fringe to many of the principal lines.

Pennell pleaded his young friend's cause, and asked to be allowed to bring Beardsley to a small reception Whistler and his wife were holding at their house on the rue du Bac that Sunday afternoon. Whistler, after much grumbling, consented ungraciously. Aubrey's second attempt to woo Whistler's favour was as unsuccessful as the first; the painter ignored his would-be disciple, but Beardsley took some consolation from the occasion. Among the guests was his admirer, Puvis de Chavannes. The president of the Academy greeted him cordially and urged him to call at his studio. Also at the party was Stéphane Mallarmé, the guiding light of symbolism, of whom Beardsley was already an admirer; indeed he had decorated his copy of *L'après-midi d'un faune* with five small drawings.

The prospect of being able to engage with Whistler at close quarters seemed to present itself when a wealthy English guest invited Beardsley and Pennell to dinner at the Café des Ambassadeurs on the Champs-Elysées, and asked Whistler to come too. The painter, having accepted, failed to turn up. For Beardsley, this was the final insult; that evening he produced a biting caricature of Whistler and presented it to Pennell.

Although Pennell's account of Beardsley's first unhappy meetings with Whistler is vivid and persuasive, it should be treated with some circumspection. Pennell, as Whistler's friend and biographer, relished his position at the master's side, and was anxious to present himself as the sole arbiter between Whistler and the world, or – in this case – Beardsley. There were, however, others in Paris that May who might have brought the two men together. One visitor to the Salons recalled a dinner party in Whistler's studio at which Beardsley was present: 'He spoke little but spent most of his time drawing quaint designs on the glass shades of the small lights that stood on [the] table.' The image, for all its piquancy, does little to alter Pennell's picture; it suggests that Beardsley had access to Whistler's circle but found scant welcome there.[12]

Even Whistler's rebuffs could not destroy the magic of the month and Beardsley returned to London elated. June saw the publication of the first serialized part of the *Morte Darthur* and also of the *Bon-Mots of Sydney Smith and Richard Brinsley Sheridan*, Beardsley's first appearance between hard covers. The subscription format of *Morte Darthur* and the trivial nature of the *Bon-Mots* volume limited their review coverage, but *The Studio* offered its support, announcing that Beardsley's work was the 'chief attraction' of the *Morte* and that 'the promise it gives of Mr Beardsley's future as a decorative artist is well sustained in this first portion'. There was no suggestion that the pictures marked a rift with the text.

A similar willingness to assume a connection between drawings and written word informed *The Studio*'s comments on the *Bon-Mots*. Beardsley's 'clever grotesques' were praised as 'an attempt to symbol- ise the jokes rather than a pictorial illustration'. The reviewer's only regret was that excessive reduction lessened the power of some of the drawings. This concerned Beardsley too, not only with the *Bon-Mots* pictures but with those for *Morte Darthur*. According to Vallance, he was disappointed with the printing and at finding 'how much of the beauty of drawing on which he had bestowed infinite pains was lost in excessive reduction'. Seeing his elaborately worked tondo of Merlin reduced almost to the size of a coin marked perhaps the beginning of his disillusionment with the project.*

The work still had to be got through, but the monthly deadlines became appointments with dread; the drawings left to the last moment and done in haste. Beardsley's temperament, Vallance regis- tered, was not suited to sustained effort: 'His mood and interests, instead of marching and developing with the leisurely passage of years, changed and leaped from one phase to another, weekly or even daily, in rapid transition.' During the summer of 1893 his mood and interests were in particularly sprightly form. He abandoned his weekly commitment to the *PMB*, and threw himself with enthusiasm into the *Salome* commission. As ever, the new project called forth a new style. To capture the play's dreamlike eroticism, he developed what he called a 'mystico-oriental' manner. The Japanese element he had been toying with remained dominant, and the familiar tropes – Burne-Jones roses, Whistler peacocks, Renaissance figures – still found a place, but they were employed with new and increasing economy. Beardsley placed his figures on stark white backgrounds and, dispensing almost entirely with the fringed border effect, used only a few simple lines to describe forms and evoke the fall of drapery.

Although the beginnings of this style were discernible in the two

* A facetious note had already intruded into his *Morte Darthur* work. The detailed drawing 'How Arthur Saw the Questing Beast' (dated 8 March 1893) included a phallus, concealed amongst the tracery of lines swirling across the foreground. Dent did not notice it.

illustrations for *Pall Mall Magazine*, Ross had no hesitation in ascribing the new austerity to his study of Greek vase painting. Inspired by MacColl's talk over the Paris café tables, Beardsley had made a close inspection of the Greek vases in the British Museum. The 'mystic' element, however, seems to have been derived from Carlos Schwarbe and the other young continental symbolists. As a further refinement, he adopted Wilde's idea that Salome should have a different face in each picture. He was delighted with this new phase of his art. Almost weekly he took his latest efforts to Lane's and Mathews' book-crammed shop in Vigo Street for inspection and admiration. The work, he told Ross, was proceeding famously.[13]

The other abiding excitement of the early summer was the family's move to a new home. Aubrey's earnings (even with the staggered payment schemes favoured by his publishers, he had earned almost £300 in ten months), together with the monies received and due from Sarah Pitt's will, made it possible for the family to take, for the first time, a lease on a house. They did not look far, moving around the corner to 114 Cambridge Street. By Pimlico standards, No. 114 was an attractive house. Although of the usual four-storey stucco-fronted style, it faced the west end of St Gabriel's church, and offered a glimpse through to the trees in Warwick Square. The lease was taken in Mabel's name as she was over twenty-one and, unlike her parents, unencumbered with debts, but its decoration was left to Aubrey.

He engaged Aymer Vallance to help him with the scheme. The previous year Vallance had completed a series of articles on 'The Furnishing and Decoration of the Home', but the quiet Morris-type good taste he had advocated there seems to have been subverted by Aubrey. The two connecting rooms on the first floor were turned into a gracious drawing-room-cum-studio. The walls (where they were not lined with book-cases) were painted orange. The wood-work, floors and furniture were painted black. The curtains were dark and heavy, and 'designed in France'. Additional colour was provided by blue-and-white-striped upholstery and a scattering of green rugs on the floor.

The furniture was simple. Aubrey always favoured a tall wicker armchair with padded wings at the top, and his desk was a simple

Regency table, painted black. The effect of the room was variously described as 'sombre', 'dark' and 'severe, almost frigid'. There was some art: a 'white plaster cast of the "smiling girl"', a few framed prints and several of Aubrey's drawings, mainly in reproduction. Two were originals. In an act of deliberate self-mythologizing, he displayed the drawing of a carnival which he had done when he was eight and given to his grandfather, and the portrait of 'Raphael' that marked the beginning of his first individual style. There is even a suggestion that he re-drew the picture to accentuate its novelty.

Although the drawing-room was the focus of Beardsley and Vallance's energies, there is mention of a little 'study' hung with a pale, vertically striped tapestry, which suggests that care was taken throughout the house.

Beardsley did little that was unconsidered, and it is tempting to read his orange colour scheme for the Cambridge Street drawing-room as a homage to the famous orange chamber created by Des Esseintes, the decadent anti-hero of Joris-Karl Huysmans' novel À Rebours. Orange, Huysmans observed, was the very hue of decadence: 'As for those gaunt, febrile creatures of feeble constitution and nervous disposition whose sensual appetite craves dishes that are smoked and seasoned, their eyes almost always prefer that most morbid and irritating of colours, with its acid glow and unnatural splendour – orange.'

Beardsley certainly seems to have been adopting a decadent pose. Already something of a dandy, he extended his calculated anti-naturalism to the affectation that he could work only by candlelight. At least one early caller at Cambridge Street did find him at work with the curtains drawn while the sun blazed outside; she recorded with some amusement that although Aubrey refused to join his mother and herself for tea on the little first-floor balcony, after Ellen had taken a cup in to him at his desk, he soon 'strolled out into the air and sat on the balustrade'. It was obvious to the visitor that 'he was dying to get out of that stuffy room all the time'.[14]

For most of the period of the move and the refurbishment Aubrey was alone in town with his father. He would have liked to have got away. MacColl, Thornton, the Harlands and others had taken a small cottage on the Normandy coast at Ste Marguerite-sur-Mer, and had invited Aubrey and Mabel to join them. But his work commitments

– to *Salome*, *Morte Darthur* and the last of the *Bon-Mots* collections – made it impossible for him; Mabel, however, was keen to go, and it was arranged that Ellen should accompany her as chaperone. Their sojourn at the GROB MacThorlander, as the Normandy cottage was jestingly christened after its various residents, gave Aubrey a vicarious presence among the company. He learnt from his mother and sister not only of the games and diversions which filled the days – the picnics, the charades and sketching parties – but of the artistic theories, plots and plans discussed over vermouth in the trellised arcade of the nearby Hôtel des Sapins.

Conder was staying at the hotel and joined in the debates. The most stimulating discussion was provoked after Conder had made a drawing to illustrate a piece Harland was writing for an English paper. He lamented that artists, when dealing with the commercial press, had to rely on the prior existence of a written story. This injustice had struck other artists, and it even appeared unfair to a writer such as Harland. MacColl took up the idea and suggested that there might be scope for a magazine which printed pictures independently of text, and text independently of pictures.

In London Beardsley was exercised by similar concerns. In his illustrations he had always striven to elude the obvious connection between word and picture, and had toyed with other means of arresting the viewer's attention. That summer he was being courted by a new magazine, *St Paul's*. The editor wanted to commission a series of biblical illustrations in his latest mystico-oriental style, and Aubrey began planning how he might introduce subversive portraits of contemporary figures into the sacred scenes. Such tricks were diverting, but he was also working towards a virtual independence between drawing and text. While Harland and MacColl were theorizing, he was making plans for a book of pictures without words, or with only a vague accompaniment of 'incidental verse'. He had been gestating this project, which was to be called 'Masques', for some time, perhaps ever since seeing *L'Enfant Prodigue*. It was to have 'a prologue to be spoken by Pierrot (myself)'. He thought he had persuaded the comic paper, *Pick-me-up* (produced by the man who was launching *St Paul's*) to serialize it, and then issue it in book form later. He hoped Ross would provide the incidental verse. Time, however, and the pressure of other work prevented Beardsley making a start. Even in London in the summer there were distractions.[15]

William Rothenstein came over from Paris. He had secured a contract from John Lane to produce a series of twenty lithographic portraits of Oxford celebrities; and although he based himself up at the University, he spent much time in London. Beardsley invited him to make use of the new studio-cum-drawing-room at Cambridge Street whenever he was in town, and their friendship grew.

They would sit on either side of the black-painted table, as at a Victorian partners' desk. Such were Beardsley's powers of concentration that he was able to keep up a stream of talk while he was drawing. They talked about art, Beardsley benefiting from Rothenstein's first-hand knowledge of, and pronounced views on, the Parisian scene. They began an unfinished collaboration on a 'dialogue'. The scrap that survives reveals how Beardsley was refining his wit and, in the face of Rothenstein's defence, his animosity towards Whistler. In the fragment, written in Beardsley's hand, M seems to stand for Me, and R for Rothenstein:

R: But what is the master doing just now?
M: Oh painting a fool's length, I suppose. I hear he is taking great pains over the face so that the portrait may be distinguished.
R: What, don't you admire Jimmy? *Entre nous*, he has influenced me considerably.
M: Oh you suffer, I know, from severe attacks of Whistlerian tremens.

Rothenstein achieved his revenge when they were discussing Burne-Jones. The influence of the great Pre-Raphaelite was waning, and Beardsley, seeking to deny his former master, suggested that as an artist he was 'too remote from life' though as a designer he remained 'inimitable'. Rothenstein hastened to correct him: 'Imitable, Aubrey,' he pressed, 'imitable, surely'. The quip delighted Beardsley and he was soon using it on his own account.

These exchanges give some flavour to the fellowship of wit and ambition which Beardsley gravitated towards. It was a charmed circle, offering the comfort of support and the edge of competition; within it the power of authority was recognized but gleefully subverted, though the subversion often borrowed its style from the magisterial examples of Whistler and Wilde.

In 1893 the group was only beginning to assemble. Ross was a member, though as a critic rather than an artist he stood at the edge of the circle. Rothenstein soon announced his discovery of a new recruit. During his stay in Oxford he had been introduced to Max Beerbohm, then an undergraduate at Merton College. He was the half-brother of the famous actor-manager, Herbert Beerbohm-Tree, and was already a poised and precocious character. He knew Oscar Wilde through his theatrical sibling, and had adopted something of Wilde's pose and paradoxical wit. Wasting little time in academic endeavour, he had secured a reputation through his wit, his ingenious caricatures and an essay on the beauty of modern dress in the *Spirit Lamp*, an undergraduate periodical edited by Lord Alfred Douglas. Rothenstein considered him the most brilliant person at Oxford, and drew his portrait for the Oxford series. When the summer term was over, Rothenstein lost no time in introducing his brilliant new friend to Beardsley, bringing him to Cambridge Street one afternoon. An instant rapport sprang up between them. They were almost twins, Beardsley being three days older, and they recognized and admired many similarities, and some differences, in each other.

Beerbohm was alarmed by Beardsley's apparent fragility, but soon perceived the febrile vigour which underlay it. He recognized too the stony common sense beneath the sparkling surface of wit and extravagant paradox. They paid each other the tribute of caricature. Beardsley comically pointed up the three-day difference in their ages by presenting Beerbohm as a baby in a top hat. And to assure his friend of a dubious immortality he added the drawing to the last batch of *Bon-Mots* illustrations.

Rothenstein, busy and gregarious, became an instant expert on the London art and literary scenes. He frequented the Domino Room of the Café Royal, the epicentre of the capital's cultural life, and initiated Beardsley into its gilded secrets. He introduced him to some of the younger members of the Rhymers' Club, a band of poets which included W. B. Yeats and Lionel Johnson, Ernest Dowson and Arthur Symons – diverse talents all seeking, in their different ways, escape from the traditions of Victorian verse. Rothenstein took Beardsley to the Vale, the art-filled house off the King's Road, where Charles Ricketts and Charles Shannon lived together, two artists dedicated to work, to beauty and to each other. They produced, at very irregular intervals, a periodical, the *Dial*, which combined their sinuous Pre-Raphaelite wood-engravings with articles on aspects of modern (particularly French) culture. Many artists were drawn to the Vale, where the hospitality was perfunctory but the atmosphere was, or could be, stimulating. Oscar Wilde described it as 'the one house in London where you will never be bored'. Ricketts admired Wilde; he had designed covers, frontispieces and illustrations for almost all of Wilde's books and this may have been the reason for a slightly strained relationship with the young illustrator who had usurped his claims to *Salome*. Certainly no intimacy grew between Beardsley and the 'Sisters of the Vale'.[16]

Aubrey enjoyed more the Sunday morning gatherings at Wilson Steer's studio in Cheyne Walk, where the radical impressionists of the New English Art Club held 'animated discussions about ways and means'. He was drawn particularly to Walter Sickert, the leader and theorist of the group, who offered to show him how to paint.

Beardsley continued to see Wilde. He went with him, Ross and Lord Alfred Douglas to the last night of *A Woman of No Importance*. Moreover, Beerbohm's fascination with 'Hoscar' seems to have sharpened Beardsley's interest. The two young dandies tested their wit against the master's. Beardsley's quip that he had caught a chill by leaving the tassel off his cane, proclaims a Wildean debt, and Beerbohm's letters to his university friend Reggie Turner are rich in such echoes. Beardsley's letters also developed rapidly in stylistic assurance and ambition. Wilde was content with this tribute of emulation. He expected no less. He enjoyed catching his own reflection. He introduced his young disciples to – among others – Frank Harris, the ebullient editor of the *Fortnightly Review*. They all dined one evening, together with Rothenstein, at the Café Royal.

Beerbohm probably introduced Beardsley to Ada Leverson, the literary hostess whom Wilde described as 'The Sphinx of Modern

Life' and 'the wittiest woman in the world'. Mrs Leverson, then in
her early thirties, lived with her conventional husband in South
Kensington. In a male world she provided a barb of feminine piquancy. Nevertheless it was with Rothenstein and Beerbohm that
Beardsley enjoyed the closest ties. With them he had the feeling of
camaraderie, the sense of shared enthusiasms and ambition which he
had previously experienced with Cochran and Scotson-Clark.*

It was a happy situation in which to pass his twenty-first birthday.
He had achieved much and felt confident that he could achieve more.
His health, though delicate, had not suffered any serious setback for
some months; there were grounds for optimism.

Lane was delighted with his work and pressing him for more.
Already looking beyond the *Salome* commission, he agreed to publish
'Masques' (accepting Beardsley's new suggestion that Beerbohm
should provide the occasional verse). He also signed him to provide
covers and frontispieces for two small volumes of short stories –
Pagan Papers by Kenneth Grahame and *Keynotes* by George Egerton.
Despite this, Beerbohm joked that Lane was quite unable to appreciate the finer points of Beardsley's art; he claimed that the publisher
had told him excitedly, 'How lucky I am to have got hold of this
young Beardsley: look at the technique of his drawings! What workmanship! He *never goes over the edges!*' The comment, though invented,
was probably characteristic. But if Lane's artistic sensibility was
limited, his commercial flair and grasp of publicity and marketing
were acute. He recognized the potential of his rising star, as he
recognized that of Rothenstein and Beerbohm. Though the trio
might make sport of him, they appreciated his kindness and his
usefulness.

When Beerbohm was twenty-one, three days after Beardsley, Lane
presented him with two proof illustrations from *Salome*. Later that
evening the publisher went with Beardsley to the Crown, the
bohemian pub off Leicester Square, where the younger poets of the
Rhymers' Club and the devotees of the music halls would congregate.
They saw Arthur Symons, the young poet and music-hall critic,

---

* Ross claims that Beardsley once said 'only four of his contemporaries interested him'.
It is quoted as an instance of his delight in 'perverse' utterance, but it is tempting to
guess at his quartet: Beerbohm, Sickert, Rothenstein and himself, perhaps?

whose volume of verse, *Silhouettes*, Lane had published that June to
a chorus of gratifyingly scandalized disapproval. Symons was self-
consciously trying to introduce French ideas and practices into his
work, attempting to create a poetry not of ideas but of 'impressions'
and 'sensations', not of conventional beauty but of strange forms.
He looked for inspiration to the poetry of Verlaine and his disciples,
and though some critics were keen to damn him as a *décadent* or
even a *symboliste*, he accepted the terms as marks of distinction.
There was much that might have drawn him to Beardsley, but their
encounter at the Crown was not propitious. Symons considered the
artist the 'thinnest young man' he had ever seen, 'rather unpleasant
and affected'.[17]

Beardsley, however, was beginning to find his place within the
cultural context mapped out by Symons and his critics. His connection with France was firmly established when the August number of
Le Livre et l'Image, a Parisian periodical, carried a brief but flattering
notice of him and his work. It 'really is awfully good', Beardsley told
Ross complacently. On 25 August the *Morning Leader*, a middle-brow
London daily, carried a small article, complete with portrait sketch
of him, on its front page. Although brief and formulaic, the notice
allied Beardsley with the avant-garde and foreign tradition, calling
him 'a symbolist and a clever one'. Though pleased with this first
piece of personal publicity in a national newspaper, he affected a
blasé horror at the 'atrocious' portrait and at the fact that the 'Brutes'
had given his 'real age'. He was already conscious that the press could
(and should) be manipulated. If he were to appear as a prodigy of
youthful talent, it would be as well to remain twenty-one for some
time. The *Morning Leader* also mentioned that Beardsley would soon
be receiving the fuller coverage of a critical article by the young poet
Theodore Wratislaw.

'Some Drawings of Aubrey Beardsley', under the pseudonym 'Pastel', appeared the following week in *The Artist and Journal of Home
Culture*, which was edited by Charles Kains Jackson, a city solicitor
and advocate of homosexuality. Jackson was also a family friend of
Gleeson White's and it seems probable that it was White's influence
which prompted the appearance of the piece. Certainly Wratislaw's
reflections were derived almost exclusively from the pictures repro-

duced in *The Studio*. He was generally enthusiastic; from the pontifical height of his twenty-two years, he noted some small deficiencies in Beardsley's technique, but excused them on the grounds of the artist's extreme youth.

The *Morning Leader* had labelled Beardsley a symbolist, but Wratislaw praised him as a decadent. Aligning Beardsley specifically and closely with the French tradition, he noted the 'curious' fact that 'for all the influence of the most modern French art on English literature, there [was] little of this influence visible in English painting'. In France he could point to Gustave Moreau, Odilon Redon and Felicien Rops as the visual counterparts of Huysmans and Verlaine; in England the literary 'decadentism' of Wilde, John Gray and Arthur Symons had not been matched until now, when 'Mr Beardsley's drawings' had appeared to 'fill up part of the vacant space'.

Art criticism abhors a vacuum. Wratislaw had perceived the 'vacant space' and drafted Beardsley in to fill it. The fashionable cultural debate about 'the modern neurosis, the delight in anything strange and depraved, the curiosity of a decadent style', which had previously been confined to literature, could – with Beardsley – now be extended into art. He ignored the *Morte Darthur* illustrations, dwelling instead on the horror of 'Salome', the weirdness of 'Siegfried', the 'mocking diablerie' of 'Madame Cigale', and the 'horrible' atrocity of the 'Kiss of Judas'. In these pictures, he suggested, Beardsley had distilled the 'neurosis of the age' and satisfied its demands for 'novelty and strangeness'. It was a verdict which placed Beardsley at the centre of the cultural stage; even though it was uttered in a specialist art magazine, it coloured future discussion of the artist and his work.[18]

Ellen and Mabel returned from France at the beginning of September, full of excitement and ideas. The friendship with the Harlands, begun in Paris and ripened at Ste Marguerite, continued in London. Mabel and Aubrey, and indeed Ellen, became regular guests at the Saturday evening gatherings the Harlands held in their flat on the Cromwell Road.

The Beardsleys, too, settled in their new home, decided to launch themselves in a modest way into the social world. They began to entertain on Thursday afternoons: Ellen, as etiquette dictated, was the nominal inviter, but her children presided. One guest remembered Mabel, 'in a dress that vaguely recalled a lady of the Italian Renaissance, seated in a carved, high-backed chair, from which she rose to receive each newcomer with graceful, if slightly mannered courtesy'. Aubrey was conspicuous, handing around cake and bread-and-butter, making people feel welcome. Max Beerbohm thought him at his best at 'these little half-formal half-intimate receptions', his natural good manners and 'inborn kindliness' shining through the gloss of affectation.

There were always, Beerbohm recalled, 'three or four drawings of his to be passed from hand to hand. Beardsley liked nothing more than the praise of his friends, and the gatherings were well attended with friends both old and new. Aubrey invited not only his new artistic *confrères* – such as Beerbohm, Rothenstein, Ross, Sickert and Stenbock – but old colleagues from the insurance office. Mabel asked fellow teachers from the polytechnic. Wilde came at least once, and so did Frank Harris.

Vincent took no part in these social gatherings; indeed the period of the move seems to have coincided with another fall from grace. His position in the family became even more marginal; he was never seen and scarcely mentioned. To all Aubrey's and Mabel's friends, he remained a figure of mystery. Stories grew up to account for his absence: that he was separated from Mrs Beardsley; that he worked in the City; that he drank, and was forced to live out of sight in the basement; that he was dead. He took no part in his son's success.[19]

Aubrey enjoyed every moment of his advancing fame, but it did not mute his sense of mischief or his delight in shocking. In September he wrote to Lane, who was in Paris for a week with Rothenstein, announcing that he planned to go to the St James's Restaurant one night 'dressed up as a tart' and meant to have a 'regular spree'. It is difficult to gauge whether this was a passing joke to alarm Lane, or whether he carried out his scheme. Several hints suggest that Beardsley might have enjoyed dressing up in women's clothes: two published pastiche caricatures showed him thus attired, and an Ada Leverson skit in *Punch* included a character called Baby Beaumont, based perhaps partly on Beardsley and Beerbohm, who confessed to a weakness for wearing dresses. There was much contemporary concern about supposed confusion between the sexes, and there seems to have been an eagerness among observers to align Beardsley with this confusion. But the attempt was often overstrained – sometimes to comic effect. One drawing Beardsley did at this time showed a fancifully chic shepherdess, above the caption 'Il était une bergère'. The phrase, 'Once there was a shepherdess', was the title of a popular French song in the repertoire of Yvette Guilbert, but some English commentators mistranslated it as 'He was a shepherdess' and thought the picture represented a man dressed as a woman, a 'woeful symbol of contemporary morals' and of Beardsley's predelictions.

Caution should be exercised. Although it is tempting to read Beardsley's interest in cross-dressing as an instance of his self-reflexive emotional stance, it perhaps belongs more properly to his delight in drawing-room theatricals and practical jokes. Such playful considerations affected even his choice of everyday clothes. In a deliberate sartorial ploy to emphasize his youth, he returned to wearing 'an Eton jacket and turn-down collar'. One journalist remarked, 'It is as good a way as another of accentuating an artistic individuality and the impression that it gives is certainly definite enough.' Dressed in this curious rig he called on Henry Harland and had himself announced as 'Master Tibbett'. Harland needed a second look to recognize the 'tall boy in the Eton jacket' as Beardsley, and Aubrey was delighted with his prank.[20]

This waywardness was also finding increasing vent in his drawings. The *Salome* illustrations offered scope for mischief, but they were not his only point of conflict that autumn: the Lucian contract with Lawrence & Bullen was terminated. Beardsley had produced only five pictures, of which three had been rejected by the publishers, probably on grounds of obscenity. He would have been happier to have kept this job and escaped some of the others. His disaffection with the *Morte Darthur* commission reached crisis point at the end of September, when he announced his intention of abandoning it. He had completed only half the illustrations.

Ellen was horrified at the proposal. She wrote clandestinely to Ross, begging him to use his influence to make Aubrey see sense. 'To me,' she wrote, 'it seems monstrous that he should even contemplate behaving in such an unprincipled manner. His "Morte" work may be a little unequal – that is his own fault and because he is wilful enough not to exert himself over what he pretends he doesn't like . . . but that is not the point, [h]e undertook to do it, and Mr Dent has spent money over it and subscribers too, and if Aubrey gives up it will be disgraceful.' Such behaviour deserved her harshest condemnation: it was 'ungentlemanly'. She lamented that Aubrey was no longer small enough to 'whip' but, given that he was not, she felt she had to rely on Ross and Vallance to 'shame him into proper behaviour'.

Aubrey soon succumbed to reason and duty. He had great respect for Ross and, besides, it is likely that there had been an element of exaggeration about his threat. Having registered his protest, he returned to the *Morte* work with ill grace. Over the next eight or nine months, each new batch of pictures was wrung from him with increasing pain. Deadlines would pass; Beardsley would make improbable excuses, announce that he had completed pictures which he had not even begun, and then 'strain every nerve, working early and late', to get the work done. Dent would be obliged to send a messenger to Cambridge Street to collect the overdue pictures, or even go himself.

On one occasion when he called in desperation, Ellen went upstairs to fetch the errant illustrator. She found him still in bed. He answered her remonstrations with an impromptu limerick:

> There was a young man with a salary
> Who had to do drawings for Malory;
> When they asked him for more,
> He replied, 'Why? Sure
> You've enough as it is for a gallery.'

His attitude to the book became increasingly cavalier and dismissive. He told Ross that he found the story 'very long-winded' and soon exaggerated this to the frank, if untrue, claim that he had never 'taken the trouble to read it' at all.

To lighten his load slightly, Dent renegotiated the specifications, allowing him to produce five double-page illustrations rather than ten full-page pictures. This spared him something in invention and required him to draw only half of each decorative border, the other half being produced in reflection, photographically. But the signs of slovenliness remain. In the double-page picture of 'La Beale Isoud at Joyous Gard' there are traces on the original drawing suggesting that Beardsley reduced a group of figures on the right of the composition to a single female. This may, of course, have been an aesthetic consideration, but there is a strong hint of corner-cutting. Dent had increasingly to reuse chapter headings to make up the bulk; he had begun this practice early and it was probably always part of his design, but it became more frequent in the second half of the book. There were moments of invention: there is interesting work among the later chapter headings, but the medieval flavour of the early designs became increasingly simplified while the tone was increasingly sensual. The relationship between the chapter headings and text, always oblique, became yet more strained and fortuitous.

Those who had seen him as the heir and hope of the Pre-Raphaelite tradition began to doubt. Vallance felt the blow most keenly, considering that his protégé had fallen victim to 'the latest charlatanisms of the hour'. In his view, Beardsley had succumbed to the influence of new interests, new haunts and new companions: 'The art of the pavement in the name of impressionism, the art of the monstrous and distorted in the name of Japan, and of all that was most insincere and corrupt in the work of the French decadents' had claimed him.

Beardsley's airily contemptuous attitude to the work in hand led also to a break with Burne-Jones. He still called occasionally on his first mentor, but found himself increasingly out of temper with the painter's pious attitude towards Arthurian romance. When Burne-Jones asked him how the commission was progressing, Aubrey replied brutally that he would be 'precious glad when it was done', he hated it so. Burne-Jones asked why he did it at all if that was his attitude, and Beardsley was only too happy to tell a man who had lived his life free of financial problems and restraints the stark commercial nature of the undertaking. He did the work, he explained, because a publisher had asked him to, not because he had any love of Malory; indeed, rather gratuitously, he added that he hated the story as he hated all medieval things.

He must have known that this would wound Burne-Jones. The blow struck home. The painter dismissed his erstwhile protégé. 'I let him see pretty plainly', he said, 'that I wasn't anxious to be troubled by him again.'* Beardsley's behaviour had been petty and vain. It had also been deliberate. One of Wilde's favourite dicta was that in art 'il faut toujours tuer son père', and there was something about the wounding candour of his last visit to The Grange that suggests attempted parricide.[21]

Beardsley, meanwhile, was attempting to commit a similar murder of Wilde, although the means he employed were slightly more subtle. Privately, for the amusement of Rothenstein and Beerbohm, he mocked Wilde's pretensions. He lampooned the supposed originality and erudition of *Salome* in a picture entitled 'Oscar Wilde at Work', which showed the playwright, corpulent and complacent, sitting at his desk surrounded by his study-aids: the works of Swinburne and Gautier, Flaubert's *Trois contes*, a 'Family Bible' and – most importantly – a French dictionary and a volume entitled 'French Verbs at a Glance'. For more public consumption he began to introduce caricatures of the intended victim into his work. Wilde, wreathed in vine leaves, appeared as Bacchus in both a chapter-heading for *Morte Darthur* (Book XI, ch. 4) and the frontispiece Beardsley drew for John Davidson's plays. When the *Daily Chronicle* suggested that the latter caricature might have been an 'error of taste', Beardsley replied airily that Wilde was 'surely beautiful enough to stand the test even of portraiture'. He ignored suggestions that Wilde's personification as the god of wine was a reflection on the playwright's drinking habits ('to put vine leaves in [one's] hair' was a euphemism for drunkenness in Beardsley's circle, and Wilde – under the pressures of work and Lord Alfred Douglas's friendship – was drinking heavily).

He also caricatured Wilde in the *Salome* illustrations. There was an element of dramatic irony in his depiction of the author, dressed as a mage, heralding the arrival of Herodias and her attendants. More subversive, however, was the recurrent appearance of the playwright's features in the Moon, the poor sad 'Moon' which, in the course of the play, was likened again and again to a 'mad', 'drunken' woman

---

* Though Beardsley had never been close to Watts, as he had to Burne-Jones, he hastened to place a distance between himself and the venerable painter. Watts, he suspected, disapproved of him; he revenged himself by confessing to interviewers that he 'greatly dislike[d]' Mr Watts. (*Book Buyer*, February 1895.)

'seeking everywhere for lovers'. Beardsley, it seemed, was transposing the sober symbolism of the play to a less elevated level, summoning the image of Wilde as the abandoned and effeminate sensualist 'seeking everywhere for [homosexual] lovers'. He also undercut the erotic charge of the drama by intruding concealed obscenities in the details. What Wilde had sought to achieve through allusive verse, Beardsley reduced to mischief.

Wilde was irritated by these pranks. A sense of hurt lay behind his quip that Beardsley's art – like absinthe – 'gets on one's nerves and is cruel'. He did not complain about the caricatures, but found the rude details trying, like 'the naughty scribbles a precocious boy makes in the margins of his copy book'. He sought artistic grounds for his dissatisfaction, complaining to Ricketts that Beardsley's drawings were altogether 'too Japanese' for a play that was essentially 'Byzantine'. Whatever the truth of this verdict, there lay behind it Wilde's uneasy awareness that Beardsley was not so much a disciple as a rival: the illustrations were threatening to upstage the text.

There was a fundamental difference in the artistic personalities of the two men, which became increasingly apparent. It was reflected in, and derived from, their modes of life. Wilde, at the height of his commercial triumph, was grown fat and florid. Together with Douglas, he had surrendered himself to sensuality. He devoted his energy and his money to an exploration of the cheaply perfumed world of homosexual vice, but strove to dress his transactions in the colours of Roman decadence. He was, *au fond*, a sentimental romantic. Beardsley looked through the purple haze of sentimentality, and adopted the cynic's view. Illness had already made him old beyond his years, and his mind was attracted to the sharp lines of wit and reason. As a mutual friend noted, 'Oscar loved purple and gold, Aubrey put everything down in black and white.' It was a combination which inevitably produced tension.

Relations between the two, though cordial on the surface, took on an undertow of competition and even spite. Wilde strove to chasten Beardsley's presumptions with wit, but a strain of malice

OPPOSITE 'The Woman in the Moon' from *Salome*; Wilde is caricatured as the moon, 1893.

weakened the thrust. Where Aubrey mocked Wilde's coarse sensuality, Wilde made play of Beardsley's freakish asexuality: 'Don't sit on the same chair as Aubrey,' he once declared, 'it's not compromising.' If Wilde resembled the Moon, Beardsley had 'a face like a silver hatchet and grass green hair'. The illustrator's pose of cosmopolitan urbanity provoked the patronizing observation, 'Dear Aubrey is too Parisian; he cannot forget that he has been to Dieppe – once.' His love of literature and admiration of Pope were condemned with a magisterial verdict, 'There are two ways of disliking poetry: one is to dislike it and the other is to like Pope.'

Beardsley was not to be drawn by these sallies. He soon realized that Wilde's knowledge of the visual arts was limited and conventional. The realization gave him confidence. He would, on occasion, reply in kind, disparaging Wilde's reputation as a cultural prophet with the observation that 'At noontide Oscar will know the sun has risen.' But for the most part he deployed his barbs in his art.

Lane became anxious about these pictorial pranks against Wilde and against the public; he feared they might jeopardize the book's commercial prospects. A certain notoriety could be useful, but obscenity would prevent the book's being advertised and sold openly. Lane took to examining the pictures with a magnifying glass, and in his alarm would sometimes spot obscenities which were not there while missing those that were. Even Beardsley, though, was obliged to admit that Lane was right to reject the first design for the contents page: a nude figure kneeling before a priapic terminal god could not appear in booksellers' windows. Confronted by 'Enter Herodias', Lane became so exercised by the nude figure on the right that he failed to spot the erection distorting the garment of the freakish attendant on the queen's other side or the array of explicitly phallic candlesticks (a graphic pun, perhaps, on 'pricket', an archaic term for a candleholder).

Beardsley was obliged to bowdlerize this drawing at proof stage by placing an elaborately tied figleaf around the loins of the naked pageboy. His impish attitude to the affair is preserved in the ditty he inscribed on at least one presentation copy of the original proof:

> Because one figure was undressed
> This little drawing was suppressed,

It was unkind, but never mind,
Perhaps it all was for the best.

Even the additions did not entirely calm Lane's fears, and he reviewed all the drawings, involving others in the process. The pictures, Beardsley claimed, had 'created a veritable fronde, with George Moore at the head of the Frondeurs'.[22]

There were further changes. Even though blocks had already been made, three more of the drawings – 'John and Salome', 'The Toilet of Salome' and 'Salome on the Settle' – were removed and replaced by three other designs, described by their creator as 'simply beautiful and quite irrelevant'. It is hard to know why the three suppressed pictures caused such offence. The subject has proved a fruitful ground for scholarship and gossip, but there have been no answers. The exposed breasts in the drawing of 'John and Salome' or the naked serving boys in the 'Toilet of Salome' cannot have been decisively disgusting as the same offences occur in several of the retained pictures. But inconsistency was a feature of Lane's censorship. The offence of 'Salome on the Settle' is even less clear. Perhaps it was discarded because it derived from one of the *Bon-Mots* grotesques, or because it bore no relation to the play, or even because Lane feared that unsavoury conclusions might be reached about what Salome intended to do with the candle she was holding.

Connection with the text does not seem to have been an over-riding concern, as Beardsley's comment about the three replacement pictures makes clear. The 'Black Cape' which took the place of 'John and Salome' looked like a contemporary fashion plate. Indeed the very oblique connection between some of the drawings and the text of the play may have encouraged Lane to invent a special designation for them: the title page, it was decided, should proclaim that the play had been 'pictured', rather than illustrated, by Aubrey Beardsley.

Nor was this the only complication that had to be addressed. Wilde and Douglas fell out over the quality of the translation. Beardsley rashly interposed and suggested that he 'thoroughly understood the spirit of the play' and could do a 'splendid' job of the work himself. Wilde was evidently so annoyed with Douglas that he overlooked his doubts about Beardsley's understanding of the play, and accepted the proposal. Beardsley worked on his translation during the first weeks of September, but by the time he showed it to Wilde the playwright's irritation with Beardsley's pictorial pranks was in the ascendant, and his tiff with Bosie had passed. Wilde, at least according to Douglas, pronounced Beardsley's version of the text 'utterly hopeless' and decided that he would rather use Douglas's translation. This was a blow to Beardsley's pride and, with the strife over the disputed drawings, made for a difficult month.

His health suffered. He had a minor recurrence of haemorrhage, but although the attack prevented him from going to see Rothenstein in Paris it did not halt his work on Salome. A friend of Mabel's recalled visiting Cambridge Street at the time; while she talked to Mabel, Aubrey worked at his table, turning occasionally to make a remark, 'then he got up abruptly, a handkerchief at his lips, and went out of the room'. There was blood on the handkerchief. Nevertheless, despite such alarms the dramas of the Salome commission were soon providing Beardsley with a pretext for wit. 'I had a warm time of it between Lane and Oscar & Co.', he wrote to Ross. 'For one week the number of telegraph and messenger boys who came to the door was simply scandalous.' He described Oscar and Douglas with theatrical exasperation as 'really dreadful people'. The verdict was neither sincere nor decisive. Wilde and Beardsley were soon joining forces to prevent Lane from using some 'quite dreadful . . . Irish stuff' for the cover of the book.

Nevertheless, the camp tone and knowing allusions are telling: telegraph boys had been a subject for double entendre among the informed ever since 1889, when a male brothel staffed by off-duty post-office messengers had been uncovered in Cleveland Street.

The letter was sent to Ross in Switzerland. He was at Davos, escaping the after-effects of an ill-concealed scandal involving himself, Lord Arthur Douglas and their rivalrous infatuation for a sixteen-year-old schoolboy with 'wonderful eyes'. Beardsley clearly enjoyed the air of danger and social subversion which surrounded the lives of his homosexual friends; and he enjoyed too the camp pose by which it was often outfaced.[23]

*   *   *

Beardsley's intellectual interest in sex was prodigious. It carried him into many of the 'courts and alleyways' of seventeenth- and eighteenth- century literature. Rothenstein recognized this, and presented him with a book of Japanese erotic prints, which he had acquired in Paris but was embarrassed to own. The combination of Japanese artistry and graphically delineated acts of sexual congress delighted Beardsley. Rothenstein's embarrassment was merely compounded; when next he called at Cambridge Street he was startled to discover the prints, neatly framed, bedecking the walls of the drawing-room.

The sexual tenor of Beardsley's work was becoming more pronounced and more noticed. It touched explicit sexual scenes, such as Salome's dance, but also quite innocuous subjects. He contributed a stylized drawing of 'Girl and a Bookshop' to the NEAC winter exhibition. MacColl, in the *Spectator*, was faint in his praise, finding the design of the bookstall 'well arranged' but 'the lady ... too calligraphic'. The critic for *Public Opinion*, however, saw rather more.

He bracketed it with the three 'eccentricities of Felicien Rops', also in the exhibition. He conceded a 'nursery book' charm in the drawing of the 'infinitely delightful' bookshop, but for the rest he was doubtful. The trees, enclosed in 'wooden cages', he thought 'conventionally degraded to meet the ends of art'. The girl herself was 'an impossible Japanese-cum-Egyptian figure' and though the overall drawing possessed charm, it was 'undoubtedly the charm of degeneration and decay'. 'These things', the review concluded, 'do not belong to the sane in body or mind, and they do not find their out and out admirers in men of robust intellect or of a wholly healthy moral tone.'

This was an extraordinary extrapolation from a 'calligraphic' representation of a girl standing in front of a 'charming bookstall'. It may well have derived its line, though not its tone, from Wratislaw's critique. Beardsley was delighted with the verdict, and wrote amusedly to Ross that the critics had set him down 'as belonging to the Libidinous and Asexual School'.

In a neatly contrived piece of orchestration, the NEAC show also contained what MacColl described as a 'delightfully malicious' portrait sketch of 'Mr Beardsley', by Rothenstein. The public was thus able to judge for itself just how 'un-sane' in body certainly, and

in mind perhaps, was the creator of the 'Japanese-cum-Egyptian' girl.
The combination of an artistic and a personal profile was telling.
The proliferating press of the 1890s was fast discovering that 'personality' rather than 'fact' was what the public craved, and the energies
of the *soi-disant* 'new journalism' were being directed increasingly
towards the invention, promotion – and indeed destruction – of new
'personalities'. For Beardsley to appear at the end of his first year of
professional endeavour in a major London exhibition, represented
by a picture adjudged to sum up the most dangerous elements of
the contemporary avant-garde, and a gratifyingly extreme portrait
representation, was a coup that could not have been expected.[24]

In 1893 there was little harm in the taint of 'degeneration and
decay'. The publisher T. Fisher Unwin recognized Beardsley's position and moved quickly to buy 'Girl and a Bookshop', thinking that
it might form the basis for an excellent poster. The artistic possibilities
of the poster were a topic of interest; there was a growing recognition
of the achievement that the French had made on this front, and a
growing desire to emulate it. Such thoughts were particularly in
mind that November when there was what Beardsley termed a 'very
jolly exhibition of French work' at the Grafton Gallery. It included,
among an impressive collection of applied and graphic art, several
lithographs by Bonnard, Vuillard and Villette, and a much admired
series of posters by Grasset, in which he made 'nature subserve a
decorative convention, and achieve[d] some notable triumphs'.

Beardsley studied these posters carefully. His restless artistic curiosity, stimulated by his time in Paris, was entering a markedly French
phase. He sought out the contemporary 'affiches' at the Grafton, but
he also began an enduring and fruitful exploration of earlier French
work. He started to collect the series of books – *Les Artistes Célèbres*
– issued in Paris by Pierson et Cie: volumes on the great and small
masters of the eighteenth century, Fragonard, Les Cochins, Les Saint-
Aubins, Les Moreaus ('simply ravishing') and Watteau. He sought
out their work, and was delighted to find a shop where 'very jolly
contemporary engravings' from Watteau, Cochin and the rest could
be got 'quite cheaply'.

The world of elegant leisure these artists conjured up – of *fêtes
galantes* and riding parties, courtly gatherings and intimate *toilettes* –

appealed to Beardsley's imagination. The figure of Watteau in particular, as revealed not only in the perfunctory facts of the *Artistes Célèbres* volume but in Walter Pater's 'Imaginary Portrait', must have seemed powerfully suggestive. Watteau was a consumptive who had borrowed and played with oriental effects in his 'Chinoiseries' rather as Beardsley had sported with Japanese art. But the practical impact of Watteau and his *confrères* upon Beardsley's work was not immediate; it needed time to percolate.

He was aware that others were deriving ideas from the same period. Young poets such as Dowson, Wratislaw and Gray, following the earlier example of Verlaine, were harking back to the vanished world of *fêtes galantes*, and painters were also drawing on this imaginary past. The Parisian-based Australian, Charles Conder, had exhibited some of his diaphanous impressions of courtly indolence in London at Goupils Gallery in September, and they had been well received. If Beardsley were to compete, he needed to be sure of his ground, to refine the vision into a personal style. It was perhaps the accomplished print work of Les Moreaus and Les Cochins that prompted Beardsley to take up Pennell's offer of an 'etching lesson', but little eighteenth-century grace showed in the bold print version he made of his portrait of Henry Irving as Becket.

The etching plate was not the only medium he was experimenting with that winter. One evening at the Empire Music Hall with Julian Sampson he dashed off a pastel sketch of the performer Ada Lundberg. He attempted a similar impressionistic treatment for a sketch portrait of the celebrated French actress Réjane. He drew her in profile, with smudged pencil and red chalk, and considered the result 'rather amusing'. He was not, however, moved to repeat the effect; his later portraits of her (and he made many) were done in pen and ink.

In November the poet Verlaine came to England on a lecture tour.* He had been hailed in some quarters as the prophet of decadence, and his arrival in London coincided with the publication of an article by Arthur Symons on 'The Decadent Movement in Literature', which tried to draw together some of the strands of this cultural

---

* Beardsley did not attend Verlaine's London lecture, but he did meet the poet at the Harlands and found him 'a dear old thing'. Perhaps he even borrowed his ravaged features for a *Morte Darthur* chapter heading (Book XI, ch. vi).

fashion. Symons's essay was part of a debate conducted fitfully in the press over the previous year. The term 'decadent' was used as abuse by some, and borne with pride by others; although it was generally agreed that the origins of cultural decadence were to be found in France, the term remained unsusceptible to definition. Symons wanted to rectify this and to suggest that there was a concerted 'Decadent Movement'. Although his article was concerned exclusively with literature, his terminology would have been intriguing to Beardsley and to those familiar with Beardsley's work.

Symons suggested that literary decadence could be divided into two strands – 'Impressionism' and 'Symbolism'. The former sought to reveal the 'essence of truth' through its 'appearance to the senses', while 'Symbolism', more nebulously, tried to show 'the truth of spiritual things to the spiritual vision'. He considered that the movement displayed all the qualities that mark the end of great periods, the qualities we find in the Greek, the Latin decadence: 'intense self-consciousness . . . restless curiosity in research', over-subtle 'refinement upon refinement . . . spiritual and moral perversity'. He described this movement of the day as a 'new and beautiful and interesting disease', which enjoyed an affinity with the corrupted body it settled on. Decadent art, he wrote, 'reflects all the moods, all the manners of a sophisticated society; its very artificiality is a way of being true to nature.'

He coloured his argument with reference to the French writers who best represented the decadent style: the Goncourts, Verlaine, Mallarmé, Maeterlinck, Villiers de L'Isle Adam and Huysmans, and included representative writers from Holland, Italy, Spain and Scandinavia. He found traces of the movement in England, in the 'morbid curiosity' of Pater's prose and the extreme impressionism of W. E. Henley's verse. Henley, an unlikely choice in some ways, was praised particularly for his poems about London: 'To be modern in poetry,' Symons wrote, 'to represent oneself and one's surroundings . . . to be modern and yet poetical is perhaps the most difficult as it is certainly the most interesting of all artistic achievements.'

Symons's article helped to crystallize ideas of contemporary decadence. The terms he employed were those already being used to describe Beardsley's work. The connection, first made by Wratislaw, was lent further, though indirect, support by the article. Beardsley's position as the embodiment of the 'Decadent Movement' became increasingly remarked. In his pose quite as much as in his art, he had encouraged it. Nevertheless, even among the 'decadent' confraternity, he remained something of an anomaly. Though he could lay claim to a 'heterogeneous style' and a mood of 'spiritual and moral perversity', his work was not tied to the world of the senses. Where others sought to discriminate their sensations with a subtlety which became almost diaphanous, Beardsley recorded his impressions in black and white. His art and his personality stood in marked distinction to the 'faint lights and faint colours and faint outlines and faint energies which many call[ed] "the decadence"' and Yeats preferred to term 'the autumn of the flesh'. It was, however, a distinction that went unremarked.

Strangely, Symons, in his listing of decadent writers, failed to mention Edgar Allan Poe, considered by many as the decadent stylist par excellence. Beardsley would certainly have made the addition: Poe was much on his mind. He had received a letter from a Chicago publishing firm, Stone and Kimble, asking whether he would draw eight pictures for a new edition of Poe's tales they were planning. Beardsley readily agreed, asking £5 each for the drawings.[25]

At Cambridge Street, as the festive season arrived, Aubrey and Mabel set up a Christmas tree and decked it with improbable conceits, including Aubrey's caricature of Whistler and some volumes of Verlaine's poems; MacColl carried off one of these as his Christmas present.

The Christmas celebrations were marred, however, by a recurrence of Ellen Beardsley's illness. She had to have an operation, and then undergo a period of convalescence at Miss Tidy's Harley Street establishment for 'Invalid Ladies'. It is an indication of Ellen's charm and her place in Aubrey's life that she received visits not only from her own friends – such as the Gurneys and the Alstons – but from Aubrey's circle; Ross and Walter Sickert visited during her recuperation.[26]

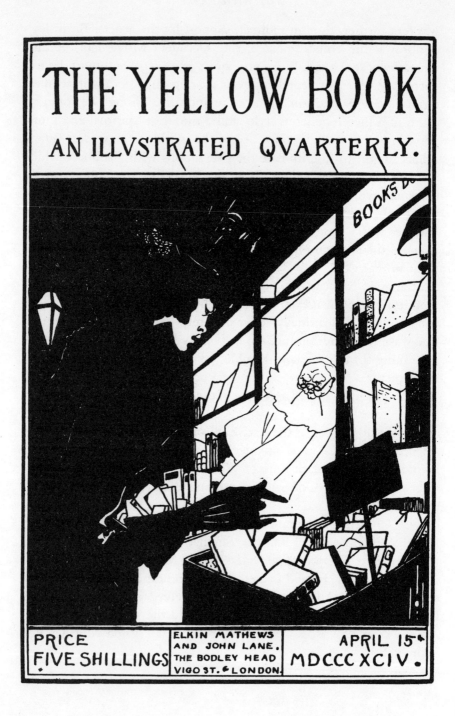

THE YELLOW BOOK

AN ILLVSTRATED QVARTERLY.

BOOKS DO

PRICE
FIVE SHILLINGS

ELKIN MATHEWS
AND JOHN LANE.
THE BODLEY HEAD
VIGO ST. & LONDON.

APRIL 15th
MDCCC XCIV.

CHAPTER VI

'The Beardsley Boom'

ON THE LAST DAY OF 1893, Aubrey and Mabel lunched with the Harlands at Cromwell Road. The day – a Sunday – was not a happy one for consumptives; the air was thick with one of the densest, soupiest and yellowest of London's yellow fogs; it muffled up the streets and shut out the weak sun. After lunch, however, the company gathered before the glowing fire and, sitting almost lost in deepening darkness, complained happily about the travails of the artistic life: the pusillanimity of editors, the tardiness of publishers, the want of a cultured public.

One particular theme recurred: the awkward yoking of pictorial art and literature insisted upon by the commercial world of book, magazine, and newspaper publishers, a theme rehearsed so often during the previous summer at Ste Marguerite-sur-Mer, and one which had prompted Beardsley to conceive 'Masques', in which pictures were to precede and dominate a meagre and incidental text. MacColl's idea of a magazine in which art and literature could appear independent of each other had simmered on in Harland's mind. He had discussed it since and, when it was revived in the post-prandial gloom of the Harlands' drawing-room, Beardsley responded with enthusiasm.

OPPOSITE Design for the prospectus of *The Yellow Book*, 1894.

Egging each other on, he and Harland spirited up the vision of a
new quarterly which would present 'Letters and Black and White
Art' as separate entities, would 'represent the "new movement"'
and, at a practical level, would provide a forum for their own work.
Harland would oversee the literary contributions, Beardsley would
look to the art. Very soon, Aline Harland recalled, they were 'plunged
into practical considerations of detail . . . Books were brought from
the study . . . new and rare editions were studied.' As a mere 'piece
of book-making', it was at once understood that the new magazine
'must be on a par too with the quality, the artistic virtue of its pages'.

And then there came the question of a name. The 'frolic of the
hour inspired Beardsley, who proposed: *The Yellow Book*. This title,
its appositeness and humour, struck all the young contingent, and it
was decided to cling to it,' at least 'until a better one was found'.
The 'appositeness and humour' of the name have long since evaporated, but they existed, it seems, on several levels. Yellow was beginning to enjoy a vogue: it was the predominant colour not only of
London fog but of several successful posters; there was irony too in
a wilfully bold publication putting on the accepted hue of cowardice;
and a joke at the expense of that other significantly coloured volume,
the *Blue Book*, which recorded parliamentary proceedings.

The main impact of the book's yellowness, however, would be
to associate it with the cheap editions of French novels which during
the 1890s were bound in distinctive yellow wrappers. Beardsley
expressly described the prospective publication as being designed to
look 'like the ordinary French novel', knowing full well that, to a
late-Victorian English readership, there was nothing remotely ordinary about French novels. The productions of Zola, Huysmans, Flaubert and the rest were regarded with alarm if not horror by the
British burghers; a periodical clad in yellow would inevitably inherit
the aura of scandalous glamour.

When Beardsley suggested the name to the excited company, the
new 'quarterly' existed only as a dream, and could easily have thinned
and faded like the London fog. But the following day Beardsley
and Harland set about transforming it into reality. They made an
appointment with John Lane to discuss the project and Lane convened a meeting over the lunch table at the Hogarth Club, around

the corner from Vigo Street. Maybe, as he later claimed, there was not room in his tiny office for the three of them, but the suspicion remains that he was even then seeking to exclude his partner, Elkin Mathews, from proceedings.

Beardsley and Harland, in states of undiminished and impatient excitement, laid out their plans. Lane saw at once the potential of the venture. 'At one o'clock precisely,' as Harland recalled, 'the three of us sat down to luncheon. At five minutes after one [Lane] had consented to back our publication with Beardsley as art editor and myself as editor.' Even allowing for Harland's fabled tendency towards exaggeration, Lane does seem to have been remarkably prompt and positive in his response. Indeed the idea of starting a review had perhaps already occurred to him; he would certainly have heard Beardsley's and Harland's ideas about art and literature before, and very probably would have been party to discussions on the subject. More significantly, he saw at once the commercial benefits of establishing a periodical that would provide a platform for authors and artists already on his list, and a magnet for newcomers.

There was general agreement on many points: the periodical should be produced as handsomely as a book; art and literature should be presented independently of each other; the content would not be a slave to 'topicality' or 'prudishness'; and Oscar Wilde, though a Bodley Head author, would not be invited to contribute. Lane later represented Wilde's exclusion as Beardsley's particular wish, claiming that relations between the two men had become and remained strained since the dramas surrounding the *Salome* commission. The suggestion that they were barely on speaking terms at the beginning of 1894 is, however, unfounded and untrue. More probably, anxiety over Wilde's domineering artistic personality, rather than animus against his person, prompted Beardsley to press for his exclusion, and persuaded Harland and Lane to agree: they feared that if they gave Wilde a part, he would take over the play.

If there was firm agreement over who was not to appear, there was a rather more tentative consensus as to who *should* contribute and, just as importantly, what they should contribute. The two editors and their publisher achieved a broad understanding that 'the chief object of the Yellow Book' should be to protest against the 'story picture' in art and 'sloppy sentimentalism and happy endings' in literature.

Harland's initial idea of a magazine that would represent the 'new movement' had rapidly expanded into something less defined. Prompted by Lane, he planned to offer a range of alternative 'movements', to include not only works by young, unsentimental realists – such as Egerton and Crackanthorpe – and young, even less sentimental decadents – such as Symons and Wratislaw – but pieces by more established writers such as Henry James, Edmund Gosse and Richard Garnett.

Beardsley, with his naturally catholic tastes, paid lip-service to this plan of operation, but he continued to regard the periodical's declared protest against conventional Victorianism largely in terms of subversion and revolt. *The Yellow Book*, he hoped, would be a haven for 'stuff' that could not be accepted in a 'conventional magazine' because it was either 'not topical or perhaps a little risqué'.[1]

In the days following the decisive lunch there was much canvassing of possible contributors, much discussion of formats, fonts and costs. The Hogarth Club became the unofficial centre of operations. The office boy at the Bodley Head recalled the scenes of bustle and excitement: Lane 'hurtling' into his Vigo Street premises, followed by Beardsley and Harland. Then moments later, all three of them sweeping out again 'as though whisked away by a gust of wind, bound for the Hogarth', Lane bearing samples of paper, cloth and type. The flair for production and design which the Bodley Head had developed was going to be applied to *The Yellow Book*.

The colour of the publication was important to Beardsley, but that it was to be a book – something 'to last longer than a quarter of a year' – was the main thing. It would not be 'like the *Edinburgh* or the *Quarterly*. Not just a *paper* thing. A *bound* thing: a real **book**, bound in good thick boards. *Yellow* ones. Bright yellow. And it's going to be called *The Yellow Book*.' Beardsley's emphasis fell always upon the second word.

The names of potential writers and artists were put forward, pressed and carried by acclamation. Despite the proposed division between art and literature within the covers of the magazine, the art editor, the literary editor, and indeed the publisher felt entitled to poach on one another's preserves or to shoulder one another's burdens. Beardsley accompanied Harland when he called on Henry James to secure a short story for the first issue.* The art editor wrote to Robbie Ross (on Hogarth Club paper) soliciting a contribution for the new literary and artistic quarterly. 'We all want to have something charming from you for the first number,' he explained. 'Say an essay, or a short story in which the heroine is not a beautiful boy.'

Beardsley also pushed the claims of Netta Syrett, a friend and colleague of Mabel's who was looking to escape from teaching into a literary career. And it was Beardsley – backed by Lane despite Harland's doubts – who insisted upon Beerbohm's inclusion in the new venture. Many years later Beerbohm recalled the occasion:

> *Scene:*   Cambridge Street, Pimlico . . . afternoon.
> *Persons:* Aubrey Beardsley and myself.
> AB: How are you? Sit down! Most exciting! John Lane wants
>   to bring out a Quarterly – Writings and Drawings –
>   Henry Harland to be Literary Editor – Me to be Art
>   Editor. Great Fun.

In the case of Beerbohm, Beardsley was only half-usurping Harland's authority; though Beerbohm was planning to launch himself as an essayist, Beardsley recognized that his artistic gifts matched his literary accomplishment and asked him 'both to caricature and write' for the quarterly. Harland and Lane were just as ready with their advice on the art front. Lane enlisted the support of J. T. Nettleship, a painter who had written a book on Browning for the Bodley Head. And it was almost certainly Harland who approached his companions of the previous summer, L. B. Goold and Alfred Thornton. Conder did not join the party; an unfortunate misunderstanding had sprung up between him and Harland over some pictures Harland had taken on consignment intending to sell. The breach was later healed, but it served to exclude Conder from the first list of proposed contributors and also denied Beardsley the services of MacColl, who had been drawn into the dispute on Conder's side.

---

* An undated letter from Harland to Lane (in the Lane archive) suggests that the publisher secured James's initial agreement to contribute.

Beardsley's own artistic contacts were centred on the NEAC, and it was to his radical *confrères* at the Club that he first turned: Sickert, Steer and, of course, Rothenstein. He also sought out Laurence Housman, a young illustrator who had recently begun designing weird Pre-Raphaelite inspired frontispieces for the Bodley Head. In line, however, with the agreed policy of broad-based eclecticism, he also approached some 'past masters'. There were several well-established talents within the membership of the NEAC to whom he could apply: R. Anning Bell, doyen of bookplate designers, was an admirer of Beardsley's work, and Charles Furse, though quite conventional, was not unfriendly. They both agreed to lend their names, and their pictures, to the venture. He also approached Rothenstein's artistic mentors, Ricketts and Shannon. They accepted initially but backed out before their names could even appear in the prospectus, fearing that involvement in *The Yellow Book* might 'lead to complications' over the new issue of their own magazine, *The Dial*, scheduled to appear in May.[2]

Beardsley had more success with Joseph Pennell, accosting him with Harland one evening at the Hogarth Club. 'We are going to edit a magazine,' Harland announced without preamble, 'and John Lane will publish it.'

'Who's "we"?,' asked a nonplussed Pennell.

'Aubrey and me,' explained Harland. 'I'll do the literary end, he'll look after the art.'

Pennell was taken aback. 'Why, you don't know anything about editing,' he exploded. 'Neither of you, not even with me, can run a magazine.'

'You will see,' Beardsley replied, with the unchallengeable confidence of youth, inexperience and drink. 'And what's more you are to do something for it.'

Pennell, surprised at finding his protégé turning the tables on him, declared, with perhaps more truth than humour, that he wanted to be the 'art editor' and have Beardsley as his contributor, but more drinks were ordered and Pennell found himself swept on board by the duo's enthusiastic account of the new quarterly. There was, as he recalled, no tedious discussion about print runs, prices or reproduction fees, only an infectious desire to make the 'best art and literary magazine' possible.

A yet more magisterial recruit was Sir Frederick Leighton. Since the previous spring, when Beardsley had found himself bound with the ageing Leighton between the covers of the first *Studio*, an unexpected bond of friendship and mutual esteem had sprung up between the 'New Illustrator' and the president of the Royal Academy. It was well known that Leighton had 'a great admiration' for Beardsley's work. The compliment was speedily returned. Beardsley sought Leighton's advice on artistic matters and (though nothing came of it) expressly asked if he could design the cover for a book on Leighton which Ernest Rhys was preparing.

The proximity of the Royal Academy and Bodley Head premises encouraged Leighton to extend his knowledge of Lane's artists. He would often call in at the shop in Vigo Street to assess the progress of the 'New Art', suggesting playfully that if he was not 'performing an R.A. duty he was doing a neighbourly one'. On one of these neighbourly calls he was poring over Beardsley's latest designs and remarked enthusiastically, 'Ah! what wonderful line! what a great artist!' before adding, *sotto voce*, 'if he could only draw.' When Lane responded neatly, 'Sir Frederick, I am tired of seeing men who can *only* draw', Leighton at once replied, 'Oh! yes, I know what you mean, and you are quite right too.' Away from Vigo Street, he championed Beardsley's work. He usually tempered his enthusiasm, but told at least one person that the art editor of *The Yellow Book* was 'the greatest master of line the world had ever seen'.

He readily agreed to supply a drawing for the inaugural number of the new quarterly, and Lane was much encouraged by his participation. He had a great respect for established authority and only limited confidence in the twenty-one-year-old Beardsley. Arthur Waugh, a young journalist and critic, recalled encountering Lane and Harland at the National Club in Whitehall Gardens during the first week of January 1894. They were having lunch with Edmund Gosse, gathering his support for the venture and seeking advice about contributors. When Lane, turning to the 'art side' of the quarterly, mentioned that Beardsley was art editor, he paused and 'looked round apprehensively' to see if there was any criticism of his choice, 'hastily throwing in the names' of Leighton and Furse to 'steady the balance'. The ploy was unnecessary. Gosse was a 'great admirer' of Beardsley and considered him an excellent choice, and 'a great draw', as did Waugh.

Nevertheless, the incident revealed Lane's curious admixture of boldness and caution, his grasp of the commercial possibilities of what was new and daring, and his anxiety lest he offend the proprieties. For the moment, however, the enthusiasm that greeted all news of the project soothed Lane's doubts and muffled any dissenting voices. Arthur Waugh contributed a regular 'Transatlantic Letter' to an American journal, *The Critic*, so news of *The Yellow Book* and Beardsley's part in it reached America almost before it was broadcast in Britain. But Lane's contacts in the London press – many of his budding poets and young conteurs survived on journalism – ensured that the British public was soon brought up to date. The embryonic periodical became, in Harland's phrase, 'the talk of the town'. A prospectus was in hand, and material was being gathered for the first number.

Adapting perhaps a drawing intended for 'Masques', Beardsley made a cover design which he considered 'wondrous'. He showed it to everyone, and everyone concurred, with one exception. Beerbohm met Oscar Wilde one afternoon in the Café Royal and learnt that Beardsley had just been in, showing off the drawing before taking it to Vigo Street. Beerbohm asked Wilde what it was like. 'Oh,' said Oscar, spotting an outlet for his pique at being excluded, 'you can imagine the sort of thing. A terrible naked harlot smiling through a mask – and with ELKIN MATHEWS written on one breast and JOHN LANE on the other.'[3]

Practical considerations were to the fore. Lane settled on the Ballantyne Press to print the text. The Swan Electric Engraving Company was chosen to reproduce the artwork. The pictures were to be printed off on hand-presses on to special grade art paper (which, in a pleasing but unintended irony, was manufactured by the Lord Mayor of London). And to further distinguish the art contents from the literary contributions it was decided to print each picture on its own right-hand page, preceded by a title-page and sheet of protective tissue. Lane arranged for the Boston publishing firm of Copeland & Day to distribute *The Yellow Book* in America; and for Robert A. Thompson & Co. to act as agents for 'the Colonies'. The format was set at 250 pages, octavo, and a first print-run of 5000 was decided upon. The price was fixed at five shillings, not cheap at a time when many novels cost 3s 6d and most illustrated weeklies could be had for sixpence, but within the bounds of a middle-class budget. The price ensured a degree of exclusivity and marked *The Yellow Book* as something distinct and significant.

It was understood from the outset that Beardsley and Harland would have responsibility for the budget. They would receive a royalty on sales and would be expected to pay all literary and artistic outgoings from this sum. They would negotiate terms with individual contributors, and any profit made after fees had been paid would be divided equally between the two editors. In the first flush of excitement, with the magazine existing only in the limitless realm of the potential, Beardsley and Harland thought they might even become rich. Such was the buzz of anticipation surrounding *The Yellow Book* that, by the end of January, the proposed print-run of 5000 was looking inadequate; Lane was preparing paper supplies for up to 15,000 copies.

The minds of the two editors turned to thoughts of possible income: with royalties of 15 per cent on the first 5000 copies, and 20 per cent thereafter, the editorial team would receive, if only 5000 copies were sold, £187 10s. If 10,000 copies were sold, the sum would leap to £437 10s. In the unlikely but not impossible event of 15,000 being taken up, the editors would clear the huge sum of £687 10s. These amounts did not of course represent profit for division between them; there was the expenditure for contributors – a considerable amount for 250 pages of top quality art and literature. They could, of course, pay contributors a tiny royalty out of the editorial fraction, but Harland and Beardsley recognized that an 'author or artist will naturally put a lower price on his wares if he is paid at once and certainly, than if he had to wait some months and then depend on chance for the amount'. Besides, with the possibility of substantial sales, the editors were reluctant to share the potential profits. Cash payment for contributors would, they thought, net them 'vastly more'.

Visions of fortune as well as fame swam before them. They estimated, however, that even with cash payments for contributors they would need £200 to fill the first volume. Roughly three-quarters of this amount would be needed to pay for the literary contents; the remaining £50 would secure the artwork. Expenses would be covered by sales of 5250 copies, a target which seemed almost paltry in the heightened atmosphere of literary gossip and log-rolling. As ever, though, the problem of cash-flow had to be considered. With an entrepreneurial zeal not often associated with *fin-de-siècle* artists, they conceived a scheme to raise £250 from private backers, which could be used to pay the contributors up-front. After publication, when royalties were paid, the backers would receive a dividend and the two editors would take the bulk of the profits. Beardsley was, it seems, continuing to keep 'the money view' of his work 'keenly in view'.

In the event the £200 to pay the contributors was provided not by independent sources but by Lane, who also revised the royalty structure. He reduced it to 10 per cent of the cover price on the first 1000 copies, 15 per cent on the next 4000, and 20 per cent thereafter; the US and colonial sales would pay only 5 per cent.

Just how much the editors paid to secure the art and literature contents for the first issue is not recorded. It was certainly close to the full £200, but some of it was paid to themselves for their own contributions. Harland included two of his short stories (probably charging about £12) while Beardsley, besides providing a cover design and title page, was planning to use three or four of his own drawings, for which he might receive as much as £30. Except in the case of cover designs, the pictures remained the property of the artist. The publishers secured a one-off reproduction right only, but owned the block made from the picture and could thus negotiate republication elsewhere. This was a good deal for Beardsley and the other *Yellow Book* artists.* Many periodicals failed to pay artists for

---

* A note from Harland to Rothenstein at Harvard shows that the artist received £5 'for the use of . . . "Portrait of a Gentleman" and "Portrait of a Lady" in the Yellow Book [volume 1]'. For his Oxford lithographs Rothenstein received £5 each, but Lane kept the originals.

their contributions; others insisted on retaining the original artwork.

With the great flowering of illustrated papers and periodicals during the early 1890s, artists became more aware of their commercial worth and strength. This awareness had achieved a point of focus at the end of 1893 with the establishment, by Joseph Pennell, of the Society of Illustrators. Beardsley became a member of this association, which in its initial form was conceived on trade union lines. It is probable that the deal he secured for the art contributors of *The Yellow Book* reflected the aims, the expectations, and even the clout, of the society.

Publication date for the first number was set for 16 April 1894. The editorial 'offices' were established in the Harlands' flat in Cromwell Road, and Beardsley spent much of his time there. Such was the pressure and pleasure of work, he would even, on occasion, stay overnight. Harland paid out of his own pocket for the services of a young would-be writer, Ella D'Arcy, who acted as the editorial assistant.[4]

In the midst of these proceedings Beardsley's reputation received a substantial fillip. At this date his published work consisted only of the *Morte Darthur* part-work, the *Bon-Mots* volumes, the *Studio* article, the insubstantial *PMB* sketches, and a handful of book covers and magazine illustrations. This had secured him the admiration of a limited public of connoisseurs and fellow artists; enough to awaken the critical interest of art periodicals and the commercial interest of publishers, but it did not represent any sort of general notoriety. He was 'fashionable' rather than famous.

The publication in February of the English edition of *Salome*, with Beardsley's startling pictures, brought him new status. Although the print-run had been limited to 755 ordinary copies and 125 'specials', Wilde's reputation and the play's notorious history guaranteed it press coverage, and Beardsley's drawings were so original and arresting as to guarantee themselves a large proportion of that coverage.

It became something of a critical commonplace that the drawings had subverted, if not completely reversed, the traditional relationship between author and illustrator. *The Studio*, not altogether approvingly, found the 'irrepressible personality of the artist dominating

everything'. The *Saturday Review* noted that Beardsley's pictures could
not be 'quite pleasing' to Mr Wilde: 'Illustration by means of derisive
parody of Felicien Rops, embroidered on to Japanese themes, is a
new form of literary torture, and no one can doubt that the author
of *Salome* is on the rack. Mr Beardsley laughs at Mr Wilde.' *The
Times* suspected that Mr Beardsley was laughing not merely at Mr
Wilde but at Mrs Grundy, John Bull and indeed everyone else. His
illustrations were condemned as 'fantastic, grotesque, unintelligible,
repulsive. They would seem to represent the manners of Judea as
conceived by Mr Oscar Wilde, portrayed in the style of the Japanese
grotesque as conceived by a French *décadent*. The whole thing', the
critic concluded, 'must be a joke, and it seems to us a very poor
joke.' Some feared that Beardsley was in earnest. Even Richard Le
Gallienne, the Bodley Head's pet critic, who wrote in the *Star* under
the unabashed soubriquet 'Logroller', shied away, murmuring that
Beardsley's art 'though "devilishly" clever' was, 'in the words of Mr
Pater . . . "What I may not see".' The sober *Art Journal* described
the book as 'terrible in its weirdness and suggestion of horror and
wickedness', advising that it was suitable for 'the strong-minded
alone'.

There was acknowledgement of Beardsley's technical accomplishment and flair for decoration. The 'Peacock Skirt' was generally
thought the finest picture in the suite, though its relationship to the
text remained a mystery. Indeed the relationship, if any, between
pictures and text became a much-debated point. Against literal-
minded plaints that there was no connection and some conflict, a
few critics suggested subtler and more allusive points of contact.
Some claimed that Beardsley was attempting something different and
distinctly modern. 'Mr Beardsley's drawings', opined the *Art Journal*,
'are thoroughly in harmony with the text and give evidence of
impressionism in illustration not hitherto accomplished or even seriously attempted.' *The Studio* posed the question of how the pictures
might illustrate the text and 'what might be their exact purpose or
the meaning of their symbolism', but then declined to consider it.
Wratislaw, however, writing in *The Artist*, perceived and described
a connection. Wilde's play, he thought, 'was a subject singularly
well fitted for illustration by [Beardsley]'. Playwright and artist, he

12 Buckingham Road, Brighton. Beardsley was born in the room on the top floor facing out to the front.

Below left Beardsley's maternal grandfather, Surgeon-Major William Pitt, in 1882.

Below right The Surgeon-Major's wife, Susan Pitt (née Lamb).

Vincent Beardsley, Aubrey's father.

Ellen Pitt at the time of her marriage to Vincent Beardsley.

Aubrey and Mabel as children.

Above Beardsley aged seven, with his toy engine.

Below An embroidered bookmark Beardsley made for his father while a pupil at Hamilton Lodge school.

Affection

Above A decorated menu-holder made by Beardsley at the age of ten.

Right 21 Lower Rock Gardens, Brighton, the house of Beardsley's great-aunt Sarah Pitt. Aubrey and Mabel lived here in 1884.

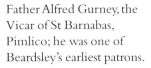

Father Alfred Gurney, the Vicar of St Barnabas, Pimlico; he was one of Beardsley's earliest patrons.

Frederick Evans, co-proprietor of Jones and Evans bookshop in Queen Street, off Cheapside. He secured for Beardsley his first book commission and, as an accomplished amateur photographer, took the well-known 'gargoyle' photograph of Beardsley.

much wrought with them, even the

Above Beardsley being struck by 'Mantegna's tremendous *Triumphs of Caesar*' at Hampton Court: a self-caricature from one of his letters to Scotson-Clark.

Left Beardsley's sketch-portrait of Edward Burne-Jones, done immediately after his first visit to the artist in July 1891.

E Burne Jones
Sunday 12th July
1891

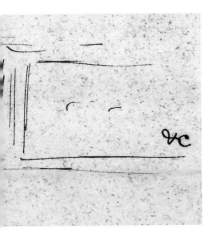

Right Robbie Ross (left),
Beardsley's great friend
and champion, together
with Reggie Turner.

Below 'Annovale della Morte di Beatrice', one of the
drawings which Beardsley showed to Burne-Jones.

Beardsley's drawing 'Hamlet Patris Manem Sequitur', or 'Hamlet Following his Father's Ghost', done under the influence of Burne-Jones.

114 Cambridge Street, Pimlico, the Beardsleys' first – and only – family home.

Gleeson White, the first editor of *The Studio*, the magazine which introduced Beardsley to the art world.

Max Beerbohm's 'Some Persons of "the Nineties"'. Front (left to right): Arthur Symons, Henry Harland, Charles Conder, Will Rothenstein, Max Beerbohm, Aubrey Beardsley. Back (left to right): Richard Le Gallienne, Walter Sickert, George Moore, John Davidson, Oscar Wilde, W.B. Yeats and (barely visible) 'Enoch Soames'.

Left Beardsley's controversial portrait of Mrs Patrick Campbell for the first *Yellow Book*.

Above Brandon Thomas, author of *Charley's Aunt*: his collaboration with Beardsley came to nothing.

Left Ada Leverson, Wilde's 'Sphinx'.

Right Edmund Gosse, the literary godfather of the nineties.

Below left Oscar Wilde and Lord Alfred Douglas at Oxford in 1893.

Below right John Lane, publisher of *The Yellow Book*.

Mabel Beardsley as Mrs
Maydew in *The Queen's Proctor*
at the Royalty Theatre, 1896.

Aubrey Beardsley photographed
by Frederick Hollyer.

Leonard Smithers with two of his authors,
C.A.E. Ranger-Gull and Hannaford Bennett,
c.1896.

Marc André Raffalovich, Beardsley's 'Mentor':
a portrait by Sydney Starr.

Above John Gray,
one of the few
contemporary
poets Beardsley
admired.

A Beardsley sketch in the manuscript of *The Story of Venus and Tannhauser*.

The wealthy Cambridge undergraduate H.C. (Jerome) Pollitt as 'Diane de Rougy'. This photograph by Frederick Hollyer was exhibited at the Photographic Salon in 1894.

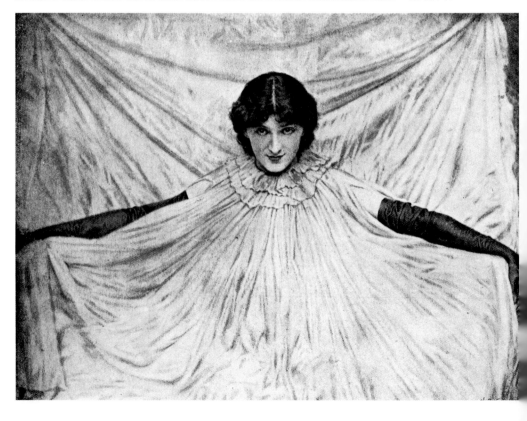

Above Bournemouth in the late 1890s. Beardsley stayed there for his health.

Below Menton, on the French Riviera, where Beardsley died on 16 March 1898.

Right Father David Bearne, S.J., who received Beardsley into the Roman Catholic Church.

A decorated initial for Beardsley's edition of *Volpone*. His use of pencil and his expressive shading marked a new – and final – phase in his art.

The last photograph of Beardsley, in his room at the Hotel Cosmopolitan in Menton with his Mantegna prints pinned up above the desk. The photographs on his bookcase include pictures of Raffalovich, Wagner and Mabel.

suggested, would each 'label himself a "decadent", for each loves the strange and fantastic, and each detests the common as well as the commonplace'.

Wratislaw recognized that Beardsley had 'not illustrated his author after the manner of Vierge' or any other conventional artist, but had 'given rein to his own fancies' so that 'it seems as if his drawings, when they do more or less coincide with the text, do so by chance as much as by design.' Only in the case of 'The Black Cape' did he feel there was no point of coincidence 'either with the book or with the remainder of the pictures', and this he felt should have prevented its inclusion.

The connection of Beardsley with decadence, impressionism and symbolism, adumbrated the previous year, was now confirmed. The view of him as a Pre-Raphaelite, adopted on the first appearance of *Morte Darthur*, was exploded. Reviewers, confronted by his extra-ordinary art and noting its novelty and power, were quick to graft it to any or all of the advanced strains in contemporary culture. The connection was certainly enhanced by the nature and subject matter of Wilde's play. The story of Salome presented many of the decadent tropes – beauty allied to cruelty, the *femme fatale*, the power of art over life – but Beardsley's treatment of the tale gave it an arresting immediacy. The anachronistic touches, such as the French novels on Salome's dressing-table, irritated many but were suggestive to some. The *Saturday Review* related them to the practice of Benozzo Gozzoli and the Italian Primitives. Wratislaw argued that, by employing such details, Beardsley had made his heroine 'modern or ancient as he pleased', presenting not a localized historical figure but 'the woman who in all times and lands has exercised the charm of her conscious beauty and the fascination of her unconscious corruption'.

Many would have concurred with *The Studio*'s verdict that Beards-ley had distilled 'the very essence of the decadent *fin de siècle*' and that his *Salome* was 'the typical volume' of the period.

He had cause for satisfaction; he had gained both a wider notoriety and a wider market. The book was noticed in Europe: the radical Belgian art-group, Le Libre Esthétique, invited Beardsley to exhibit the illustrations at its first salon in Brussels. America took note; Beardsley's illustrations received wide, if scandalized, coverage in the literary and artistic periodicals. The Boston Public Library put its copy of the book 'under lock and key' in the 'Inferno', much to the alarm of Herbert Copeland, who began to fear that he and F. Holland Day might end up 'in jail'. Sales on both sides of the Atlantic were brisk, and the edition was soon taken up, at fifteen shillings for the ordinary copies and twice that for the large-paper issue.[5]

Wilde's misgivings have been noted and could only have been confirmed by the reviews. Nevertheless, he had the sense to realize that, once the play had been published, public complaint would be useless and counterproductive. His public verdict was that the drawings were 'quite wonderful'. Despite his unspoken exclusion from *The Yellow Book*, the friendship continued between him and Beardsley, though never without its undertow of competitive unease.

They went together to the St James's Theatre to see Mrs Patrick Campbell in the hit of the season, Pinero's *The Second Mrs Tanqueray*. From their box Wilde sent a note backstage to the star, informing her 'Mr Aubrey Beardsley, a very brilliant and wonderful artist, and like all artists a great admirer of your art, says that he must once have the honour of being presented to you, if you will allow it.' He asked permission to bring his brilliant young friend to her dressing-room after Act III, adding with a lordly air, 'He has just illustrated my play of *Salome* for me, and has a copy of the *edition de luxe* which he wishes to lay at your feet.' Beardsley might not have appreciated the tone of condescension, but was delighted to meet Mrs Campbell and introduce her to his work. Perhaps she was aware of it already. Beardsley's fame was advancing on all fronts. The cover design he had provided for George Egerton's *Keynotes*, a collection of proto-feminist short-stories, achieved a wide circulation when the book became a popular and critical success. When *Punch*, at the beginning of March, produced a parody of the work as 'She-Notes' by 'Borgia Smudgiton' it was supported by a 'Japanese fin de siècle illustration by Mortarthurio Whiskersley'. A first appearance in the pages of *Punch* was confirmation of established fame.[6]

Lane was well pleased with the publication of *Salome*, as indeed was his partner. Although Beardsley's first and closest contact at the Bodley Head was John Lane, he also established friendly relations with the slightly older and much more retiring Elkin Mathews. Mathews lived in the self-consciously Aesthetic West London suburb of Bedford Park, and with his wife was part of its self-consciously artistic life. It was probably through Mathews that Beardsley became acquainted with some of the members of this set, among them Dr John Todhunter, father figure of the Rhymers' Club, and Florence Farr, a captivating and intensely spiritual actress and author. Four years previously Farr had taken the leading role in Todhunter's *Sicilian Idyll*, a verse-drama produced, to considerable critical acclaim, in the clubhouse-cum-theatre at Bedford Park. The beginning of 1894 found Farr preparing for a new Todhunter production. Backed by Annie Horniman, a wealthy and imaginative theatrical patron, she was planning to put on *A Comedy of Sighs* and a curtain-raiser by the young poet and Bedford Park dweller, W. B. Yeats. Farr asked Beardsley to design a poster which would also serve as a programme cover.*

It was an attractive proposition. The burgeoning of poster design during the latter years of the nineteenth century was everywhere apparent. On the hoardings of Paris, Cheret, Grasset, Lautrec, Willette and others had established a style which was finding an echo on London billboards with the work of Dudley Hardy, Maurice Greiffenhagen and John Hassall. There was a recognition that these productions, while being popular, were also art. Posters by Cheret and others had been displayed at Goupils Gallery the previous year, and Beardsley had admired the boldness of their massed colours.

Strength of colour is one of the key effects in a successful poster, yet for his own first effort Beardsley (while indicating a dark and light green colour scheme) chose to make the design in black and white, advising Farr that once a 'zinc block' had been made it could be printed in any colour she chose. If Beardsley's method was timid, his design was bold: a dark-haired and sensual-lipped woman in a décolleté gown, standing half-obscured, half-revealed in the gap between two spotted gauze curtains. The picture (after a short delay while the Avenue Theatre was confirmed as the venue) was

* The *Studio* diarist makes it clear that the idea of using the same image for poster and programme cover was an innovation: 'The smaller version', he adds, 'is emphatically to be preferred to the large.' (*Studio* 3, 1894, pp. 60–1.)

reproduced not by zinc block but by lithography in blue, green and creamy yellow. Although *The Studio* sniffed at the colour scheme, the effect was undoubtedly arresting. It was pasted up at the beginning of March, and immediately drew attention. It marked, as Gleeson White remarked, 'probably the first introduction of Mr Beardsley to "the man in the street"'. It was a memorable, if not entirely happy, encounter. The image aroused public 'ridicule' and public 'anger'. *Punch* could not forbear from comment; under a pastiche of Beardsley's drawing, Owen Seaman contributed a ditty addressed to 'Mr Aubrey Beer-de-Beers' whose 'Comedy of Leers, you know,/Is posted all about the town.'

The poet considered the 'Japanee–Rossetti girl' was 'not a thing to be desired'. Just as the so-called 'New Humour' was new only in that it was not humorous, so, he suggested, 'New English Art' (of which Beardsley was a paid-up practitioner) was new only in that it was not art. It was certainly artificial and unnatural: 'A beauty reared on Nature's rules,' the poet sighed, would be 'worth a dozen spotted ghouls'. The perceived ugliness of the 'woman' was a recurring theme. The critic from the *Globe* admired the design, finding it 'an ingenious piece of arrangement, attractive by its novelty and cleverly imagined', but complained that the 'mysterious female' looming 'vaguely through the transparent curtain' was 'unnecessarily repulsive in facial type'. The *Pelican* found her 'bilious, lackadaisical, backboneless, anaemic, "utter" and generally disagreeable'. It was said that 'even the cab horses shied' at sight of her. The *Artist*'s verdict upon this 'artistic poster' and its reception was that it 'conclusively proved that art is exclusive not popular'. The magazine's diarist found it 'delightful to observe the way in which the spotted lady set up the backs' of all those semi-cultured burghers 'who thought themselves artistic'. To have taken the most vital, popular art form of the day and – at a first attempt – to have produced something 'exclusive' was a notable achievement.

His poster quite upstaged the two plays it advertised. Nevertheless, Todhunter's piece was nothing if not self-consciously modern: one critic suggested that the author's intention 'seems to have been to

OPPOSITE Design for the Avenue Theatre programme and poster, 1894.

AVENUE THEATRE

Northumberland Avenue,

Charing Cross, W.C.

Manager :

Mr. C. T. H. HELMSLEY.

NO FEES OF ANY KIND.

Any Attendant accepting a Gratuity
will be instantly dismissed.

Designed by AUBREY BEARDSLEY

get the scent of *Keynotes* over the footlights, and some pretty strong whiffs of it certainly reached the nostrils'. By designing a cover for *Keynotes* and a poster for the *Comedy of Sighs*, Beardsley established himself at the vortex of modernity. Newness was one of the obsessions of the moment. The epithet 'New' was attached with significant emphasis to almost every area of human endeavour. *Punch* lampooned the trend as the 'New Newness' and suggested that the proverb would soon have to be amended to 'There's nothing old under the sun'. Beardsley found himself – almost at a stroke – in close connection with all the arresting novelties of the hour: the New Fiction, the New Drama, the New Woman and the New Art. Through Owen Seaman's satire upon his work he even found himself touched by the New Humour. Beardsley's growing fame was reflected on to *The Yellow Book*.[7]

Interest in the periodical continued to mount. The prospectus was issued with another of Beardsley's strange 'Japanee–Rossetti' girls on its cover. The drawing showed a predatory female browsing among the boxes outside a curious bookshop, recognizable to familiars as the Bodley Head premises in Vigo Street. Standing in the doorway, regarding her with an air of petulant disapproval, was an elderly Pierrot, perhaps recognizable to the same cognoscenti as Elkin Mathews.

Inside the prospectus the editors proclaimed their aims with broad conviction:

> *The Yellow Book* is to depart as far as may be from the bad old tradition of periodical literature, and to provide an Illustrated Magazine which shall be beautiful as a piece of bookmaking, modern and distinguished in its letterpress and its pictures, and withal popular in the best sense of the word. And while [it] will seek always to preserve a delicate, decorous and reticent mien and conduct, it will at the same time have the courage of its modernness, and not tremble at the frown of Mrs Grundy. Altogether, it is expected that the Yellow Book will prove the most interesting, unusual and important publication of its kind that has ever been undertaken. It will be charming, it will be daring, it will be distinguished.

Of the three closing claims, it was the second which appealed most to Beardsley – he would be 'daring'. Aided and abetted by Beerbohm, he was bent on a campaign of subversion, careless of the wrath not only of Mrs Grundy but of his artistic masters.

Max had produced a satirical essay on Oscar Wilde, entitled a 'Peep into the Past'. The mock-historical piece – which viewed Wilde as a half-forgotten relic of the 'early Victorian era' who had achieved a modest success through 'Northern grit', 'unremitting effort' and unconscious plagiarism – delighted Beardsley, as another sly blow in their campaign to escape Oscar's authority. It even shared, if it did not borrow, the jesting allusion to messenger boys which Beardsley had made in his letter to Ross at Davos. The piece, how-ever, was far too indiscreet and hurtful for publication. While Lane was happy to exclude Wilde as a contributor from *The Yellow Book*, he did not wish to traduce him within its pages. The article was vetoed. Beerbohm offered instead an essay on the 'Philosophy of Rouge' that had been intended for the *Pall Mall Gazette*. It was a flippant reworking of Baudelaire's 'Eulogy on Cosmetics', one of the key texts of the decadent canon.

Beardsley also had to be restrained. Among his own drawings for the first number was a picture of a fat woman seated before a bottle at a café table. The composition was an echo of Degas's 'L'Absinthe', given an additional *frisson* by the fact that the woman was alone, perhaps waiting for a 'client'. Lane passed it for publication but then learnt that the figure was a portrait, and a far from complimentary one, of Whistler's wife, Trixie. He was not prepared to provoke the ire of the litigious butterfly, and he withdrew the drawing. Beardsley wrote to the publisher threatening suicide or demonstrations in Trafalgar Square if the picture were not reinstated: he suggested mischievously that should it be retitled, in the Whistlerian manner 'A Study in Major Lines', it could not possibly hurt anybody's sensi-bilities. Lane, however, remained adamant.

Beardsley's other contributions, although less obvious, also carried an edge of personal spite or sought in more general ways to shock and confuse. He made an eccentric title-page design of the back view of a woman standing in an open field at an upright piano. The image took the very symbol of Victorian domestic respectability and transferred it *en plein air* as though it were the easel of some dangerous impressionist.

Whistler may have escaped the frontal assault of the 'Fat Woman', but in 'A Night Piece' Beardsley paid oblique and mocking tribute to the master's *Nocturnes*. Whereas Whistler in his night-pieces had allowed the dusk to throw a veil of romantic mystery over the Thames-side scenery, Beardsley – with glib cynicism – set his wash-drawn scene in Leicester Square and, against the background of commercial buildings struggling through the gloom to transform themselves into palazzi, he showed a slender, décolleté woman wandering alone. Any *mondain* contemporary would have recognized her as a street-walker, though perhaps only a few would have read the black butterfly bow around her neck as a pastiche of Whistler's signature.

Beardsley also aimed a barb at his other erstwhile mentor, Burne-Jones. His drawing for the bookplate of John Lumsden Propert which, together with one of Anning Bell's *ex libris* designs, was to celebrate the form, proclaimed an essential kinship with the Pre-Raphaelite and Morrisian belief in the application of art. Its image, however, of a timid pierrot kneeling at the feet of an epicene *femme fatale* recalled the pose but inverted the dynamic of Burne-Jones's 'King Cophetua and the Beggar Maid'.

Beerbohm was particularly taken with Beardsley's drawing, 'L'Éducation Sentimentale'. 'It haunts me,' he told his friend Reggie Turner, describing in excited detail the 'fat elderly whore in a dressing-gown and a huge hat of many feathers . . . reading from a book to the sweetest imaginable little . . . girl, who looks before her, with hands clasped behind her back, roguishly winking.'

As something of a departure Beardsley also included a portrait drawing of Mrs Patrick Campbell. Perhaps it had been prompted by his backstage visit, or perhaps the idea preceded the call. Soon after that *entr'acte*, however, he made arrangements with her for a sitting. Although Harland had denounced mere topicality as one of the trite vulgarities which *The Yellow Book* would be eschewing, the two editors had enough commercial sense to recognize the benefits of including a personality as famous and fascinating as 'Mrs Pat' in their pages. If justification were needed, there was a certain controversial

modernity in representing actresses artistically. In the previous twenty
years, the half-world of the stage had been taken up by artists and
writers as a new and daring subject. Degas had his ballet dancers,
Lautrec his cabaret artistes, Sickert his music-hall singers, Arthur
Symons his chorus girls. The realists embraced the stage for its modernity, the decadents for its artificiality.[8]

Beardsley expended considerable time on the picture of Mrs Pat.
He took his portrait work with a seriousness which was not often
guessed or appreciated. 'What is a portrait good for,' he quizzed,
'unless it shows just how the subject was seen by the painter? In the
old days before photography came in a sitter had a perfect right to
say to the artist: "Paint me just as I am." Now if he wishes absolute
fidelity he can go to the photographer and get it.' Mrs Campbell
gave him many sittings at the theatre, but it was only when he was
standing in the pit one evening, watching her perform as Paula
Tanqueray, that he finally 'caught her expression' and was able to
set it down with pen and ink. He knew that for all the stylization
of his representation – a long, thin, hunch-shouldered figure seen in
profile – he had captured Mrs Patrick Campbell 'herself'.

On both technical and theoretical fronts Beardsley's designs
marked a fresh advance: his forms became simpler and bolder, his
subject matter more contemporary and metropolitan. It was perhaps
the company of Sickert, Rothenstein and other NEAC impressionists
that encouraged him in this direction. Although impressionist painting now tends to be defined in terms of its attempt to capture the
evanescent effects of light, to an 1890s' mind it was simplification of
detail and the use of modern subjects which were regarded, quite as
much, as the movement's significant characteristics. In his *Yellow
Book* drawings, Beardsley embraced both these traits. He did not
absolutely abandon his Pre-Raphaelite heritage, still employing some
of the fluid decorative conventions he had learnt from Crane, Burne-
Jones and Morris. Indeed his 'new idea', as he stated it, was 'to apply
the decorative style to modern life, modern dress, modern costume'.

Technically, however, he imposed a self-challenging limit. He
wanted to see 'how far it [could] be done in black and white.
In other words to sacrifice half-tones.' Although in some of his
night pieces he did resort to dark grey washes, he preferred to use

unadulterated masses of black ink on white paper. He considered that 'when dead black is used feelingly and artistically it can be made to express almost anything' – even colour. He quoted Boccaccio's image, 'The grass was so green it was nearly black,' to illustrate the point. He evolved, too, from Botticelli, a new theory of 'the value of line'. As he explained painstakingly to one journalist, 'As you know, artists are in the habit of using thin lines to express backgrounds, and thick lines to express foregrounds. Now what I say is this. If the same value of line is kept, that is, if the background and foreground are drawn with lines of the same thickness . . . a better effect will be produced.'

Beardsley, besides completing his own drawings, was much occupied with his editorial duties, assembling work from fellow artists: two pictures from Rothenstein, two from Sickert, one from Pennell. In what appears to have been a snub to Lane, he chose, as Laurence Housman's contribution, a drawing entitled 'The Reflected Faun' which the publisher had refused as a frontispiece for a book of poems. He kept a close watch over the block-making process and examined the proofs with care. There was also publicity to consider. Perhaps prompted by the notoriety of the Avenue Theatre hoarding, Lane asked Beardsley to produce a small poster for *The Yellow Book*.[9]

Paragraphs were already appearing in the press about *The Yellow Book*, but these piecemeal comments and casual speculations were overridden when Beardsley and Harland gave an interview to *The Sketch* on 'What the "Yellow Book" Is to Be'. Beardsley even provided charcoal sketch portraits of himself and Harland to accompany the piece. The article gave the editors a chance to reiterate and amplify the claims of their prospectus. So far as the hard and fast division between art and literature was concerned, an exception was tentatively admitted 'if one man [were to be] the author of both' and 'both were part of the same work'. There was also a suggestion that, although the art in the first number would be in black and white, colour might be used in the future. Whatever the hue, however, the sole criterion for acceptance would be artistic distinction; the treatment not the subject was crucial. 'If you were to bring us a bad picture of the Crucifixion,' the editors explained, 'we should not take it; but if you brought us a good picture of a pumpkin, it's highly probable we should.'

As publication day approached, Beardsley and Harland became quite irrepressible. On 6 April, ten days before the launch, they dined with Lane and others at the Hogarth Club. Spirits were high. Lane left sometime after midnight; his companions were still carousing but he was staying with a friend and did not wish to be in too late. Perhaps he had made a point of needing his rest. Beardsley and the others, having carried on drinking until two, sent Lane a telegram 'requesting the date of the publication of the first volume' of *The Yellow Book*. Delighted at the thought of their publisher being dragged from his bed to receive this daft request, they retired, only to be woken in their turn by Lane's telegraphed reply. The humour of this practical joke did not perhaps survive the moment, but the incident reveals something of the charged and happy atmosphere in which *The Yellow Book* was brought into the world.

The first number was published on 16 April. It was a Monday. On that morning the distinctive glare of yellow flecked the railway bookstalls and the windows of the bookshops. At Jones & Evans, copies stood open at the Beardsley drawings, and Evans pointed them out to his customers with pride. At the Bodley Head, the window was dressed entirely with volumes of *The Yellow Book*. The effect of this 'mighty glow of yellow' was, according to the memory of the office boy, as though 'the sun had risen in the West'. A splash had been made; sales were brisk.

That evening there was a celebratory dinner at the Hotel d'Italie, in Old Compton Street, Soho. There were some absentees: Henry James and Joseph Pennell were abroad, as were Symons and Crackanthorpe. Le Gallienne was lecturing in Liverpool; Gosse and Egerton were indisposed; Leighton stayed away; Netta Syrett was in mourning. And Elkin Mathews had not been told of the event. Nevertheless, some fifty contributors, would-be contributors, wellwishers and supporters did turn up. The crush increased the jollity of the occasion. It was enhanced too by the informal heterogeneity of costume. Some of the men were in dress suits, others in bohemian tweeds; the women wore evening dresses or 'tailor gowns'.

George Moore, flushed with champagne and the excitement of his novel, *Esther Waters*, being banned by W. H. Smith on grounds of obscenity, was 'gaily conspicuous', seated between his sometime collaborator, Pearl Craigie, and the youthful beauty, Olivia Shakespeare. Ernest Rhys and his wife came; she sat next to the cantankerous Scottish poet, John Davidson, but found him in humorous and anecdotal mood. Theo Marzials, the chloral-addicted Parnassian, silenced Yeats briefly with a disquisition on the balladeers of yesteryear. Alfred Thornton was next to the sober, silent Steer. Down the table was the far-from-silent Sickert. Ernest Dowson had abandoned a backlog of unfinished translation work to attend. Dr Garnett, sole representative of the older contributors, sat half-concealed in a corner, whereas Beerbohm, the youngest author present, was full of suave assurance. Kenneth Grahame looked more than a little startled at finding himself in such a throng.

Beardsley surveyed the scene from the high table: Mrs Pennell, in the absence of her husband, had the place of honour, between him and Harland. To Harland's right sat Menie Muriel Dowie, a tall, fantastically coiffed travel writer, with Lane on her other side. She perhaps owed her place to the fact that her husband was Henry Norman, literary editor of the *Daily Chronicle*. It was generally agreed that 'the dinner, qua meal, was bad, bad, bad', but this in no way diminished the merriment of the occasion. Amid the general chatter, Beardsley sat unaccustomedly silent, not touching his food, anxious about the speech he was to make. When the moment came, however, for the 'sharp salvo of short speeches', he displayed a dandy's poise, beginning his address with the cool assertion, 'I am going to talk about an interesting subject, myself.' The phrase struck, as Thornton recalled, 'a new note in that time of simpler manners and less advertisement'.

Harland then spoke, and Lane blandly apologized for the indisposition of his partner, eliciting at least one cry of 'Shame'. It was generally agreed that the best contribution was extemporized by Sickert, who rose to say that he 'looked forward to the time when authors would be put in their places by being compelled to write stories and poems round pictures, which should be supplied to them readymade by their task-masters the artists'. The ordeal of oratory safely passed, Beardsley was carried off happily into the flood of talk. His place at the heart of the enterprise was acknowledged by all, though not with universal approval. Lionel Johnson, the diminutive Rhymer and an upholder of classical traditions in art, was an early dissenter. He spent the evening piping in boy-like tones, 'I abominate Aubrey Beardsley.' But, for the present at least, he found no one to take up the refrain. When the dinner broke up, Beardsley went with Lane, Harland, Beerbohm, Mrs Pennell and two or three others to Vigo Street to admire the window display and show off the home of the magazine. Unwilling to let the evening end, the party then moved on to the basement of the Monico, where they toasted again the success of the venture.[10]

The critical reception of *The Yellow Book*, though not generally favourable, was gratifyingly loud. The well-orchestrated pre-publicity campaign assured it a share of attention and envy. Despite the disingenuous editorial claims that the quarterly would 'preserve a delicate, decorous and reticent mien' and not become 'precious or eccentric', reviewers claimed to find otherwise. *The Times*, the authoritative organ of record, found the prevailing note of the new journal an unhappy 'combination of English rowdiness with French lubricity'. The inclusion of some established names among the young, modern contributors was noted but lamented. 'On the whole the New Art and New Literature appear to us to compare unfavourably with the old and we doubt if the representatives of the latter will relish the companionship.'

Most of the literary and artistic periodicals were even more reactionary. The *National Observer* managed praise for Henry James's short story, but dismissed the rest of the contents at some length as 'nonsensical and hysterical matter'. The *Speaker*, in a review which Harland thought might be libellous (and might be by George Moore), devoted two pages to excoriating the 'farrago of aspiring affectation and preposterous incompetence'. The *Spectator* threw up its hands in horror when confronted by the 'jaundiced-looking indigestible monster'. Mr Punch, in his displeasure over the 'bilious book', was moved to verse. The University publications showed the innate conservatism of the undergraduate spirit: *Granta* thought *The Yellow Book* no more than 'a collection of semi-obscene, epicene, sham erotic and generally unimportant literary and artistic efforts'; *Isis* found it 'dull and foolish'.

There were some words of praise, but even those offering approbation tended (like those pouring scorn) to focus upon the quarterly's modernity. Le Gallienne, writing in the *Star*, applauded the periodical's 'general air of being piquant and up to date'. A piece in the *Weekly Irish Times*, probably written by Katharine Tynan, another Bodley Head author, was almost an encomium: the 'exquisite new quarterly magazine [was] a sumptuous feast [of] English modernity'. The insistence on the daring modernity of the publication by both its supporters and detractors in the press inevitably focused attention on the magazine's most modern contributions: Beerbohm's essay and Symons's poem both came in for abuse, the essay being memorably called 'the very rankest and most nauseous thing in literature'; the poem received a briefer epithet: 'disgusting'. These literary offences were seen expressly as 'relat[ing] to the evil work in the sister art of painting as expressed by the New English Art Club' and exemplified by the contributions of Sickert, Rothenstein and Beardsley – particularly Beardsley.

As Beardsley himself remarked, in the storm that raged over the first number, 'most of the thunderbolts fell on my head'. His drawings were taken as the index of all that was most modern, piquant, lubricious and decadent. The most spectacular assault was launched by the *Westminster Gazette* which commented, 'We do not know that anything would meet the case except a short Act of Parliament to make this kind of thing illegal.' Others were quick to join the fray, and each of Beardsley's contributions was battered in turn. The cover design, which he had 'hoped folk [would] like at once, because it's to be permanent', was at once – and heartily – disliked not only by *The Times* (which supposed that it was intended to 'attract by its very repulsiveness and ugliness') and the *National Observer* (which castigated its 'audacious vulgarity and . . . laborious inelegance'), but also by *The Artist* which, though offering praise elsewhere, found the cover 'ugly'. The *Whitehall Review* said it was like a poster 'drawn by a schoolboy for a peep show of a fat woman', and the 'Literary Lounger' in the *Sketch* condemned it more obliquely as 'probably the nearest approach Mr Aubrey Beardsley is capable of making to a likeness of Sir William Harcourt [Chancellor of the Exchequer]'.

It was admitted, even by the *Westminster Gazette*, that Beardsley had 'technical skill'. There was acknowledgement too of his 'faculty for designing piquant bookplates', but his most conspicuous ability, it was claimed, lay in 'reproduc[ing] the leer of calculating licence'. Beyond this recognition of a cynical sexual tone, however, there was a general refusal to comprehend Beardsley's work. His drawings were called 'meaningless and unhealthy' by Frederick Wedmore in the *Academy*, and 'objectless abominations' by *Punch*. To the *National Observer*'s jaundiced eye, Beardsley's women resembled 'nothing on the earth or in the firmament'. *The Artist* insisted that 'Night Piece' was 'interesting but incomprehensible', and wondered whether it might be a practical joke.

'L'Education Sentimentale' was perhaps spared some critical fire by not being understood, though it was a specific cause of the *Westminster Gazette*'s call for government intervention. The other, intriguingly, was the picture of Mrs Patrick Campbell. Indeed, the portrait of the actress was undoubtedly the most abused item in the magazine. The drawing seemed to confound critical expectations of what a portrait might be. *Vanity Fair* insisted that it was a hideous caricature rather than a 'portrait'. The *Athenaeum* declared it 'libellous', and the stylized attenuation of the figure provoked a *Granta* wag to ask:

> Pray Mr Beardsley, tell us why
> Your elongated fancy made you
> Depict this lady nine feet high?
> What influence conspired to aid you?

Punch set her slenderness down to exhaustion, and produced a spoof version above the caption, 'Played Out, or "The 252nd Mrs Tanqueray" – trained down very fine after a long run'.

The most cleverly barbed shaft was launched by the *Daily Chronicle*. Henry Norman repaid the honour done his wife at the celebratory dinner with a review of guarded praise for the new quarterly. In passing, however, he complained that, much to his regret, the portrait of Mrs Patrick Campbell had been omitted from his copy: 'the fly-leaf announcing it precedes one of Mr Beardsley's strange *crises de pinceau*.

To those who know the trials and tribulations of processing and editing, this is very explicable.' Beardsley rose to the bait and dashed off an apology to the editor of the paper, assuring him that all other copies did contain the portrait. His letter was promptly published, with a note, 'Our own copy, it is true, contained a female figure in the space thus described, but we rated Mrs Patrick Campbell's appearance and Mr Beardsley's talent far too high to suppose that they were united on this occasion.'

Mrs Campbell seems to have taken against the picture in the wake of press opinion. Beardsley presented her with a copy of *The Yellow Book*, inscribed to 'Mrs Patrick Campbell from Aubrey Beardsley', to which she added the descriptive qualification, 'who is an unwholesome and incompetent fellow'.* Wilde, however, admired the picture so much he bought it and hung it in his drawing-room.

Beardsley, after falling into the *Chronicle*'s trap, soon regained his poise; he knew, from the example of Whistler and Wilde, that the papers were an important fan for igniting the embers of controversy, and that he had to make another attempt. He wrote an elegant letter to the *PMB* defending himself against the press and those 'private persons' who had taken exception to the 'unpardonable affectation' of the *plein air* pianist on his title page. He quoted an account (quite probably invented) of how Gluck, 'in order to warm his imagination and to transport himself to Aulis or Sparta, was accustomed to place himself in the middle of a field'; and how in this situation 'with the piano before him, and a bottle of champagne on each side, he wrote in the open air his two "Iphigenias", his "Orpheus", and some other works.' What, Beardsley asked, would the critics have said had he 'introduced those bottles of champagne? And yet we do not call Gluck a decadent.'[11]

The reaction in America to *The Yellow Book* was similar in tone, though on a smaller scale. Reviews were confined to the artistic periodicals the *Dial, Chap Book, Book Buyer, Critic* and *Modern Art*. There was consensus that the book, for all its 'brazen inessentiality',

* This may have been ironic. Margot Peters, in her life of Mrs Patrick Campbell, *Mrs Pat* (London, 1984), records that the actress kept a collection of Beardsley pictures throughout her life.

was worthy of attention and that Beardsley was its presiding genius. Indeed, he was dubbed the 'Yellow Bookmaker'. More ominously, however, another name was attached to the new quarterly; the reviewer for *The Critic*, casually perpetuating the association between Beardsley and Wilde established with *Salome*, dubbed *The Yellow Book* 'the Oscar Wilde of periodicals'.

Wilde would have been as unamused as Beardsley at this unfortunate phrase. Excluded from the quarterly's pages, he had turned his wit upon it. To Ada Leverson he complained it was 'horrid and not yellow at all'. For Ricketts' amusement he rehearsed an involved anecdote about how he had tried to discard his copy on three separate occasions only to have it returned each time. To Bosie Douglas he wrote, with brutal relish, that it was 'dull and loathsome, a great failure. I am so glad.'

A failure, however, it was not. The small tempest raging around it on both sides of the Atlantic was a source of both amusement and gratification to Beardsley; he confessed to 'enjoying the excitement immensely'. Meanwhile the public, intrigued by the furore, hastened to discover its cause. The magazine was the wonder of the hour. It was discussed everywhere, and everywhere it was discussed Beardsley's name was to the fore. At the London meeting of the Brighton Grammar School Old Boys on 17 April a copy of the quarterly 'went round and drew forth emphatic and curious criticisms'. But it was not only his schoolfellows who took an interest. In five days the entire first edition of 5000 copies had been exhausted, and a further thousand were printed. Towards the end of May, Lane announced a third edition in the pages of the *Academy*. Sales of 7000 copies would assure the editors a joint profit of £50 over and above the fees for their own contributions. It represented a healthy slice of income, especially if it were to be repeated four times a year.

From an editorial perspective the critical storm brought problems in its wake. The literary duo, Katherine Bradley and Edith Cooper, who wrote under the name 'Michael Field', withdrew their poem. George Moore, with typical peremptoriness, announced that he would not contribute to the second volume, claiming that he 'loathed the sight' of Beardsley's drawings. Mrs Craigie, despite Harland's blandishments, also refused to contribute again. A more serious defection was Frederick Leighton. He confessed that he had been so 'slated' by his friends that he 'dare not contribute any more to *The Yellow Book*'.* If the president of the Royal Academy withdrew his support, who knows what other 'senior' artists might be reluctant to contribute?

Beardsley sidestepped the problem by persuading Henry James to lend the portrait of himself by John Singer Sargent for the second number of *The Yellow Book*. James was away in Venice but authorized Beardsley to collect the picture from his rooms so that a block could be made from it. The diffident novelist had been rather alarmed by the reception of *The Yellow Book*, but, as he told his brother, he had consented to appear in it again, 'for gold and to oblige the worshipful Harland'. His attitude to Beardsley was ambivalent. He liked the artist, finding him 'touching and extremely individual', but considered his 'productions . . . extraordinarily base' and hateful. Nevertheless, he did recognize some exceptions and even wished to acquire one of Beardsley's portraits of Réjane. Sargent, though admitting privately to an admiration for Beardsley's work, was no friend of *The Yellow Book*, but bowed to James's judgement and allowed the picture to be reproduced.

Anxious to recruit more contributors, Beardsley also called on Walter Crane at his distinctly Aesthetic home in Holland Street, a house crowded with such a variety of artefacts – Japanese fans, Indian idols, plaster casts, Renaissance prints, Morris textiles – as to stretch even Beardsley's admiration for cultural eclecticism. Since their first meeting at Mrs Gleeson White's 'At Home', Crane had taken an interest in Beardsley and his work. He had admired the 'rich and inventive' designs for *Morte Darthur* and recognized the power of the japonesque, 'morbid' illustrations for *Salome*. When he was asked to expand and publish his 1889 lecture on 'The Decorative Illustration of Books', he made flattering references to Beardsley's work in the genre. He readily agreed to contribute to *The Yellow Book*, and Beardsley came away with permission to reproduce Crane's 'divine' version of 'The Birth of Venus' ('his only great thing,' Aubrey melodramatically proclaimed).

* Leighton's admiration for Beardsley's work did not prevent him from being vexed by his pose. He was moved to complain to Lane after the reception of *The Yellow Book*, 'Young Beardsley is going off his head with affectation. A pity – he is fit for better things.'

Sickert could be relied upon, and Steer was now ready. They were both used to controversy and Sickert – at least – relished it. Other men from the impressionist arm of the NEAC rallied to the cause – Alfred Thornton, Bernhard Sickert (Walter's brother) and Sydney Adamson. Beardsley also approached two promising young black-and-white illustrators – A. S. Hartrick and E. J. Sullivan – with whom he had worked on the *PMB*, and both promised pictures. From his friend Aymer Vallance, he cajoled designs for a set of playing cards.[12]

He was also content to rely on his own powers, though Harland was less sure. At the height of the critical bombardment which greeted the first number, the literary editor had written to Lane insisting that 'Aubrey must modify himself in Vol II'. Beardsley, however, was not to be moved: he had gained a reputation for shocking the public and did not intend to surrender it. His only modification was stylistic. His designs became increasingly bold in their massing of unbroken areas of black against unbroken areas of white. This new simplicity was apparent even in the pictures he submitted for the last parts of *Morte Darthur*. The wearisome task was approaching its close, and in the early summer he seems to have found a last reserve of energy if not enthusiasm.

Novelty, however, he always preferred, and in the wake of *The Yellow Book*'s success he took up several new one-off commissions. Like most freelance artists, he found it hard to turn down an offer. He agreed to do a cover design for a Cambridge undergraduate magazine, though he charged ten guineas for it; he produced an amusing picture of a fashionably attired female golfer, attended by a pierrot caddie, as an invitation card for the opening of the Prince's Ladies Golf Club at Mitcham, Surrey. The Poe illustrations had still to be done for Stone and Kimball, and the London publishers, Henry & Co., commissioned a frontispiece for the pseudonymous Jocelyn Quilp's *fin-de-siècle* fantasy, *Baron Verdigris*.

Lane was prepared to tolerate Beardsley's private commissions, but was jealous of other publishers. Impressed by the impact of *Salome* and the sales of *The Yellow Book*, he wanted to monopolize Beardsley's talent by providing him with a steady supply of work. The success of George Egerton's *Keynotes*, with its distinctive Beardsley cover, encouraged Lane to reproduce the formula and the format. He proposed to publish a short novel by Florence Farr called *The Dancing Faun* as the second volume in a Keynotes series. Beardsley, it was agreed, would provide the cover illustration and the signature 'key' (composed of the author's initials) for this and subsequent volumes.

He accepted the task readily, but used it to point up the subtly altered balance of his relationship with Lane. As the acknowledged star in *The Yellow Book* firmament, he was conscious of his power. The design he submitted was an obvious caricature of Whistler as a mincing faun perched on the end of a sofa. Lane had been able to ban the satirical portrait of Mrs Whistler from *The Yellow Book*, but he was now powerless to veto this drawing of Whistler himself. To emphasize the point, Beardsley gave the newspaper *To-Day* permission to reproduce the censored 'Fat Woman' to accompany their interview: 'A New Master of Art: Mr Aubrey Beardsley'.

The interview provided Beardsley with his first real opportunity to present himself to the public. Interestingly, he did not adopt the role of the 'decadent' artist. He preferred to announce himself as a prodigy who had sprung fully formed from nowhere. 'Nothing in [his] surroundings' had prepared him for a career in art, and even the development of his personal style (represented by the drawing of 'Raphael', which he promptly produced) had happened 'suddenly without any effort'. He disclaimed the Japanese influence on his work, asserting that although his drawing was 'said to recall the methods of the East . . . [he] knew nothing of their style of art till quite lately, beyond of course, the fans and vases which meet one's eye everywhere'. His real inspiration, he said, came from Congreve's plays and 'the eighteenth-century schools of artists and writers', particularly from France.

In passing, he mentioned his admiration for modern French art, but eschewed all theories. The perceived strangeness of his pictures, he insisted, was entirely the result of personal vision. 'I represent things as I see them . . . I fear people appear differently to me than they do to others; to me they are mostly grotesque and I represent them as I see them. I can do no more.' He got his models where he found them. 'All humanity inspires me,' he said. 'Every passer-by is my unconscious sitter; and strange as it may seem, I really draw folk as I see them. Surely it is not my fault that they fall into certain lines and angles.' He set a distance between himself and the Pre-Raphaelite tradition: the only label he would accept was that of 'Realist', in the sense that his work was realistic.[13]

The Yellow Book made Beardsley a celebrity. His art polarized opinion: it was extravagantly abused and extravagantly praised. There could be no neutrality. He achieved fame in almost the modern understanding of the word: such fame was a new phenomenon, made possible only by the rapid proliferation of the printed media and the great attention it focused on London life, and even then was more usually accorded to stars of the stage than to artists. But it was granted to Beardsley; suddenly his name and his face were everywhere. He was caricatured in the press and sung about in the music halls. He was written about, talked about, pointed out. More satisfactorily, he was invited out. That season, his mother recalled, he was much sought after by the London lion-hunters. Hostesses were delighted to find him an excellent talker; their guests were struck by how closely he resembled his drawings: elongated,* monochromatic and unhealthy. Was he, they wondered, as decadent as his creations?

He delighted in the game, honing his affectations with audacious care. His pose of cultivated anti-naturalism reached its apogee when he invited Ada Leverson to come early to Thursday tea so that she might 'scent the flowers'. She arrived to find her host spraying the gardenias with tuberose. He promptly presented her with some frangipani and urged her to perfume the stephanotis. He even sought to outface his physical condition with the mask of wit, declaring with dandiacal sang froid, 'Really, I believe I'm so affected, even my lungs are affected.'† Although the mask was assumed, Beardsley wore it with increasing regularity, and even kept it on in church. It seems that sometime in 1894 he ceased attending St Barnabas and began, though still an Anglican, to frequent the Roman Catholic Brompton Oratory. The flirtation with Rome at this stage appears to have been

---

* Because of his angular thinness, Beardsley perhaps appeared taller than he was. Scotson-Clark (in an 1895 article) gives his height as 'three inches under six foot'.
† Another of his affectations was smoking. Both Penrhyn Stanlaws and Jules Roques, who visited him at Cambridge Street, record him with a cigarette in his hand.

mere modishness. The conversions of Ernest Dowson and Lionel Johnson, Verlaine and Huysmans, not to mention Watteau, had established
Roman Catholicism as the artist's, if not the decadent's, creed. Perhaps
Beardsley was simply tasting its glamour; he hardly seems to have been
drawn by an exclusively religious impulse.

The Oratory, he claimed, was 'the finest of our modern buildings
. . . a true product of the town. It is the only place where you can
go on a Sunday afternoon and quite forget it's Sunday.' Even among
its fashionable congregation, he cut a figure. On one occasion, after
mass, he startled his fellow-worshippers by exclaiming as they
emerged into the spring sunlight, 'What a dear day.' Mabel followed
(or perhaps led) Aubrey to the Oratory. She, too, was developing
affectations. Fired by the reflected glory of her brother's achievement,
and supported by the knowledge of his increased earnings, she handed
in her notice at the Polytechnic School at the end of the summer
term. When quizzed by Netta Syrett on what she intended to do,
she replied, 'Go on the stage and become a society beauty, dear.'
Her first dramatic creation was herself. Syrett noticed that freedom,
if it did not immediately provide theatrical engagements, had an
immediate impact upon Mabel's looks. She had always been handsome in a fresh-complexioned way, but she now developed a striking
attractiveness. Her figure became 'slim and willowy', her hair (with
only 'a very little touching up') deepened from 'ginger' into alluring
'titian', and her hazel eyes beamed with new radiance in her well-
chiselled face. Aubrey was delighted with the transformation, and
took her with him everywhere.

He enjoyed too the money which *The Yellow Book* provided,
indulging himself with beautiful books and rare prints. He ordered
new suits, but his desire for a white overcoat with a pale pink lining
remained a happy fancy. He lavished hospitality and gifts upon his
friends with a generosity that bordered on the profligate. In his glory
he did not abandon former friends. He took care to welcome old
acquaintances from the insurance office to his Thursday At Homes,
and invited Mr King to dine with him when he was in town.

Though delighted by fame, he recognized something of what
Beerbohm termed the 'vulgarity' of success and was content to treat
it as a lark. When faced with the breathless demands of autograph

hunters, he could sometimes not resist mischief. Brandon Thomas, author of *Charley's Aunt* and a close friend of the Leversons, recalled Beardsley showing him an autograph album which had been sent to him for inscription. On one of the pages was a piece of music set down and signed by 'an eminent composer'; Beardsley unobtrusively added a succession of jarring sharps and flats to faze anyone who attempted to play it.[14]

The happy and established social round continued: the Harlands' Saturday nights, the Pennells' Thursday evenings, the literary gatherings in John Lane's rooms in Albany, the bohemian parties given by the Australian journalist Douglas Sladen at his flat in Addison Mansions, dinners with the Leversons and with the Brandon Thomases. But there were now new addresses: he became a regular at Edmund Gosse's Sunday At Homes, where the established names of literature and a smattering of younger talent talked 'Art' and gossiped among the teacups. There were also grander events. He can be glimpsed attending a Chelsea garden party given by the wife of the proprietor of the *Daily Chronicle*. Among other lions of the moment such as Anthony Hope (author of *The Prisoner of Zenda*), Arthur Conan Doyle, Bernard Shaw, and Marie Corelli, Beardsley flitted – pale and very interesting.

It was part of his pose to seem a man of leisure. Callers would never find him busy at his desk; there was always time for talk. Afternoons were passed in conspicuous idleness: lounging, perhaps, with Max in the regency ambience of Angelo's fencing school; sitting in the Domino Room of the Café Royal with Frederick Sandys, the ageing Pre-Raphaelite draughtsman, imbibing the atmosphere, the draught lager and the fading spirit of the 1860s. From the disreputable old artist he learnt something of the fascination of hair (the dominating motif of Sandys's work) and the bohemian trick of running up a bar bill without being able to pay it and then sending a messenger out asking a friend to rescue him. The proximity of the Bodley Head to the Café Royal made Lane a ready target on these occasions.*

---

* Lane preserved one pencil note from Beardsley: 'Please send me some cash. Café Royal refuses to cash your cheque. Bill is just under £1. 1s.' Sandys's admiration for Beardsley's work found an outlet in pastiche; he made an excellent drawing of 'Circe and the Swine' for the *Sketch* (26 September 1894, p. 501).

Beardsley delighted to dress up in his evening clothes and set out on the town. He loved music hall and the theatre: *Madame Sans Gêne* at the Gaiety, starring the *jolie-laide* Réjane, was the hit of the season. He went with Rothenstein to the first night of Shaw's *Arms and the Man* when it replaced the failed *Comedy of Sighs* at the Avenue. (Beardsley's poster was reused for the new production, with the result that the play was soon labelled by the wits, 'Shoulders and the Woman'.) He was quick to recognize and enjoy Shaw's combative genius, laughing so loudly he provoked comment. But he would have provoked comment anyway. After the shows there were suppers to eat and clubs to go to. Beardsley's favoured haunt was 'Jimmies', the St James's restaurant on Piccadilly Circus. There, in the louche gilded atmosphere, he could sit with Beerbohm or Rothenstein, Grant Richards or Robbie Ross, eating oysters and kidneys until after midnight, drinking in the hard, sensual faces of the tarts and their gentlemen friends, the elaborate effects of the women's dresses and the classical solemnity of the men's clothes – and transforming them into the distinctive lines of his own grotesque vision.

For all his pose of idleness, Beardsley was constantly at work with his eyes: 'No man', said Beerbohm, 'ever saw more.' Even in the midst of bustle and activity he maintained a detachment which allowed him to observe clearly, and beneath his leisured exterior there pulsed an energy of extraordinary intensity. To a friend who reprimanded him for being out on a bitter winter's night without a coat, he replied, 'Oh, no, I never wear an overcoat. I am always burning.' It was a fire that both drove and consumed him. Time, he knew, was short, and there was much he wanted to do. Away from the attention of others he worked hard. He had to: immediate concerns were pressing. The Poe commission needed to be completed, and he had to produce his pictures for the second *Yellow Book*. A new cover design, it had been decided, was required. Indeed, turning necessity to account, Beardsley announced that a new cover for each issue would be another of the innovations and features of the new quarterly.[15]

For his other contributions he drew on his current interests: 'Les Garçons du Café Royal', which he characterized as 'an astounding piece of decorative realism', proclaimed its provenance as well as an awareness of the graphic work of Felix Vallotton and the French artists of the Nabis School; 'The Slippers of Cinderella' had a theatrical flavour, but not so strong as that of the three mysterious, erotically fraught scenes from 'The Comedy-Ballet of Marionettes performed by the troupe of the Théâtre Impossible'. The thespian theme was completed by a new portrait of Madame Réjane. As a re-statement of principles the contents pages were retitled 'Literature' and 'Art', rather than 'Letterpress' and 'Illustration', but the clear division was undercut by the inclusion, beside the portrait, of an article about Réjane.

Each new picture was brought into the Bodley Head for inspection and admiration. A young journalist recalled walking into the Vigo Street shop one afternoon and finding Beardsley, huddled over a table with Harland and Lane, explaining his latest offering in 'quick eager sentences, with darts of long, tapering fingers, now at one part of the picture, now at another'.

Concentrating on his own work (and his own pleasure), Beardsley let his editorial duties slide. The initial commitments from Sargent, Crane, Steer and others had not yet become a definitive line-up. Harland, who was trying to paginate the new volume, grew frantic. He badgered Beardsley, but was eventually reduced to writing to Lane in triple-underlined exasperation, 'Why doesn't Aubrey send me his list [of contributors]?' It was an early but indicative instance of Harland presenting himself to Lane as the senior and responsible figure in the editorial partnership.

The pace of Aubrey's life, half stimulating leisure and half scheduled work, inevitably took a toll on his fragile health. The desire to shine was a self-imposed strain, which Beerbohm was one of the few to detect; its effects soon became clear to all. At one dinner, Max recalled, not long after the launch of *The Yellow Book*, Beardsley was 'the life and soul of the party' until, 'quite suddenly, almost in the middle of a sentence, he fell fast asleep in his chair, his narrow face as white as the gardenia in his coat.' There is a poignant vignette in the autobiography of Maude Ffoulkes. As a young woman with literary aspirations, she attended one of Mrs Gleeson White's At Homes during the summer of 1894. Wandering into an apparently empty room she settled herself on a long sofa, before noticing, at

the other end of it, 'a pale weird-looking youth', apparently wrapped in deep and not altogether pleasant reflection. To make conversation, she remarked that she hoped Mr Aubrey Beardsley was 'really coming' to the party, she wanted to see him 'because he is so much *en l'air* at present', though she feared that she would not like him.

'"And pray, why not?", remarked the pale young man.

'"Well, because I think his soul is revealed in his work. His brain must do nothing but weave tissues of beautiful wicked thoughts, for he always seems to discover the canker in the rose. Besides, I think he must be very conceited, and rightly so, though I do wish he thought a little less of his own importance and came to At Homes at a reasonable hour. I suppose he wants to 'take the stage' alone."

'"He doesn't want to do anything of the kind," said the young man, curiously stung to anger by [these] words. "I am Aubrey Beardsley, and I didn't feel well enough to turn up before, and now I'm as seedy as I can possibly be, that's why I'm sitting *here*."

'"I'm very sorry," [Miss Ffoulkes] apologised. "But you know, Mr Beardsley, that all celebrities have the reputation of doing exactly as they please."

'"Well," [Beardsley] acknowledged ungraciously. "If you weren't aware who I was, you are perfectly at liberty to express your opinion of me, but candour hurts occasionally."'

With that Beardsley rose and left. His sense of hurt at the personal encounter is telling. He relished as his artistic due the generalized opprobrium of the press, Mrs Grundy and the bourgeois; he could even accept that some individuals might not appreciate his work. But he hated not to be liked. Indeed – though he seems to have made an exception in Miss Ffoulkes's case – he generally exercised an unconscious charm to win over all who met him, even those who frankly disliked his work.[16]

Beardsley ignored the signs of his declining health; he ignored too the doctor's admonitions to rest. Life was too exciting. Perhaps the greatest excitement of the summer was the Wagner season at the

OPPOSITE 'Garçons de Café', one of six Beardsley drawings in *The Yellow Book*, Vol. II, 1894.

Theatre Royal, Drury Lane. Klafsky and Max Alvary, after their triumph of 1892, had been reunited for the occasion. In four weeks from late June to late July they performed *Die Walküre, Siegfried, Tannhäuser, Tristan und Isolde,* and *Lohengrin.* Aubrey and Mabel went to everything; when tickets were hard to get, they sat on the gallery stairs with fellow enthusiasts from 4.30 to 7.30 to secure places.

The performance of *Tannhäuser* held a particular resonance for Aubrey. He had begun a project of his own inspired by the legend of the repentant *Minnesinger.* (His plans for 'Masques' seem to have been subsumed into *The Yellow Book.*) The first hint of the new scheme came at a merry post-theatre supper that March, given by the Brandon Thomases. Among the guests were Aubrey and Mabel, several actors, and a strange figure whom Brandon Thomas introduced as the 'Weird'. The 'Weird' was a fortune-teller who had enjoyed much success in the Green Rooms of London's theatreland. He duly went round the dinner table and made several small hits. When he came to Aubrey, he 'excelled himself'. He announced that Beardsley was 'engaged on a book (sensation) that no one had yet heard about (greater sensation)'. Beardsley was astonished. 'Perfectly wonderful!', he said. 'I *am* trying to write a book, no one knows about it, I have not even told my sister, Mabel.'

It was then revealed, amid further merriment, that the soothsayer's success had been sheer luck. Brandon Thomas confessed to having coached the 'Weird' about the guests' activities; he had told him of Aubrey's connection with the impending *Yellow Book,* and this nugget had been transmuted into what seemed like a reference to the newly conceived *Tannhäuser* project. From the start, Beardsley considered it – like a Wagner opera – as a total work; he would provide not only pictures but the text. It was an attempt to reassert and make public his love of literature and his desire to write. In this, as in so many other schemes, there appears to have been an axis of encouragement running between Beardsley and Beerbohm. Max was trying to carve out a similar double path; in the wake of his literary success in *The Yellow Book,* he was contributing caricatures to the *Pall Mall Budget* and *To-Day.*

OPPOSITE 'The Wagnerites', one of four Beardsley drawings in *The Yellow Book,* Vol. III, 1894.

The Tannhäuser myth had a particular attraction for the art brigade of the nineties: the account of an artist who succumbed to the lure of the senses and finally sought forgiveness was richly suggestive. Baudelaire, Swinburne and Pater had all touched on the theme; Beardsley acknowledged the tradition and looked beyond it. In his retelling, he announced, 'the ending will be slightly altered, but will in no wise resemble Wagner's bastard version'.

The book, he was soon telling Evans, would 'astonish everybody' He was concerned that Leighton, who had expressed interest in seeing the work-in-progress, might not entirely approve, but it is unlikely that he had yet decided to make the book into the erotic − if not pornographic − fantasy it eventually became. His wildly varying descriptions of the project suggest that he had not fixed its final form. To one reporter he described it as a realistic retelling of the old German legend; to another he said, 'the book will be in verse, illustrated by twenty drawings'. Only gradually did it resolve itself into a 'rococo rendering of the tale' and then into something so risqué it could lead to prosecution and imprisonment. In its early stages, however, it could be shown, with only modest demur, to men such as Leighton and Dent. Lane, recognizing that 'Masques' would never be undertaken, was happy to accept *Venus and Tannhäuser* in its stead. The book gave a focus, if only a nominal one, for Beardsley's energies, and provided a constant among the shifting demands of his one-off commissions.[17]

The appearance of the second *Yellow Book* in July did not, of course, provoke such a storm as the first number. There was some grudging praise and some conventional abuse. The general tone of the magazine was recognized as saner, the general effect as duller. The number of staid contributors − in the literary section at least − outnumbered the more unruly representatives of the 'new school'. Beardsley was included in this muted assessment: the new cover design was adjudged not as offensive as the first; the new frontispiece was allowed to be possible. Though there was some sniping at his 'vapid and vulgar attempts at French chic', there was resigned recognition that such affectation was to be expected.

After the ephemeral caricatures in the *Sketch*, the *Morning Post* and the *Pall Mall Budget*, Sickert's full-length oil sketch of 'Aubrey Beardsley' – an angular, dandified, restless figure flitting across the page – provided a more artistic representation of the notorious art editor. This was, moreover, the first likeness published in America, and drew a comment from one critic that 'if it be a good likeness, [it] accounts for much that is eccentric in Mr Beardsley's work.' His eccentricity in the second *Yellow Book* was considered less apparent. Although the 'Comedy-Ballet of Marionettes' was not exactly applauded, its perverse narrative passed unremarked.* After the howls of protest that greeted his portrait of Mrs Patrick Campbell, that of Madame Réjane was received with something like satisfaction. One critic considered it the best likeness ever made of the 'graceful but ugly actress'. (William Archer suggested that Beardsley's success was due to Réjane's being the 'one woman in the world' who actually looked like a Beardsley drawing.)

Certainly Réjane herself saw more ugliness than grace in Beardsley's depiction; the sight of one of his portraits is said to have made her scream and burst into tears, complaining of its awful 'Cytherian grin'. Frederick Evans recognized the quality of the *Yellow Book* portrait. When the artist brought the drawing to show him, he at once offered to buy it. Beardsley accepted a large white £5 note which he tucked nonchalantly into his breast pocket. The money, unsurprisingly, had disappeared by the time he reached home; as Evans remarked, it was 'the sort of lost property that no one ever returns'.

This blasé attitude to money was part of Beardsley's pose. It was, however, supported by substantial earnings. The second number of *The Yellow Book* sold only 5000 copies and so produced no bonus for the editors. But Lane renegotiated the contract with Beardsley and Harland, doing away with royalties and giving them straight fees for their editorial work. On the financial front Beardsley also received several lucrative poster commissions. The success of the Avenue Theatre design prompted others to employ him. The publisher T. Fisher Unwin asked Beardsley to convert the 'Girl and a Bookshop'

---

* The first tableau, indeed, was deemed innocuous enough to be used, after slight amendment by the artist, as an advertisement for Gerandel's pastilles.

drawing he had bought the previous year into a coloured poster for his popular-fiction series, the Pseudonym and Autonym Libraries, and also commissioned two further designs. *To-Day* wanted to engage his services as, less expectedly, did Singer Sewing Machines.

Beardsley was delighted. He claimed to prefer poster work to both book illustration and bookplate design. He told one reporter, 'it pays well and it's interesting. I enjoy the colour.' Though he might enjoy it, he admitted to having no great care for colour, but recognized that it was essential for posters. 'I myself', he explained, 'only use flat tints, and work as if I were colouring a map, the effect aimed at being that produced by a Japanese print.' He preferred to work 'in little' and then have the design photo-mechanically enlarged. This preference was confirmed (and his workmanship revealed) when a large-scale coloured design which he had done for Unwin was accidentally thrown away at the publisher's New York office where it was thought to be a reproduction rather than the original.*

Beardsley took the trouble to crystallize his thoughts on posters in a mock-Whistlerian essay on 'The Art of the Hoarding'. It was considered for the second number of *The Yellow Book* but was placed instead in the July issue of William Heinemann's *New Review*, alongside two other pieces on poster design – one by Cheret, the other by Dudley Hardy. Beardsley's brief essay began with the neatly ambiguous assertion, 'Advertisement is an absolute necessity of modern life.' Although he was ostensibly alluding to the proclamations of soap manufacturers, there remained a suggestion that his real concern was the self-advertisement of the artist. The article worked best as a parade of wit: 'distance . . . lends enchantment to the private view'; 'the popular idea of a picture is something told in oil or writ in water'; 'our modern painter has merely to give a picture

---

* The undignified demise of this drawing perhaps inspired the comical (and surely apocryphal) legend of a discarded Beardsley poster being used to wrap washing for delivery to a Chinese laundry in Philadelphia. Mr Sam Lee, the laundry owner, rescued it because it reminded him of his native Peking. He subsequently auctioned it for US$100 to Wan Fo Li, the proprietor of the Chinese theatre in New Jersey. Mr Li exhibited it and cleared over $500 in gate money. Afterwards he sold it to a wealthy San Francisco Chinese, in front of whose house it hangs with a lamp burning before it night and day, 'as though it were powerful "joss"'. (*Westminster Gazette*, 9 August 1894/17 March 1898; *Daily Mail*, 18 March 1898.)

a good name and hang it.' The argument was slight. Although obliged to surrender the decadent position that art should be useless, Beardsley managed to adopt a paradoxical pose. 'Still,' he wrote, 'there is a general feeling that the artist who puts his art into the poster is *déclassé* – on the streets – and consequently of light character.' He, however, likened the 'poor printed [poster] left to the mercy of sunshine, soot, and shower', to an 'old fresco over an Italian church door'.

Beardsley claimed that the billboard and the sandwich-man were better settings for art than crowded galleries where a painting had to compete against 'the company of somebody else's picture' and a 'background of striped magenta paper'. The recent profusion of posters, far from disfiguring the town, had brought new beauty to its streets; telegraph wires were no longer the sole joy of the modern metropolitan's aesthetic perceptions. Of the technicalities of poster design, he said nothing, taking instead a broad Whistlerian swipe at those who would presume to teach or criticize art. The article confirmed his position as a wit if it did not reveal his views on art. But then his views were never fixed; he had no regard for consistency. And for all the strictures against conventional easel painting expressed in the *New Review* article, he never quite relinquished an ambition to be a painter, and even made an attempt to tell a tale in oil paint. Under Sickert's guidance he produced a muddied impressionistic rendering of the first tableau of the 'Comedy-Ballet of Marionettes' before abandoning it and painting on the unprimed back of the canvas a splendidly bizarre picture of a masked woman 'contemplating a dead mouse'. Neither experiment encouraged him to persevere. The canvas was stowed away and forgotten.[18]

Another of his passing ambitions was even less easy of achievement. He wanted, so he claimed, to be a 'Romantic poet'. The desire seems to have been as much symbolic as real, a wish to ally himself to the example and the image of Keats. Certainly the summer of 1894 was heavy with Keatsian echoes. On the afternoon of 16 July, Beardsley attended the unveiling of a memorial bust of Keats in Hampstead Parish Church, one of a large crowd which had gathered to celebrate the memory of a poet who, despite dying at twenty-five from tuberculosis, had confounded his self-penned epitaph that he was one 'whose name was writ on water'. Beardsley had long identified with

Keats as the image of doomed and youthful genius, and had begun to measure the probable term of his life in relation to the poet's. He told one friend, with 'the shadow of a smile', 'I shall not live much longer than did Keats'.*

The service in Hampstead must have reinforced the feeling of association. It also awakened it in the minds of others. After the ceremony Beardsley was a conspicuous figure: elegantly attired in black morning coat and silk hat, his lemon-coloured kid gloves held loosely in his hand, he stumbled, short of breath, over the graves, seeking a short-cut out of the churchyard and away from the oppressive throng. The scene seemed portentous.

Soon after the service at Hampstead, Frederick Evans made his two photographic portraits of Beardsley. Evans was at first unsure how to pose his subject, remarking facetiously, 'There's not much to be done with a face like yours . . . you're only a gargoyle, you know?' Beardsley responded by putting his hands to his face and assuming the pose of the famous Stryge on the roof of Nôtre Dame. Evans recognized the reference at once: 'That's it,' he exclaimed, and made the first exposure. The repose of the pictures conceals Beardsley's frailty. The pressures of his work and life had brought him to a point of crisis. It occurred after a particularly lively afternoon at Cambridge Street, with Beerbohm and others, when Beardsley had displayed 'even more than his usual wit and imagination, as he paced up and down the room, talking of all things, in his brisk assured manner, making his odd abrupt gestures'. When the guests had gone, Aubrey collapsed, suffering a dreadful haemorrhage. The doctor was summoned; Ellen and Mabel sat at his bedside through the night, fearing that he would not see the morning.

He survived but rest became imperative. Though he chafed at the idea, it was decided that he should leave London for a regime of country air and rustic seclusion. Friends were canvassed, advice sought, and Haslemere in Surrey decided upon. For one thing, it would be convenient if he needed to return to London on *Yellow Book* business. Accompanied by Ellen, Aubrey went down to Surrey

---

* In his last years Beardsley 'professed to hate' Keats and Rossetti. He did move from their immediate influence back to the eighteenth century, but Wilde was probably right to call this pretension 'sheer perversity'. (Vincent O'Sullivan, *Aspects of Wilde*, p. 120.)

towards the middle of August. They had taken rooms at Vale Wood Farm, and Aubrey tried to convince himself that the scenery would provide him with backgrounds for *Tannhäuser*. This conviction soon evaporated. As Ellen wrote to Ross, Aubrey 'took a dislike to the place directly he got there and wanted to rush back to town at once'. When Ross tried to cheer him with references to 'Dame Nature', he replied, 'Damn Nature'. With difficulty, his mother persuaded him from day to day to stay on for two weeks. But after he had sunk into a deep depression she relented and they returned to London.

The move lifted his gloom and stimulated his fancy, but was not beneficial to his health. There was soon 'a slight return of haemorrhage'. Despite this, Aubrey was left alone at Cambridge Street for most of September. Mabel was away; she had secured her first professional engagement as Lady Stutfield in a touring company production of *A Woman of No Importance*. Ellen, with the hapless Vincent, went back to Brighton for a fortnight's holiday.

For Aubrey there was no holiday. The cycle of quarterly publication was ever-turning, and his contributions and editorial selections for the third *Yellow Book* were already falling due.[19]

The status of *The Yellow Book* and Beardsley's position within it was confirmed by the next literary excitement of the hour. On 15 September a novel appeared provocatively entitled *The Green Carnation*. Its author remained anonymous, its two main characters – under their fictional names of Esmé Amaranth and Lord Reggie Hastings – were clearly recognizable as Oscar Wilde and Lord Alfred Douglas. Though framed as a conventional romance, and brightened by cod-Wildean epigrams, the story detailed vividly, between the lines, the homoerotic infatuation which held Wilde in Douglas's thrall.

Beardsley received a passing mention. To those with the *clef* to the *roman* something of Wilde's piqued fascination for the art editor of *The Yellow Book* was discernible in Mr Amaranth's decision to stay at home and read the latest issue of the '*Yellow Disaster*'; 'I want to see,' he declares, 'Mr Aubrey Beardsley's idea of the Archbishop of Canterbury. He has drawn him sitting in a wheelbarrow in the garden of Lambeth Palace, with . . . the motto *J'y suis, j'y reste*. I believe he has on a black mask. Perhaps it is to conceal the likeness.' For the wider public, the passage confirmed the assumed connection between Wilde, Beardsley and *The Yellow Book*.

It was soon revealed that *The Green Carnation* had been written by Robert Hichens, a young music journalist on the outer fringes of Wilde's circle. Its borrowed wit and knowing air made it a popular success. For those in the inner circle there was some anxiety that it revealed too much: that it stirred up the rumours of homosexual intrigue which already eddied about Wilde and Douglas, and gave ammunition to Douglas's homophobic father, the Marquess of Queensberry, who was bent on breaking up the association between his son and Oscar Wilde. Many contemporary commentators, how-ever, did not read the effeminacy displayed by Esmé Amaranth and Lord Reggie as homosexuality. It was seen, rather, as a phenomenon of the age, which found its concomitant in the increasing masculinity of women. The sexes, it seemed to the *fin-de-siècle* Jeremiahs, were in a state of flux, and were flowing together; Beardsley's drawings were readily taken as both a description and a reflection of this deplorable trend. The hermaphrodites and androgynes of the *Morte Darthur* chapter headings and the *Bon-Mots* grotesques did belong to a world of sexual confusion, but these drew far less comment than his depictions of contemporary women.

Although the link in the public mind between Beardsley and the 'New Woman' established by his cover design for *Keynotes* continued, there was tension in the association. During the course of 1894 a new type emerged: the 'Beardsley Woman'. His vision of woman-hood, though apparently new, was essentially ancient. Certainly it was very different from that of Egerton and other female writers of the period. Both were threatening. The New Woman held her power through education, through control of property, through her ability to use a typewriter or ride a bicycle. The Beardsley Woman wielded her power through sex. She was intelligent (he often showed her with a book in her hand), she had some control over her resources (she was always stylishly dressed), yet beneath the gloss of contempor-ary chic she remained essentially a *femme fatale*. The basis of her power was sex.

Sex was an obsession for Beardsley. His friends, on no very sound scientific basis, ascribed this to his medical condition. His theoretical knowledge, derived from literature and art, was prodigious. His practical experience was considerably less. Frank Harris, in his famously unreliable memoir, *My Life and Loves*, claimed that Aubrey had once told him, 'It's usually a fellow's sister who gives him his first lessons in sex. I know it was Mabel ... who first taught me.' For all its improbability, this passage has, over the years, fuelled much happy speculation about an incestuous relationship between Aubrey and his sister. There have been strained attempts to link the foetus motif in Aubrey's work with a putative abortion of Mabel's, the sad result, it is suggested, of their illicit union. No evidence exists to support such theories. If Harris's anecdote has any basis in fact, it is more likely to concern the general biological information that an elder sister might pass on to a near-contemporary brother.[20]

Whether Aubrey was a virgin at twenty-two is impossible to know. The accidents of his life and his illness seemed to preclude any full and satisfactory relationship: as a fragile demi-invalid living with his parents and sister, his opportunities were limited. There have been attempts to link his name with Ada Leverson's but Mrs Leverson's arch, flirtatious manner ensured that she was credited with numerous non-existent liaisons, of which the Beardsley connection was probably one. Emotionally Beardsley seems to have developed a sense of self-sufficiency and containment. The images of the hermaphrodite and of the cross-dresser perhaps engaged his imagination because they suggested a parallel completeness. The searing, highly charged operas of Wagner, with their themes of incest and lust, offered him contact with a world of sexual emotion. It was widely assumed that he 'hastened' his physical decline 'by masturbation'. The pathology is doubtful and the imputation of self-abuse, though highly plausible, must remain uncertain.

Beardsley was well aware that his sex life was the subject of speculation. On occasion he referred to himself ironically as the 'solitaire', an epithet he used also for Titurel de Schentefleur, the *chef d'orchestre* in his story of Venus and Tannhäuser: 'What were [Titurel's] amatory tastes, no one in the Venusberg could tell. He generally passed for a virgin [the MS also suggests, as a variant, 'he generally passed as being chaste'] and Cathos had nicknamed him "The Solitaire".' The description is deftly ambiguous.

The vast London population of professional and semi-professional prostitutes – met with on the promenade at the Empire, in the cafés and bars of Piccadilly, on the pavements of the Strand – might have been a possible constituency. Aubrey was fascinated by them. He startled the office boy at the Bodley Head by enthusing about a 'wanton' he had just seen in Regent Street, 'expatiating upon her visible, and speculating upon her invisible, charms in embarrassing detail.' However, this monologue merely convinced the young clerk that Beardsley's dissoluteness was largely mental.

What was in Beardsley's mind, however, was soon transmuted into art. It was an established tenet of both the decadent and realist schools that art could treat of forbidden subjects and that no realm of human experience should be left untouched. Sex uncloyed by sentimental idealism represented a terra incognita to be explored: sex fired the poetic impressionism of Arthur Symons and the more overheated experiments of Theodore Wratislaw. Sex drove forward the bleak short stories of Hubert Crackanthorpe, and stood behind Sickert's paintings of deshabillé models in unfurnished rooms. In his drawings of women alone on the streets at night, or unaccompanied at café tables (in 'Les Passades', 'Night Piece' and 'Waiting') Beardsley approached the subject directly. But for the most part his tactics were less obvious. Sex infused his subjects with a palpable but mysterious aura, and during *The Yellow Book* period his subjects were almost exclusively women. There was sex in the confident pose, the lazy droop of the eye, the pert flare of a nostril or the full curve of a mouth, proclaiming its presence and its power.

This was what made his drawings so shocking: the Victorians had devoted decades to obscuring and denying the power of sex. In recent decades there had been constant attacks on their pudic fastness, but direct assault could be met directly. Beardsley's campaign was insidious: sex pullulated from every stroke of his pen. It was sex allied not to conventional beauty but to unconventional ugliness. Beardsley's creations were perceived by an alarmed public as ugly and bizarre. Some critics pretended that this arose merely from the artist's inability to draw people. The thick-lipped 'Beardsley mouth' came in for particular censure as being 'inexpressive and ugly' and anatomically improbable; it had, the wags suggested, been borrowed from Africa and applied incongruously to the Anglo-Saxon face. Beardsley's handling of other features was not much better regarded. One newspaper described an imagined gathering of Beardsley's men and women: 'some of the ladies have not brought their faces with them, while the larger number of men have had their noses unscrewed and their foreheads duplicated. Extension necks are conspicuous and eyes are cut on the bias . . . The belle of the occasion wears forty pounds of black hair in an alligator-skin valise suspended from her ears, and has elbows in her swanlike throat . . . The general complexion is that of scrambled eggs.'[21]

A more general view considered the ugliness of Beardsley's figures as the outward and visible sign of their sinfulness, and to the Victorian mind a picture of sin must be either a warning against it or an inducement to it. Few hesitated to place Beardsley's work in the second category. The disillusioned Burne-Jones went so far as to denounce his former protégé's *Yellow Book* drawings as 'immoral'. Even Beardsley's allies recognized the supposedly connected elements of sex, ugliness and evil in his work. Various attempts were made to explain or excuse their presence. Both Vallance and Evans were bemused that someone in his early twenties could produce the 'monstrous images' he did. Evans tried to account for it by the theory of 'demonic obsession', which Wilkinson used to account for the images created by Blake. Vallance likened him to Walter Pater's description of La Gioconda, who betrays 'a vampire's hoary veteranship of vice' despite her age. Rothenstein and Beerbohm set it down to a youthful – and not unnatural – desire to shock. Yeats evolved an elaborate theory of 'victimage', suggesting that Beardsley, after the manner of a medieval saint, took on 'the knowledge of sin' to enable 'persons who had never heard his name to recover innocence'. A more common line was that Beardsley, in depicting the ugliness of evil, was satirizing it. He was proclaimed a modern Hogarth.

Beardsley denied such arguments. When it was put to him that his work was 'inspired by rage against iniquity', he replied merely, 'If it were so inspired the work would be in no way different.' He claimed that his drawings were not satires upon life but 'life itself':

'What I am trying to do', he told one interviewer, 'is show life as it really is.' He admitted that his vision was personal and idiosyncratic: 'I see everything in a grotesque way. When I go to the theatre, for example, things shape themselves before my eyes just as I draw them – the people on the stage, the footlights, the queer faces and garb of the audience in the boxes and stalls. They all seem weird and strange to me. Things have always impressed me in this way.'

Once when Ellen complained mildly of one of his drawings, 'Oh, Aubrey, this is dreadful', he replied, 'Vice is dreadful, and should be made or depicted so.' It was the hypocrisy about vice not vice itself which he sought to confront. Mabel told Yeats that her brother 'hated the people who denied the existence of evil, and being so young he filled his pictures with evil. He had a passion for reality.' His images shocked because they were true, and truth was usually denied. 'Of course [people] are furious,' he explained to Ellen, 'they hate to see their darling sins.' People, he claimed, *were* 'ugly', life *was* 'offensive'. The 'harlot' was the representative type of the age, the subject of plays, novels, paintings, and his own modest drawings. 'She fills the public eye,' he said. 'Centuries ago it was the Madonna . . . but today the old Madonna has become the new Magdalen. It is she whom I see and whom I try to describe.'

He allowed that the mood of his current work 'disappointed and disgusted' some, and even announced that the mood was rapidly drawing to a close, but he defended his right to express it while it lasted. The 'true artist should be given every liberty of expression'.

Beardsley's arguments in defence of his art were not without qualifications and inconsistencies. The Beardsley Mouth, the ugliness of which he disputed, was, he thought, technically interesting as design and aesthetically pleasing as a mouth. 'The beauty' of his technique was that he drew the mouth 'with one line': 'The idea is, I think, my own.' As to the mouth itself, he said, 'Let them criticize. It's my mouth not theirs.'

On another tack – asserting the claims of formal beauty over moral worth – he claimed that prostitutes and loungers were suitable subjects because they were the best-dressed people in London. And although he loudly disclaimed the title of satirist, he does seem to have been intrigued by the irony that proscriptive art allowed, even demanded, the detailed elaboration of the evils it denounced. In his mock introduction to *Venus and Tannhäuser* he pretended to excuse the 'venery' of his tale on the ground that it led to 'the great contrition' of the story's hero in the last chapters. It was, perhaps, a similar delight in the double standard that drew him to Juvenal and prompted his improbable plan to illustrate the book of Leviticus.[22]*

The appearance, in October, of the third number of *The Yellow Book* was a fresh challenge to the critics. It was the first to be produced in name, not merely in fact, under the sole imprint of John Lane. By the end of September the growing rift between Lane and Elkin Mathews had been formalized by a 'divorce'. The list had been divided between the partners, with Lane inevitably taking *The Yellow Book*, *Salome*, the Keynotes series; indeed all the projects with which Beardsley was connected. Mathews kept the premises at Vigo Street, but with unbusinesslike generosity gave the Bodley Head sign and name to Lane. He was horrified when his erstwhile partner promptly took up the lease of a shop across the way. It was from these premises that Volume III was issued.

It marked an advance in boldness. Most of the more extreme members of the perceived decadent clique were represented: Arthur Symons with his poem 'Credo' and Wratislaw's 'Salome of St James'; Ernest Dowson, whose lyric 'Cynara' was establishing itself as the most eloquent expression of *maladie fin-de-siècle*, contributed a short story. Lionel Johnson offered a precious disquisition on the pleasure of a poet's life within the ivory tower; there was a grim short story from Hubert Crackanthorpe and another facetious essay from Max Beerbohm. The most-discussed literary contribution was John Davidson's 'Ballad of a Nun', a poetic adaptation of a medieval legend in which a nun deserts the sheltered cloister to worship 'sinful man'. Among the 'Art' was Steer's 'Skirt Dancing' and Sickert's 'Charley's Aunt'.

---

* It has even been claimed – albeit by a doubtful authority – that Beardsley made a (now lost) illustration to Leviticus, chapter XVIII, verse 23 – 'Neither shalt thou lie with any beast to defile thyself therewith; neither shall any woman stand before a beast to lie down thereto: it is confusion.' Jack Smithers, *The Early Life and Vicissitudes of Jack Smithers* (London, 1939) p. 39.

Despite these distractions, it became increasingly clear that Beardsley was the dominant presence. The *Artist* claimed that 'to most Mr Aubrey Beardsley is the *Yellow Book*', while *The Studio*, more cautiously, averred that 'the Art of *The Yellow Book* is the art of Aubrey Beardsley'. Even his allies at *The Studio*, however, while acknowledging that he was probably the best illustrator then at work and praising the 'powerful expression' of his line and the 'boldness' with which he deployed his masses of black and white, found fault with his subject matter and his attitude. His one text, Gleeson White lamented, was 'Frippery and Frailty', his abiding tone one of degradation. Humanity was displayed always at its ugliest and most bestial. In Volume III, besides the now expected new cover design and title page, Beardsley gave four readings from the book of 'Frippery and Frailty': 'La Dame aux Camélias', a 'Portrait of Himself', 'Lady Gold's Escort' and 'The Wagnerites'. Of these, he recorded that the last two – extreme essays in the use of black – were 'particularly noticed'. They were not, however, particularly liked.*

Beardsley had intended to continue his portrait series with a drawing of Lillian Russell, the American singer, starring at the Lyceum in *The Queen of Brilliants*, a musical comedy adapted from the German by Brandon Thomas. But for some reason the drawing was never completed, and, in what appears to have been a fallback position, he reused a picture which had already appeared as 'Girl at her Toilet' in the April issue of *St Paul's*. He now retitled it 'La Dame aux Camélias', neatly allying it to the two theatrical productions of Dumas' play in London that summer, one starring Bernhardt, the other Eleanora Duse.

The 'Portrait of Himself' provoked much irritation. After the startlingly immediate Sickert portrait in the previous number, this was self-advertisement through self-concealment. Beardsley, his head

---

* Sickert had a theory that there was a 'law of aesthetic satisfaction that may be stated thus: where an effect is obtained by placing black lines, patterns, patches or dots on a white ground, the pleasure of the observer begins to be lessened as soon as the amount of black, being the pattern, tends to exceed the amount of white being the ground.' He disliked the 'Wagnerites' on this account, and discouraged Beardsley from continuing his essays in this line. (W. Sickert, 'The Future of Engraving' in *A Free House*, pp. 262–3.)

swathed in a large turban, was almost entirely hidden by the bed-clothes of a canopied bed. Adding a further note of mystery, or mystification, an inscription in the top left-hand corner read, 'Par les Dieux Jumeaux tous les monstres ne sont pas en Afrique'. The reviewer in the *Artist* called it an impertinence, and lamented that Beardsley was wasting his talent in abandoning the 'wall-poster for the four-poster'. *Punch* labelled the picture 'Portrait of the Artist in Bed-lam', and Owen Seaman provided a sub-Rossettian verse accompaniment which began:

> Under a canopy as dark-hued as – well
> Consult the Bilious Book page 51 –
> Lies pallid Whiskersley's presentiment done
> By Whiskersley's own weird unearthly spell.

Such squibs were now to be expected. The new *Yellow Book*, how-ever, was not without its surprises. Together with the art contri-butions of Sickert, Steer, and George Thomson, there was a severe classically drawn profile of 'Mantegna' ascribed to Philip Broughton, and a slight impressionistic sketch of a woman 'From a Pastel' by Albert Foschter. Both works and artists were the inventions of the art editor.[23]

Beardsley watched with delight as his critics rushed to acclaim his inventions. Although Beerbohm's recollection of a reviewer urging Beardsley to 'study and profit by the sound and scholarly draughts-manship of which Mr Philip Broughton furnishes us another example in his familiar manner', is perhaps too good to be true, the fiction was slight. The *Saturday Review*, after complaining of Beardsley's 'freakish' contributions, pronounced favourably on the 'Mantegna' ('a drawing of merit') and 'From a Pastel' ('clever study'). The *National Observer*, the *St James's Gazette* and others blundered down the same impasse, to Beardsley's gratification. A fellow artist who visited him at the time said, 'I never, before or after, saw him in such a happy frame of mind.'

His drawings were inescapable during the autumn of 1894. Apart from *The Yellow Book*, they could be seen in *To-Day*, *St Paul's* and *The Idler*. The 'gargoyle' portrait of him by Frederick Evans was one of the successes of the Photographers' Salon in October, and many of his *Morte Darthur* drawings and *Bon-Mots* grotesques appeared in

an exhibition of black-and-white art put on by J. M. Dent at the Royal Institute Galleries. They provided a graphic record of the speed of his development and the breadth of his stylistic range.

At the end of October, London's first major show of posters was mounted at the Westminster Aquarium by an entrepreneur, dealer and paper manufacturer named Edward Bella. The International Artistic Pictorial Poster Exhibition was a celebration of the newest and most vital contemporary art form; some 200 posters and poster designs were on view, the majority from France. Toulouse-Lautrec, who had overseen the French selection (and came over for the exhibition), was represented, as were Cheret, Grasset, Willette, Bonnard and Steinlein. Among the English contributors were Crane, Greiffenhagen, Hardy, Raven-Hill, Steer, and Beardsley. The Avenue Theatre poster and the design for Unwin's Pseudonym and Autonym Libraries were prominently displayed; they were already achieving the status of classics. *The Studio* considered Beardsley 'at his best' in such work.

The exhibition enhanced his status in France. Jules Roques, critic for the *Courrier Français*, came to see the show and was full of praise for his work. He also sought out the artist and gathered some material for a brief profile for the *Courrier*'s '*Artistes Anglais*' series. It was a propitious meeting: the beginning of a close association between Beardsley and the French periodical. Nor was Roques the only foreign visitor at Cambridge Street. A young German art-historian, Julius Meier-Graefe, also came, perhaps to solicit interest in a new art periodical he was planning. Beardsley's fame was spreading rapidly, and so was his influence.

The strength and extreme individuality of Beardsley's style set him apart; some of his young competitors in black and white resented his success and derided his genius. R. A. Bell, however, who was already working in a similar vein of post-Pre-Raphaelite pen and ink when he encountered Beardsley, admitted to having borrowed much from the younger artist, but on his immediate *confrères* – Sickert, Steer and Rothenstein – his influence was less tangible and he received as much as he gave; pen and ink was not their medium and they could take little from the technical side of his art.

OPPOSITE 'Portrait of Himself' from *The Yellow Book*, Vol. III, 1894.

His distinctiveness, however, made him a beacon for art students, amateurs and parodists. Competition entries printed in *The Studio* each month revealed the strength of his influence, and the difficulty of handling it successfully. The results were seldom happy. One of the very few artists to use Beardsley's influence successfully was the American, Bill Bradley. Although his early work occasionally borders on pastiche, he was not 'entirely dominated by Mr Beardsley's intensely personal art'.[24]

Beardsley's bold simplification of form was readily misconstrued as simplicity of method. To a Victorian public which instinctively revered diligent workmanship, Beardsley seemed guilty of sharp practice. This, of course, was a line of critical attack that had run since Ruskin had accused Whistler of flinging a pot of paint in the public's face. It was used against all the impressionists of the NEAC, but with the advance of Beardsley's fame and the development of his *Yellow Book* style the fire was concentrated increasingly upon the young art editor. When a pavement artist was sentenced for vagrancy at Wandsworth police court on the grounds that his 'pictures' were 'mere meaningless smudges of chalk', a newspaper satirist penned an ode consoling the unfortunate artist with the suggestion that his 'black patch and a couple of white smears . . . Aubrey Beardsley would delight'; and with the thought that 'soon each genius of the Yellow Book will haste to call you fellow'.

The deceptive simplicity of Beardsley's method also provoked *Punch* to produce an 'Art Recipe', purporting to explain 'How It Is Done':

> Take a lot of black triangles,
> Some amorphous blobs of red;
> Just a sprinkling of queer spangles,
> An ill-drawn Medusa head,
> Some red locks in Gorgon tangles,
> And a scarlet sunshade spread:
> Take a 'portière' quaint and spotty,
> Take a turn-up nose or two;
> The loose lips of one 'gone dotty',
> A cheese-cutter chin, askew . . .
> Take an hour-glass waist, in section,

Shoulders hunched up camel wise;
Give a look of introspection
(Or a squint) to two black eyes . . .

There were many who were delighted to stir these ingredients to produce parodies of Beardsley's art.* The Westminster Aquarium exhibition even included a spoof poster for the Oxford University production of W. S. Gilbert's *Pygmalion and Galatea*. *Punch* was seldom without a Beardsley parody from the pen of E. T. Reed or Linley Sambourne. Indeed few artists can have been lampooned so often, or so frequently rechristened: 'Mortarthurio Whiskersley', 'Danbrey Beardless', 'Awfully Weirdly', 'Daubaway Weirdsley', 'Weirdsley Daubrey' – the names rolled on.

This parallel career in derision, though sometimes irksome, provided another avenue for Beardsley's fame. It assured his position as the most conspicuous exponent of the 'New Art'. The work of his more strictly impressionist contemporaries was less easily distinguishable, less easily parodied and less easily reproduced. Sickert, for example, although accounted a radical in art quite on a par with Beardsley, received not infrequent mentions in *Punch* but was never accorded the glory of a pastiche picture.[25]

Early in November, Aubrey suffered another debilitating haemorrhage. Dr Symes Thompson recommended his immediate removal to Dr Grindrod's hydropathic clinic in the wooded hills above Malvern. Beardsley struggled against the prescription; he hated to be away from London, but his doctor was adamant. On 14 November Ellen took the invalid to Paddington and handed him over to Dr Grindrod. He was very depressed at parting. Sitting in his third-class railway carriage opposite the doctor he looked like 'a little white mouse

* The American work ethic was affronted by Beardsley's dramatically pared-down style. Several satirical poems touched on this: one told of 'Jim Smears', a rude yokel who cleaned his paint brushes on a barn door and then sold the accidental result to a city-type who took it for a Beardsley poster. (*Echo*, 3, 1895, p. 224.) Another oft-reprinted ditty ran: 'Said a Beardsley boy to a Bradley girl/Whom he met on a poster blue:/"I haven't an idea who I am,/But who the deuce are you?"/Said the Bradley girl to the Beardsley boy:/"I'll tell you what I think;/I came into being one night last week/When the cat tripped over the ink."' (*Clack Book*, 2, 1896, p. 49.)

caught in a trap'.* His distress was possibly caused as much by his
prospective cure as by his advancing illness. The doctors were still
pronouncing favourably on his overall condition, suggesting that
there was no deep-seated disease, and that total rest would provide
a complete return to health.

Rest, however, was anathema to Beardsley, and he needed
distraction from the miseries of the Malvern regime. 'Pity me,'
he wrote to Lane, 'with nothing but cold baths and mustard plas-
ters and scenery all around me.' Although he was not supposed
to work, he spent much of his time 'moping and worrying'
about his *Venus and Tannhäuser* story and was soon working up
a 'picture of Venus feeding her pet unicorns'. He also managed to
produce a 'chaste' and elegant cover design for Lane's forthcoming edition of *Sappho*, but these small acts of defiance were few.
Ellen's anxiety that he would 'rush home in about a week and say
he couldn't stand it' was not realized, but he did not stay beyond
a month. And even after his submission to Dr Grindrod's mustard-
plaster regime, his health remained delicate. He accepted an invitation
from Lane to go and stay over Christmas at St Mary's Abbey, beside
Lake Windermere. The house belonged to Lane's friends, the Barnards, who had urged Lane to bring a friend, or friends, for the
festive season.†

Although over 200 miles from London, Windermere was readily
accessible by train. And St Mary's Abbey, despite its romantically
medieval name, was a large and comfortable house. A studio had
been set apart for Beardsley so that his work would not come to 'a

---

* It is intriuging that within weeks of Beardsley making a painting of 'A Woman
regarding a dead mouse' his mother should be regarding him as a 'mouse caught in a
trap'.
† In his account of Beardsley and *The Yellow Book*, Lane says that Beerbohm and the
poet William Watson were also in the party, but a letter of 17 November 1920 at
Princeton shows that Lane asked Professor Barnard for a reminder as to who had been
there. Barnard dated the visit erroneously to 'the summer or autumn of 1894' and said,
'Present, I believe, yourself, Beardsley, Max Beerbohm and Watson.' Although Lane
adopted this account, merely moving the occasion to Christmas, Barnard's memory
seems to have been faulty on this point too (as well it might after twenty-five years).
Beerbohm and Watson *were* at Windermere with Lane and the Barnards for Easter 1897,
as a letter from Beerbohm to Reggie Turner makes clear. It is probable that Beardsley
was Lane's only guest in December 1894.

standstill'. There was, he lamented, 'a tremendous amount of old as well as new work to get through'. His promised bookplate for Evans was still not done. And he had rashly agreed to produce one for Dent too. His spirit of goodwill towards his various friends also led him to moot the idea of illustrating Edmund Gosse's 1892 fantasia, *The Secret of Narcisse*, and he had gone so far as to clear the matter with Heinemann, Gosse's publisher.

Beardsley made an excellent impression on his hosts. Professor Barnard remembered him with affection as 'excellent company and an especially charming guest'. He was, moreover, 'of all the art people' who visited St Mary's Abbey, the only one to recognize the Barnards' collection of Constantin Guys drawings for what it was. Guys, a refugee from France in 1842, had been engaged to teach French to Barnard's mother and uncle and had left a body of his drawings to the family. Guys, as the subject of Baudelaire's seminal essay on art, dandyism, and the anti-natural, 'The Painter of Modern Life', was a key figure to Beardsley, who perhaps considered himself The Draughtsman of Modern Life. On seeing the drawings, he had impressed his host at once by exclaiming: 'Oh, these are by Guys!' – a feat not achieved 'even [by] York Powell'. Beardsley, it seems, pressed home his advantage, and persuaded Professor Barnard to allow him to reproduce some of the pictures in a future *Yellow Book*. The fourth number of the periodical was even then on the point of going to press. Harland, left in London, was guiding it along the critical path. He wrote on the eve of Christmas to assure the Windermere party that the 'pull' of Beardsley's picture 'The Repentance of Mrs . . .' looked fine. Beardsley, meanwhile, was in the studio putting the finishing touches to 'A Frontispiece to Juvenal', which was going to be a special fold-out page. In what seems to have been a spirit of mischief, he wrote to Elkin Mathews asking him to look out and send an 'early edition of Gifford's translation' of the Roman satirist – for reference purposes.

Amid the work and the festivity, he made a point of attending the nearby church 'regularly and devoutly'. Perhaps his recent illness had recalled him to a deeper concern for spiritual matters, or perhaps it was merely habit. The rector, Canon Crewdsen, for a long time afterwards did not fail to make enquiries after 'that devout youth'.

For all its comforts, however, Beardsley's stay at Windermere was brief. By the end of December he was back in London, celebrating the arrival of the new year at Cambridge Street.

As a final confirmation of the year's achievements, the Christmas supplement of *Punch* carried an elaborately worked cartoon of 'Britannia à la Beardsley' by 'Our Yellow Decadent'. The drawing (by E. T. Reed) was as much homage as parody. Britannia was transformed into the image of the Beardsley Woman, with 'turn-up nose', 'loose lips', 'cheese-cutter chin' and 'hour-glass waist'. She sat, beneath heavily tasselled swags, proudly surveying the Channel (or, perhaps, looking to France for inspiration). Beardsley had stamped himself on the nation's psyche as well as the nation's symbol.[26]

CHAPTER VII

'A Declaration of War'

EARLY IN 1895 Max Beerbohm wrote to Ada Leverson recalling, with cod nostalgia, the distant days of the year just passed. 'What fun we had and how long ago it does seem. I feel so old . . . Younger men, new ideas have come into being since the days of Aubrey Beardsley. I don't profess to keep pace with them.' Beerbohm's tone was archly ironical, but the valedictory note about 'the days of Aubrey Beardsley' was truer than he knew. The extraordinary pre-eminence Beardsley had achieved during 1894 was about to be abruptly and dramatically curtailed.

On the surface all seemed set fair for another year of bourgeois-baiting, newspaper attention and artistic achievement. The fourth *Yellow Book* appeared in January and provoked the usual outraged comment. One picture in particular, 'The Mysterious Rose Garden', depicting a naked woman being addressed, if not propositioned, by a wing-slippered messenger, produced a 'peculiar feeling of revolt and horror among the art gentlemen of the Press'. Beardsley took great pleasure in proclaiming his innocence: the drawing, he explained, was 'the first of a series of biblical illustrations, and represent[ed] nothing more or less than the Annunciation'.

In *Punch*, accompanying a sustained spoof of *The Yellow Book*'s

OPPOSITE 'The Abbé', 1895.

233

literary contents by Ada Leverson,* Linley Sambourne pastiched the
'Frontispiece for Juvenal' as 'A Puzzle Picture to preface Juvenile
Poems, or nothing in particular'. In place of the monkey footmen
carrying a sedan chair in the original, Sambourne had Beardsley
dressed in an elaborate lace frock, pulling a cartload of leering harlots
past a billboard advertising *A Doll's House*. The sides of the cart were
emblazoned with notices for *The Yellow Book* as published by 'The
Bogey Head'. The cartoon confirmed (if confirmation were necessary) that Beardsley was the quarterly's guiding spirit and most out-
rageous representative.[1]

On other fronts too Beardsley's reputation was growing. His covers
for the expanding Keynotes series began to establish a personal style
and to draw notice. He gave a well-received and much-discussed
lecture on Art at the home of the Annan Bryces in Bryanston Square.
His drawings were being reproduced on a regular basis in the *Courrier
Français*, and an article on him appeared in the Italian art journal,
Emporium. His work was included in the second salon of La Libre
Esthétique, and he also exhibited a drawing of Réjane at the Glasgow
Institute of Fine Arts. There were plans afoot for a trip to America.
Lane had been quick to recognize the enormous commercial possi-
bilities of the US market. He was impressed with the sales achieved
by Copeland & Day, and was planning a visit to assess the viability
of an office of the Bodley Head in the States. He proposed that
Beardsley should accompany him; a sea-crossing would do him good.

There would be plenty of scope for fun: Beerbohm was already
there, travelling with his brother's theatre company in the unlikely
capacity of 'secretary'; there might be a chance of meeting up with
his old friends, Cochran and Scotson-Clark. There would, too, be
the chance for self-promotion. Wilde's American lecture tour of 1882
was Beardsley's proposed model: he planned to lecture on 'Italian
Art' and 'Ugliness' and even prepared some witticisms ready for
departure; when he was assured that the Americans would make
much of him, he replied, 'I hope to make much of them.' News of

---

* She claimed, in a parody of Beerbohm's essay '1880', that 'Max Meerboom' had
been 'impelled' to a study of 1894 on seeing 'a sketch of a lady with a Mask on, playing
the piano in a Corn field, in a low dress, with two lighted candles, and signed "Aubrey
Weirdsley" '.

the proposed visit was greeted with excitement by the American press. Scotson-Clark penned a sympathetic account of his old school-friend in the *Bookbuyer*, assuring Americans that they need not be alarmed at Beardsley's approach; his manners were excellent, he had 'the good sense to be modest when talking of himself and his work', had no 'conceit', and was generally 'one of the most delightful companions'. Notices appeared in the east coast press and – in a fine display of New World materialism – there was much candid speculation about Beardsley's earnings. American art students, it was announced, had become 'infected with Beardsleyism'.[2]

On 3 January 1895 Aubrey and Mabel were conspicuous in the Leversons' box at the Haymarket for the first night of Wilde's *An Ideal Husband*. It was a gala occasion; the Prince of Wales was there. The fashion correspondent for *The Lady* noted 'with special pleasure and a good deal of curiosity, Miss Beardsley, the sister of the distinguished artist of *The Yellow Book*, resplendent in a pale mauve gown trimmed with bunches of pink heliotrope'.

The play's plot centred upon a successful man whose life concealed a dark and potentially devastating secret. To the company sitting in the Leversons' box, the resonance between the play's storyline and the playwright's situation was obvious, though in the context of the moment it added only a *frisson* of irony to proceedings. Certainly the majority of the audience was unaware of the double life Wilde led; the play was a great success. Within six weeks Wilde had capped even this triumph. *The Importance of Being Earnest* opened at the St James's Theatre on 14 February. Once again Aubrey and Mabel were in the Leversons' party. The night was bitterly cold, with flurries of snow, but the theatre was all brightness, glitter and warmth. Wilde had commanded that his friends should wear lily-of-the-valley as a 'souvenir' of Bosie, who was away in Algeria. It is unlikely that Aubrey complied.

He could scarcely fail to be amused by the comedy, but found Wilde increasingly irritating. Success and the tyranny of Lord Alfred Douglas had made the playwright coarse. At the end of Act II, Wilde appeared in the Leversons' box – fat, bejewelled and flushed with success. Seeing Aubrey and his sister together he remarked, with more imagination than tact, 'What a contrast the two are: Mabel a daisy, Aubrey the most monstrous of orchids.' After the play the Leverson party went on to supper at Willis's, a restaurant so fashionable it had been mentioned in the play. Wilde did not join them. Beardsley, however, almost certainly learnt from Mrs Leverson something of the concealed drama of the evening: how the Marquess of Queensberry, father of Lord Alfred Douglas, had planned to disrupt the performance; how Oscar had cancelled his ticket and barred him from the theatre. Perhaps he even learnt that the Marquess, disappointed in his attempts to gain admission, had left a large bouquet of vegetables for Wilde at the stage door.[3]

Beardsley suffered a disappointment of his own. His plans for America collapsed; his health, it became clear, could not support the exertion. Lane would travel instead with Richard Le Gallienne. Before Lane's departure Beardsley designed an invitation card for a 'smoke' which the publisher held in his rooms in Albany on 22 February. He was, of course, one of the fashionable literary throng that attended.

He found a greater relief from his disappointment – and an assuagement too for his irritation with Wilde – in a new project he began at this time. Brandon Thomas had produced a triple bill of short plays prior to *Charley's Aunt*; one of the three had worn less well than the others and Thomas suggested that he and Beardsley collaborate on a play to replace it. Beardsley was thrilled. It was decided that the piece should be 'a skit on the artistic affectations of the day'. Thomas mapped out a 'slight' plot-line which they could embroider together, adding details and dialogue. The costumes and scenery were to be designed by Beardsley.

There were frequent working sessions at the Brandon Thomases' flat, and Mrs Brandon Thomas recalled that she had 'never . . . seen a play written under such conditions. There was no privacy about it. Mabel and I were admitted to the study and every line was received with shrieks of laughter from us all.' The four of them talked 'of nothing but the play'.

Although satirizing contemporary culture, the play was penned along stylized lines, related to the stylizations of Beardsley's art. He wrote to Thomas about a possible title: 'Since the keynote of my pictures is pose & attitude, why not call the play "ATTITUDE" – & the characters "POSERS".' The letter ended excitedly, 'I long to have another talk with you . . . I have 1 or 2 ideas.'[4]

The ideas were probably never heard. On to the scene of animated endeavour at Cadogan Gardens exploded the news of Oscar Wilde's libel action against the Marquess of Queensberry. Queensberry, thwarted at the St James's Theatre, had left a card at Wilde's club, addressed with reckless disregard for spelling but close understanding of the limits of libel: 'To Oscar Wilde posing somdomite'. Harassed beyond measure by this fresh insult, Wilde was persuaded (by Ross and Douglas) to begin proceedings for libel, and Queensberry was duly arrested and charged on 2 March. His trial began on 3 April. By that time the Marquess and his team of private detectives had found several witnesses – stable lads, valets, hotel porters and an erstwhile office boy from the Bodley Head – willing to testify that Wilde had had sex with them. Wilde's case collapsed after two days; Queensberry was acquitted, and the matter was hurried before the Public Prosecutor. Wilde was arrested that evening at the Cadogan Hotel, and charged under the Criminal Law Amendment Act with more than twenty counts of gross indecency with young men. He was denied bail and sent to Holloway Prison to await trial. He was held there for three weeks.

Against the lurid background of these much-publicized events, Beardsley's professional life began to fragment. He had at first sought to maintain a distance from the drama. At the commencement of proceedings he wrote with poised wit to Ada Leverson that he 'look[ed] forward eagerly to the first act of Oscar's new tragedy' though he feared that 'the title *Douglas* ha[d] been used before'. As matters developed, however, it became increasingly difficult to sustain this air of detachment; Beardsley felt a real sympathy for Wilde ('Poor dear old thing') in his trouble. His animus against the playwright evaporated. To one correspondent he confided: 'Poor dear old Oscar, how horrible it all is. I am really upset about it – more than I think perhaps.'

Alarmingly, he found himself being drawn into the drama. In the heated debate over Wilde's (supposed) conduct, some began to equate Beardsley and Beardsley's art with Wilde and Wilde's crimes.

They were all manifestations, the press claimed, of an evil tendency in contemporary cultural life, a far from comely decadence. Every recent artistic development which had challenged the old mores was 'lumped' together and condemned. But within this agglomeration the link between Wilde and Beardsley was the most obvious. Beardsley had achieved his first public acclaim as the illustrator of *Salome*, and first impressions are the most lasting.

Their connection was confirmed in ironic circumstances at the very climax of events. On 5 April, even as Wilde was leaving the Cadogan Hotel in the company of the two detectives, he had picked up the book he was reading: *Aphrodite* by Pierre Louÿs. An 'ordinary French novel', Beardsley might have called it; it was bound in yellow covers and to English eyes that hue proclaimed only one publication. It was reported that Oscar Wilde had been arrested with *The Yellow Book* in his hand, and, as the press was for ever reiterating, '*The Yellow Book* is Aubrey Beardsley'. The relationship between Wilde, Beardsley, *The Yellow Book* and the Bodley Head was thus decisively confirmed in the public mind.[5]

The timing could not have been worse. John Lane stepped off the SS *Umbria* in New York to be greeted by banner headlines: OSCAR WILDE ARRESTED: YELLOW BOOK UNDER HIS ARM. A mob gathered in Vigo Street and stoned the windows of the Bodley Head. On the day after Wilde's arrest, a deputation of the high-minded Alice Meynell and the weak-minded William Watson called on Lane's lugubrious and self-important deputy, Frederic Chapman, demanding action. Their first concern was the immediate removal of Wilde's name from the Bodley Head list. Failing this, they would withdraw their own works. The threat was unnecessary; Lane had come to the same conclusion, and his telegram withdrawing the Wilde titles crossed with Chapman's urging him to do so. Within two days, the self-appointed moral guardians realized that they had not gone far enough. Wilde's polluting influence was, they considered, living on in Beardsley. They returned to demand the art editor's exclusion from all future numbers of *The Yellow Book*.

Watson was being urged on by the best-selling novelist and indefatigable busybody, Mrs Humphry Ward, with promises of 'private help' should he succeed. Mrs Meynell had not even this excuse. She simply disapproved of Beardsley. She supported her antipathy with chiromantic evidence; he had, she said, 'a line in his hand'. She found his art expressive of 'infernal evil' and 'sneering hatred of the body'. Although she had never approved of *The Yellow Book* and had refused to contribute to it, she now wanted Beardsley dismissed from its pages. In the absence of any real justification for this demand, there was a resort to bluster. She announced that it 'must follow' inevitably upon Wilde's exclusion from the list, as though the confusion of Beardsley's art with Wilde's crimes was an established fact. Watson was 'immovable' on the point. It appears that there was a comical (and successful) attempt to convince Chapman that Beardsley's cover design for the forthcoming *Yellow Book* – a drawing of a faun reading to a girl on a river bank – contained a concealed detail so obscene it could not even be mentioned. Watson telegraphed directly to Lane: 'Withdraw all Beardsley's designs or I withdraw all my books.'

Lane was bemused by the 'extraordinary' demand; it would be 'an injustice to Beardsley'. Le Gallienne, Beerbohm and Kipling, who all happened to be in New York, concurred. Lane cabled to Chapman for 'advice'; Chapman cabled back advising 'concession'. Watson's 'defection just now' would be 'most damaging'. He also asked for permission to delay publication of Volume V of *The Yellow Book*, which was even then being proofed. Harland was in Paris, but had entrusted this last editorial chore to Ella D'Arcy. Beardsley, besides his cover design, had provided four drawings. Lane, on the other side of the Atlantic, relying on telegrams and American newspaper reports, was unable to judge clearly. He suspected that he did not know all the facts. Had Beardsley been mentioned (however unreasonably) at the trial? His own name had been brought up; it had been claimed in court and 'widely reported in [the] press' that Lane had introduced Wilde to Edward Shelley, the one-time Bodley Head office boy. Although Lane had previously treated remarks about the risqué nature of Bodley Head publications as nothing more than useful publicity, he now took fright. Perhaps the firm would collapse under the weight of the scandal.

If Watson and Mrs Meynell deserted the standard, others would follow. Lane might find himself with nothing more than Wilde's backlist and the prospect of Beardsley's *Venus and Tannhäuser*. He

acted on Chapman's advice and cabled his agreement to Beardsley's removal; at the same time he wrote expressing doubts about the wisdom and justice of the action. He urged Chapman to defend Beardsley as a 'satirist, in the manner of Hogarth', should he be attacked in the press.* He hoped *The Yellow Book* would not be delayed. On 11 April, Maundy Thursday, Ella D'Arcy arrived at the Bodley Head with the corrected proofs of *The Yellow Book* ready for press. Chapman accepted them without mentioning the decision against Beardsley or the need to delay publication. Nor, indeed, did he tell the art editor of the decision.[6]

Beardsley was blithely unaware that the transatlantic cables had been humming with his name; his attention was elsewhere. Ada Leverson kept him informed of Wilde's plight, and he had been busy with arrangements for the NEAC spring exhibition. He was on the 'selecting jury', with Sickert, Steer, Hartrick and others. Of his own works he chose 'Black Coffee', one of the drawings for Volume V of *The Yellow Book*. The picture was another variation on the Degas 'L'Absinthe' theme, with two women sitting at a café table, a single cup of coffee before them. The title perhaps echoed the revelation that the drink on the table in Degas's picture was in fact black coffee, and suggested the dangers of trying to interpret an image. On Easter Sunday Aubrey probably attended the Oratory; he had made friends there with Father Williamson, an urbane, Eton-educated cleric who lived most of the year in Venice. He sent the priest a ticket for the NEAC show.[7]

On the Tuesday after Easter when Ella D'Arcy called to see how production of the quarterly was progressing, Chapman bent the truth and told her that Lane had just cabled from America ordering the suppression of Beardsley's drawings. D'Arcy was 'astonished'. Though she had never cared for Beardsley's pictures, she could see little wrong with them; certainly nothing that merited the treatment

---

* Interviewed in the *New York Times* (12 April 1895), Lane adopted this line, likening Beardsley to a modern Hogarth, and suggesting that his caricatures of Wilde had done much to discredit the playwright.

OPPOSITE The suppressed cover-design for *The Yellow Book*, Vol. V, 1895.

Lane now ordered. Nevertheless, she set about replacing his four illustrations. Swan Electric held blocks of several pictures planned for future editions and she hunted up some of these. She returned to Vigo Street the following morning with the four new pictures, expecting that publication could now proceed. Chapman was 'obliged to tell [her]' that it was delayed. A new cover was necessary. D'Arcy protested that Beardsley's cover seemed perfectly fine, indeed was one of the few drawings by him that she 'really liked'; Chapman then hinted with an embarrassed but mysterious air that it was 'the most improper thing Aubrey Beardsley [had] ever done'.*

Commissioning a new cover was not in D'Arcy's power; as the art editor, Beardsley should have been consulted. D'Arcy's loyalties, however, were to Harland, and she telegraphed him in Paris, urging his immediate return. Harland came at once. He met Chapman and D'Arcy the next morning at Vigo Street and immediately took matters in hand. He does not seem to have pressed hard for Beardsley's reinstatement: his loyalties were to *The Yellow Book*, not to its art editor. A 'young draughtsman', F. H. Townsend, was 'captured' and set to work. By ten o'clock that evening a new cover had been completed. Chapman telegraphed Lane that all was well. (Due to an oversight, Beardsley's back cover and spine decorations were left unchanged.)

How and when Beardsley learnt of all these clandestine dealings is not clear. It was probably Harland who finally informed him of his removal from the quarterly, but the action was presented as a temporary and extraordinary measure necessitated by circumstances. Harland returned to Paris immediately after his trouble-shooting mission and Beardsley, it seems, accompanied him. Certainly he was with the Harlands soon afterwards. At first, the sudden drama excited rather than alarmed him. Paris worked its familiar magic upon his

---

* Beardsley mocked those who read imaginary obscenities into his drawings. In a suppressed passage of *Venus and Tannhäuser* he recounts how the guests at Venus's banquet indulged in 'a general criticism of the decorations, everyone finding their own peculiar meaning in the fall of a festoon, turn of twig and twist of branch'. In a fine display of 'insight and invention' one character explains what was 'intended by a certain arrangement of roses'. To confirm the connection Beardsley added a marginal note: '[c.f.] my own drawing'.

spirit, and he was soon 'having a charming time'. His true position at the Bodley Head was obscured by the work he was still doing for the Keynotes series: even in Paris he received requests from Chapman for coverwork and 'key' designs. However, as he dwelt upon his predicament, its true injustice dawned with awful force. The public, he realized, when faced with the fact of his dismissal – and when the fifth number appeared, shorn of his designs, the fact would be clear to all – would conclude that there was indeed evidence to connect him to Wilde and Wilde's supposed crimes. The connection, far from being broken, would be confirmed.*[8]

He realized that he had lost for good his position on *The Yellow Book*, and with it his largest and most regular source of income. In return he inherited a deleterious and enduring association with a type of criminalized vice which, though it may have amused his imagination, had never dictated his actions. He seems to have suffered a *crise*. He left Paris and travelled overnight to London; there he consulted Mabel. She advised him to call on a young man named Marc André Raffalovich. Mabel's advice was surprising: she knew Raffalovich only slightly, and Aubrey had scarcely met him. Their only contact had been at Aubrey's lecture on 'Art', when he had been in the audience. Why then did Beardsley call on him?

In 1895 Raffalovich was thirty years old. The son of a cultured Russian-Jewish émigré banking family, he was born in Paris but had come to England when he was eighteen and had lived in London ever since. He was accompanied by a formidable Scottish governess, Miss Florence Truscott Gribbell, who over the years metamorphosed into his housekeeper, companion and confidante. Miss Gribbell was a recent convert to Catholicism and a visitor to the Oratory. It is possible that Mabel had come to know her – and of Raffalovich – through her own visits there. Raffalovich possessed a large private income and a small literary talent. He poured the former into hospitality and the latter into several slim volumes of even slimmer verse. His poetry was not appreciated and his generosity did not go unpunished. Many unkind things were said of him. It was told that he had

* Although the wags claimed that, after Beardsley's dismissal, *The Yellow Book* 'turned grey overnight', it continued for nine more issues, not without distinction.

been sent to England because his mother found him too ugly to keep with her in Paris. In one of his less generous quips, Wilde declared that he had come to London to found a salon but had succeeded only in establishing a saloon.

He and Wilde had briefly been friends during the 1880s. Raffalovich was exclusively homosexual and Wilde, though recently married, was fascinated by homosexuality. They enjoyed many 'nice improper chats', until Raffalovich, shocked by Wilde's indiscretion, broke the connection. The rift had widened in 1892 when Raffalovich took up Wilde's protégé John Gray, and paid for the publication of his first book of verse. Gray's realignment had been precipitated by the rejection he felt at Wilde's growing infatuation with Lord Alfred Douglas, and by his inability to come to terms with his homosexual nature, or to reconcile it with his recently embraced Catholicism. Raffalovich, while acknowledging his own sexual orientation, seems to have striven to sublimate it. Perhaps he followed the example of Ricketts and Shannon in embracing an ideal of chaste companionship and shared dedication to art, and tried to forge such a partnership with Gray. They both wrote poetry; they collaborated on small-scale dramatic pieces, and Raffalovich installed Gray in a flat around the corner from his house in South Audley Street. Beyond poetry and drama, Raffalovich maintained an interest in sexual deviancy, and contributed articles to the *Archives d'Anthropologie Criminelle*.[9]

Beardsley presented himself at Raffalovich's house on the morning of his arrival in London, only to be told that the master was out making an early call. He announced that he would wait, and was shown into an elegant drawing-room, amongst the treasures of which was a painting by Gustave Moreau of 'Sappho'. Beardsley was admiring this when Raffalovich entered. He at once explained his business. He was 'in a fix', and wondered whether Raffalovich could advise or help him. The nature of the 'fix', the advice and the help remain tantalizingly unspecified in the account of the interview preserved by Raffalovich. Was it financial? personal? psychosexual?

There has been a tendency to assume that it was exclusively the first. Raffalovich, as a wealthy art-lover, was certainly a useful contact for a young artist in need of pecuniary assistance. But Beardsley's dramatic arrival from Paris, his urgent call at South Audley Street, and the future course of his friendship with Raffalovich all suggest a more complex motive. The spring of 1895 was a time of anxiety for many young men about their sexual natures. It was a period of rapid realignments and emphatic gestures: some fled to France; others took the simpler course of getting their hair cut and subscribing to *The Times*'s Shilling Cricket Fund. Beardsley's orientation was always considered, by those who knew him, to be heterosexual. But his fascination with the homosexual milieu must have reflected some part of his nature. Perhaps he had become unsure of his position. And perhaps this uncertainty had prompted him to consult Raffalovich, an acknowledged 'expert' on the subject of 'unisexualité', to find a point of reference.

Whatever advice Raffalovich gave, it seemed reassuring. Beardsley returned to Paris, where he continued to be 'capital company' for the Harlands. News of Wilde's trial reached them there. It began on 26 April and ended in deadlock on 1 May, with the jury unable to agree a verdict. The whole process would have to be gone through again. Beardsley finally left Paris on 8 May. Back in London, he looked forward to renewing his collaboration with Brandon Thomas. But again he found himself thwarted by the pervasive influence of Wilde's disgrace. The events of Oscar's tragedy had struck an unfortunate echo in the intended plotline of the play. On grounds of taste the piece, it was agreed, had to be abandoned. It was another setback and, although Beardsley recognized its necessity, it confirmed Wilde's place as a blight in his life. Wilde was out on bail, staying quietly at the Leversons' in South Kensington. It is possible that Aubrey visited him there, in his nursery quarters at the top of the house; Mabel, at least, saw Ada Leverson during this troubled period.

Whatever Aubrey's sense of anxiety, Mabel too found herself in need of reassurance. On 13 May she took the decisive step of joining the Roman Catholic Church. She was received by Father Sebastian Bowden of the Brompton Oratory (a priest who, seventeen years earlier, had almost secured the conversion of Oscar Wilde). She took Philippa as a middle name, in reverence for St Philip Neri, the founding father of the Oratorians. Ada Leverson toyed with the idea of following suit. She wrote to her friend Francis Burnand, the editor of *Punch* and of the *Catholic Year Book*, seeking his advice. He counselled her to 'consider well – if you decide "yes", *don't delay but do it*; if you decide "no" – dismiss it.' Decisive action was not, however, her forte. It is hard to believe that Aubrey was not touched by these happenings; he had shared his religious life with Mabel and the bond between them was still strong. Mabel's conversion drew her into closer intimacy with Mrs Gribbell, who became her godmother, and stood as sponsor at her confirmation in July the following year.[10]

Aubrey's intimacy with André Raffalovich was growing too. He kept up a bi-diurnal stream of notes and letters thanking his new friend for gifts of books, chocolates ('a great support'), flowers, lunches, theatre trips, walking sticks, and even a 'sonnet'. Raffalovich had a late-Victorian enthusiasm for intense poetical friendship and his association with Beardsley allowed him to indulge it: 'he arrested me like wrought iron and like honeysuckle,' Raffalovich recalled; he offered the attractions of 'hardness, elegance, charm, variety' and, of course, fame or, more properly, notoriety. Raffalovich was happy to bask in its reflected glow: 'Wherever we went he was gazed at. They sang about him at the Gaiety; Max caricatured him; strangers credited him with unfathomed perversity; acquaintances all recognized his simple boyishness.'

From the outset, the friendship was given a poetic gloss and a defined colour by the use of pet-names: Beardsley addressed Raffalovich as 'Mentor' and signed himself 'Télémaque'. The allusion (as the accents make clear) was not so much to the *Odyssey* as to François Fénelon's moral tale of 1698, *Aventures de Télémaque*. The dynamic of the relationship, however, was the same in Fénelon and Homer: Mentor was the moral guide and guardian of his young companion. And though the allusion was probably not untouched by irony (no allusion of Beardsley's ever was), it must have reflected something of the truth of the situation. Certainly it supports the view that Beardsley sought out Raffalovich for advice rather than money. The direction of the advice is suggested by some of Raffalovich's presents. Among the conventional and comestible gifts Beardsley received, there were also some more intriguing items: he acknowledged receipt of Raffalovich's pamphlet *L'Uranisme: Inversion Sexuelle Congénitale*, finding its 'study of inversion . . . quite brilliant'. He also looked forward to Raffalovich's work in progress, a monograph on *L'Affaire Oscar Wilde*.

Despite this area of shared interest, the friendship also had its practical aspect. Raffalovich sought work from Beardsley and paid for it; he bought drawings from him. There was talk of a portrait commission ('It must be in pastel on brown paper – full length', wrote Beardsley). He also made an exquisite frontispiece for Raffalovich's latest volume of poems, although the publisher, David Nutt, refused to use it, considering that the figure at the centre of the design 'whatever [Beardsley] might say . . . [was] hermaphrodite'. Perhaps, too, there were gifts of money; his friends thought so. Vallance wrote to Ross as early as 23 May suggesting that Raffalovich was 'financing Beardsley to any amount'. His intimacy with Raffalovich inevitably brought him into contact with John Gray. Gray was evidently sufficiently sure of his place in Raffalovich's affections not to feel threatened by Beardsley, and an easy friendship sprang up between them. Beardsley had a genuine admiration for Gray's poetic gifts.[11]

The Wilde débâcle, while stimulating Raffalovich's curiosity and gratifying his sense of justice, was having a profoundly upsetting effect upon Gray. The young poet was in a state of nervous distress. He had a barrister (paid for by Raffalovich) with a watching brief at the trials, in case his name should be mentioned. More significantly, the drama precipitated a spiritual crisis. It is said that, perhaps prompted by the news of Wilde's arrest, he hurriedly entered a church and knelt down in prayer before the image of the Virgin Mary. 'A few minutes later, as it seemed to him, an old woman bearing keys approached and told him that she was going to lock up. It was night. He had been on his knees all day.'

Gray's distress increased Raffalovich's animus against Wilde, and this was a hostility that did not allow of contradiction. The ultimatum, 'You cannot be Oscar's friend and mine', marked 'a certain stage' in Raffalovich's friendships. Beardsley recognized and accepted the situation. But it put a strain on his other relationships, and introduced an element of duplicity into his conduct. Beerbohm, Rothenstein, Ross, Dowson and the other young artists of the movement remained fiercely loyal to and protective of Wilde. And although they recognized that Beardsley was suffering unjustly from his supposed connection with the disgraced author, the fault, they considered, was scarcely Oscar's. Beardsley was obliged to wear different masks with different companions.

The division should not be overstated. Ada Leverson, Wilde's staunchest friend and ally, had an amicable relationship with Raffalovich. Nevertheless, the dilemma existed, and had to be faced. For the sake of his new friendship, Beardsley calmly denied his former friend.

At the beginning of Wilde's retrial, Raffalovich and Gray had taken evasive action and gone to Germany. Beardsley wrote to them there, after the jury had finally convicted the poet: 'I suppose the result of the Oscar trial is in the German papers – two years' hard. I imagine it will kill him.' The tone was wilfully brutal, and perhaps there was a hint of self-punishment in it. Wilde's conviction confirmed the puritan backlash against artistic experiment in general and Beardsley in particular. The tide of public sentiment turned against art and culture. A new and brash philistinism – coarse, perfervid and jingoistic – characterized the second half of the decade. Harry Quilter, in an influential article, 'The Gospel of Intensity', condemned as one of the manifestations of contemporary malaise the perverted distortions of Beardsley's art; others were quick to join the chorus. Burne-Jones, writing to a friend, said, 'We shall be in clearer air now [Wilde] is ended and others must go too – all the same lot who hang on every good thing and try to drag it into their own perverted depths.' There can be no doubt that he regarded his erstwhile protégé as one of those who 'must go'. Beardsley, however, was staying put.

Raffalovich and Gray had invited Beardsley to join them in Germany, but the invitation had to be declined; Beardsley's 'many business engagements' did not allow of it, but his work proceeded falteringly, hampered by small obstructions and constraints. Nutt's refusal to print the frontispiece for *The Thread and The Path* was merely an irritation, since Raffalovich would buy the original drawing, but it was indicative of the indignant puritanism that followed the Wilde trials.[12]

Beardsley continued to produce designs for the Keynotes series, but they became increasingly muted and decorative. There is a suggestion that this tendency towards floral patterning was prompted by a desire not to risk offence. Arthur Machen, though delighted with the 'very charming' abstract design which Beardsley produced for the cover of his novel *The Three Impostors*, remarked obliquely to Lane, 'I suppose he has abjured figures for the present.' Beardsley's position was not helped particularly by the appearance in *Punch* towards the end of May of Ada Leverson's comic skit, 'The Scarlet Parasol'. The story – printed over three weeks – was about Alan Roy, a young harpist of prodigious ability and extreme youth, who was clearly based on Beardsley. The title paid homage to Beardsley's drawing, 'A Scarlet Pastorale', which had appeared in *The Sketch* the month before, and the illustrations made the connection explicit. The mannered dialogue ('You look like a Botticelli in a Paris dress') confirmed Beardsley's connection with Wilde's pose if not with Wilde's crimes. The skit had been meant as a piece of fun; its timing was unfortunate.

In literary circles much of the blame for Beardsley's predicament was laid at Lane's door. Certainly his friends considered the publisher responsible. Vallance referred to him as 'the viper', and Beardsley seems to have harboured resentment. He felt justified in calling at Vigo Street while Lane was still in America and 'borrowing' the suppressed *Yellow Book* designs and two of the *Salome* drawings. These he sold to raise funds. Nevertheless, it soon became clear that the expenses of a household were overstraining his resources. Before the end of May he had put Cambridge Street on the market and was proposing 'to live by himself in Conduit Street'. In the event, he preferred Knightsbridge to Mayfair and company to solitude. At the end of June Aubrey and Mabel took a short-term lease on a house at 57 Chester Terrace. Friends rallied round to help with the décor. Mrs Savile Clark, an intimate of the Leversons, sent some 'art muslin' for curtains; Aubrey facetiously suggested that he would have it made into a suit ('so nice and cool in the hot weather').

The house was not far from Will Rothenstein's studio in Glebe Place and Beardsley often called there in the morning, 'hastily dressed and without a collar'. Frustrated in his drawing, he tried to direct his energies into writing. The Tannhäuser project had been interrupted, though its imminent appearance was proclaimed in the advertisement pages of the Bodley Head list, and he had told several friends it was all but finished. Other schemes kept presenting themselves to his mind, and on one visit to Rothenstein's he wrote a poem. He took to idling away his evenings with Rothenstein's friend Conder, and with Ernest Dowson. They were bohemian company, fond of the pubs and dives round Leicester Square and Soho; fond, too, of the cheap prostitutes who frequented them.* Although some of Beardsley's friends expressed concern at his dissolute life, it is easy to suppose that he was seeking to escape his supposed connection with Wilde in the indulgence of conventional vice. Despite such ploys, and despite the support of his many friends, he continued to feel his vulnerability. There was never any question of social ostracism, but he was morbidly alive to slights and snubs – real or imagined.

When a hostile article appeared in St Paul's accusing him of being 'sexless' and 'unclean', he was provoked to respond. Writing to the editor, he retorted, 'as to my uncleanliness, I do my best for it in my morning bath, and if [your art critic] has really any doubts as to my sex, he may come and see me take it.' The letter was not published, but it healed the breach with the art critic in question, a faintly absurd and thoroughly pompous ex-soldier, Haldane MacFall. Indeed it initiated an unlikely friendship between the two men.

Beardsley's touchiness and sense of disequilibrium also revealed themselves in a brief *froideur* between him and Raffalovich on the latter's return from Germany. Raffalovich, himself oversensitive to imagined slights, took exception to Beardsley's 'lack of social courage', when he failed to rebuke a fellow guest for discourtesy to an American woman at some social gathering. The procession of dinners, gifts and letters was abruptly broken off, both parties feeling aggrieved, and the hiatus lasted three months.[13]

*   *   *

* Not all their recreations were bibulous. Edgar Jepson records an excursion made by Beardsley, Conder and Rothenstein with George Moore, on the 'knife-board of an omnibus' to Dulwich. Moore made them all get off at Peckham because, he said, 'I've written about Peckham.' He was surprised to find it very different from his description. 'That is the fate of the realist!' he exclaimed. 'He writes about a field and a haystack in Peckham, and there are no *field* and no *haystack* in Peckham.' (*Memoirs of a Victorian*, p. 256.)

Into this vacuum stepped the splendidly louche figure of Leonard Smithers. Smithers was a large, pale-eyed, pasty-faced solicitor from Sheffield, who had abandoned his profession and his native city (though not his Yorkshire brogue) for a career as a bookseller in London. Unprepossessing in appearance, he was compelling in personality. In 1895 he was thirty-four. During the late 1880s he had befriended the traveller and polymath Sir Richard Burton, and assisted him in plans to publish 'scholarly' English editions of oriental erotica such as *The Perfumed Garden* and the *Kama Sutra*. Smithers, a classical scholar, then proposed launching his own publishing venture: editions of the suppressed works of Roman authors. He had begun in 1890 with a collection of poetic epigrams addressed to Priapus, the god of fertility, supported by a substantial and lubricious apparatus of notes and appendices dealing with every sexual act and deviancy. This – and various subsequent volumes of erotic tales – supplemented his second-hand book and print dealing business. His stock, although it included substantial holdings on the American War of Independence and the career of Napoleon, was more noted for its 'curiosities' and limited editions. On more than one occasion he offered a book bound in human skin. His selections from the clandestine French literature of the previous century were extensive and choice. Wilde described him as 'the most learned erotomane in Europe', and suggested that he did not confine his interest to theory.

Beardsley had encountered Smithers the previous year, lured into his shop in Effingham House, off the Strand, by a display of Fragonard prints. This 'perfect little museum of erotica' soon became a preferred browsing-ground. He had come away from his first visit with a small but expensive volume of eighteenth-century fables; on subsequent calls he not only bought but sold. On one occasion he offered Smithers several desirable items with the explanation that he was taking a girl out to dinner and needed the cash. Beardsley was a readily recognizable figure, and Smithers cultivated the acquaintance.

In 1895 Smithers was expanding his publishing operations and moving them above the counter. He had been prompted in this direction by Arthur Symons. Symons's third collection of verse, *London Nights*, had been rejected by John Lane as being too frank in manner and too lewd in matter, and other established publishing houses had agreed. The hostile climate surrounding the Wilde trials made publication problematic. In his frustration Symons approached Smithers. To a man with long experience of pornography and the profits to be made from it, Symons's poems of 'light love' must have seemed tame and commercially viable. He also perhaps saw an opportunity. With the Bodley Head retreating in disarray, he could become the publisher of the 'movement'. Symons certainly encouraged him, urging him to give up pornography for poetry and ensure himself a place in the history of late nineteenth-century literature.[14]

Beardsley's sacking from *The Yellow Book* presented an immediate and obvious opportunity. Smithers had the idea of establishing a new periodical, a rival to the 'bilious' quarterly, which might provide a showcase for Beardsley's art, Symons's poetry and the work of other avant-gardistes. Symons could be literary editor while Beardsley took charge of the art. Symons readily agreed and an interview was sought with Beardsley. The prospective art editor was temporarily out of action. After a bad 'haemorrhage of the lungs', he had been 'sent to bed' by his doctor. The project, however, was too exciting to delay, so Symons – if not Smithers – hurried around to Chester Terrace.

He thought he had arrived too late; Beardsley was 'lying out on a couch, horribly white'. On hearing Symons's proposal, however, he revived and was at once 'full of ideas, full of enthusiasm'. The possibilities rose up before him: it would provide a focus for his energies, a chance to bury *The Yellow Book*, and the comfort of a regular (if not a fixed) income.

Time, however, was short. Smithers hoped that the first issue might be ready before the end of the year, and the canvasing of contributors needed to begin at once. With the summer well advanced, London was emptying. Symons himself was leaving on a visit to Dieppe. Poor health and Keynotes commitments kept Beardsley in town. He saw much of Smithers and the band of young writers and artists gathering around the reprobate publisher. Wratislaw had rallied to Smithers' standard when Lane turned down his volume of poems. Dowson and Conder followed, as did Arthur Machen, author of two volumes in the Keynotes series. Herbert Horne, the poet and art historian, became an intimate. Even Beerbohm moved within the orbit of the group. It became Smithers' proud boast that he would publish 'what the others were afraid of'. They spent evenings among tarts and lushes at a seamy supper club called the Thalia (sometimes referred to as the 'Failure'), drinking brandy and talking a bit about art but rather more about sex. In its dining-room one evening, Beardsley made a drunken attempt to ravish Horne's mistress.[15]

Of importance at this time was the contact Beardsley made with a wealthy Cambridge undergraduate, Jerome Pollitt, a figure of some repute even beyond the Cam. His tastes for decadent art, maquillage, and cross-dressing had all marked him out from his fellow students. His rooms at Trinity were decorated with Beardsley reproductions. As a leading member of the Cambridge Footlights he had established a reputation with his skirt-dancing act, which he performed under the extravagant *nom-de-théâtre* of 'Diane de Rougy' (his tribute to the genius of the Parisian cabaret star, Liane de Pougy).

A striking transvestite portrait of Pollitt had been exhibited at the Photographers' Salon alongside Evans's 'gargoyle' portrait of Beardsley, and this association perhaps encouraged Pollitt to approach him. He wrote, asking whether the artist would make him a bookplate. Beardsley, despite having publicly proclaimed that he would never produce another bookplate, accepted the task, and suggested a meeting.

Beardsley seems to have been at once drawn to the 'gilded youth' who, despite being a student, was a few months older than himself. Pollitt offered the glimpse of a parallel world; he had so much that Beardsley lacked and craved: wealth, good looks, good lungs and a university education. They shared something too: youth, pose and a great admiration for Beardsley's art. It was a happy basis for a new friendship, different from the semi-rivalrous associations with Beerbohm, Sickert and Rothenstein or the quasi-filial relationships with Raffalovich and Smithers.

Beardsley's health returned and his work progressed. In mid-August he set off 'touring all over the world', as he put it with more flair than accuracy. He went, it seems, briefly to Germany, perhaps desiring to absorb the Thuringian atmosphere as a background to his tale of Tannhäuser. Or he may have been prompted by the travellers' tales of Raffalovich and Gray. Almost nothing is known of his itinerary. He perhaps called on Meier-Graefe in Berlin, to discuss a contribution to the periodical *Pan*, and he did, it seems, stay at the Englischer Hof in Cologne; certainly he used their writing paper for his compositions. It was one of his affectations at this time to claim that he was 'unable to draw anywhere but in London'. He therefore devoted himself to literature, working diligently at *Venus and Tannhäuser*.

He had resolved that the book, although contracted to Lane and announced in his catalogues, would be published by Smithers, and would appear initially, in serial form, in the new periodical. To ease the transfer, Beardsley suggested retitling the work 'The Queen in Exile', saying, disingenuously, that under such a banner 'Lane would not suspect it was his book.'

Towards the end of August he arrived in Dieppe and found Symons and Conder there. Smithers had been shuttling back and forth; Dowson was expected; Herbert Horne was coming too, perhaps with his mistress. Beardsley installed himself at the Hôtel Sandwich and wired Mabel to join him.[16]

Dieppe in the 1890s had a magical aura, boasting a romantic past and offering a delightful present. It had been the resort of kings and emperors, of artists and musicians. Delacroix had visited it; Liszt had passed a summer there, but it remained untouched by vulgar tourism and unconstrained by tedious smartness. For all its summer trade, it had the mundane aspect of an old Norman seaport, with market place and fish market, a castle, two old churches, and a quaint row of 'rather primitive' white-boarded hotels on the front. The hub of life was the peppermint-brick Casino and the terrace in front of it. It was there that everyone gathered – in the morning at the bathing quay, on selected afternoons at the Bal d'Enfants, in the evenings at the concert, and all day at the gaming tables. Even the gambling had a magical air; the holiday crowd put their money on the 'little horses': a mechanical hippodrome in miniature.

Several distinct social groups gathered at Dieppe. It was preeminently popular among the French bourgeoisie; there was also a smarter French set, and the respectable English. But along with these there was the distinctly literary and artistic crowd of which Beardsley was part. This set was unusual in that it comprised British and foreign elements. One of its leading lights was Fritz Thaulow, a vast, red-bearded Norwegian painter; with his statuesque wife and their two statuesque children, he had settled permanently in the town. The hub of the group was a Frenchman: Jacques Émile Blanche, a charming, well-connected painter in his mid-thirties. His family had long had a villa at the Bas Fort Blanc, which had established a reputation as a gathering place for artists and writers over two generations. Its walls were filled with paintings by Corot, Degas, and Manet. The studio where Blanche worked had been decorated by Renoir with scenes from the Tannhäuser legend. At the end of the garden was a small wooden pavilion where talk might flow and ideas take flight.

Blanche, brought up in the French tradition of intellectual hospitality, made it his business to gather in the young English painters and writers who came to Dieppe and introduce them to their French counterparts. He recognized early on the genius of Sickert; he sought out Conder, having admired his paintings in Paris; he took up Symons. When Beardsley arrived, he was immediately added to the circle.

Although Blanche was repelled by what he knew of Beardsley's work, and disapproving of his connection with the lightweight *Courrier Français*, he was charmed by the person and personality of the artist. He was also impressed by Beardsley's knowledge of French literature: his enthusiasm for Molière, Corneille and Racine, his ability to recite the choruses of *Athalie* and *Esther*, his close study of George Sand, Chateaubriand and, of course, Balzac. Blanche's grandfather had known Balzac, but Beardsley, the Frenchman remarked, 'knew the personage of *La Comédie humaine* like members of his own family'. Beyond the charm of erudition, Blanche interpreted the Englishman's unhurried pose as generosity of spirit. Though born with 'the most divine gifts' and with 'all possibilities' at his command, Beardsley was content to 'smile' and make himself agreeable to his friends. He was happy to pass the time in joking and gossip, pointing his quips with a rap of the thick cane he carried, improvising stories 'so daring it would have been better had he told them in Greek'.[17]

Beardsley became an established presence in the pavilion at Villa

Bas Fort Blanc and a welcome guest in the studio. He was seen too on the terrace at the Casino, and around the tables at the Café des Tribunaux. Although a seaside gaiety pervaded the scene and the season, much of import was discussed. It was at these alfresco gatherings that Beardsley and Symons laid the plans for their periodical. A title was needed; finally Mabel suggested *The Savoy*. The name took immediately; it combined the smart and theatrical with a topographical allusion to Smithers: the Arundel Street shop was in an area of London once known as Savoy. It also offered a double-edged reference to the magnificent hotel which had opened in 1889 as the acme of chic modernity, but had figured prominently in evidence at the Wilde trials as a scene of seduction and licence.

There was discussion too about the tone and direction of the magazine. In the wake of the Wilde tragedy, and the philistine reaction it had provoked, should they retreat or advance? Should they proclaim their right to deal with forbidden subjects, to explore unusual artistic forms, to seek out unusual beauty? Or should they seek safety in conformity? Beardsley had clear views: indeed Conder initially thought that he, rather than Symons, was the editor. He was all for defiance, and his expression of it was sometimes overemphatic. Conder confided to Rothenstein that Beardsley was being 'very pompous about it all'.

It was understood that Beardsley should have a prominent position: he would provide the cover designs and title pages, and would also write for the publication both verse and prose. Some considered that Smithers had established *The Savoy* simply as an outlet for Beardsley's talents. As to other contributors, Beardsley began to gather in the usual suspects: Rothenstein and Conder were at hand, as was Blanche. Beerbohm and Pennell were in London, while Sickert, though in Venice, could be relied upon for his support. In what might have been a ploy to add more established names to the list, Beardsley commissioned an article from Pennell on the illustrators of the 1860s, thus allowing the reproduction of two examples by Sandys and one by Whistler.

One new recruit was Charles Shannon. His scruples about appearing in publications other than *The Dial* had gone, or perhaps Rothenstein, who had exhibited with him the previous year, used his powers of persuasion. He contributed a lithograph. In tone, as in personnel, the art side differed little from that of the early *Yellow Book*. Steer was the only notable absentee. Beardsley had not looked beyond the coteries of Dieppe, the Café Royal and the NEAC. It was left to the more doctrinaire Symons to mould the quarterly and define its tone. Although he too sought material from his friends – an article on Zola's novels from Havelock Ellis, two poems and a story from his new intimate, W. B. Yeats, an essay on Criticism by Selwyn Image, some verse and prose from Dowson – he recognized the need to reach beyond the limits of the clique, soliciting an article from Bernard Shaw and another from a prominent critic, Frederick Wedmore.

Symons also composed a pre-emptive 'Editorial Note' claiming, 'All we ask from our contributors is good work, and good work is all we offer our readers . . . We have no formulas, and we desire no false unity of form or matter. We have not invented a new point of view. We are not Realists, or Romanticists, or Decadents. For us, all art is good which is good art.' Symons's disclaimer, 'We are not Decadents' was thought necessary, in the harsh climate of the day, for a magazine fronted by Beardsley and himself. Beardsley himself had become increasingly irritated by a term which served no purpose except to link him to Wilde.[18]

Since his arrival in Dieppe, Beardsley had persisted in his affectation of being unable to draw except in London. He would, he announced, console himself with literary endeavour. There were poems he wished to compose; he planned an essay on *Les Liaisons Dangereuses* or a longer piece on J. J. Rousseau. He even entertained hopes of translating the *Confessions*, but the plans changed rapidly and most were left undone. The one enduring project was the Tannhäuser tale: he wandered around with a morocco-bound, gilt-tooled, Louis XIV folder containing the manuscript. Sitting in the writing-room at the Casino, or (with his back to the sea) on the shaded terrace, he might add a phrase or an episode, pile on another epithet or, forgetting his proclaimed incapacity, sketch a figure passing on the promenade. Although he added a fanciful casino scene in homage to his surroundings, the story was developing, perhaps under the influence of Smithers' recherché stock of erotica, almost into a piece of rococo pornography. Smithers – though he would doubtless have

enjoyed the account of the satyrs' orgy or the touching episode of Venus pleasuring her pet unicorn – must have realized that the story was unpublishable. It would need to be expurgated before it appeared in *The Savoy*. It would also, as Beardsley had pointed out, need a new title to save it from legal action by Lane.

Eventually the title *Under the Hill* was agreed. It provided a knowing anatomical allusion to the *mons veneris*, with a more personal reference to More Adey's family house, 'Under the Hill' at Wotton-under-Edge, Gloucestershire; there was perhaps, too, an echo of Kate Greenaway's popular collection of rhymes, *Under the Window*.* Beardsley would also have taken pleasure in the effect it might have on his own mother's aunt, Wilhemina Underhill, in Edinburgh; even when Smithers had edited out the explicitly pornographic passages, the extravagance of the prose carried an erotic charge calculated to raise a great-aunt's eyebrows.

The names of the protagonists had to be changed too. Venus became Helen, and the Chevalier Tannhäuser was transformed, first into the Abbé Aubrey and then into the less blatant Abbé Fanfreluche. Beardsley's self-identification with his hero was not, however, obliterated: Abbé echoed the French pronunciation of his initials.[19]†

*   *   *

* Item 1260 in Smithers' *Catalogue of Rare Books No. 8* (1896) is Kate Greenaway's *Under the Window* 'bound in levant morocco by Rivière'. Smithers often sold books for Beardsley, and the camp notion of having a children's picture book bound in leather seems plausibly Beardsley-esque. Greenaway did not return Beardsley's admiration; after seeing his work at the NEAC show in 1894 she wrote, 'I HATE Beardsley more than ever.' (Quoted in Rodney Engen, *Kate Greenaway*, London, 1981, p. 181.)

† Fanfreluche in the original manuscript is the name of a dissolute courtier; in *Under the Hill* he appears as 'Sporion'. The word 'fanfreluche' is French for 'bauble' but it is interesting to note a volume in the Private Case at the British Library titled *Les Fanfreluches* by Prosper Blanchmain (Bruxelles, 1879). One of Venus/Helen's attendants is, moreover, called 'Blanchmains'. Such allusions abound in the text: the courtier 'Marisca' derives her name from a passage in Smithers' edition of *Priapeia* on 'Sodomy with Women': 'the poet [Martial] describes the anus of a youth as a Chian fig, that of a woman as a *marisca*. The Isle of Chios was famous for the fine quality of its figs; the *marisca* was a large-sized fig of inferior flavour.'

OPPOSITE 'The Bathers', an illustration for Arthur Symons's article on Dieppe, 1895.

Symons, ever alive to what he called 'impreshuns and sensashuns', was composing an impressionistic *causerie* on Dieppe and a poem comparing the sea to absinthe. He was sceptical of Beardsley's literary efforts. He saw in Beardsley's application no natural aptitude, only 'pathetic tenacity'. Later he recalled how Beardsley had spent 'two whole days' on the grassy ramparts of the old castle at Arques-la-Bataille working at a short poem for the magazine, striving by 'sheer power of will' to produce a *tour de force*.

The poem tells (as its title proclaimed) of 'Three Musicians': a Polish pianist, 'a soprano lightly frocked', and a 'slim, gracious boy' whose aspirations are divided between a desire to enjoy the favours of the soprano and desire for '*réclame* and recall' at Paris and St Petersburg, Vienna and St James's Hall. They are wandering on a sun-filled day through the drowsy countryside near the soprano's château. The Polish pianist 'lags behind' and, plucking some poppies, begins to conduct an imaginary band; the way is clear for the seduction of the soprano, and the inadvertent scandalization of a passing tourist.

> The gracious boy is at her feet,
> And weighs his courage with his chance;
> His fears soon melt in noonday heat.
> The tourist gives a furious glance,
> Red as his guide-book grows, moves on, and offers up a prayer for
>   France.

Beardsley claimed that the voluptuous soprano was based on Sophie Menter, a German pianist of the time; there was perhaps something of himself (and much wishfulness) in the 'gracious boy' at her feet. The image of the erubescent tourist stumbling upon a scene of languorous dissipation clearly recalled the excursion to Versailles with Joseph Pennell and the other Salon watchers two years previously. Despite these echoes, the setting of the poem remains dreamily unfixed: the figure of the Polish virtuoso conducting a field of flowers was borrowed from an episode recorded by George Sand of Liszt walking in the countryside. It was a scene, fantastical and whimsical, which clearly fascinated Beardsley; he would return to it again.

As the weeks at Dieppe flowed on, he abandoned the pose of

being unable to draw. The extended period of rest had given him a chance to adjust his bearings. He was in search of a new style, a new mode of expression. He wished to confound expectations: he told one acquaintance that he planned to change his style, 'fearing lest he found a school'. Although he had claimed the French eighteenth century as one of his major influences in the *To-Day* interview the previous year, it had not been apparent in his work; now it began to dominate his artistic practice. His long study of Watteau, Lancret, St Aubyn, Cochin, Dorat and the rococo masters of French illustration provided the direction for his drawing.

He worked on a cover design for *The Savoy* governed by this new influence and the old sense of mischief, producing a startling image of a woman in a riding cape in a lush, overgrown classical garden; at her feet a robed cherub stands poised to urinate upon a discarded copy of *The Yellow Book*. The simple disposition of bold masses of solid black against areas of white, common to almost all *The Yellow Book* drawings, was abandoned in favour of an elaborately worked and variegated surface. For almost the first time since his schoolboy drawings he tried to render shade and shadow. In a punning picture he did for Smithers of Siegfried wielding a blacksmith's hammer, he even employed cross-hatching for the first time. The effect of these new techniques was to make pictures which to some degree mimicked the eighteenth-century prints he adored and collected, rather as his early drawings for *Morte Darthur* had approximated to the fifteenth-century woodcuts of German and Italian artists, or his posters to Japanese prints. He delighted in the confusion and subversion of media.

Blanche noted his immersion in the eighteenth century, and thought it even affected his appearance. The artist's two brown moles were like the beauty patches worn by the beaux. Blanche captured something of this in the elegant portrait he made of Beardsley that summer – a symphony in silver grey with notes of pale pink. (It was more successful than the portrait Conder attempted, in which Beardsley looks like a disinterred banker.) Blanche was persuaded to take Beardsley to Le Puy to meet Alexander Dumas *fils*, author of *La Dame aux Camélias*. With the advance of his illness and the misfortune of his 'disgrace', the sad story of Marguerite had assumed for

Beardsley a 'special significance'. To Blanche's amazement, Beardsley was able to charm the inhospitable Dumas with a flow of informed questions and skilful compliments. At parting, the author presented his young admirer with an inscribed copy of his famous novel. Aubrey embellished the gift with a drawing on the title page, and it became one of his most cherished possessions.[20]

He was unable to tear himself from the charmed atmosphere of Dieppe. What had been intended as a fleeting visit stretched to over a month. He had changes of clothes sent to him. He delayed his departure, claiming he lacked money for a return ticket, and begging Smithers to send him funds. Eventually, towards the end of September, he embarked for home.

In London, he changed his living arrangements again. He sold the lease of Chester Terrace and, separating from Mabel (whose theatrical commitments meant she was increasingly out of town), moved into rooms at Geneux's Private Hotel, 10 & 11 St James's Place. His new address was closer to Smithers' shop in Arundel Street, and more convenient for town. It also offered privacy and independence, but it could scarcely be counted an economy measure. It was, moreover, a relocation fraught with peculiar significance. The address was notorious. Oscar Wilde had rented the same rooms from October 1893 to March 1894. He had written most of *An Ideal Husband* there. And, as the jury at the Old Bailey had heard, he had used them for assignations. Yet Beardsley, suffering from the assumed connection between himself and Wilde, installed himself in the same suite. The move can only be understood as a pose: the choice of his new address, like the choice of the title for the new periodical, seems to have been a ploy to explode the association with Wilde by exaggerating it to absurdity.* It was not mere coincidence. The supposed connection with Wilde and the injustice he had suffered because of it

---

* On other fronts, however, Beardsley exaggerated his *distance* from Wilde. It became one of his affectations that Wilde's books were 'bad luck'; he refused to have them near him. (Frances Winwar, *Oscar Wilde and the Yellow Nineties*, p. 180.) He was perhaps able to offload the offending volumes during his move to St James's Place when he sold off part of his library through Smithers.

OPPOSITE Unexpurgated design for the front cover of *The Savoy*, 1895.

continued to plague him even after his return from Dieppe, and it continued to spur him on his course of wilful dissoluteness.

Yeats recalled that Beardsley had for a while a beautiful mistress.* On one occasion, however, he arrived early in the morning at Symons's rooms in Fountain Court, accompanied by a tart called either 'Twopence Coloured' or 'Penny Plain'. Beardsley was still a little drunk from the night's excesses and his mind kept returning to the injustice of his dismissal from *The Yellow Book*, though it had happened some six months previously. Leaning his head against the wall, he stared into the mirror and contemplated his face. The sight depressed him further: 'Yes, yes,' he muttered with resignation, 'I look like a Sodomite.' (Which, as Yeats remarked, he certainly did not.) 'But no,' he added, 'I am not that.' Then he began railing against his ancestors, back to and including the great Pitt, accusing them of all manner of crimes and blaming them for his sorry situation.

He sought also to advertise his spiritual distance from Wilde through his work. *Under the Hill* contained several allusions to the disgraced playwright: the quaintly ridiculous figure of Venus's fat *fardeuse*, with her 'short respiration . . . corrupt skin . . . great flaccid cheeks . . . chin after chin' and voice full of 'salacious unction' was strongly reminiscent of Wilde. His illustration accentuated the likeness. Perhaps, too, Wilde's famous description of the liaisons with London renters as 'feasting with panthers' was bathetically undercut by the image of Venus's dinner-guests clad in 'tunics of panthers' skins . . . over pink tights'.[21]

Soon after his return, Beardsley sought an interview with Edmund Gosse, his literary godfather, to ask 'a blessing . . . upon my new quarterly'. Plans were progressing well, as were his drawings. The privacy of his rooms and the luxury of living alone were conducive to concentration. He was able, as he boasted, to 'get through an astonishing amount of work'. But the *Savoy* drawings were extremely time-consuming. He planned to do three illustrations for the opening instalment of *Under the Hill* as well as six other pictures for the

* The girl's identity remains unknown. Martin Birnbaum claimed that Beardsley was 'engaged' to the actress Pauline Chase, but as Ms Chase was only born in 1885, the report seems untenable.

periodical, and his new style required infinite pains and infinite patience. There was, moreover, other work to be done. It would be wrong to imagine that Beardsley's dismissal from *The Yellow Book* had made him unemployable except by Smithers.

Lane, returning from America and realizing the effect of his actions not only on Beardsley's life but on his own reputation, strove to limit the damage. There was no question of offering Beardsley his post back, but Lane did commission two book covers from him.* Beardsley accepted the work, but insisted on advantageous terms. Several independent-minded publishers and editors also saw their chance in the artist's break with the Bodley Head quarterly. Heinemann commissioned a small poster; Pennell asked him to contribute to an anthology of poems and pictures celebrating the work of the London County Council,† and a coloured lithograph of 'Isolde' was published in *The Studio*. Elkin Mathews asked him to design a frontispiece for Walt Ruding's novel, *An Evil Motherhood*. Probably pressure of work, together with an ironic sense of justice, led Beardsley to try to pass off on Mathews 'Black Coffee', one of the drawings suppressed in the fifth *Yellow Book*. He knew that a block had been made of the drawing and, as 'time was pressing', he thought to use it. There was the spice of revenge in this because, technically, the reproduction rights to the picture, and the block itself, still belonged to Lane.

When Mathews saw the picture, however, he thought it 'unsuitable' for a frontispiece. Certainly it had no point of connection with the novel. The situation was exacerbated when Lane learnt of the planned subterfuge, and was quite prepared to believe that Mathews had encouraged this attempted piracy. There was, Beardsley told Smithers, 'a blaze up with Lane-cum-Mathews', and he was obliged to produce a new design at 'the sword's point'. He made a more

* Lane offered the post of art editor to D. S. MacColl, who 'sent him away with a flea in his ear', explaining that, as a friend of Beardsley's, he could not possibly supplant him after his shabby dismissal. To escape further rebuffs – and to reduce expenditure – Lane then took on the duties himself.
† The anthology was intended as election propaganda for the ruling 'progressive' party in London. But, as Pennell recalled, 'when the votes of the members were counted, it was found the progressives had lost twenty-five seats. Such was the power of Art in England. I was told Beardsley lost us a lot of votes.' (*Adventures of an Illustrator*, p. 255.)

suitable drawing of a young man in an armchair, using (Mathews claimed) Walt Ruding as his model.

His own portrait by Blanche was exhibited in the Royal Portrait Society's exhibition in October. Beardsley himself submitted a wash drawing of a lady on a horse as a portrait of the Comtesse d'Armail-hacq – whom he seems to have invented. By such means he kept himself and his image before the public.[22]

As plans for *The Savoy* progressed, a prospectus was required. For the cover he produced a picture of Pierrot, tripping across a stage clutching the first number of the periodical, but Smithers found the image whimsical and frivolous. He suggested that 'John Bull' and the great British public 'would like something serious'. Beardsley forthwith transformed the flippant Pierrot into 'John Bull' himself. This new 'superior' drawing was printed on pink paper and issued, with Symons' 'Editorial Note' and details of the publication ('120 quarto pages of letterpress . . . six or more illustrations independent of the text together with illustrated articles', all for two shillings and sixpence – half the price of *The Yellow Book*). Most of the eighty thousand copies of the prospectus had been distributed before George Moore's scrutiny of the Beardsley drawing revealed that John Bull was in 'a condition of strained sexual excitement'. The bulge in his breeches was small but unmistakable. Moore, listed in the prospectus as a contributor, was horrified at this latest jape which could capsize the venture at its outset.

He consulted with his young friend and neighbour, Edgar Jepson, who himself hoped to write for the magazine. A meeting was convened at Jepson's rooms in King's Bench Walk. Moore, Herbert Horne, Selwyn Image, Bernard Shaw and Teixera de Mattos attended. Not everyone shared Moore's and Jepson's righteous indignation. Indeed, there was a general feeling of regret among the gathered contributors that 'their attention had been drawn to the matter' at all. As it had, though, something had to be done. Shaw was elected 'fighting man in chief' of the scandalized authors. He went to remonstrate with Smithers and to demand the withdrawal of the offending prospectus. Smithers was amazed; he considered that John

OPPOSITE Design for the front cover of the prospectus of *The Savoy*, 1895.

Bull's state of arousal could only increase his appeal to the public. However, he saw no point in antagonizing his authors and, not having any copies left, diplomatically agreed to the circular's suppression.

Peace was restored, and Beardsley produced a John Bull of 'a more tepid temper', for a second issue. Nevertheless, the incident revealed the continuing nervousness of the artistic community in the post-Wilde world – it also exposed its hypocrisy. Ernest Dowson was quick to point out that Jepson, for all his vociferous outrage, had submitted a story to the periodical, so 'confessedly indecent that he was afraid to sign it, lest it compromise his academic reputation'. Nor was suppression of the prospectus the only censorship of Beardsley's *Savoy* drawings. His cover was judged a liability. The discarded *Yellow Book* and the poised penis of the impish *putto* were both excised from the original design. George Moore considered the details offensive, while Smithers was perhaps unwilling to allow the rival quarterly a place, however undignified, on the cover of his periodical.

Nevertheless, the literary gossips were in no doubt that the new quarterly would not be shy of offence. One of the first notes of advance publicity was sounded by Owen Seaman's poem in the *National Observer*. The ditty suggested that although *The Yellow Book* had lost all its 'spice' when 'Aubrey went' the 'New Quarterly Blue Book' would be more highly seasoned than its progenitor had ever been, and that the 'racier journal' would 'stamp its pages/With Beardsleys braver far'. Seaman's poem appeared in November and it was hoped that the quarterly would follow directly, but the alterations to the cover, coupled with last-minute changes to the literary contents, and the myriad complications attendant upon launching a magazine, postponed the intended publication date. Even though Beardsley had drawn a densely worked, if conventionally conceived, Christmas card for insertion in the first number, it became clear that *The Savoy* would not make its appearance until the following year.*[23]

The last months of the year saw a *rapprochement* between Beardsley and Raffalovich. The thread of friendship was picked up, and the

* The Christmas card was one of two Beardsley drawings exhibited at the 25th Exhibition of the Glasgow Institute of Fine Arts (3 February – 4 May 1896).

round of dinner invitations, concert parties and theatre trips recommenced. The planned pastel portrait was mooted again and in every note Beardsley announced its imminent commencement. The tone of their correspondence altered by degrees. Raffalovich shifted from 'My dear Mentor' to 'My dear André'; Beardsley ceased signing himself 'Télémaque' and became, less coyly, 'Aubrey Beardsley'. Raffalovich sealed the friendship by presenting him with his latest production, *L'Affaire Oscar Wilde*; Beardsley offered Raffalovich news of the forthcoming *Savoy* ('a new magazine I am bringing out') and an introduction to its publisher. Raffalovich had the neglected manuscript of a novel he had written some years previously and Beardsley used his influence to get Smithers to accept it for publication.

The frustration of *The Savoy*'s delay and the piecemeal nature of Beardsley's work for it reawakened in him a desire to illustrate a book. He had not produced a sustained piece of illustration since *Salome*. *Under the Hill*, he realized, would not be finished quickly if at all. His plans to illustrate Edmund Gosse's *Secret of Narcisse* had, despite good intentions, never matured into ink and action. Gosse, modest about his work, was not concerned by this failure. He urged Beardsley to move on from it, and pressed him to illustrate not some 'ephemeral work of the day' but an acknowledged masterpiece of 'old English literature', which might be 'in his own spirit'. To such prompting Beardsley had replied – in what Gosse called 'his eager, graceful way' – 'Set me a task – tell me what to do and I will obey.' Gosse, who relished the role of literary godfather quite as much as Beardsley enjoyed the mask of suppliant son, suggested three subjects: Pope's 'Rape of the Lock', Ben Jonson's *Volpone* and Congreve's *Way of the World*. The Congreve at once 'jumped' to Beardsley's eye; he knew the play well and loved it. He had illustrated his Mermaid edition of Congreve's works at school. *The Way of the World*, he announced, would be his first care. The other two titles he could not 'see' with the same clarity.

He brooded upon them, however, and found his mind or his 'eye' returning most often to 'The Rape of the Lock'. Perhaps he saw in it a chance to obliterate Wilde's flippant jibe at his admiration for Pope, or he may have been encouraged by Smithers, who certainly supported his decision to illustrate Pope's poem. Nevertheless, the publisher also had his own ideas for suitable (or unsuitable) titles. While Beardsley was havering between Congreve and Pope, Smithers suggested Aristophanes' *Lysistrata*. The play, about a sex strike called by the women of Athens, was suggestive to a pornographer. Though usually left in the obscurity of the Greek language and the library cupboard, it had recently been in the news. An experimental production had been staged at the Cracow Theatre and was reported to have been 'brilliant beyond expectation'.

An illustrated edition of *Lysistrata* could not be published openly, but it would, Smithers was confident, command a select market and a high price. Beardsley was excited by the idea; his imagination raced off on the story's possibilities. With a restless energy, increasingly typical, he began both projects at once: Pope and Aristophanes. On 16 December he announced to Smithers that '*Lisystrata* [sic] goes beautifully. [I] will bring you [the] first finished drawing tomorrow morning.' Only a few days later he told Raffalovich that he had begun illustrating 'The Rape of the Lock'.

Even in the midst of these two projected works, he was mapping out a third. For Heinemann, he proposed to make a series of twelve illustrations for *Cinderella* to be issued monthly (perhaps in the *New Review*). But this scheme was not begun. Smithers was an increasingly jealous guardian, and proposed paying Beardsley a weekly wage in return for exclusive rights to his work. Although this sum has been quoted as £20 a week, records suggest that it was £12. Even this amount, however, was handsome; it gave Beardsley an illusion of security, a space to work.

At the end of the year Beerbohm published an essay in *The Pageant*. He embroidered the themes and phrases of his letter to Ada Leverson. Looking back on his brief career, he announced his retirement, ceding his place to 'Younger men, with months of activity before them'. 'I feel myself to be a trifle outmoded,' he sighed. 'I belong to the Beardsley period.'*

By the end of 1895 it was indeed a past era.[24]

---

* Beerbohm's phrase has become famous; it was used as the title of Osbert Burdett's 1925 book on the 1890s. It is interesting to note, however, that when Beerbohm was interviewed by the *Boston Herald* (30 March 1895) about his admiration for Beardsley's work, he replied, 'It is inevitable [that I should admire it] . . . Is he not of my period?'

CHAPTER VIII

'The Hardworking Solitaire'

ON THE EVENING OF 22 January 1896, Leonard Smithers gave a small dinner party at the New Lyric Club on Coventry Street, to launch the first issue of *The Savoy*. It was an intimate gathering, quite unlike the rowdy, crowded affair which had ushered in *The Yellow Book*. Only a handful of the contributors could – or would – attend. Smithers presided, Beardsley and Symons were there, together with Beerbohm, Yeats and a young writer named Roudolf Dircks. A gloss of female company was provided by Mabel Beardsley and, in a rare public appearance, Smithers' small, buxom wife, Alice.

As the company stood about in the little private dining-room waiting to be seated, and Mrs Smithers made nervous small talk about the bamboo wall-coverings, Symons, in the spirit of controversy, produced two letters sent to W. B. Yeats. They were from high-minded literary friends, who condemned roundly Yeats's connection with the new quarterly and its publisher. Symons read out the first note, from the earnest Rhymer, T. W. Rolleston, accompanied by Smithers' rising cries of 'Give me the letter, give me the letter, I will prosecute the man.' Symons dodged the publisher's arm, finished the document and, tucking it into his pocket, proceeded to read the

OPPOSITE 'Puck on Pegasus', the title-page decoration for *The Savoy*, nos. 3–8, 1896.

second note. It was from George Russell, the Irish poet, and its strictures were even more severe. Russell denounced the new magazine as the very 'organ of the incubi and succubi'.

Beardsley listened closely. Then, perhaps perceiving Yeats's embarrassment at being the conduit for these attacks, he went up to the poet and said, 'You will be surprised at what I am going to say to you. I agree with your friend.' He confessed that he had always been haunted by what he called 'the spiritual life', and recounted his childhood vision of the bleeding Christ over the mantelpiece. Nevertheless, with casuistic agility, he suggested that there was grace in working even for the 'organ of the incubi and succubi'; 'after all,' he said, 'I think there is a kind of morality in doing one's work when one wants to do other things far more.' Beardsley's confession to a sympathy for the 'spiritual life' perhaps encouraged Yeats to sound him out on his own great passion of the moment: the occult. Once seated, Yeats discoursed with the art editor in 'deep, vibrant tones' across the table, of 'the lore and the rites of diabolism' – or 'dyahbolism', as he pronounced it.

The lure of 'magic' in its various forms was strong in the 1890s: an extreme reaction to the disorientating claims of modern science. It seemed to many that far from making the workings of life clearer, science had supplanted the simple certainties of faith with less certain credos – material, relative and harshly Darwinian. Faced with a new, disparate and contingent world, the desire for unity, certainty and the life of the spirit reasserted itself. Some clung to the comforts of established religion. Others sought new ways into the unified spiritual realm. Magical and spiritualist societies abounded across Europe: Egyptian, Kabbalistic, Hermetic, Rosicrucian, Theosophic and Masonic. Yeats had begun the spiritual search early, founding the Dublin Hermetic Society in 1885, and had joined Madame Blavatsky's Theosophists two years later. In 1890 he became an initiate of the Hermetic Students of the Golden Dawn, and regularly spent his evenings in fancy dress, balancing arcane symbols above his head in the hope of being vouchsafed a vision.

Beardsley's early drawings, particularly the two he made for the *Pall Mall Magazine*, often led people to assume that he shared the comtemporary interest in the occult. Indeed, he did dabble on it:

fringes, experimenting occasionally with a 'planchette' (a pictorial ouija board) and even obtaining some startling results. Nevertheless, confronted by Yeats's portentous utterings, he was not to be drawn. With that 'stony commonsense which always came upmost when anyone canvased the fantastic in him', he made it clear (to Beerbohm, if not to Yeats) that he thought 'Dyahbolism' silly. He greeted each of Yeats's fantastical pronouncements with a brisk, 'Oh really? How perfectly entrancing' or 'Oh really? How perfectly sweet.'

At the other end of the table Symons was doing his best with Mrs Smithers, expanding upon the delights of various continental capitals and expressing amazement when she confessed to never having visited them. Symons's contention, that the peripatetic was 'the best of all possible lives for the artist', provoked Yeats to break off his disquisition upon the occult. He declared emphatically that 'an artist worked best among his own folk and in the land of his fathers'. Symons defended his position with the claim that 'new sights and sounds and odours braced the whole intelligence of man and quickened his powers of creation'. But Yeats began to batter him with argument. Mrs Smithers, with the delicate tact of a suburban hostess, sought to calm the situation. She asserted sweetly, 'Mr Symons is like myself. He likes a little change.' The bathos of the phrase effectively terminated the debate, but the truth of her sentiment lingered. There was a prophetic irony in the exchange: Beardsley had spent his short professional life claiming that he could work nowhere but London; in 1896 he would find himself continually driven to seek 'a little change'.

The 'Bombe glacé à la Venetienne' and the 'Champignons sur croûtes' having been consumed and the menu cards signed, the party returned to the Smithers' rooms in Effingham House, above the shop. But Beardsley's strength was giving out. At the flat, he all but collapsed with a minor haemorrhage. He reclined, 'grey and exhausted', propped on two chairs in the middle of the room while the party continued around him. Smithers, sweat pouring from his face, was turning the handle of a hurdy-gurdy piano, while Yeats looked on with ill-concealed distaste and wondered when he could decently leave. Beardsley, however, would not let the music stop; between visits to the bathroom to spit blood, he urged Smithers on with rapturous exclamations over the instrument's 'beautiful tone' and 'incomparable touch'. Beardsley survived the half-comic, half-infernal evening, and *The Savoy* was launched upon the world.[1]

The reception of the first number by press and public was 'for the most part unfavourable'. The editor professed himself flattered by the abuse, taking it as the inevitable reward of true art in a philistine world. The reaction was, however, a muted affair when set beside the storm that assaulted the first *Yellow Book*. There were no calls for suppression, no demands for the publisher's head. But, inevitably, there were comparisons: scarcely a review failed to mention *The Yellow Book*. Not infrequently, these comparisons were mildly favourable to *The Savoy*: the *Sunday Times*, *Academy* and *Athenaeum* all found in favour of the newcomer. *The Times*, however, damned it with faint praise, suggesting that *The Savoy* must be a 'disappointment' to those hoping for something 'more antinomian than its now respectable parent'. Of the English press, the *Star* was the most frankly hostile. Given 'Logroller's' close connection with the Bodley Head, it was not surprising that he denounced the rival publication as 'dull – at once eccentric and insipid'.

The noted eccentricity was almost entirely attributable to Beardsley. And, despite the presence of Shaw, Yeats, Symons and the rest, it was Beardsley who came to dominate public perception of *The Savoy* as he had done with *The Yellow Book*. He had provided the cover, which was at once recognizable as a 'Beardsley' and at once suggestive of the bizarre. Inside the cover, he was represented not only in drawings but also in prose and verse.

Artistically he was still characterized as a decadent. The connection – emphatic in the pre-publicity – was maintained after the magazine's appearance. The *Sunday Times* (which Beardsley told Smithers '[is] always so friendly to me') praised the 'splendid decorative effect' of the artist's 'compositions, his patterns, his "idea"', but admitted that it was exercised in the service of an 'audacious decadence'. Despite such terminology there was tentative recognition that Beardsley's work had developed. His French-inspired eighteenth-century style was received with guarded praise. The *Sketch* was 'glad to notice' that he had 'discovered a new type of woman' who, unlike her predecessors, was 'almost pretty'. Gabriel Lautrec, writing in the

Courrier Français, found the work less morbid, and suggested that Beardsley had found a 'new soul'.

Under the Hill was less easily judged. The *Athenaeum* found it 'the chief feature' of the first instalment but did not trust itself to an adjective. The *Academy* considered the story 'a little too fantastic for us'. The *Star*, to Beardsley's amusement, pronounced a strong distaste for the experiment. But it was left to the puritans of the New World to wield the strongest epithets: the New York *World* denounced the novel as a 'Fresh Eruption of Beardsleyism', while the *Sunday Times-Herald* of Chicago, unwilling or unable to break the fateful connection, said it must have been written by 'one who is at present nameless in England'[2].

Ada Leverson offered Beardsley and his colleagues the advertisement of satire. She asked Burnand if she might provide a spoof for *Punch*. In an aside that revealed how far public interest in artistic ventures had eroded since 1894, Burnand wondered whether anyone would 'know anything about the *Savoy* – sufficient that is to warrant a parody'. Nevertheless he acquiesced in Mrs Leverson's pleas, and she produced a cod-appraisal of 'The Book of the Week – "The Saveloy"', focusing on the work of 'Simple Symons', 'Max Meerboom' and 'Daubaway Wierdsley'. In an inversion of the critical consensus, she lauded Mr Wierdsley's prose work, 'Under Ludgate Hill', for 'its terse, vigorous style, its absolute truthfulness to nature, and – more important than all the rest – its high moral tone'.

Beardsley was delighted with her parody, not only for its play upon his work but for its creation of 'Simple Symons'. He eagerly adopted the soubriquet: relations between Beardsley and Symons were already becoming strained. There was perhaps a tinge of professional jealousy in Symons's attitude, a resentment that Beardsley should be trespassing in the realm of letters. Beardsley seems to have enjoyed emphasizing his literary aspirations: when Symons put him up as a member for a library, he insisted on designating himself on the application form 'a man of letters'.

Symons, however, ascribed the tension 'à cause, à cause d'une femme . . .' Perhaps some rivalry over a chorus girl at the Thalia provided sufficient cause for a quarrel. Although Beardsley's social life maintained a decorous veneer with lunches *chez* Raffalovich and jolly dinners at the Leversons, he was seeking more and more the relief of dissipation, spending sodden evenings at the Thalia with Smithers and a seedy crowd of bibulous poets. Almost a year on from the Wilde débâcle he still felt vulnerable, and remained acutely conscious of the 'snubs and cold shoulders' he met with in general social intercourse. He needed the companionship of cronies.

Despite this taxing schedule of 'pleasure', he found time to draw. In the first months of 1896 he was at work on some of the most complex and most finished pictures he had ever attempted. The illustration of 'The Rape of the Lock' became his chief charge. In style, the pictures were a refinement and simplification of the over-wrought illustrations for *Under the Hill*. Beardsley's delight in fashioning elaborate furniture and elegant costume was held in check by a classical severity. Balance was maintained: the dense cross-hatching of the parquet was offset by ingenious use of dotted lines to suggest lace, embossing and embroidery, and the confident return of large areas of white and (occasionally) black. There was aptness in Smithers' decision to describe the poem as 'embroidered' rather than illustrated. Beardsley was pleased with this stylistic departure and took some early examples to Joseph Pennell for assessment. In the Pennells' drawing-room, he was disconcerted to find Whistler. Relations between the two had not developed after their first meeting in the spring of 1893, but Beardsley affected unconcern, as did Whistler.

He produced his portfolio and began to show Pennell the new work. Whistler looked on, indifferent, as the first of the 'Rape' drawings was produced, then with interest, finally with delight. He announced with measured formality, 'Aubrey, I have made a very great mistake – you are a very great artist.' At these words from his hero, Beardsley (if we believe Pennell) 'burst out crying'. Whistler reiterated his verdict – 'I mean it, I mean it' – over the sobs.[3]

Early in February, Beardsley went to Paris with Smithers and a girl from the Thalia for a bacchanalian excursion. They met up with Dowson, who was already there, and spent much time with Gabriel Lautrec, a young French critic and humorist. In his review of *The Savoy*, Lautrec, with a sounder sense of fun than of criticism, had

OPPOSITE 'The Battle of the Beaux and the Belles', for *The Rape of the Lock*, 1896.

suggested that much of Beardsley's early work might have been produced under the influence of opium. It was a charge of which Beardsley was innocent, but the recollection of it perhaps prompted him to make an experiment with drugs. The experiment seems to have been more conducive to riot than to art. On the evening Beardsley took 'haschish for the first time', he went on to dinner with Lautrec, Smithers and Dowson. His laughter became 'so tumultuous' that it affected the rest of the party, who had not taken 'haschish'. They all 'behaved like imbeciles' and, had they not been in a *cabinet*, would have been 'turned out' of the restaurant.

There were several such jolly evenings, although the fun was sometimes undercut by an air of tension. Not infrequently Beardsley would become exasperated with Dowson's shambolic manner, lack of dress sense, and apparent ignorance of personal hygiene. He admired Dowson's poetry, but found the poet's way of life incomprehensible and inexcusable. He complained to Smithers that it was unfair to inflict such a shabby and malodorous figure on a smart restaurant, and, when forced to spend an evening with Dowson, he was likely to sink into silence or flare into rudeness. Dowson remained unstung by such behaviour. With a fine sense of fun, he dedicated his rollicking rustic ditty about love in a dairy ('Soli cantare periti Arcades') to Beardsley, and continued to seek him out.

On 11 February, the two attended the première of Wilde's *Salomé*, produced by Aurelien Lugné-Poe at the Théâtre de l'Oeuvre. It was a 'triumphant' occasion. The presence of the play's first illustrator did not, it seems, go unnoticed by the French avant-gardistes. In his review, Jean Lorrain, the decadent poet and *conteur*, regretted that the producer had not asked Beardsley to design the 'costumes and décor'. The following day Dowson, seeking sea air, solitude and cheap accommodation, left for the Breton village of Pont-Aven. Smithers had already returned to London to attend to business, but Beardsley resolved to stay in Paris. He discovered that – like Symons and Mrs Smithers – he liked a little change. Free from the demands of London life, he was able to concentrate on work.

He took rooms in the Hôtel St Romain, in the rue Saint-Roch, close to Les Pyramides, where he continued to work diligently at the 'Rape' pictures. He avoided almost all social commitment, sending one 'lying note' to escape a lunch party, and keeping a low profile in the hope of avoiding the Leversons' friend, Clara Savile Clark, who was then in Paris. He eschewed too (as he told Smithers) the louche delights of the rue Mongé and its brothels. He strove to stay within his means, giving up his rooms at St James's Place and living the life of a 'hard working solitaire'. But economy proved beyond him. Dining at the modestly priced chain of Duval restaurants became 'loathsome and impossible', and his natural extravagance soon asserted itself. Even as Smithers was selling off some of his library, Beardsley was haunting the bookstalls, acquiring new and expensive books. He complained of being 'swindled abominably' over a copy of Diderot's dialogue on art and amorality, *Le Neveu de Rameau*.[4]

Practical preparations for the second *Savoy* were left largely to Symons and Smithers in London. The printing was taken away from Smithers' erstwhile partner, H. S. Nicholls, and given to the Chiswick Press. The format was expanded and it was decided that Symons's name should appear on the cover as designated editor. Nevertheless, Beardsley maintained an influence from across the Channel. He undertook to design a new cover and to provide his contributions in prose and line, and the 'art contents' as a whole continued to carry the distinctive stamp of his direction. There were pictures from Pennell, Rothenstein, Shannon and Beerbohm; Sickert sent a drawing of the Rialto from Venice, and, before leaving London, Beardsley had accepted some curious work by a BGS old boy, W. T. Horton, whom he had encouraged so generously the previous year.

On the literary side too there was evidence of his will. Clara Savile Clark, whom he had been avoiding in Paris, was to contribute a short story under the byline 'A New Writer', and it was Beardsley's advocacy that secured the acceptance of John Gray's poem, 'The Forge'. His own contributions had been delayed by the 'Rape' illustrations. Perhaps to reduce the burden, it was decided to ask permission to reproduce the drawing of 'The Comtesse d'Armailhacq' bought by Charles Holme from the show at the Society of Portrait Painters. When Holme refused the request, wanting to save the picture for use in *The Studio*, Smithers adopted a more expedient measure: in a deft piece of early publicity he included the title drawing for 'The Rape of the Lock'.

Beardsley's central place among the contributors was to be confirmed by the inclusion of two portraits – a caricature by Beerbohm
and a fanciful self-portrait, showing himself tethered to a slender
herm. The image carried a suggestion of an artist tied to venery and
the world, and, indeed, given that he was contemplating work on
Aristophanes' *Lysistrata* – a play given over to herms and their phallic
properties – the image was apt enough. Nevertheless the bonds
looked decidedly light, and the captive blithely at ease.

Smithers kept in close touch with Beardsley; an almost daily flow
of letters crossed the Channel. Towards the middle of February he
arrived in Paris, planning, after a few days of fun, to go on to visit
dealers in Brussels and buy stock for his next catalogue of curiosities.
Beardsley went to see him off; at the Gare de Lyon, on a sudden
whim, he decided to go along too. Without luggage, leaving his
possessions at the Hôtel St Romain, he boarded the train for Belgium.
The excitement of the jaunt did not last long. After a few days of
'Flemish lewdness' and 'Belgian lubricity', during which Beardsley
seems to have embarked on a liaison with a girl called Rayon, disaster
struck. His health collapsed; he suffered a succession of bad haemorrhages, and was confined to bed in his hotel. Smithers tended him
briefly, but was obliged to return to London.

Beardsley was left in Brussels too weak to travel, but not quite
abandoned. He had contacts there, and an associate of Smithers'
former partner, Nicholls, was staying nearby. None the less, it
was a frightening predicament. He was unable to leave his room,
scarcely able to rise from his bed. He tried to find solace in
work but was in a state of distracted anxiety. As he told Smithers,
'I'm as nervous as a cat, and am torn in a thousand directions, so
don't be surprised if you get a mixed collection of drawings from
me.'

Despite his nerves and his lungs, he produced the new cover
design, a drawing of the 'Ascension of Saint Rose of Lima', which
he considered had 'a sort of charm in it' that he had 'never given to
any other drawing',* and an 'elaborate piece of nonsense' illustrating

---

* Saint Rose of Lima, the first saint of the New World, was a Peruvian maiden who,
in Beardsley's phrase, 'vowed herself to perpetual virginity when she was four years
old.' There was an image of her at Brompton Oratory.

the 'Third Tableau of the Rheingold'. He also submitted a poem, 'The Ballad of the Barber', which (like the two drawings) was supposed to form part of *Under the Hill*. All were sent to Effingham House. The poem – about a court coiffeur who, finding his skill disorientated by desire for the young princess, is obliged to kill her – was a distillation of decadent attitudes to art, artifice and desire. Beardsley had already begun the illustration for his poem when Smithers told him that Symons thought the ballad 'poor' and wanted the last verse reworked. Beardsley was horrified at what he considered an act of presumptuous intervention. He suggested printing the poem pseudonymously under the nom-de-plume 'Symons'[5].

His irritation was temporarily alleviated by the arrival of Mabel, who came over to nurse him; her presence provided a happy alternative to worry and work. She escorted him on short forays from the hotel, and, with a fine disregard for economy, they lunched at the Café Riche and enjoyed a bottle of Latour Blanche 1874. Aubrey, encouraged by Smithers, had become something of a wine snob. He described the Latour Blanche as 'the most insidious and satisfying thing imaginable', and his letters to the publisher were flecked with similar pronouncements on rare vintages tasted and important bottles drunk.

Mabel's career was not spectacular, but she had recently been performing at the Royalty with Arthur Bourchier's company, in the *Chili Widow*, and there was the prospect of further work from the same quarter. Indeed, this ensured that her stay in Brussels was brief. She stayed only a week. The report of her brother that she took back to London cannot have been good. Ellen, 'utterly wretched' at the thought of her son an invalid in a foreign land, had him 'prayed for' at St Barnabas. She hoped that prayer might help him and console her: on the latter score she was disappointed; she told Ross, 'When I heard his name [read out] I was heart-broken.'

Mabel left Vincent O'Sullivan, a young American-born writer of Smithers' circle, to watch over Aubrey. O'Sullivan had just arrived and was staying at the Hôtel Emperor; he was soon joined by Smithers and Mrs Smithers. Beardsley's semi-invalid condition prevented any

AUBREY BEARDSLEY.

resumption of riotous indulgence, but there was scope for gentler pleasures. On one evening all four went to *Carmen* at the Opera, and the evening was enlivened by a man in a box falling 'with a thud' for the conspicuous charms of Mrs Smithers, who jokingly returned his ardent looks. Afterwards, as the party supped at a nearby restaurant, the man reappeared, took a table opposite and resumed his impassioned ogling. Beardsley missed the dénouement of the drama. His strength was failing and O'Sullivan took him back to the hotel. Smithers afterwards boasted that he had fixed a price with the man for the enjoyment of his wife's long-vanished 'virtue'.

In this typically Smithers atmosphere, it was decided that the *Lysistrata* illustrations should be the next major product of Beardsley's pen. He announced his intention of starting on them as soon as Smithers returned to London, but found that he lacked the will and the strength for the task. He became 'desultory', toying with ideas for *Under the Hill*, but drawing little. He did make an elegant cover motif for Smithers' edition of Dowson's *Verses*, and Dowson was delighted with the design, though Beardsley privately joked that the simple arabesque marked out a 'Y' – for 'Why was this book ever written?'

Another small drawing made at this time was similarly allusive: 'Puck on Pegasus', which became the title-page ornament for all the later *Savoys*, had a strong autobiographical tone. Beardsley identified with Puck, the master of mischief and confusion, and the presence of Pegasus sounded an echo of that important article on 'drawing' by Walter Crane, where it was claimed that a 'pen, once mastered, may prove a quill from the wing of Pegasus himself'. Sure enough, in Puck's quiver are a quill, plucked from the winged horse, and a drawing pen. Beardsley was asserting his status as master of his chosen medium.[6]

In the more mundane aspects of his life he felt anything but magisterial. He was being subjected by the local doctor to an uncomfortable regime of 'blisters' – a treatment which made him 'furious' but which

OPPOSITE 'The Coiffing', illustrating Beardsley's poem 'The Ballad of a Barber', 1896.

had some effect, distracting him from his other ailments. Soon he announced that he was able to walk again without too much difficulty, and hoped to return to London at the beginning of May. He instructed Smithers to find him a high-up room in a hotel with a lift; he wanted the benefits of clear air without the problem of steep stairs.

His doctor thought the return journey would soon be manageable, but in the meantime increased Beardsley's miseries by forbidding him to eat fish or drink wine, and putting him on a regime of 'creosote pills'. This was another irritation to add to a long list: the 'filthy weather' made walking impossible; the hotel was emptying of interesting guests, but the staff was entirely taken up with preparations for the marriage of the proprietor's daughter. Moreover, news of his sorry plight was being touted around London with increasing exaggeration. By the time it crossed the Atlantic the American press were ready with his obituary.

The one pleasant distraction was the arrival of Raffalovich, who sought out Beardsley and took him to lunch. They had not seen each other for several months, and since their last meeting Raffalovich had been received into the Roman Catholic Church. His conversion had been a *coup de foudre*. He had previously shown scant interest in the faith and – indeed – had disapproved of Mrs Gribbell's conversion. Interestingly, he had marked his independence from her by ignoring the claims of the Oratory. He was baptized by Father J. M. Bampton at the Jesuit Fathers' church in Farm Street, Mayfair. He had since made a pilgrimage to Loretto, in Italy; it is possible that his visit to Brussels was the final stage of his journey home.

Raffalovich had the zeal of a new convert. While at Loretto, he had arranged for masses to be said in the Santa Casa for the conversion of various friends – and indeed enemies. Oscar Wilde's name was put forward, and it is more than probable that Beardsley's was too. Certainly Raffalovich's conversion forged another important Roman Catholic link in Beardsley's life. Vallance and Ross were both converts; Mabel had been received the previous year; John Gray had returned to the practice of his faith with new energy and feeling. Vincent O'Sullivan had been brought up a Catholic, and Dowson had converted in 1891; though his observance was imperfect, he carried a small crucifix which he dipped into his wine before drinking. Aubrey's 'leanings' towards Rome were already well established, but from this time they became more marked.

His immediate concerns, however, were not spiritual but practical: how to escape from Brussels. Unable to travel without assistance, he telegraphed Mabel asking her to pilot him home, but she was tied to her theatrical commitments. Ellen asked Ross whether he might undertake the chore, but he too had to decline. As a last resort, Ellen, though in delicate health, made the journey herself, but arrived in such a state of exhaustion that a day's recovery was needed before she could escort Aubrey back to London. Ross had meanwhile proved himself useful, renting a set of rooms for Aubrey at 17 Campden Grove, Kensington, and sending around a sofa upon which the invalid could recline.

It was a necessary item of furniture: Aubrey would spend many of the coming days horizontal. Dr Symes Thompson was consulted as soon as Aubrey reached London, and his prognosis was most unfavourable. Aubrey had pinned much hope on returning to the care of his first doctor; this bleak pronouncement caused unlooked-for alarm. He was, for the first time, really 'depressed and frightened' about his condition. He came to view his trip to Brussels as the turning-point in the struggle against his disease: he was now forced to regard himself as an invalid. Of course, he remained susceptible to the accesses of optimism – and sudden bouts of depression – common to tubercular sufferers; he also enjoyed sudden and unexpected remissions and apparent recoveries of health. But from May 1896 his course was fixed, and he seemed to know it.[7]

There were happier occurrences to distract him. With a celerity that might astound modern publishers, Smithers had produced finished copies of *The Rape of the Lock*. It looked wonderful. Beardsley, with a letter of elaborate mock-modesty, dispatched a copy at once to Edmund Gosse, the volume's dedicatee and inspirer. Gosse was delighted with the 'delicious golden book, and its inscription', saying that Beardsley had never had a 'subject which better suited [his] genius, or one in the embroidery of which [he had] expended more fanciful beauty'. Ellen's friend, Lady Alston, was so taken with the book that she presented a copy at the wedding of Princess Maud and Prince Charles of Denmark. These notes of private praise were soon echoed in the press.*

The *Manchester Guardian* ruled that Beardsley's art was perfectly in harmony with the spirit of Pope; this verdict was endorsed by the *Saturday Review*. Even the usually disapproving *Times* found the illustrations 'ingenious', and there was agreement that in the depiction of his heroine Beardsley had made a 'first concession to conventional ideas of a pretty face'. Few publications found fault with the production, although *The Studio*, Beardsley's first champion, was muted in its praise. The unsigned review (possibly by Holme) took issue with the artist's new style, finding too much labour expended upon 'insignificant detail'. The force of Beardsley's 'indispensable' line had been lost in over-elaboration. His illustration of parquet flooring came in for particular censure as being 'unpleasant', 'wearisome', and 'commonplace'. 'The Toilet' was praised as the most successful picture in the suite, because of its well-balanced and contrasting masses. Only the *Metropolitan Magazine* of New York dismissed the drawings out of hand as 'absurd failures'.

Despite the approving notices, *The Rape of the Lock* was, of course, a small-scale, exclusive production. Smithers had set the print-run of the ordinary edition at 1000 copies, but initially printed off only 500. The numbers were comparable to Lane's edition of *Salome*, but the impact made was much less. *Salome* had marked a moment, combining the notoriety of Wilde, the acumen of Lane, and the novelty of Beardsley. The press had recognized and proclaimed the point. The reissue of a classic poem with illustrations which tended towards conventional prettiness could not expect to compete. Smithers, however, knew how to make small editions pay, and was sufficiently encouraged by the book's reception to propose a miniature 'bijou' edition, reusing

* Another who received a presentation copy was Yvette Guilbert, the celebrated French *diseuse*, who was then appearing at the Empire. Guilbert, like Beardsley, was regarded as an embodiment of *fin-de-siècle* decadence. Jean Lorrain had urged Guilbert to acquaint herself with Beardsley's work (*Poussières de Paris*, 1er series, p. 150), and she did so. Symons, who had befriended her on her first visit to London in 1894, sent her a copy of the second *Savoy*. She wrote back with discerning praise for Beardsley's distinctive designs. Symons subsequently introduced them. (Karl Beckson, *Arthur Symons*, p. 112.)

all Beardsley's pictures much reduced and thus securing a second harvest on the artwork. Such ploys may have seemed necessary, since Beardsley's future output was uncertain.[8]

Dr Symes Thompson was insisting upon the necessity of 'quiet and change', so Aubrey was sent to a substantial Victorian boarding-house, 'Twyford', in the 'depths of country stillness' at Crowborough in Sussex. His fellow boarders ('various good ladies') were unexciting, but the rooms were pleasant, and he liked the place. It was near enough to London for Mabel, Ross and Smithers to come to see him. Though his cough lingered, strength gradually returned. But all drawing was 'stopped on doctor's orders'. This was a serious inconvenience. The deadline for the third number of *The Savoy* was approaching and the magazine's star illustrator had produced almost nothing beyond a cover design and frontispiece. Perhaps the shortage of his work obliged Symons to pass the 'Ballad of the Barber' and its illustration, but Beardsley continued to fret over the poem and to make alterations until the last moment. It was his only significant contribution to the issue.

The poem was published under his own name, but separate from *Under the Hill*. A publisher's note announced the temporary discontinuation of the novel's serialization due to the author's ill health. The 'Ballad', for all Symons's doubts, was well received. Beardsley was particularly amused by George Moore's enthusiasm for it. Nevertheless the halting of *Under the Hill* was a blow. Down at 'Twyford' he brooded long on his plans for the 'continuation' of the story. Progress, however, was slow; instead, he read.

Smithers had sent him (perhaps at Mabel's or Raffalovich's prompting, but just as likely at his own request) a six-volume edition of Bourdaloue's sermons, and the exhortations and opinions of the seventeenth-century French cleric provided a salutary diet. But, as Beardsley wrote to Smithers, enclosing an order for the works of Shelley, Matthew Arnold and (surprisingly) Wordsworth: '[Man] can't live by Bourdaloue alone'. Smithers seems to have been optimistic about Beardsley's prospects. Encouraged by the good reception of the second *Savoy* and healthy subscription of the third, he announced plans for turning the quarterly into a monthly. This, as Beardsley remarked to Gray, would involve 'a tremendous amount of additional work', but he seemed more excited than daunted by the thought.⁹

Beardsley stayed at 'Twyford' for only a fortnight; his initial liking for the place swiftly evaporated. And though Ellen urged Ross to encourage him to stay ('Enlarge on the beauties of the place and its many advantages; he thinks a great deal of your opinion, *and naturally doesn't think much of mine*') he was not to be swayed. He returned to London for a consultation, and after various delays it was decided to find a new and more permanent resort. He favoured Brighton, the place of his birth, but the doctors recommended Epsom. It marked another return: over ten years before Ellen had taken Aubrey to the little town to 'get strong'.

He was now installed in 'two palatial rooms' at the Spread Eagle Hotel in the centre of town. The air on the downs was 'lovely' and the hotel had the advantage of a 'pretty little restaurantish dining-room'. Cheered by these surroundings and by the change of scene, he embarked, at last, upon the illustrations for *Lysistrata*. In just three weeks (and despite an 'iron rod' falling on his head), he completed eight full-page drawings. For all the indecorum of their details, the pictures were conceived and worked with severity. There was a pagan frankness about the images of the sexually confident women and the frustrated mentulate men very different from the salacious voyeurism pervading the work of Rops and other late nineteenth-century eroticists. Beardsley drew deeply on his knowledge of Greek vase painting and oriental art, and the influence of Japanese manga prints is discernible in the tone of licentious fun, in the stylizations of the giant phalluses, and even in the detail of the anal fusillade delivered by the women defending the citadel. As in Greek vase painting, the figures stand against blank grounds.

The control of the drawings is the more impressive when set against the continuing break-up of his health. The Epsom doctor confirmed that Beardsley's left lung was 'breaking down altogether', and the right was 'becoming affected'. He prescribed some 'wondrous medicine' which had little effect but to make the patient's 'shit black

OPPOSITE 'The Lacedaemonian Ambassadors', for *Lysistrata*, 1896.

AUBREY BEARDSLEY

and head ache'. Beardsley was soon 'too weak to walk or to exert himself'. He struggled to maintain a bantering note in his almost daily correspondence with Smithers, but there were moments of doubt and dread. He drew some consolation from a copy of John Gray's *Spiritual Poems*. The book was mainly translations from Latin, Spanish, German and French devotional poems and prayers, tempered with Gray's poetic meditations on spiritual themes. Beardsley considered the book 'really admirable'; it became something of a personal talisman. He felt the need of such support. When Smithers came to visit him on 17 July, Beardsley asked the erstwhile solicitor to draw up and witness his will. Everything was to go to Mabel.

His work, not unnaturally, was affected by this mood of dread. The *Lysistrata* having been completed, Smithers put him to work on illustrations for a Christmas gift book of *Ali Baba and the Forty Thieves*. Beardsley began with a picture of the frightened Ali lost in the depths of a dark wood, which spoke eloquently of his sense of fear and uncertainty. There was a suggestion of posthumous memorializing about his plans to gather up a slim volume of his 'table talk', and an even more elegiac note was struck in a beautiful drawing entitled 'The Death of Pierrot'. Beardsley's known identification with 'the white frocked clown of Bergamo' gave the image a ghastly pathos. The drawing was intended for the fourth *Savoy*, but Beardsley became anxious that it would be his only contribution. Perhaps he feared that, presented alone, it would be read as his epitaph, and he asked for it to be held over. The issue appeared at the end of July with no illustrations by Beardsley apart from a new cover and the repeated title page of 'Puck on Pegasus'.

The omission was hardly helpful to the magazine's cause. The conversion to monthly publication was not proving successful: it had been dealt a cruel blow at the outset. Soon after the appearance of the third number, W. H. Smith announced that they would not be ordering future issues. Symons had hurried round to their offices to remonstrate. W. H. Smith controlled all the railway bookstalls and their influence on the book trade was enormous. It was widely supposed that Beardsley's work must have provoked Smith's action, even though his contribution to Volume Three had been minimal.

When Symons queried the company's decision, the firm's manager produced a copy of *The Savoy* and turned up what he considered a particularly offensive illustration. Ironically, it was a picture not by Beardsley but by William Blake, one of four illustrating an article by Yeats on 'Blake as an Illustrator of Dante'. It showed the giant Anteus, unfortunately nude, 'setting Virgil and Dante upon the verge of Cocytus'. Symons's restrained observation that Blake was 'a very spiritual artist' provoked the response, 'Mr Symons, you must remember that we have an audience of young ladies as well as an audience of agnostics.' With unabashed hypocrisy the manager added that he might reconsider if 'contrary to our expectations, *The Savoy* should have a large sale'. There was no reprieve. Without the support of Smith's distribution, sales fell away. The print run was reduced to 2400 for the fourth issue.[10]

Meanwhile, though the doctors considered that their patient was making progress, the haemorrhages resumed, and by the end of July, a change of scene was once more being plotted. Dieppe was suggested, but Beardsley confessed to Smithers that he was fretful about going back to France, lest he be arrested for leaving his bill at the Hôtel St Romain unpaid. Once again he pressed for Brighton, but was overruled. Boscombe, near Bournemouth, was the medics' choice. Mabel undertook to travel down to the south coast to find a 'little home' in the town for her brother.

Aubrey told Raffalovich of the proposed move; he, Gray and Mrs Gribbell were staying near Epsom, at Weybridge, for the summer. It had been hoped that Aubrey might go to visit, but ill health had prevented this. Beardsley had introduced a slight formality into his dealings with Raffalovich. He did not tell his friend of the *Lysistrata* drawings until they had been completed and dispatched; even then, he dropped the reference casually, fearing that Raffalovich might disapprove. Raffalovich's conversion, however, had not led to any prudishness on his part. His fascination with sexual deviancy – his own and other people's – continued, although he strove to accommodate his interests and inclinations within the framework of his new religion. He at once expressed an interest in the *Lysistrata* drawings, wondering only, with typically well-informed nicety, whether they were illustrative of Aristophanes' play or the recent French version by Maurice Donnay.

The position Beardsley adopted between Raffalovich and Smithers was deliberately divisive. After his tentative attempt to bring them together over Raffalovich's novel, *Self-Seekers*, he seems to have worked at keeping them apart. He exaggerated the piety and pomposity of Raffalovich to Smithers, and downplayed his dealings with Smithers to Raffalovich. There was probably some necessary tact in this course, but there is no doubt that he encouraged the divide, preferring to keep his friends in separate compartments.

His interest in the *Ali Baba* project did not outlast his stay at Epsom. With Mabel seeking rooms in Boscombe, and Ellen preparing to take on the duties of nurse, he announced that he wanted his next project to be an illustrated edition of Juvenal's satire 'Against Women'. He had, of course, made one illustration for Juvenal already: his last published contribution to *The Yellow Book* had been the double-page 'Frontispiece for Juvenal', but he had not taken it further. Smithers, too, had an interest in the Roman poet, having prefaced his 1894 edition of the *Carmina of Catullus* with a mention of plans for a 'literal and unexpurgated' English rendering of Juvenal's works. After a lapse of two years, the two returned to the scheme, with Beardsley planning to produce not only the pictures but the translation.

It is difficult to judge his attitude to Juvenal. He had always disclaimed the title of satirist, though many had been keen to bestow it. Yet, by taking up Juvenal, he was allying himself with the greatest satirist of classical antiquity. There was little in his relations with women to suggest why he should wish to 'scourge' them. He had enjoyed the tarts at the Thalia; his sister was his closest confidante; though he might resent his increasing dependence on his mother, he acknowledged her loving care; in Ada Leverson he had found an intellectual companion and equal. His surviving correspondence with Mrs Leverson ceases in early 1896 and it is possible that some rift occurred which might have sharpened Beardsley's resentment 'Against Women'. But it seems unlikely: there is no echo of such an occurrence in the correspondence of their mutual friends.

The first illustrations he made serve only to confuse matters further. The drawing of 'Juvenal scourging woman' presented a bizarre image of the poet – with a three-line whip, vulpine leer, and the 'magnificent spout' of a tumescent penis – laying about a stolid female strapped to the top of a column. The poet appears as a figure of vicious licence; the woman has a lumpen unsensualized dignity. It was almost as though Beardsley were satirizing the satirist. The subsequent picture was not of a woman at all but of Bathyllus, the Greek dancing boy whose performances, according to Juvenal, provoked Roman matrons to a state of sexual frenzy. The abandon of the women is left to the imagination; the lewd posturing of the effeminate mime is carefully delineated. Bathyllus was something of a cult figure among *fin-de-siècle* decadents. Jean Lorrain had written a homoerotic poem about him; W. H. Mallock, in his satire of contemporary fads, *The New Republic*, had made the claim that, to the aesthetic school, 'the boyhood of Bathyllus is of more moment than the manhood of Napoleon'. Given that the life of Napoleon was one of Smithers' favourite topics, it is tempting to see a shared joke between publisher and illustrator in the choice of subject.

There was, however, a more immediate resonance. Beardsley's drawing depicted the dancing boy in the part of Leda (the role in which Juvenal mentions him). The elements of female impersonation and dancing would have had a direct appeal for Jerome Pollitt, Cambridge University's best-loved terpsichorean transvestite. As Pollitt was the eventual purchaser of the picture, it seems likely that Beardsley did the work with him in mind.[11]

After sundry delays, Aubrey was moved to Boscombe around the middle of August. Mabel had ignored the claims of the large, well-established and expensive Boscombe Chine Hotel, and taken rooms at Pier View, a smart little redbrick guesthouse on the undercliff above the beach. The front rooms had trim white balconies looking out to the sea and, of course, the pier. Aubrey was pleased.

The rooms were made pleasant for him: besides a bedroom he had a 'charming' combined sitting-room and workroom overlooking the sea. Some of his furniture was sent down, including two Chippendale settees of which he was proud. He decked the walls with his inspirations of the moment: prints by Watteau, Pater and Lancret. His 'studio', as he liked to call it, comprised a table and the two beloved Empire ormolu candlesticks. He began work at once.

Beyond the walls of his rooms, Boscombe seemed a 'strange place', but not in any interesting way. He was, he announced with Wildean hauteur, 'so disappointed with it'. He had, however, the consolation of his sister's presence, as well as his mother's; Mabel stayed on at Pier View for the first month.* A few days after his arrival, Smithers came to visit. He too was in the midst of upheavals, relocating his shop from Arundel Street to the fashionable Royal Arcade on Bond Street. He found Beardsley in poor shape, distressed by a troublesome cough and by the Boscombe doctor's 'bad account' of his condition. With knowledge of the causes of and cures for tuberculosis still vague, each new doctor was apt to dismiss all previous opinions and prescriptions. The Boscombe physician was no exception. His regime, over the following months, included a plethora of new measures: astringent doses of gallic acid and arsenic, the application of iodine to Beardsley's chest and the more familiar blisters to his back. His general tone, however, was pessimistic. At the first consultation he made it clear that it was unlikely he would be able to 'stop the mischief'.

Perhaps this sense of hastening and irreversible decline prompted Smithers to suggest producing an album of Beardsley's best work as a summation of his achievement. This idea, far more than the Boscombe air, served to perk the patient's spirits in the coming weeks. Energy returned, and his correspondence is full of plans and thoughts for the album. He dispatched letters to 'all the publishers, and private persons, etc., etc., for the right to reproduce work', and it was decided that Mabel should call in person on Dent and Lane to secure permissions from them. Beardsley's mind raced over which drawings to include – his poster designs he considered important – and how many. Fifty was the number decided upon. To give the book an additional mock gravitas he decided to ask Vallance, his first champion, to produce a complete list, or 'Iconography', of his drawings. He also wanted several portraits of himself included.

It was probably a desire to chase up pictures and permissions for

---

* Vincent Beardsley seems to have played no part in his son's last years. He is not mentioned by either Aubrey or Ellen and it must be supposed that he was living away from the family at the time; a letter from Gray to Raffalovich (10 October 1904) refers to 'the wickedness of Beardsley père'.

the album which led him to make a visit to London at the end of August. Calling on one magazine editor to retrieve a drawing, he was asked how he was: 'I'm at death's door,' he replied cheerily, 'but that's no matter.' Looking at his picture on the wall, he then exclaimed with innocent delight, 'How good! How good. What a clever boy I am.' The trip ended in disaster. His health broke down again, and he had to be taken back to Boscombe, where he was confined to his rooms for a month.[12]

The setback was severe. All who saw him at this time wondered if he would live more than a few weeks, and he himself began to doubt that he would pull through the winter. But from his sickbed he continued to direct the compilation and production of the 'Book of 50'. Almost everyone was proving helpful: Dent was positively 'gushing' in his eagerness to assist; Pennell, Beerbohm and Clara Savile Clark were all keen to lend their drawings. Lane, after a short delay, gave permission to reproduce three *Salome* illustrations. Only Charles Holme at *The Studio* was obstructive, refusing to allow any of his drawings to appear. In his irritation, Beardsley planned to re-draw at least one of the embargoed pictures. For, despite his poor health, he continued to work; the weekly cheques from Smithers were a necessity and he felt that he had to try to earn them. He produced a binding-block design for Smithers' edition of the memoirs of Marie Antoinette's hairdresser, and a frontispiece for a collection of short stories by Vincent O'Sullivan. He also began some drawings for the forthcoming *Savoy*.

Amazingly, though all these designs were undertaken during a period of physical debilitation and nervous exhaustion – and many were probably executed in bed – there was no falling off in quality. He was particularly pleased with a drawing of a naked woman inspecting a trayload of books held by an attendant dwarf. It was, he thought, 'a very good example of the improvement of my drawing of late', and decried the notion that his early work was his best.

As a present for Dent, who amidst all his generous help with the album had expressed a desire to have 'a little personal thing' from him, he produced 'Tannhäuser returning to the Venusberg'. It was a reworking of an early drawing which Dent must have seen and admired. The image of the haggard *Minnesinger*, denied absolution

and struggling through thorns back to his beloved Venus, had taken
on a deeper resonance than when Beardsley sketched it in 1891.
Dent was overwhelmed by its moral power and autobiographical
insight: 'All the spirit that is in me', he wrote to Ellen Beardsley, 'is
moved to its depths by this most beautiful, most pathetic drawing –
God save the boy's life!' Under the influence of its power, he conceived the idea that Beardsley should illustrate *Pilgrim's Progress* and
wrote suggesting it: 'Don't laugh! Just take it up and read it. If you
could do it I believe it would be your monument for ever, and you
know what real suffering is.' Beardsley acquired a copy of the book,
but there is no evidence that he ever took it up and read it. The
Dent drawing was not Beardsley's only repayment that autumn. He
produced a title-page motif for Will Rothenstein's and Gleeson
White's annual, *The Pageant*, a 'scroll' for *The Parade*, and a tailpiece
for the catalogue of Lord Carnarvon's library.

Smithers did not encourage such acts of generosity. Already he
was getting 'practically no return' on his weekly investment (though,
as he remarked brutally to Frederick Evans, 'after [Beardsley's] death
prices will rise'). He forbade Beardsley to design a new poster for
Unwin. Another casualty, though from a different cause, was
Juvenal's 'Sixth Satire'. After the twin achievements of *The Rape of
the Lock* and *Lysistrata*, he was finding it difficult to settle to a third
book, and the project began to lose momentum. He had embarked
upon it without a very clear scheme and, having produced two
pictures of Bathyllus, two of Messalina and one of the 'Impatient
Adulterer', as well as the frontispiece, his interest fizzled out. Like
Under the Hill, *Table Talk*, *Ali Baba* and *The Secret of Narcisse*, Juvenal
was set down to be taken up – later.

A new project rapidly took its place. Having introduced a brief
description of *Das Rheingold* into *Under the Hill*, he now thought to
expand upon the subject by producing a short, illustrated prose account
of the Rheingold story as the first in a series of 'play books'. Anxious
that he should produce something publishable, Smithers approved.[13]

The news of *The Savoy* was less than satisfactory. Sales, after an initial
surge, had continued to fall. The print-run had been reduced to just
1500 copies, and Smithers had begun to gather up back numbers for

resale as a bound volume. Beardsley's contributions were marginal: he provided new cover designs for each issue, but that was all. A half-tone drawing of 'The Woman in White', published in the September issue, was an 1894 drawing borrowed from Frederick Evans; the 'Death of Pierrot' was pressed into service the following month.

Beardsley, though he continued to push (unsuccessfully) for the inclusion of Gray's poems, seems to have relinquished editorial control over the 'art contents'. Horton's pictures continued to appear, but increasingly Symons and Smithers relied on old and existing artwork: eighteenth-century bookplates, Rossetti paintings, Blake illustrations. A rare innovation was the appearance in the October number of a cartoon by Phil May. May had claims to rival Beardsley as the period's exceptional draughtsman. A comic 'guttersnipe' realist to Beardsley's dandiacal aesthete, he nevertheless adopted a similar course: adapting Japanese conventions to a modern sensibility, and a highly individual style. They had several friends in common – Brandon Thomas, Douglas Sladen, and Will Rothenstein – but there is scant evidence to suggest they met. It was probably Smithers who sought the connection with May. Certainly May had admired the bijou edition of *The Rape of the Lock*. Beardsley was less easily persuaded: he thought May's contribution to *The Savoy* looked 'very out of place'. May's presence was not enough to raise the fortunes of the magazine and Smithers was obliged to announce that *The Savoy* would cease at the end of the year, after two more issues.

In the literary and artistic circles of London there was little doubt about the reasons for the periodical's failure. Hubert Crackanthorpe urged Grant Richards to buy up the title and make him editor. If *The Savoy* could but make a fresh start and 'break away from the Beardsley tradition', it would have a 'very fair chance of success'. Yeats reluctantly recognized the truth of this verdict. 'We might have survived,' he wrote later, 'but for our association with Beardsley.' The point was brought home to him when he wrote to a 'principal daily newspaper' complaining of the W. H. Smith action towards the magazine, and was told that his letter would not be printed because it alluded to Beardsley: 'the editor had made it a rule never to mention Beardsley's name.'

By the autumn of 1896 Beardsley was regarded as a non-person by the popular press and as an outworn liability by his contemporaries. But Smithers was unrepentant. As a mark of defiance (or a measure of economy) it was decided that the last issue of *The Savoy* should be made up entirely of contributions by the art and literary editors. Beardsley, after his near-total absence from the previous numbers, was fired by the thought, and announced his intention of producing some 'scorching' pictures for 'No. 8'. For the penultimate issue, however, he had prepared a third poetic offering. Symons's disparagement of 'Ballad of the Barber' never ceased to rankle, and he determined to smother it beneath the laurels of another triumph. The valedictory thread running through his work from the 'Death of Pierrot' to 'The Return of Tannhäuser' continued in this literary endeavour: a translation of Catullus's graveside hymn, 'Carmen CI'.

The choice of poem was suggestive, the choice of poet expedient. Smithers' 1894 edition of the *Carmina* contained, alongside the Latin text, convoluted verse translations by Sir Richard Burton, and more restrained, sympathetic prose versions by Smithers himself. Beardsley leant with his full weight on Smithers' prose:

> Through many a folk and through many waters borne, I am come, brother, to thy sad grave, that I may give the last gifts to the dead, and may vainly speak to thy mute ashes, since fortune hath borne from me thyself. Ah, hapless brother, heavily snatched from me.
>
> But now these gifts, which of yore, in manner ancestral handed down, are the sad gifts to the grave, accept though, drenched with a brother's tears, and for ever brother, hail! for ever, adieu!

And deftly transformed it into

> By ways remote and distant waters sped,
> Brother, to thy sad grave-side am I come,
> That I may give the last gifts to the dead,
> And vainly parley with thine ashes dumb:
> Since she who now bestows and now denies
> Hath ta'en thee, hapless brother, from mine eyes.
>
> But lo! these gifts, the heirlooms of past years,
> Are made sad things to grace thy coffin shell,
> Take them, all drenched with a brother's tears,
> And brother, for all time, hail and farewell!

The economy of Beardsley's method reveals the richness of his poetic gift. He was pleased with the result, and eagerly inquired for Symons's verdict. Gray, he reported, was full of admiration.[14]

The poem, and an accompanying illustration, provided Beardsley with a sense of achievement when much else was vexing him. 'Tonic, milk, retirement and Boscombe air' were availing nothing in controlling the blood. The haemorrhages persisted. The weather had turned damp, exacerbating his condition and ruining at least one drawing. There were plans to remove to the South of France, but, however beneficial the change of climate might be, it was thought that his strength was insufficient for the journey. There were also several minor financial worries: Mr Deman, whom he had borrowed money from in Brussels, was requesting repayment; while Doré, the fashionable tailor, was suing for the settlement of a large unpaid bill. As a final irritation, production plans for the Album were being dogged by delay.

At the beginning of October a friend, probably Pollitt, came to visit for a week. Company had a beneficial effect, and despite gales outside Aubrey's mood brightened briefly. The 'scorching' drawings for the last *Savoy* were being assembled; Beardsley's progress had been slower than he wished. The bulk of the collection had to come from the series of vignettes intended for his version of *Das Rheingold*. There were pictures of Erda, Flosshilde, Alberich, and the Rhinemaidens. Of these, the drawing of Erda, the full-breasted earth goddess, was the most 'outspoken' and that of Alberich the most freighted with meaning.

Beardsley may have felt closer associations with other Wagnerian characters – with Tannhäuser, or Loge, the flickering mutable god of fire – but Alberich was the original German form of the name Aubrey. He could not ignore the claims of his namesake, the despised and dwarfish Nibelung who renounced love to win power. Beardsley gave the dwarf a nose very like his own. He showed Alberich after he had been tricked of his treasure and his power by Wotan and Loge, bound but protesting, uttering his terrible malediction upon the ring which has been taken from him. The picture is a study of enraged frustration. Though it does not allow of a literal interpretation, it suggests something of Beardsley's predicament: he had sacrificed much to fulfil his genius; now illness was stealing everything.

Besides the borrowed Rheingold drawings, the abandoned *Table Talk* was plundered for caricatures of Mendelssohn and Weber, but there was also some new work. The Wagnerian theme was revived in a delicate wash drawing, 'A Répétition of "Tristan and Isolde"' – one of a series of pictures inspired obliquely by music. He produced, too, a trio of notable literary libertines: Molière's Don Juan; Count Valmont from *Les Liaisons dangereuses*; and – in a sly subversion of the type – Mrs Pinchwife, the transvestite heroine of Wycherley's *The Country Wife*. There was also a drawing, 'Et in Arcadia Ego', which was a punning jest on Smithers' new business address and perhaps partly another reminder of the artist's mortality.

Beardsley had been brooding. Dwelling on his hateful condition, he had sunk into one of his periodic depressions. His mother felt excluded by these bouts of uncommunicative gloom, so, seeking an outlet in uncomplicated affection, she bought some canaries. The birds delighted her, and even amused her son, providing him with a rich subject for lewd allusions in his letters to Smithers.[15]

At the end of October, after a brief respite, Beardsley began to suffer a recurrence of haemorrhage. This time, he struggled to conceal the attacks from his mother. He was anxious not to alarm the family. Mabel had signed up for an American tour with Bourchier's company and he feared she would forgo the opportunity if she thought his condition was deteriorating.

The strain of the attacks and of their concealment took much out of him. Ellen, perplexed at his withdrawn fretful manner, suspected that he was worried about money, and feared that Smithers was no longer maintaining the weekly payments. News of her concern reached Robbie Ross, who promptly offered help. Though Mabel did not know the worst, she was certainly concerned at her brother's condition. It was perhaps at her prompting that Raffalovich began to write more often, sending both letters and presents. His generosity took the familiar forms: chocolates and flowers; he also encouraged Beardsley to list any 'bookish wants'. His letters were full of theatre

OPPOSITE 'Alberich', intended for 'The Comedy of the Rheingold', 1896.

ALBERICK

trips, concert outings and the latest debates on sexual deviancy. He continued to send copies of his anthropological publications, and Beardsley continued to regard him as a fount of knowledge on such matters. When Pollitt sent 'three very interesting photographs' for his comments or captions, it was Raffalovich (rather than Smithers) that Beardsley wished might see them.

To these common intellectual pursuits, and to the many acts of practical generosity, Raffalovich added a new note: his letters were touched with earnest concern for Aubrey's spiritual wellbeing. Aubrey responded readily to this new element. He already knew the 'beautiful' Catholic Church at Boscombe (perhaps he had accompanied Mabel to it), but he welcomed Raffalovich's offer to put him in touch with the local Jesuits. Father Charles de Laposture called at the beginning of November, and Beardsley found him 'most charming and sympathetic'. Contact was not kept up only because the priest left Boscombe on holiday soon afterwards, but a Catholic tone was maintained with the unexpected arrival of Vincent O'Sullivan, who was staying nearby in Bournemouth.

Smithers' fortunes continued to rise. The move to the Arcade was barely completed when he pulled off a 'good stroke of business with America'. It must have been a very good stroke indeed for he decided to buy a mansion in Bedford Square. Beardsley was much amused and delighted by the news, not least because, with Smithers in funds, the continuing sequence of post-dated cheques was assured.

The last *Savoy* drawings having been gathered together, a new project had to be decided upon. The opportunity to design a cover for Balzac's *La Fille aux Yeux d'Or*, illustrated by Conder, he declined. Their relations – both personal and artistic – stood 'very much in the way of any collaboration'. Yeats was a more attractive proposition. Whatever the poet's thoughts about Beardsley's responsibility for the collapse of *The Savoy*, he continued to admire his work. He had used the Avenue Theatre poster design as the frontispiece for the published version of *The Land of Heart's Desire*, and he wanted the artist to illustrate his new symbolist drama, *The Shadowy Waters*. Beardsley was intrigued by the notion, but other projects were also in his mind. He favoured, as a first task, a cheap illustrated edition of Dryden's *Metamorphoses*, and even began a drawing for it of Apollo and Daphne. His thoughts then raced to Gosse's suggestion of *The Way of the World* before being firmly directed by Smithers towards Dowson's verse-playlet, *The Pierrot of the Minute*. He affected to despise the piece, calling it a 'filthy little play'. But the care he lavished upon the five elegantly dotted decorations, and the fact that he finished the commission when so many others were left undone, suggest he had some feeling for both the play and its author. Perhaps he was spurred by the fact that Mabel had appeared as the Moon Maiden in a private production of the piece.[16]

Mabel was much in his thoughts as her departure for America approached. Ellen went to London to see her off, and Aubrey was left alone to enjoy the unseasonable spell of 'stunning weather' and to fret whether he would ever see his sister again. The spate of haemorrhages was lessening and he was able to walk along the front. The influx of 'winter people' at the guesthouse enlivened the atmosphere, perhaps even more than the acquisition of a bagatelle board for the downstairs smoking-room. His natural amiability asserted itself. 'Everyone here', he told Smithers with camp complacency, 'adores me.' He was popular with the children, and had made a particular friend of Mrs Towle, daughter of the eminent high-Victorian civil servant Sir Henry Taylor. She was full of accounts of all 'the great Victorian people' and promised to take him up to Shelley Park to meet Lady Shelley (wife of the poet's nephew) and to see the memorabilia of the great Romantic.

The decoration of Dowson's play having been completed, Beardsley announced that he was anxious to start work on something more substantial. All previous plans were abandoned. He applied to Raffalovich and Gray for suggestions. Their list included *L'Histoire d'une Grecque moderne* by Prévost, Stendhal's first novel *Armance*, and Benjamin Constant's *Adolphe*. The last appealed most, but Beardsley announced that he would first tackle Laclos' *Les Liaisons Dangereuses*. Since producing his *Savoy* picture of 'Count Valmont', he had reread the novel. It seemed to him attractive, and started several 'new ideas for drawing'. After the clear lines of *Lysistrata* and the multi-dotted technique of *Pierrot of the Minute*, he seems to have been planning a new style of 'line and tint'. Having recently discovered the work of Pierre-Paul Prud'hon, the French painter of the Revolution and First

Empire, he wanted to introduce some of that artist's 'erotic yet expressive' power into his pictures, letting the 'decorative element', so dominant in his recent work, take 'a back seat'.

The project was entirely to Smithers' liking, and he engaged Dowson to make the translation. Beardsley would provide a series of illuminated initials and ten full-page drawings. However, for all the excitement, the work was never begun. Beardsley had to wait, he said, until he had seen Dowson's translation before he knew which initial letters to make. Instead he started on a picture for Yeats's play, but this too went unfinished.[17]

The approach of winter produced in Beardsley a feeling of vague 'anguish'. The blood held off through the latter part of November but he was plagued by toothache and neuralgia. Writing to Ross, urging him to visit, he lamented, 'I am a poor shadow of the gay rococo thing I once was.' He placed himself in the hands of a 'charming and skilful' dentist, who undertook to deal with the problem. A course of phenacetin did not alleviate the discomfort, and even Ross's visit could not distract him from his misery. As soon as his friend left for London, Beardsley went back to the dentist and insisted on 'taking gas' and having the tooth out. It was a 'huge rock of a thing' as he wrote proudly to both Smithers and Raffalovich. More, he feared, would have to follow. Nevertheless, despite such horrors, he hoped to be allowed up to London. Raffalovich was offering to make a room ready for him at South Audley Street. Beyond his teeth, his strength, he thought, was reviving.

On 10 December, Ellen took him for a morning walk. They had nearly reached the top of the hill which led to the cliff path when he suffered a 'sudden burst of haemorrhage'. They struggled down to the little summerhouse at the bottom of the hill where there was a drinking fountain. Their route, Ellen told Ross, might have been tracked in blood, so profuse was the flow. At the summerhouse Aubrey was able to drink a little, and the cold water checked the blood. Ellen left him in the charge of a passing couple, while she set off to find a bath-chair. He was dragged back to Pier View and to bed, where he lay stretched out, racked by shivering fits, until he ebbed into sleep.

The drama of the incident and its long aftermath (the bleeding continued intermittently for almost a week) alarmed Ellen more than Aubrey. With Mabel away and Robbie Ross in London, she felt isolated and vulnerable. Aubrey perhaps sensed her fright, and with touching solicitude wrote to Smithers ordering a book for her Christmas present.

Aubrey himself brushed off the significance if not the seriousness of the attack. He wrote lightly of the incident to Smithers ('I expected I should make an "Al fresco" croak of it'). Nevertheless, in the wake of it he found himself plunged back into depression, a condition which seemed to him 'next door to the criminal'. He dispelled it, so he claimed, by hard work, though this must have been largely mental; he may have mulled over his plans for the *Liaisons*, but did not produce any drawings. Other distractions probably played a part in lifting his gloom: Zola's *Rome*, with its 'very ludicrous passages about Botticelli'; a presentation copy of Beerbohm's *Caricatures of Twenty-Five Gentlemen* ('Of course,' Beardsley wrote in his letter of thanks, 'I like my own portrait best'); unexpected winter sunshine and the even less expected excitement of an earth tremor ('a fruitful subject of conversation' at breakfast); presents from Raffalovich; long letters from Mabel; and a visit from the Pennells, who were spending Christmas at Bournemouth.

Joseph Pennell was the dedicatee of Beardsley's album of *Fifty Drawings*, advance copies of which, after long delay, had arrived. Beardsley underplayed his pride in the volume by lamenting the 'many faults' in the book's get-up due to the 'perfectly indecent haste in preparation'. The faults were not apparent to others, and the book's production values were unlikely to dominate any discussion of it.

The November issue of the *Magazine of Art* had carried an article by Margaret Armour on 'Aubrey Beardsley and the Decadents'. It sought belatedly to confirm his position at the heart of a movement which had all but expired. In Beardsley's drawings, the author claimed, 'we have the most complete expression of what is typical of the [decadent] movement – disdain of classical traditions in art and clear traditions in ethics; the *fin de siècle* outlook on the husk of life, and brilliant dexterity in portraying it.' Beardsley might 'say

almost without arrogance, "l'Art décadent, c'est moi."' The blight,
Armour considered, had its origins in the reaction against 'the somewhat emaciated purity of the Pre-Raphaelites' and in the pollution
of 'tainted whiffs' from 'across the channel'. She was, however, prepared to acknowledge some ground for optimism. Despite strong
words about the 'hectic vice' and 'slimy nastiness' of Beardsley's
Yellow Book work, she 'joyfully hailed' the 'improvement' of the *Rape
of the Lock* and *Savoy* illustrations. It is doubtful that Armour's joy
would have survived the final number of the pink-tinted periodical.*
Beardsley's pictures, particularly his Wagnerian illustrations, provoked outrage within a modest sphere. The reviewer in the *Academy*
considered them 'hideous – nothing less'. 'There is no reason,' he
wrote, 'why Mr Beardsley should not make such a drawing as that
entitled "Erda" if he likes, but there is every reason why the editor
of a magazine avowedly artistic should decline to publish it.' Even
Max Beerbohm regretted that his friend seemed to be trying 'in a
spirit of sheer mischief, to scandalize the public': 'An artist should
not do that.'[18]

Beardsley enjoyed such squalls. He knew that even Smithers had
considered the 'Erda' drawing 'outspoken' on first acquaintance, but
he was irritated by the *Magazine of Art* article, writing to Raffalovich
that he felt he 'owe[d] an apology to all his friends for it'. Nevertheless, though he professed to dislike the epithet 'decadent', he continued to present himself, on occasion, in a decidedly decadent
fashion. As part of the publicity drive to promote the *Book of Fifty
Drawings*, he was interviewed for *The Idler*. Although the piece did
not appear until the following March, it provides an index of his
attitudes at the end of 1896.† He put himself forward in the mask
of the unrepentant dandy-decadent, avoiding the term but proclaiming the tenets. He advanced the virtues of art and artifice, the beauty
of ugliness, and the value of decoration. The pose was designed to

* *The Yellow Book* outlasted its rival but only by two issues, ending with Volume XIII
in April 1897.
† In a letter to Ross, Beardsley claimed that he had been 'interviewing himself' for
The Idler; he obviously prepared his answers but, from the description of Beardsley's
room, it would seem that Arthur Lawrence, the nominal interviewer, at least called at
Pier View.

startle: he admitted the fanciful notion that he could draw only by artificial light, and that, if he wished to work during the day, he had 'to pull the blind down and get [his] candles' in order to begin.

He refused to confine his comments to pictorial art, remarking that he was 'equally fond of good books, good furniture, and good claret'. He blithely advised his interviewer to lay down some bottles of Château Latour 1865, a notion which had the dual effect of shocking journalistic notions of economy and projecting Beardsley's desires into an uncertain future. When asked to name his favourite authors, he supposed they were 'Balzac, Voltaire, and Beardsley', while confessing to a current enthusiasm for the works of the French Catholic Divines. Of his art, he remarked, 'Of course, I have one aim, the grotesque. If I am not grotesque I am nothing.' In the face of economic necessity and grim physical constraint, he claimed 'as a proud boast' that he had always maintained a dandy's pose; 'I have always done my sketches, as people would say, for the fun of the thing . . . I have worked to amuse myself, and if it has amused the public as well, so much the better for me.' He would not admit the limits imposed by illness (or acknowledge the facts of his position): 'How can a man die better than by doing just what he wants to do most? It is bad enough to be an invalid, but to be a slave to one's lungs and to be . . . sniffing sea breezes and pine breezes with the mistaken idea that it will prolong one's existence, seems to me to be utter foolishness.'

The approach of Christmas provoked a sharpening in the split between the halves of Beardsley's world. To Raffalovich he wrote feelingly of 'the most beautiful of all the feasts', regretting that in its social and commercial aspects it should have 'grown to be so displeasing a season to almost everybody'. To Smithers he exclaimed with pagan exasperation, 'Ye gods what a feast is Christmas.' But to Raffalovich he fretted that he would be unable to attend midnight mass and would not witness the 'great festival' in the 'adorable' surroundings of the Brompton Oratory. With Smithers he adopted a note of strained impropriety, introducing into their correspondence puerile references to 'wet dreams' and 'cockstands'. He enclosed an obscene limerick about a 'young lady of Lima/Whose life was as fast as a steamer', claiming that he had sent it to a woman who had requested some 'verses' upon one of his pictures. For a Christmas card, he sent his publisher a lace-trimmed devotional portrait of one of the virgin-martyrs with an account of the lewd uses to which Monsieur le Frère de Louis XIV had put such images. Intriguingly, the reference was from Raffalovich's book, *Uranisme et Unisexualité*.

Christmas Day did not pass off without excitements and dramas at Pier View. At breakfast Beardsley found a pile of little presents beside his plate – gifts from fellow guests, particularly the children. He delighted the little girls by his grave display of surprise and grati-tude; he bowed over them and kissed their hands with elaborate courtesy. And he took pleasure in the antics and the excitement of the children as they opened their own presents. Gray sent him a copy of the Vale Press edition of an *Imaginary Conversation* by Landor. Gosse wrote a letter full of praise for the 'beautiful work' Beardsley had done in 1896, and assuring him of his place in the 'art history of the century'. Raffalovich sent a volume on Watteau and a 'kind' but unspecified gift – almost certainly a cheque. It marked the begin-ning of his generous and regular financial help.

Aubrey was too weak for any church service. The only overtly religious element in the day's proceedings was provided by Ellen. She gave her son a life of Jacques Bossuet, the seventeenth-century Jesuit controversialist, and a copy of St Alfonso Liguori's 'little book on the Blessed Sacrament'. Although still a High Anglican, Ellen was evidently much intrigued by, and far from disapproving of, her son's growing interest in Roman Catholicism.

At Christmas lunch, Aubrey was overcome by a 'horrid chill', which made him 'fly from the dinner table' and take to his bed, in a state of 'pain and fever'. It seems to have been the prelude to another tubercular attack. He was prescribed arsenic, but the cure proved worse than the disease; the drug 'disagreed most dreadfully' with him. Matters reached a climax. The year ended with prep-arations for 'a grand specialists' consultation' around Beardsley's bed to decide upon future action and treatment.[19]

CHAPTER IX

'An Invalid's Delay'

THE VERDICT WAS NOT GOOD. Beardsley had 'collapsed in all directions' and was 'frightening the doctors not a little'. It was decided to move him again. Aubrey hoped that his deterioration was due to nothing more than influenza, and clung to the hope that he would be allowed to return to London. The doctors proposed a less radical relocation: two miles west to Bournemouth.

Despite their proximity, in the eyes of the medical world, Bournemouth held various 'sanitary advantages' over its neighbouring resort. A sheltered position between low hills gave it an unusually favoured climate: the temperature between January and July was supposed never to fall below 45°F; the town boasted the lowest winter rainfall in the country. And beyond the meteorological benefits, there were the 'health-giving properties, especially for pulmonary diseases, of the pine woods, with the incense of which the air is thoroughly impregnated'. Although the town had grown rapidly as a health centre, achieving within fifty years a population of 38,000 and a reputation for fashionable modernity, the wooded walks and open parkland spaces had been preserved. The myriad pines lent the town an evergreen, almost Italianate, character.

His transfer to this pine-embosomed haven was, however, delayed.

OPPOSITE 'The Return of Tannhäuser to the Venusberg', 1896.

On 17 January, after arranging for his books to be packed and stored by a local bookseller, he collapsed again. For a week his life hung in the balance; he was too frail to be moved. In the midst of the crisis, news came from Mabel that she was extending her sojourn in the United States: the Bourchier tour had ended but she had been engaged by Richard Mansfield's company. The engagement was less the result of her thespian prowess than her personal charm and connections: Mansfield's business manager was Aubrey's friend, Charles Cochran. But the news of Mabel's delayed return added new terror to Aubrey's wretchedness: he feared she would not find him alive when she came back.

Perhaps the fear lent him strength. At the end of January he was carried downstairs in an invalid chair and jolted to Bournemouth in a heated coach. With Ellen, he was installed near the centre, in an ugly yellowbrick guesthouse at the corner of Exeter and Terrace Roads, close to the front, the pier, the pleasure gardens and the Winter Gardens. The house had been named 'Muriel', a name curious enough in itself but one which had the added distinction of belonging also to Herbert Horne's mistress, Muriel Broadbent, whom Beardsley had tried to 'ravish' in the supper-room at the Thalia. 'I suffer a little', Beardsley wrote to Gray, 'from the name of this house. I feel as shy of my address as a boy at school is of his Christian name when it is Ebenezer or Aubrey.' It was one more thing to bear.

He found himself in the care of a new physician, Dr Harsant, who pronounced most unfavourably on his condition, telling Ellen that her son would not last another winter and might die at any moment.

With a fine display of civic chauvinism, if not medical insight, he laid the blame for Aubrey's sorry state upon the climate and position of Boscombe. Pier View, exposed to the winds, was, he announced, particularly 'badly situated for a consumptive'. Only the timely removal to Bournemouth had preserved his life. The move certainly did have a beneficial effect. The patient was roused from illness and depression; Dr Harsant was impressed, and was soon allowing the possibility of a sojourn in London during the spring.

The thought of London was better than medicine for Aubrey. Resuming his correspondence, he was a-buzz with plans for where he might stay. He canvased advice from Raffalovich and Smithers: a studio in Bloomsbury? a little flat where he and Mabel might live together? a hotel perhaps? or a lodging-house? Anxious to make light of his recent crisis, he took an interest in the ailments of his friends. Smithers had been having trouble with his leg (gout, perhaps); Raffalovich had an injured hand.[1]

Beardsley made himself comfortable in his new surroundings, assembling and ordering his belongings. He made up his little 'studio' table, laying out the pens and pencils. Ellen was amazed and delighted to witness these signs of interest and activity. Among his drawing materials, he also set out a small watercolour paintbox which he had recently acquired. His first essay in the new medium was a mauve-tinted wash drawing of Théophile Gautier's cross-dressed heroine, Mademoiselle de Maupin. The eponymous novel was one of the key works of the period: Swinburne had called it his 'Golden Book'; Baudelaire had revered it; Wilde would not travel without a copy. The story was an unrepentant hymn to the amorality of art and the joys of sensual beauty – a telling subject for Aubrey to select for his first picture of the new year.

The most recent breakdown of his health had, it seems, provoked an intensification of his concern for the 'spiritual life'. But it was an influence he struggled to accommodate. He had come to view his religion as something not merely separate from but opposed to and exclusive of his art. Writing to Gray about two priest-artists – Father Sebastian Gates and Father Felix Philpin de Rivière – he exclaimed perplexedly, 'What a stumbling-block such pious men must find in the practice of their art.' In another letter he expressed his envy of Raffalovich's butler, who was planning to convert and 'whose conduct of life puts no barriers in his way to the practical acceptance of what he believes in'.

Beardsley did believe. But he considered that his 'practice of life' (or, rather, practice of art) imposed real barriers to the practical acceptance of faith. The separation of art and morality insisted on by the artists of the 1890s had transformed itself in his mind into an opposition between art and morality. Ignoring the instances of Fra Angelico, John Bunyan, Palestrina and any number of others, he called upon Pascal as the great example to all artists and thinkers faced with a like predicament; the French philosopher 'understood that, to become a Christian, the man of letters must sacrifice his gifts, just as Magdalen must sacrifice her beauty'. Having established this credo in such stark terms, Beardsley was understandably reluctant to act. The sacrifice of his art was one he felt unwilling or unable to make.

It is unlikely that Raffalovich would have agreed with this framing of the equation. He had maintained his professional interests after his conversion; the arguments of the Farm Street Jesuits had shown him how he might do so with a clear conscience, and it is probable that he adopted a similar line with Aubrey.

Beardsley was acutely conscious of his work during the first months of the new year. The *Book of Fifty Drawings* was published in January, in an edition of 500 with fifty large-format specials. Beerbohm reviewed it enthusiastically in *Tomorrow*, praising its 'unique exuberance', and Haldane MacFall contributed some broadly complimentary waffle in the pages of *St Paul's*, but it received scant notice, and scanter praise, elsewhere. The *Athenaeum* damned it in a few sharp paragraphs, suggesting that the drawings were remarkable only 'for the pains the draughtsman has expended in the search for ugliness and deformities'. The *Daily Telegraph* regretted that he 'should be content still to envelop himself in an atmosphere of miasma such as to infect with its exhalations well-nigh everything that he creates'. Beyond these squibs, there was no outcry. The critics had grown weary of asserting that he did not know how to draw, and the gossips had found new subjects.[2]

Gray and Raffalovich came to Bournemouth for a few days in the third week of February, and Beardsley's spiritual wellbeing was one of the topics of their visit. By the time they departed, Raffalovich had arranged for Father David Bearne, a Jesuit priest from the nearby Oratory of the Sacred Heart, to call upon the invalid. Raffalovich was keen to address his practical welfare too. He had already made more than one generous gift of money, but now he formalized his generosity into a regular allowance of £100 a quarter.

It is difficult to compute the Beardsleys' income and expenditure at this time. With Bournemouth boarding-houses charging a daily rate of about eight shillings per person, the bare essentials of bed and board must have cost at least £6 per week. Smithers' cheques had become infrequent and irregular, and, perhaps to precipitate them, Beardsley, in writing to his publisher, often mentioned small but pressing debts. Raffalovich's allowance (which Beardsley certainly did not mention to Smithers) removed the spectres of anxiety and want. It would be too easy to link the payment of the allowance and the visits of Father Bearne, suggesting that Beardsley, caught at his lowest ebb, was blackmailed into the arms of the 'designing Jesuits' by Raffalovich's offer of an assured income. Smithers certainly had his suspicions on this score (and others have held them since). Intellectually and aesthetically Beardsley had long been attracted to Roman Catholicism. Its trappings and traditions he knew. He was drawn towards it, but was fearful of the attraction. Father Bearne, a convert and a 'man of letters', was well placed to offer reassurance. Beardsley pronounced the priest 'most charming', and accepted from him, at their first meeting, a 'long life of Saint Ignatius of Loyola'.

Bournemouth, as a haven for the terminally ill, was well provided with churches, and there was some rivalry among the denominations. Father Bearne's visits at 'Muriel' did not go unnoticed, and Beardsley received several lengthy lectures from 'pillars of the Anglican faith' about his communication with the kind fathers of the Sacred Heart. But it was not the attractions of Anglicanism which held his progress towards Rome in tension; it was the continuing claims of the amoral realm of art.

At the end of February Jerome Pollitt announced his intention of coming to visit for a couple of days. The young connoisseur was basking beneath an aureole of reflected glory: he was generally taken to be the model for the eponymous hero of E. F. Benson's facetious novel of undergraduate life, *The Babe, B.A.* In this borrowed fame, moreover, he was allied with Beardsley. The 'Babe' was described as having decked his rooms with 'several of Mr Aubrey Beardsley's illustrations from the *Yellow Book*', while on another page he went so far as to wish that he could 'look as if Aubrey Beardsley had drawn [him]'. Beardsley was delighted with the references and their testament to the endurance of his fame. He was also delighted at the prospect of his young patron's visit. He mentioned to Smithers that, should he see Pollitt in town, he might 'say something to him about the dignity of art and the necessity of artists', adding, as an aside, 'Insinuate a reference to Maecenas.'

Pollitt's generosity needed no such prompting. None the less, the young Maecenas arrived in Bournemouth on a mission: he wanted his bookplate. He had paid for a Beardsley *ex libris* in October 1895 and had yet to receive it. Aubrey was shamed into immediate action. Though there was no time to make a new picture, he suggested a compromise. The beautiful drawing he had produced of the naked woman selecting a volume from a dwarf-borne tray had appeared in the *Book of Fifty Drawings* as the 'Book Plate of the artist'. This could, however, be amended. The drawing was at Smithers' shop in London, but Pollitt had brought his copy of the album (one of the large format issues, printed on Japanese vellum). The artist duly doctored the printed picture, inserting Pollitt's name in the blank space at the top of the composition; he also added a facetious erratum on the facing page. Pollitt was able to take the lettered illustration to a block-maker and have a reduced format bookplate made from it.[3]

Beardsley had little else that he could show his friend, other than a couple of unfinished Juvenal illustrations, but tempted him with tales of the *Lysistrata* suite. Pollitt admired both the Bathyllus picture and the drawing of the 'Impatient Adulterer' and Beardsley under-took to complete them. (It might be noted that Bathyllus, according to tradition, was the beloved of Maecenas: Pollitt, in desiring the drawing, was living up to his classical soubriquet.)

Immediately after this visit, Smithers came down, grateful for some healthful coast air after his tribulations with his leg. In an outburst of holiday spirit, he, Aubrey and Ellen had their pictures taken by the local photographer, W. J. Hawker. Hawker was, it transpired, an old friend of Cochran's. The two images he made of Aubrey in a thick tweed suit at his work desk, were, even in the sitter's view, 'quite a success'. The look of studious composure he achieved for the camera was deceptive. By the time the prints were ready he had suffered another haemorrhage – his first since the move to Bourne-mouth. The worst was soon over but, despite an astringent course of Dr Harsant's specially formulated 'haemorrhage mix', the blood continued to 'ooze' through the first weeks of March.

The doctor's mounting alarm was increased when Beardsley began to haemorrhage afresh 'via the bum'. Dr Harsant's diagnosis – that Beardsley had developed tuberculosis of the liver – has been questioned. Haemorrhoids were, it seems, the more probable cause, but the incident was disconcerting for both doctor and patient. It had, too, the serious effect of throwing out plans for a stay in London. Better climes were needed. A long journey being out of the question, Dr Harsant suggested Normandy or Brittany, but feared that even these would have to wait until Aubrey had recouped his strength. Recovery was slow. An old anxiety returned when Doré, the tailor, issued a writ for the balance of his account. Beardsley was obliged to ask Pollitt to advance him twenty guineas in expectation of 'Bathylle' and a hand-coloured set of the *Lysistrata* illustrations.

A happier incident was the arrival of a young actress who had been on the Bourchier tour in America. She brought interesting news of Mabel and her doings, but Aubrey was concerned to learn that his sister had been worrying about him and determined to 'write her a good account' of himself. In truth, his spirits were lifting, and with them his health. By 18 March he was able to attend an afternoon symphony concert in the Winter Gardens, Dr Harsant sitting at his side 'in case of calamity'. It was, he declared, a great treat after his 'long exile from music'. Happily, even the excitement of Beethoven's Fourth did not provoke the feared relapse.

The appearance of *The Idler* interview created a gratifying little splash, and served to recall Beardsley to his friends as much as to the general public; he was particularly glad to receive a note from Mr King in Blackburn.* There were other reminders of recent achievement: Dent was planning a pocket edition of *Morte Darthur* which would reuse some of his illustrations; and advance copies of *The Pierrot of the Minute* arrived, looking 'delightful'. There were hints too of continuing endeavour. Even in the days of blood-oozing debilitation, Beardsley produced a portrait drawing of Balzac for the back of Smithers' planned edition of *Scènes de la Vie Parisienne*. He

---

* At Brighton Grammar School his reputation, though still upheld by Mr Payne, no longer received enthusiastic sanction from Mr Marshall. The headmaster had become increasingly antipathetic to Beardsley's 'occult taste for the morbid' (B. Muddiman, *Brighton & Hove Society*, 7 September 1907; p. 1037).

also began to consider his next real project. He found drawing exhausting, 'on account of the mere physical exertion required' when he tried to bring anything to completion. But he could plan and sketch out ideas, and he could write. He had been reading the fantastical *contes* of Jacques Cazotte, the eighteenth-century anti-rationalist, and was minded to make an essay in a similar vein, complete with coloured illustration. He began his story, 'The Celestial Lover', and the first picture almost simultaneously, but could finish neither. He redrafted endlessly the first page of the opening chapter; the wash drawing of his heroine was spoilt or abandoned. He did, however, finish his wash drawing of Mademoiselle de Maupin. It was sent to Smithers, who considered binding it into a copy of the novel to make a unique and desirable object. The image continued to haunt Beardsley though, and he announced his intention of illustrating the whole novel 'come what may'.

Even as he was announcing this plan, his resolve to convert to the Roman Catholic faith was crystallizing. He recorded several 'good talks' with Father Bearne, and many acts of kindness. The Jesuit, recognizing the literary bent of his charge, plied him with books from the Oratory library, saints' lives, ecclesiastical histories and devotional works. Aubrey studied them carefully. He also began taking 'instruction'; he spent two hours one morning closeted with Bearne having the creed of Pius IV explained 'most fully'. Although he had an intellectual desire for faith, he struggled sometimes to respond emotionally. 'My soul', he wrote to Pollitt in a moment of self-castigation, 'has long since ceased to beat.' To Raffalovich he lamented his 'dryness and difficulty in prayer', but hoped that these failings would be corrected with time and practice. First, the decisive step had to be made.[4]

He took it on the last day of March, perhaps hastened by his imminent departure for France. Dr Harsant had persisted in this recommendation, but, with Beardsley's condition improving, he now contemplated the Riviera as a possibility as well as Normandy. Beardsley was received into the Church that morning. He was too weak to go to the Oratory, but Father Bearne came to 'Muriel' to perform the ceremony, and to help him through his first confession. A first communion was brought to him that Friday.

He wrote at once to Raffalovich, addressing him as 'Dearest Friend and Brother', and giving him a very brief and 'very dry' account of what he called 'the most important step' in his life. In a note to Gray, he expressed his happiness and relief at being 'folded after all [his] wandering'. He wrote to Mabel, too, knowing that she would be delighted. (She herself had just delighted Aubrey with the news that she would be back in England by the end of May.)

The sincerity of Beardsley's conversion is beyond doubt. It was attested to by those who knew him well; even Lionel Johnson, a fellow convert who might have been disposed to doubt, was convinced. Although the poet did not go to Bournemouth, he heard much of Beardsley on the Catholic and the artistic grapevines, and he reported the consensus: 'I can say, emphatically, that [Beardsley's] conversion was a spiritual work and not an half-sincere aesthetic act of change, not a sort of emotional experience or experiment: he became a Catholic with a true humility and exaltation of soul, prepared to sacrifice much.' There were also things he hoped to gain: Father Bearne recorded that Beardsley sought 'the staying principle of authority and, above all, the sure grace of the sacraments'. Such hopes were understandable. Beardsley had always looked for father-figures, and, with his health and life fragmenting about him, the certainty of assured grace had an urgent attraction. Nevertheless, he found it impossible to accept such boons without reservation. He courted authority only to subvert it.

He could not deny his artistic life completely. To Smithers on the day of his reception, he wrote briefly about business arrangements and the weather, ending with an oblique, gallicized admission of his new status: 'je suis catholique and ever yours, A.B.' It was as far as he was able to go.[5]

Arrangements for his move to France were confirmed. He was to travel to London, spend the night at the Charing Cross Hotel and then cross to France before progressing, via Paris, to Menton. That, at least, was the plan. The prospect of London, however, was so exciting that he resolved to extend his stay to two days. A quieter hotel than the Charing Cross was needed, and Raffalovich found rooms for him at the Windsor in Victoria Street.

Beardsley travelled to London on 7 April. There had been a slight return of bleeding and Dr Harsant had become anxious that the journey to Menton might be too much. Dr Symes Thompson was consulted for a second opinion and Raffalovich, as further support, offered the services of his own physician, Dr Phillips. Both the London doctors concurred with Harsant's anxieties. They favoured France but feared that the journey to the Riviera would be too taxing. As a compromise, Paris was decided upon for the spring. The news provided an additional fillip for Beardsley's spirits. London was already doing him good. He passed two 'bright and happy' days in the 'dear little flat' at the top of the hotel. Raffalovich gave him a collection of 'beautiful pi books', and arranged for Father Bampton to call. The priest was disappointed that Beardsley was hurrying on so soon; he would otherwise have arranged for Cardinal Vaughan to confirm him. Smithers called with plans for a third, even smaller edition of *The Rape of the Lock*, with the illustrations reduced to 'well-nigh postage stamps'.

Nevertheless, despite such excitements, behind the brightness lay unspoken recognition that this was Beardsley's farewell to London. He saw Vallance and throughout the visit maintained a ready cheerfulness, but the compiler of the 'Iconography' knew that it was goodbye.[6]

Aubrey and Ellen travelled to France on 9 April, accompanied by Dr Phillips. Raffalovich had made all the arrangements and they travelled 'en prince'. The sea was 'beautifully calm and unruffled' and on the train from Calais to Paris Beardsley felt his spirits rise with every passing mile. They were booked into the Hôtel Voltaire, an old establishment opposite the Louvre, overlooking the river. It had been – though Beardsley may not have known it – the scene of Oscar Wilde's honeymoon. He made no allusion to the fact; he was too delighted with the views of the *quai* and the Louvre Palace. There was no lift, but the porters were happy to carry him up and down the stairs. He stayed downstairs for most of the day, so much inconvenience was avoided.

Paris at once exerted its spell, and Aubrey found himself able to walk unassisted for the first time in months. On his first morning he patrolled the streets, so he told Smithers, 'as pertinaciously as any tart'. He lunched in a restaurant and felt the constraints of invalid life recede. Ellen was less taken with Paris. She confessed to feeling like a fish out of water. 'I don't like Paris,' she told Ross. 'I'm afraid I'm very British.' But she was delighted with Aubrey's progress, and could scarcely believe the sight of him 'prancing about as if he had never been ill'. She wondered how long this 'miracle' would last.

Even in the midst of his excitement, Aubrey sought out the nearest place of worship: the church of S. Thomas d'Aquin, in the rue du Bac. He made himself known to the incumbent, the Abbé Vacossin. Easter was approaching and, although Beardsley hoped he might then be well enough to attend services, he made arrangements for the sacrament to be brought to him at the hotel. The connection with St Thomas Aquinas was fortuitous, but it awoke Beardsley's interest in the great Dominican who had striven to reconcile pagan thought with Christian Faith. He asked Raffalovich to pray that Aquinas might intercede for him. He also made his own requests. He undertook a pilgrimage to S. Sulpice, his favourite Parisian church, and spent half an hour in 'stumbling and imperfect' prayer.

Whether from moral conscience or forensic anxiety, one of his first acts was to settle his long-unpaid bill at the Hôtel St Romain. He then devoted himself to the cafés and the boulevards, luxuriating in the spring sunshine. He haunted the bookstalls and printsellers of the quai Voltaire, and found himself drawn into a stimulating round of social calls. He was too fragile for evening entertainments, but lunches and afternoon visits were possible. The young critic, Henry Davray (at Dowson's prompting), sought him out, as did Octave Uzanne, editor of Le Livre. Raffalovich provided him with introductions to several important figures, though it is not known whether Beardsley took up the chance to meet Huysmans.

Raffalovich also put him in touch with the elderly Mrs Ian Robertson and her daughter, who were staying in Paris. She was a keen medical amateur, and had already expressed interest in Aubrey's condition. She decided to take him in hand, and had no doubt that a strict regime of roast beef and hot water would effect a complete cure. Aubrey was taken with her and her plan; he remarked archly to Raffalovich, 'I have a personal experience of hot water and know what wonders it works.'[7]

Raffalovich was in Paris at the end of April; he, Gray and Mrs Gribbell were en route for a holiday in Touraine. Ever solicitous, he devised schemes for Aubrey's amusement and edification. They attended the Goncourt sale, where Aubrey bought two 'delicious dix-huitième engravings' – 'Toilette du Bal' and 'Retour du Bal' – after de Troy. He also hosted a lunch at Lapérouse, so that Aubrey might meet Rachilde, the Egeria of the Parisian decadents and the author of such lurid tales as *Monsieur Vénus*, *La Marquise de Sade* and *Madame la Mort*. She held a salon every Tuesday evening, but Aubrey had not been able to attend. On this occasion, the salon came to him. Rachilde was accompanied by what Aubrey described as 'some long-haired monsters of the Quartier'.

Beardsley was accepted and admired in Parisian artistic circles with a readiness he had never experienced in London. His work had appeared frequently in the *Courrier Français*, and an article about him had been published that month in *L'Ermitage*. Though flattered by the attention, he maintained an air of ironical detachment; he was suspicious of fads. The 'monsters' all presented him with copies of their books; he found them quite unreadable. Nevertheless, there were some points of contact between his art and that of his hirsute *confrères*.

Among the monstrous crew around the table at Lapérouse was the troll-like figure of Alfred Jarry, a protégé of Rachilde's. His extraordinary play, *Ubu Roi*, had been performed the previous December at the Théâtre de l'Oeuvre, and Beardsley almost certainly knew of it. Symons and Yeats had been in the audience, and Symons had reviewed it as 'A Symbolist Farce' in the *Saturday Review*. Jarry's use of actors as 'marionettes' would have engaged the attention of the creator of the 'Comedy-Ballet of Marionettes as performed by the Theatre of the Impossible'. And Jarry's theories of 'deformation' as the fount of art must have interested the acknowledged 'Apostle of the Grotesque'.

Beardsley's work was much admired by Jarry. The French author even fixed his admiration in an experimental novel on which he was then engaged. The story's hero, Dr Faustroll, had among his defining possessions books by Baudelaire, Mallarmé and Verlaine, posters by Bonnard and Toulouse-Lautrec, and 'a portrait' by Aubrey Beardsley.* When these chattels are seized by the bailiff, the doctor flees the law in a magical sieve and travels to a series of imaginary lands, each dedicated to one of Jarry's artistic heroes (or hates). Faustroll's second port of call is 'The Land of Lace'. The chapter is dedicated to 'Aubrey Beardsley', and the land offers a poetic evocation of Beardsley's world, in which 'The King of Lace' draws out 'the light as a rope-maker plaits his retrograde line, and the threads tremble slightly in the dim lights, like cobwebs'.[8]

Besides launching Beardsley into these fashionable artistic circles, Raffalovich addressed his medical and spiritual wants, introducing him to Dr Prendergast, an English physician practising in Paris, and Father Coubé, a sympathetic Jesuit. The Jesuits, though not officially permitted to operate in France, had a large establishment in the rue de Sèvres, and it was there that Beardsley went to make confession.

Although he was established in a 'pleasant' pair of rooms at the hotel, Aubrey had done almost no work in his little studio. He produced a cover design for the new miniature edition of *The Rape*, but was not pleased with it. When Heinemann called on him and asked whether he might do an illustration for a *History of Dancing*, Beardsley offered the Bathyllus drawing promised (and paid for by) Pollitt. Heinemann, however, wanted something less provocative, and Beardsley, conscious that he could no longer rely on Smithers' cheques, agreed to make a new picture for him. The clandestine commission had barely been accepted when Smithers arrived in Paris, anxious for the sight of fresh work. There was nothing to see. Beardsley had made no progress with the *Mademoiselle de Maupin* illustrations, though Smithers, in readiness, had had the original wash drawing expensively reproduced. 'The Celestial Lover' had been abandoned. The Juvenal project had not been revived.

---

* This imaginary drawing of the imaginary Dr Faustroll has been parlayed into an actual (but lost) Beardsley picture of Jarry. Beardsley did sometimes make sly portraits of his friends (such as the caricatures of Pennell and Beerbohm), but there is no evidence to suggest that he drew Jarry.

Beardsley's sprightly health, however, seemed to offer hope of future drawings, and Smithers urged him on. The result of his visit was that the long-neglected scheme to illustrate *Ali Baba* was revived. Beardsley had completed only one drawing for the story at Epsom, but now undertook to make more. It was perhaps to discuss this that the pair had arranged to lunch on 4 May. Smithers was delayed, but Beardsley had invited Henry Davray to join them, so the occasion was salvaged. He and Davray had become warm friends, and it was decided that Beardsley should take French lessons from the critic, though, as he told Raffalovich, 'it will cut away my last excuse for not being able to speak French.'*

It was a Tuesday, so they went on after lunch to Rachilde's in the rue de l'Échaude, where a company of determined *symbolistes* and *décadents* jostled, 'all caught,' as one guest remembered, 'in the lassoo of Rachilde's great laugh'. The great laugh died when news was brought of a terrible disaster at a grand charity bazaar being held in a marquee near the place des Vosges. There had been a fire; indeed it was still raging. A spark from an ether-operated cinematograph had started the conflagration; with appalling speed, the bunting had taken, the gaily-painted stalls and booths, all of wood and canvas, had followed, as had the marquee itself. Flames had leapt to the straw hats and taffeta gowns of the fashionable women who thronged the narrow aisles and manned the loaded counters. Panic raced as quickly as the fire; within thirty minutes 127 people were burned or trampled to death. Only five were men. Paris was stunned by the tragedy. That evening the cafés and theatres were almost empty. Within the circles of Aubrey's acquaintance, everyone had lost somebody. Blanche wrote the next morning putting off a luncheon engagement; 'several of his friends [had] been burned'.

Beardsley sought solace in work. Within a week he produced a 'sumptuous' cover design for *Ali Baba*: a fat bejewelled figure, variously seen as the robber baron, Ali Baba, after he had enjoyed the

---

* Although Beardsley read French well, and was erudite enough to be able to correct the pedantic Francophile Andrew Lang on his 'medieval French', he spoke the modern language with less confidence. Thus, he often adopted a proto-Franglais approach: one of his favourite expressions was 'Je suis stoné', to announce the fact that he was 'stony broke'.

thieves' treasure or 'an eastern potentate'. But with Smithers back in London the pace was not maintained. His nerves were too frayed to allow of concentrated effort. Paris was striving to obliterate the awful memory of the bazaar holocaust, and Beardsley strove with it. He went with the symbolist author Jean de Tinan to a reception given by the poet Jerome Doucet. He dined with Raffalovich and the others when they passed through Paris. He saw the American actor Clyde Fitch, and considered him 'really quite pleasant'.

He was delighted to receive a visit from William Rothenstein. The bustling impressionist found Beardsley 'much changed', not so much in looks ('he was always delicate') but in manners. 'All artifice had gone,' Rothenstein recalled. He was 'gentle and affectionate'. Beardsley told his friend that he had found peace after years of rudderless vanity. He spoke with regret of some of his past work, and talked wistfully of what he might do if time were allowed him. He was anxious, it seemed, to efface a self he now considered (or wished) was 'no more'. His moods were not constant, however, and his old self was apt to revive, but on that afternoon he impressed Rothenstein with his sincerity, with 'a new beauty in his face . . . a new gentleness in his ways'. Rothenstein produced his chalk and made a lithographic drawing of his friend, sitting pensively at the window. Beardsley thought the portrait admirable.[9]

Despite such diversions, Beardsley realized that he had to move again. Paris was expensive; it was also exhausting, and too much stimulation was taking its toll. His lungs had began to 'creak'. One or two 'little relapses', while not serious, impressed upon him the need for quiet and, if possible, warmth. Octave Uzanne fired him with tales of Egypt 'as a winter home'. It would, he claimed, be possible for Beardsley to live well at Luxor on ten shillings a day. Luxor, however, like winter, was a long way off.* A closer, short-term alternative was St Germain-en-Laye, a little summer resort east of Paris on the edge of the Bois. Aubrey and Ellen visited it and were charmed by its

---

* In healthier days Beardsley had not valued the charms of Egypt. He told the *Sketch*'s interviewer, 'I can never understand why people should seek Egypt in search of the Sphinx and the Pyramids, when they can visit Euston Station and survey the wonders of the Stone Arch.'

eighteenth-century aspect; the wood, Aubrey announced, was 'simply Elysian', the air deliciously pure and fresh. There was even a lift from the station up to the town. They found rooms in an unimaginably pretty hotel, the Pavillon Louis XIV, which had a garden, was scarcely fifty yards from the terrace and the park, and but a little further from the sumptuously ornate church. There was, as a final point of recommendation, a 'coiffeur' almost next door.

Although the hotel had not opened for the season (it was only the middle of May), the proprietors agreed to accommodate them from the end of the week. Their rooms were charming and, just as importantly, cheap (four and three francs a day respectively). Preparations were slightly hampered by a bout of food poisoning. Aubrey succumbed only briefly, but Ellen was so stricken that it was decided Aubrey should go without her. The American woman with whom the Robertsons were staying lent her servant to assist with the packing and transport, and to reduce his luggage and supplement his funds Aubrey set aside some thirty books to be sent to Smithers for sale.

Even so his departure was marred by the theft of a hundred-franc note. Aubrey felt 'wretched' about it, not, as he explained to Raffalovich, 'on account of the loss', but because of its sad reflection upon human nature. He had 'really been most generous' to all the hotel servants during his visit. He was delighted to reach St Germain-en-Laye. The cycle of move-recovery-relapse began again. Within moments of arriving, he pronounced himself 'better already'. The charm of the resort had not been illusory, and there were fresh pleasures to be discovered. The cooking at the hotel was particularly good, though 'rather expensive'. A charming fair was in progress with 'theatres for Guignol and all sorts of fantoccini under the trees'. Everything was near at hand. Aubrey was able to sit in the sunshine on the terrace, enjoying the fresh air, and contemplating the polluted haze over Paris. The 'creaking' in his lung disappeared.

The curator of the local museum called, aware that a distinguished artist had arrived, and presented him with a pass for the collection. Father Coubé had written to an old Jesuit priest in the town and Aubrey received a visit from Père Henri, whom he found 'the most friendly person imaginable'. The priest undertook to manage Beardsley's spiritual wants, and arranged for communion to be brought to him at the hotel. Aubrey was much taken with 'dear Père Henri', he was frequent in his confessions, and they spent hours talking of religious matters and of life. He was also delighted by the priest's naivety; on one occasion Père Henri asked whether Aubrey had completed his military service and he had 'felt quite ashamed' to explain that in Britain one was not expected to do anything for one's country.[10]

Father Henri's benign presence did much to strengthen the religious and even the religiose side of his nature. Report reached Ernest Dowson in Brittany that Beardsley was 'living surrounded by crucifixes and images'. Nevertheless, as was so often the case with Beardsley, an assertion in one direction demanded and provoked an opposite reaction. Even while forging a friendship with the elderly Jesuit, he began a close and enthusiastic study of Casanova's memoirs, which he had bought in Paris. Soon he was proclaiming the indefatig-able libertine as 'perfectly stunning', 'a great person and a great writer'. Casanova's exploits stimulated his imagination, and he enquired whether Smithers might want some 'erotic drawings', per-haps to be inserted into an English edition of the memoirs that Smithers was planning.

The drawings were never made. Beardsley was still unable to settle to his work and was 'living upon thorns', plagued by nervous anxiety. He tried to rationalize this to Smithers (who owed him money) as his 'mortal funk of the pauper's life and death', but its origins seem less specific: an unspoken dread that his health was about to collapse again. Other physical problems were distracting him too; he had a pain-ful ulcer on his tongue. Dr Edouard Lamarre, the local practitioner, had a high reputation and Beardsley took the opportunity to consult him not only about the ulcer but about his 'more serious trouble'. Pre-dictably, the new doctor, after much prodding and tapping, overturned all previous diagnoses and prescriptions, and 'raised his hands in horror' on learning that Beardsley had spent time at Bournemouth. Nothing, he declared, could have been worse, except perhaps the South of France. 'Mountain air' was the answer. Or, at a pinch, 'forest air'. If these could be obtained, there was every chance of recovery.

The terrace was put out of bounds. Beardsley was to embark on a strict regime of rest, sleep and forest walks. He was to rise every morning at four o'clock and 'take two hours' airing in the Bois'. He was never to be out of doors after five o'clock in the afternoon, and had to retire to bed early. Aubrey was much impressed by the forcefulness and confidence of Dr Lamarre's pronouncements. But his regime had to be delayed. Only a few hours after the consultation Beardsley had a bad attack of 'blood spitting' and was confined to bed. The ever-optimistic Dr Lamarre thought the attack a great boon. It had 'relieved' the congestion and done a lot of good. Beardsley, he announced, was well on his way to rude health. The plan for early-morning walks had, however, to be abandoned. All Beardsley's St Germain acquaintances thought it mad and, as he informed Gray, he slept 'better between four and six in the morning than at any other time'.

Dr Lamarre was not downhearted: Beardsley's room was close enough to the forest for an open window to give the required intake of dawn-fresh woodland air. Later in the morning the hotel page-boy would carry a chair out to some 'charming shady spot' and leave Beardsley there until lunchtime. More beneficial than forest breezes was the arrival of Mabel, who had disembarked at Liverpool and hurried at once to St Germain, arriving unexpectedly on 4 June. Aubrey thought his sister looked wonderfully well considering her long journey and had not changed at all. The slight trace of an accent he detected had, he thought, been 'acquired *since* she left America'.

Mabel was 'amazed' at the apparent improvement in his condition, and was of course happy to greet him as a fellow Roman Catholic. That Sunday they attended the Chapelle of the Pensionnat S. Thomas, and took communion together. 'You cannot imagine', Aubrey told Raffalovich, 'how happy the service made both of us. I shall always attend S. Thomas' Chapel in future.' Mabel's visit was 'jolly' but all too brief; the prospect of work took her back to London after only a week.[11]

An element of doubt had entered into Beardsley's relations with Smithers. He had been surprised to learn from Gray that his drawing, 'Venus between Terminal Gods', was for sale at the Royal Arcade when he had not even known that Smithers possessed it. He asked Mabel to call on Smithers and to check on the sale of his library.

With Mabel gone, St Germain seemed dull. There was no English colony; occasionally friends came from Paris to enliven the monotony. But after lunch they would return. As a diversion Aubrey and Ellen began to take German lessons. Aubrey found the grammar 'quite inaccessible', but with characteristic impatience was trying to read Goethe in the original. His health continued to hold up in the June sunshine, but soon he was expressing fresh anxieties. His confidence in Dr Lamarre's optimism was on the wane. Ellen wrote to Dr Phillips seeking advice. He sent a prescription for a 'tonic' and recommended that they consult Dr Prendergast in Paris.

Aubrey and Ellen hurried to see him. He was less sanguine about Aubrey's condition than Lamarre; the left lung had, in the euphemistic terminology of medical science, 'consolidated generally', but the right was still in 'very fair working order'. There were additional complications: Beardsley's liver was considerably enlarged and this was the probable cause of his weakness, depression and anxiety. Dr Prendergast was not impressed by talk of forest walks or mountain retreats. He recommended 'more bracing air' and plenty of exercise. Trouville, Boulogne, Dinard were suggested, but in the end Dieppe was chosen. It was not too fashionable and Aubrey knew it to be 'amusing and inexpensive'.

They made the move almost within the week, returning to St Germain only to pack and say their farewells. Aubrey was sad to leave Father Henri; the old priest was sad too, not least because he had no high regard for the spiritual amenities of Dieppe. Jesuit confessors would not readily be found there. The journey passed off without medical incident, though there was an altercation at the Gare St Lazare when they boarded a boat-train express. The stationmaster insisted that, since they were not travelling on to Newhaven and London, they could not ride. But since the next train would take seven hours to get to Dieppe, they stuck to their seats with 'overwhelming obstinacy' and prevailed.

They found Dieppe basking in bright sunshine, softened by gentle winds. Aubrey's room, in the Hôtel Sandwich on the rue Halle au Blé, was, he claimed, the largest he had ever slept in. It doubled as a 'very pleasant sitting-room'. He began taking Dr Phillips's tonic, but once again the real tonic was the novelty. Fresh sights and sounds stimulated fresh hopes, and he tried to establish a regime of early rising. He took breakfast at a little café at half-past eight and then sat enjoying the morning air. In the afternoon he stayed in his room to read, write and rest.

Père Henri's concern over the limited religious life of the town proved not unfounded: Dieppe's two churches, S. Remy and S. Jacques, though old and beautiful, were not 'well-served'. Aubrey put himself in the care of the Abbé Georget of S. Remy, but was not impressed. He sought a fuller consolation in the constant presence of the Blessed Sacrament in the church; it lent his private devotions an 'extraordinary joy and content'.

Dieppe offered rather more on the secular front. The holiday season was underway, and the town was abustle with life. Old friends were there: Blanche and Thaulow and Conder. Dowson was on his way from Brittany. Mabel had been obliged to put off a visit when she landed a part in a play, but Smithers was expected at any moment. With so many of the cast reassembled it was inevitable that memories of the Dieppois summer of 1895 should be stirred. Those weeks when *The Savoy* had been planned were tantalizingly close. Two years on, though the seaside scene was the same, much else had changed: illness had advanced, fortune had dwindled, and work had slowed. Nevertheless, for Beardsley there was still something of 'the joy of life' to be seized. Sitting, muffled up on the terrace, under a coloured umbrella, a glass of milk at his elbow, a book in his hand, he could conjure up a world of imaginary pleasures.

His enthusiasm of the moment was Denis Guibert's *Memoirs pour servir à l'histoire de la ville de Dieppe*. He amused Blanche and Conder with its rich and curious catalogues of the town's past. Some of the descriptions of medieval religious festivals and processions he knew by heart. Everything was vivid to his fancy: 'An amazing town,' he declared, 'I can see medieval Dieppe, and the Dieppe of the Renaissance and the town of powdered wigs and sedan chairs. I see it as clearly as the Rue Aguardo at the period of the Dame Aux Camélias and the Empress Eugénie. We ought to organize pageants . . . I should undertake the staging.' When Blanche suggested that any revival of pageants should really be the job of the natives of Dieppe, Beardsley dismissed the idea, pointing out, 'The French have no imagination, that's proved by the plays they produce at the Casino.' Besides. 'For centuries the English here have been on conquered soil. We shall re-animate the people's ancestral taste for religious processions, for military and naval parades, for firework displays on board a ship out of commission.'[12]

On to this scene of fanciful festivity a new and unlooked for firework exploded: Oscar Wilde. In the summer of 1895 he had been in prison, in the summer of 1897 he was in Dieppe. Released from gaol the previous month, he was staying a few miles down the coast in the village of Berneval-sur-Mer, under the conspicuous alias of Sebastian Melmoth. However, his visits to Dieppe were frequent, and his presence unmissable. He provoked alarm among the bourgeois British holiday-makers and the French restaurateurs. He was snubbed often and occasionally turned away, but his fellow artists welcomed him. The Hôtel Sandwich was his forwarding address and base in Dieppe, so it was inevitable that he and Beardsley should meet. They certainly encountered each other at a dinner given by the Thaulows, and greeted each other as friends.

Wilde had been putting the final touches to his poem, 'The Ballad of Reading Gaol', and was looking for a publisher. Smithers was the obvious (if not the only) choice: the man who would publish what others were afraid of. Dowson may already have suggested him; Beardsley would have confirmed the recommendation and told Wilde of the publisher's imminent arrival. When Wilde next saw him, Beardsley was accompanied by Smithers. The publisher was very intoxicated but amusing, 'Aubrey . . . was looking very well, and in good spirits.' Wilde asked Beardsley to dine at Berneval the following week; it is possible that he went, but the invitation was awkward. On the day he accepted it, he received a cheque from Raffalovich for the next quarter's allowance. The £100 was essential to his existence. There could be no doubt that his benefactor would disapprove of the renewed friendship with Wilde. Raffalovich's dictum, 'You cannot be Oscar's friend and mine,' did not allow of ambiguity.

In desperation Beardsley proposed to move to another hotel, telling Raffalovich obliquely, 'Some rather unpleasant people come here.' The plan, however, had to be delayed when news arrived that

Ellen's mother was very ill in Brighton and Ellen was obliged to leave her invalid son to visit her invalid parent. Aubrey remained at the Hôtel Sandwich in the care of Mrs Smithers, and could scarcely avoid Oscar. On one of Wilde's visits at the beginning of August, they went on a spree together. Wilde made Beardsley buy a hat 'more silver than silver', telling him he was 'quite wonderful' in it.

Beardsley confided something of his predicament to Vincent O'Sullivan. O'Sullivan later said that Beardsley had no 'dislike' of Wilde, but tried to avoid him because of 'receiving a pension from a man who was an enemy of Wilde's'. Avoiding a great man in a small town is a difficult business: on one unhappy afternoon Beardsley was with Conder and Blanche when he saw Wilde in the distance and steered his companions into a side street. The manoeuvre, unfortunately, was observed. Wilde had received many slights since coming out of prison, but his spirit had not become dulled to the pain. If anything, he grew more acutely sensitive with each stab. He felt Aubrey's snub, and in later years returned to probe the wound, seeking an explanation for his own sense of hurt as much as for Aubrey's unkindness.* His immediate reaction, however, was to ignore the cut. He continued to hope that Beardsley might design a frontispiece for his ballad, believing it would be 'a great thing' to have such an embellishment to the work. Beardsley agreed to the commission, but in a way which convinced Smithers at least that, as with so many other plans, it would never be done.[13]

Beardsley suffered his own moment of rejection. Sitting at his shuttered window one afternoon he saw the Pennells, recently arrived with Whistler, pass by. The Pennells called on him later, but Whistler,

---

* Recalling the incident later to Vincent O'Sullivan, Wilde exclaimed, 'It was *lache* of Aubrey . . . a boy like that, whom I made. No it was too *lache* of Aubrey . . . If it had been one of my own class I might perhaps have understood it.' The snobbery is unconvincing, and was as unworthy of Wilde as it was unjust to Beardsley. Wilde subsequently resolved his feelings more satisfactorily as paradox. Laurence Housman, in *Echo de Paris*, recorded Wilde's claim, 'The worst thing you can do for a person of genius is to help him: that way lies destruction . . . Once only did I help a man who was also a genius. I have never forgiven myself . . . when we met afterwards he had so greatly changed that, though I recognized him, he failed to recognize me. He became a Roman Catholic, and died at the age of twenty-three, a great artist – with half the critics and all the moralists still hating him. A charming person.'

fastidious in the face of illness, did not accompany them. There were other tensions in the air. The friendship with Conder, never without its undercurrent of antipathy, produced some brittle moments. To Beardsley, the fastidious invalid with scarcely a year to live, the brash figure of Conder, lounging complacently in his checked coat, riding breeches, boots and even spurs, seemed an affront to tact and taste. The disparity in their conditions grated on Beardsley and repelled Conder. Once, at Blanche's, when Beardsley accidentally drank from Conder's glass, Conder, with 'an involuntary gesture of repulsion that shocked the party, carefully wiped the rim'. Beardsley repaid the slight with an uncharacteristic outburst: 'I'm going to die, with all I might have done left undone, and you're going to live on and on – it's an intolerable thought.'

Aubrey buried himself in work, returning to the notion of illustrating *Mademoiselle de Maupin*. After plunging into the task, however, he suddenly thought he might do Casanova instead. And there were other projects to distract him: he offered to make a cover for O'Sullivan's new book, *The Houses of Sin*; and he was working on the promised picture for Heinemann's *History of Dancing*. Smithers despaired of getting 'any connected work out of him of any kind'.

Ellen returned after two weeks, and Aubrey, prompted by Raffalovich, sent Mabel money for a ticket. She disembarked in rain and wind to find Aubrey 'very tired'. Dr Caron (a recommendation of Blanche's) was summoned, and insisted on rest and quiet. Perhaps the better to achieve these, the Beardsleys moved to the Hôtel des Étrangers, which was quieter than the Sandwich. Sheltered from the wind, it had the attractions of a covered terrace, good food – and scant chance of meeting Oscar Wilde.[14]

Medical opinion was not in short supply. A Dr Dupuy, who was staying at the hotel, was encouraging of Beardsley's scheme to move to Paris for the early part of the winter; his views were promptly confirmed by Dr Phillips, who arrived in Dieppe on holiday. He was delighted to note the improvement in his patient's condition, and predicted that, with care, Beardsley might 'get quite well' and have 'a new life'.

The gravelled terrace at the hotel was a haven. Beardsley passed his afternoons sitting in the shade of an old acacia tree, the sounds of the distant promenade muffled and dulled by high ivyclad walls. Among his fellow guests, he was befriended by the Johnson family from New York. Mr Johnson was an assistant editor on *The Century Magazine*, and a great admirer of Beardsley's work. Another enthusiast was the Russian ballet impresario, Serge Diaghilev. He was part of the summer crowd that season and he took care to make Beardsley's acquaintence. Pollitt came to visit for a few days; if he hoped to claim his 'Bathyllus', he was disappointed.

Another visitor was a wealthy young poet named Douglas Ainslie. A friend of Mabel's, he had a great love of French literature, and often sat on the terrace with Aubrey telling tales of Gautier, Baudelaire, and Barbey d'Aurevilly. It seems that Aubrey had lost none of his zest for talk or flair for wit. Ainslie recalled his 'wonderful capacity for creating atmosphere', his pellucid brevity when talking of art, 'his clean-cut gestures', and his 'blazing brown eyes,' set in the 'long ascetic-looking face rendered so tragically keen by illness'. Aubrey rapped out his anecdotes and reflections 'like a prince throwing down golden ducats'. The talk, though 'alas, unprintable', was 'dazzling in the extreme: it was like a sun-glass that concentrate[d] such intense light . . . one felt . . . it would set the subject aflame.' Unfortunately it often scorched Beardsley too. His enthusiasm and his laughter would soon 'summon too much colour into his cheeks', and the session would have to be brought to a close.

Once established at the Étrangers, and perhaps stimulated by Ainslie's enthusiasm for Gautier, Beardsley 'immersed' himself in his drawings for *Mademoiselle de Maupin* – using grey washes to give a new richness to the work. One afternoon he produced some of the illustrations for Ainslie's inspection, after 'a rapid circular glance' to make sure they were undisturbed. Ainslie was struck by a Longhi-esque vision of a lady at her dressing-table; Beardsley remarked that the dark-eyed, full-lipped figure was the nearest he had 'been able to get to a beautiful woman'.

Ellen was making preparations for the coming months. Paris would be the first stopping-place, after which she hoped they would move further south. Perhaps in a spirit of mischief, Aubrey suggested Naples, where Wilde had recently gone to visit Alfred Douglas. Ellen did not feel up to going so far; with the doctor insisting he 'must not be left', some nearer resort would have to be found. She was also anxious about money, and unhappy about living on charity and off her son's earnings. She hoped to find some teaching work in Paris, as a private tutor or 'nursery governess'. Prospects were not encouraging, but she refused to be disheartened.[15]

The move to Paris was accomplished at the end of the second week in September. Aubrey was sad to leave Dieppe, and confessed to shedding some bitter (if 'invisible') tears at parting from that 'most charming spot on earth'. They took rooms at the Hôtel Foyot, near S. Sulpice, where he was well pleased with his bedroom looking over the Luxembourg Gardens. Although there was a 'whole host of people to see', a chill confined him to his room and allowed him to work steadily.

For some weeks he had been receiving the intensely expressed literary effusions of a new correspondent. She signed herself 'Opal' or 'Wilde Olive', but her name was Olive Custance, an aspiring poetess in her early twenties. She favoured pink as a colour and poetry as a way of life, and sometimes carried a sheaf of white arum lilies. She was prone to poets: John Gray had been the first object of her adoration (her 'Prince of Poets'); Richard Le Gallienne had conquered her heart with a single look; she went on to marry Lord Alfred Douglas. A poem of hers had been published in *The Yellow Book* (after Beardsley's departure), and Lane had agreed to bring out a collection of her verse. She hoped to meet Beardsley through Lane, but there is no evidence that she did; the relationship seems to have been literary and one-sided; Beardsley was apt to express his exasperation at 'Silly little O' and her screeds. (Faced with one 'huge letter' he remarked, 'She must buy me in large paper if she expects me to read her letters.') He did, however, write back. Perhaps excited by the forthcoming publication of her first collection, *Opals*, Custance wrote asking him to design her a bookplate. He must have had some fondness for her (or she must have bought several large-paper copies of *The Pierrot of the Minute*) for he accepted the commission and fulfilled it. He was pleased with his delicate pencil drawing of a mysterious woman in profile: Custance paid £10 for it.

He made progress too with his *Mademoiselle de Maupin* illustrations. The idea of illuminated initials was abandoned in favour of full-page drawings, three per part. By mid-October he was able to send Smithers the first trio (which included the 'Lady at the Dressing Table' so admired by Douglas Ainslie), and his suggestion for the next subjects.

Although he claimed that 'nothing but work' amused him, he did not lead a hermit's existence. He went often to the Louvre, though his afternoons of study in the chalcographical department could be accounted work. He visited Paris churches, and attended a special mass at S. Sulpice celebrated by Cardinal Vaughan. He sought out Father Coubé and saw much of him. Dowson visited and remarked how well he was looking. He became 'rather *lié*' with Charles Whibley, Henley's erstwhile lieutenant on the *National Observer* but now the Paris correspondent for the *Pall Mall Gazette*. Blanche asked him to comment on the colour scheme for his new house at Auteuil, and happy hours were spent discussing Saint Theresa with Vincent O'Sullivan.

One evening Beardsley dined with O'Sullivan in the restaurant attached to the hotel. O'Sullivan recalled that, at the end of the evening, when they were alone but for a somnambulant waiter, the door opened and a little woman came in and sat down at a table facing them. She was dressed in the style of 1850. Out of a huge reticule she drew a snuff-box, took a pinch of snuff and set herself to examining a bunch of papers by the aid of a candle in a silver candlestick which she had told the waiter to set on the table. Beardsley could not keep his eyes from her; she had, he said, come walking out of a book by Balzac. 'Now, if the *Savoy* were going,' he added wistfully, 'there would be a picture.' The wistfulness had an edge: Beardsley was becoming increasingly anxious about Smithers' ability – if not will – to publish his drawings.

The use, for the *Mademoiselle de Maupin* drawings, of wash and pencil rather than plain pen-and-ink, though artistically effective, was commercially problematic. Half-tone reproduction was required, and half-tone blocks were expensive. Even with part-work publication, a considerable outlay would be needed for each instalment. Smithers could ill afford the expense; he had over-extended himself, and was faced with an inevitable cash-flow crisis. He havered; Beardsley, though marooned in Paris, knew that all was not well. Cheques from the Royal Arcade had become rarities and the artist reasoned that if Smithers could not afford to pay *him*, he could probably not afford to pay the Swan Engraving Company either.

Beardsley became 'utterly cast down and wretched'. Time was always against him: *Maupin* was to have been a *chef d'oeuvre*, perhaps his last, but if Smithers could not meet the expenses of block-making, printing and binding, the project would never materialize. The drawings might 'hang about hidden' in Smithers' shop 'till Doomsday'; given that they had delicate, easily smudged pencil-work, there was every chance of their being spoilt. Anxieties crowded in on him. Mabel tried to be his eyes and ears in London: she called on Smithers and must have relayed some account of his position to Paris.

Aubrey wrote to Smithers suggesting that *Maupin* be put on hold until the following year. In the meantime, they should aim at 'some small work' illustrated in line which could 'appear complete in the immediate future' and might even be popular. Returning to a favourite theme, he put forward Tannhäuser; Smithers proposed the twice-abandoned project of *Ali Baba*. In the end, Beardsley settled on the third of Edmund Gosse's recommendations, Ben Jonson's *Volpone*: 'Such a stunning book it will be,' he told Pollitt. He confided to Mabel the heretical thought that he would perhaps hold on to any pictures he did, rather than let Smithers have them. Others would be keen to publish him. Heinemann, indeed, had just been over in Paris, full of praise for Beardsley's drawings. And Robert Johnson, the nice American, was keen to take his work for *The Century Magazine*.

The commencement of *Volpone* had, however, to wait; a fresh upheaval was in prospect. The weather had turned cold, and Dr Dupuy was insisting that the Beardsleys move south at once. There was much debate as to the competing merits of Menton, Cannes, Biarritz, Arcachon and Bordighera. Every fresh person consulted had fresh places to suggest. Aubrey's room became 'littered with guide books to the health resorts of the Riviera'. After many changes of mind, Menton was decided upon.[16]

CHAPTER X

'The Death of Pierrot'

THE JOURNEY SOUTH WAS FRAUGHT. Dr Dupuy had forbidden Aubrey to travel overnight and had insisted that the journey be broken at Marseilles. Such precautions were of small account: the train had barely reached Dijon when the first blood appeared on Aubrey's handkerchief. It was, he pretended, divine 'punishment' for bringing Gibbon to read on the train. In future, he would never set out without the *Imitation of Christ* – or 'at least' Saint Theresa. The sight of his blood terrified him for the rest of the journey, and he arrived at Menton (or Mentone, as he called it in deference to its Italian past) 'nearly dead'.

He had been prepared for what he would find there. The guidebooks were grimly cheerful about the pleasures of the town:

> It is a common notion that Menton has rather a depressing effect, on account of the number of invalids; but the proportion of this class of visitor among the winter population is not so large as is generally supposed. It must be remembered, too, that the character of Menton has changed a great deal of late years. Compared to many of the smaller stations on the Mediterranean littoral . . . it is now a decidedly gay place. In fact, the remark attributed to an Irish visitor, that 'but for the occasional funeral there would be no life

OPPOSITE 'The Death of Pierrot', 1896.

in the place,' may be regarded simply as an amusing instance of Milesian hyperbole.

Menton's popularity with the hale and the sick depended on its mild climate, its sheltered position in a natural amphitheatre, its low rainfall, and its proximity to Monte Carlo. Within the vast curve of the hillside, the Hôtel Cosmopolitan, where the Beardsleys were staying, held a high and sheltered position on the west bay. Though Aubrey had only a single room, it was quite 'palatial' and Ellen busied herself to make it attractive. She bought flowers and pinned his Mantegna prints along one wall. His few books were lined up in a little bookcase, and the two much-travelled candlesticks placed on either side of a crucifix on the desk. Framed photographs were on display: Mabel, Raffalovich and Wagner.

Aubrey's enthusiasm for *Volpone* survived the journey, and he was at once eager to start. Although he told Smithers of his plan to 'develop a new style' for the project, his doubts about the publisher persisted. He told Mabel that he hoped he might have 'the strength of mind' and the opportunity to get all the drawings done before dispatching any to Smithers or anyone else. For the opportunity he depended upon his 'pension' from Raffalovich. This posed its own problems: the allowance, initially paid because of his inability to work, had been continued to release him from the pressure of having to. Raffalovich, himself something of a valetudinarian, recognized the vital need for rest if Aubrey was to make a recovery. He therefore disapproved of Aubrey's continued drawing and was apt to 'scold' him on the point. As a result Beardsley – anxious not to appear ungrateful, perhaps even fearful that the allowance would be stopped – kept all news of work from his benefactor. In Paris that spring he had told Raffalovich that he was drawing 'a little', but that had been a rare and isolated admission.

His letters to Raffalovich from Menton were about everything except his plans for *Volpone*; his letters to Smithers contained almost nothing else. His anxieties on the subject were probably over nice, but they served to maintain the tension between the poles of his life.

To Raffalovich, he enthused about the weather ('wonderful sun-

OPPOSITE 'Volpone Adoring his Treasure', 1897.

shine'), described his symptoms ('much less troublesome') and set out his regime (sitting 'all morning' by the sea or in some 'beautifully shaded' spot in the hotel grounds). He fretted over the mosquitoes ('They have attacked me atrociously') and reflected on his reading (St Augustine's *Confessions*); he talked of the town ('so gay and amusing'), and of his fellow guests. He was particularly pleased with a 'dear old German novelist' who, knowing nothing of Beardsley's 'modest fame . . . presaged a brilliant future and success' for him. Beardsley's needs were met: Dr Campbell, one of two English doctors in the town, was consulted, and Beardsley sought out a place of worship. There were several churches nearby; he favoured a little chapel close to the hotel.

To Smithers, he wrote with extraordinary practical energy about *Volpone*. His plans grew and matured with almost every post. After the difficulties with the *Maupin* wash drawings he resolved to return to the more cheaply reproducible simplicity of black-and-white line work, albeit in his 'new style'. His first attempt, a boldly composed but closely-worked picture of 'Volpone Adoring His Treasure', was, he considered, 'one of the strongest things' he had ever done.

Perhaps he surprised even himself. The success of the picture fired him with 'excitement'. The coming year, he announced, would see either his 'death' or 'chefs d'oeuvre'; he hoped it would be the latter. The book would be something 'great and compelling', brought out in the 'grand style'. In format, he thought it should be a companion volume to *The Rape of the Lock*, and he mapped out a plan for twenty full- and half-page illustrations, in line, with half-tone frontispiece. In his enthusiasm the 'strength of mind' he had mentioned deserted him utterly: he could not resist sending the first picture to Smithers, together with a decorative cover design. They could, he suggested, be used for a 'handsome' prospectus. In a further effort to assure himself that he would produce the drawings, he urged Smithers to announce the book in the *Athenaeum* at once. The publication date would be May or June.

The physical exertion of drawing was, however, a heavy burden, and he was able to do only three or four hours of work a day. He strove to make up in regularity what he lost by resting. He looked, too, for help from above, urging Mabel and Pollitt to light candles for the success of the project. Gradually, however, he reduced the limits of the task, planning fewer full-page illustrations, and taking up (from his *Liaisons Dangereuses* scheme) the idea of decorative initials. The book engrossed him completely. When he was away from the drawing-board, he pored over the play. He carried it with him and could 'dream of nothing else'. He began working on an introductory note for the prospectus, reading Swinburne's *Study of Ben Jonson*, Taine's *History of English Literature*, and William Gifford's textual commentary, to stimulate his thoughts. The note Beardsley produced was revealing. Although he characterized the play as a satire – 'more full of scorn and indignation', indeed, even than Juvenal's work – he found Volpone 'a splendid sinner, [who] compels our admiration by the fineness and very excess of his wickedness' . . . 'We are scarcely shocked by his lust, so magnificent is the vehemence of his passion, and we marvel and are aghast rather than disgusted at his cunning and audacity.'

There was perhaps an echo of Smithers in the description. It shows, nevertheless, that for Beardsley, in this instance at least, morality was still subservient to style.[1]

Smithers was delighted with Beardsley's zest for work, but he had seen plans flare and die before. He tried to restrain the artist's impatience while channelling his energies. The prospectus and *Athenaeum* announcement, Smithers suggested, would best be left until the new year, but in the meantime he had blocks made of the cover design and first illustration. His cash-flow problems seem to have eased; not only did he send cheques on receipt of the first *Volpone* drawings but he proposed producing the book in a larger format than even *The Rape of the Lock* (which pleased Beardsley greatly). More significantly, he suggested that the illustrations could be half-tones rather than line drawings.

The suggestion 'upset' Beardsley's plans 'for the better'. He had been working on a first decorative initial, of an 'elephant bearing on its well-dressed back a basket of fruit and flowers. Round about it all a scroll and the letter "V" over everything.' Rich already in its black-and-white conception, with the additional use of pencil and wash half-tones it could become 'stupendous'. He returned in part to the style of the *Maupin* illustrations, and planned to 'press into service' at least one of them.

His new technique, however, was at once stronger and more severe. He considered that he had 'definitely left behind all former methods'. The book, 'as illustrative and decorative work', would be a 'marked departure . . . from any other arty book published for many years' and as such would 'create some attention'. His half-tone work was far more elaborate than his line drawing and more time-consuming. He soon recognized that if the optimistic plans for May publication were to be met, he had to scale down further the number of illustrations and decorations. Instead of twenty, he now suggested 'say fifteen (including initials)'. In the midst of these swiftly changing plans, Smithers unhelpfully started off on another tack, announcing a new periodical – *The Peacock*. It might be thought that this was the product of late-night discussions at the Thalia, except that Smithers wanted Aubrey not only to design the cover but to be the editor.

Beardsley took the idea on the wing, agreeing in principle, on the not imprudent condition that Oscar Wilde, 'anonymously, pseudonymously or otherwise', would have nothing to do with the magazine. He was, however, concerned that schemes for *The Peacock* would distract Smithers from *Volpone*, and he begged that this should not happen.

As Christmas approached, the bright December sun gave way to rain. Beneath grey skies, the town was decked with 'horrid pseudo-Christmas gaiety'. A visitor to Menton recorded how he saw 'for a wet second, a yellow skeleton in waterproof fighting an umbrella on the steps of a chapel . . . and recognized Aubrey Beardsley'. For the most part, however, Beardsley kept to his room. To his friends in London and Paris he sent copies of a photograph of himself, sitting in his room surrounded by books and prints, a crucifix set prominently against the wall. It projected an aura of studious severity more wished for than real.

On Christmas Day, communion was brought to him at the hotel by the Abbé Luzzani, an Italian priest who lived in a villa nearby and had taken an interest in Beardsley's case. Smithers sent a beautifully bound set of Racine's works and a tie-pin, but otherwise there was little to cheer him.

The year went out in a 'pitiless drench of rain' but it did bring
the hoped-for cheque from Raffalovich – and a visit from Vincent
O'Sullivan. With American disregard for European distances, O'Sullivan had made the journey specially; there were plans to discuss. In
a 'weak moment, and little dreaming he would accept', Beardsley
had suggested that he contribute a critical preface to *Volpone*. O'Sullivan had seized the chance; their meeting was only slightly marred
by O'Sullivan's having caught a 'horrid chill' on arrival.

Beardsley continued with the initials: 'V', 'M', 'S', another 'V'.
As they progressed, so did his command of the pencil. The tentative
modelling and shading which had first appeared in some of the *Savoy*
drawings was handled with growing confidence and to greater effect.
In the spirit of this new realism, he asked Smithers to send him 'an
inexpensive handbook of perspective, and a ditto of anatomy'.
Smithers persisted with his perverse plans for the new quarterly, and
Beardsley tried to be interested. He suggested a strong editorial line:
on the art side he thought they should 'attack *untiringly and unflinch-
ingly* the Burne-Jones and Morrisian medieval business, and set up a
wholesome seventeenth and eighteenth-century standard of what
picture making should be'. On the literary side he wanted to explode
the established traditions of *The Yellow Book* and *The Savoy*. Instead
of 'impressionist criticism and poetry, and cheap short storyness', he
proposed that a rigorous 'critical element' should dominate. He did
not care for Smithers' title, preening and overly aesthetic, preferring
the chastely prosaic *Books and Pictures*. The brisk tone of his recommendations, as much as their content, suggested a man hurrying away
from his past in an effort to convince himself that he has a future.

He sought such assurance everywhere. He thought he detected it
in the features of one of his fellow invalids at the Cosmopolitan. He
wrote excitedly to Raffalovich that the man, 'a famous Egyptologist
. . . looks like a corpse, has looked like one for fourteen years . . . is
much worse than I am, and yet lives on and does things. My spirits
have gone up immensely since I have known him.' But the unspoken
fear that all was coming to an end hovered above him. His thoughts
about *The Peacock* swept off in a new direction. He confided to Mabel
that unless Smithers was willing to make it 'a Catholic magazine', he
would not be interested. He himself was convinced that a 'well-

conducted Catholic quarterly review (quite serious)' would have a market. The pictures would be few: illustrations to poems such as Robert Southwell's 'Burning Babe'; there would be little hagiographical sketches and, occasionally, designs for church decorations. The reviews should deal not only with English Catholic works but with interesting productions from all over the world.

He realized (as who could not) that Smithers would need a 'lot of talking to' before he would agree. Beardsley's enthusiasm for the project seems wilful, a strained attempt to assure himself (and Mabel) that the future still existed. Perhaps, too, there was – at this late moment – a desire to reconcile the spiritual and artistic sides of his life, always previously held in opposition. Mabel was eager to see the possibilities of the project; she was beginning to extend her talents into journalism (she was writing a piece on 'Bohemianism' for *The Idler*) and perhaps saw a Catholic magazine as an attractive opportunity, and one which might link her with her brother even at a distance.

The plan had no chance to evolve. A mild attack of rheumatism in his right arm halted Aubrey's drawing, and then, on 26 January, he suffered a slight haemorrhage and took to his bed. The attack had not been bad but it refused to end; over the following days the blood continued to ooze. This ceaseless bleeding was made worse by his agony of mind over not being able to work on the *Volpone* illustrations. He could not admit (even to himself) that the project might have to be abandoned. He wrote enthusiastically to O'Sullivan about the preface, and sought to explain the delay to Smithers by pretending that the rheumatic attack had worsened. He maintained the same fiction to Raffalovich and Mabel; only to Pollitt did he confess the true reasons for his 'exile from design'.

To those about him, the seriousness of his condition was inescapable. He could not leave his room and was rarely able to rise from his bed; he was too weak to shave. Concerned visitors tried to lift his spirits. The cadaverous Egyptologist kept him company, and the Abbé Luzzani with another priest, Father Orchmans, called in rotation to chase away the 'papillons noir' of depression. A less expected visitor was Constance Wilde – Oscar's estranged wife – with their young son, Vyvyan, on exeat from his prep school at Monte Carlo.

Ellen had been suffering with toothache, but once the offending molar was removed, she devoted herself to Aubrey's care. His particular pleasure was for her to 'read aloud, a few sentences at a time', from the works of St Alfonso Liguori, so that he could then meditate on them. Despite such apparent signs of resignation, however, he continued to struggle against his fate. He began – but did not finish – a poetic reverie entitled 'The Ivory Piece', and though Dr Campbell had forbidden work, he made one final attempt. Propped up in bed, he asked his mother to bring him his drawing things, but the effort of work was beyond him. Ellen returned to find him lying with his face to the wall, the pen sticking like an arrow from the floorboards where he had thrown it.

The awfulness of incapacity was brought home to him again when, soon afterwards, he received a request for an illustration from the *Revue Illustré*. Though tempted by the thought of appearing in a journal so '*répandu* all over Europe', he was so feeble he could do no more than sign a courteous note of refusal.[2]

On 6 March, despite some days when he seemed to be making a slow recovery, he suffered a catastrophic haemorrhage. The disease, according to Ellen, 'had touched an artery, and it was tragic'. Dr Campbell strove to conceal the fact, but it was clear that the final crisis had arrived.

Although the true seriousness of Aubrey's condition remained unknown to his friends in London, Ellen telegraphed to Mabel, who had just opened in a play at the Garrick, urging her to come at once. Aubrey survived the night. He had, however, as Gray termed it, come 'face to face with the old riddle of life and death'. Under the awful presence of its gaze, his elaborately and carefully maintained pose cracked. The division between the two sides of his life collapsed: he abandoned art and surrendered completely to faith. Penitence and the possibility of redemption had always been present to him. The images of Mary Magdalen and Tannhäuser were among the first he had chosen for his personal pantheon. With such models before him, he knew how to assume the mask. From Raffolivich he had received a preservative 'girdle' dedicated to St Thomas Aquinas. He wore it at all times. March 7 was St Thomas's 'feast day', and the significance of the date perhaps stirred Beardsley to one final act of renunciation. Taking up his pen for the last time, he wrote urgently to Smithers:

Jesus is our Lord and Judge.

Dear Friend,
I implore you to destroy *all* copies of Lysistrata and bad drawings. Show this letter to Pollitt and conjure him to do the same. By all that is holy *all* obscene drawings.

He signed it with the melodramatic subscription, 'Aubrey Beardsley. In my death agony.'

The letter was addressed and sent by Ellen. Aubrey's agony was not short. Mabel arrived to find her brother hopelessly ill. The haemorrhages continued, frequent and severe; his breathing was an agony of effort, he was unable even to raise his head without assistance. He maintained an unfractured 'patience and courage', supported by the new mask he had assumed, and also – perhaps – by Dr Campbell's frequent ministrations of morphia. After one troubled night he murmured to his mother, as she bent over him, 'Read me the *Te Deum*.' His spiritual anguish was extinguished by the arrival of a telegram from Smithers announcing that all the obscene drawings had been destroyed. The message was of course untrue; Smithers had too strong an appreciation of Beardsley's genius, and too ready an understanding of the worth of the pictures once Aubrey was dead, to destroy them. Nevertheless, Beardsley, a crucifix and a rosary clutched to his creaking breast, the girdle about his waist, heard the news with relief. He would die in peace.

Two nurses were in attendance for the final days. Ellen and Mabel, worn down with care, spent much time kneeling at the bedside. Their vigil enhanced the religiose aspect of the scene. All were touched who saw Aubrey at the end. The hotel waiters, scarcely a sentimental breed, revered him. The hotel proprietors thought him 'a benediction in the house'.

On 14 March Beardsley received the last rites, and the end came in the early hours of 16 March.* He died, Mabel told Ross, 'as a

---

* The date on his death certificate is 13 March, a clerical error, perhaps caused by the homophony of 'treize' and 'seize'; Robert Ross strayed even further in his book, saying that Beardsley died on 25 March.

Saint . . . full of love, patience, and repentance'. The hotel proprietor dealt with the civic formalities and practical necessities, and Father Orchmans made arrangements for the funeral. Mabel, her dramatic sensibilities unimpaired, laid Aubrey's copy of *La Dame aux Camélias* inside the coffin.

A requiem mass was held in the town's small baroque cathedral with one of the regular clergy officiating. Mabel wrote to Raffalovich letting him know how beautiful everything had been. The 'dear heart himself would have loved it. There was music.' Under cloudless skies, they followed the coffin on foot up the steep, winding road to the hill-top cemetery. It was a long and solemn procession, with many of the hotel staff and most of the few remaining members of the English colony.

Father Orchmans conducted the burial service. Aubrey Beardsley was laid to rest in a grave hewn out of the rock – 'a true sepulchre'. Cut on the very edge of the hill, it looked out from beneath cypresses and among roses over the town to the waters of the Mediterranean. Ellen mournfully called it 'a lovely spot as he would have chosen'.

Perhaps he would have selected it, but the choice would have marked the triumph of his aesthetic over his spiritual nature. In a bureaucratic oversight, Beardsley – as an English citizen – had been assigned a plot in the Protestant part of the cemetery.[3]

Epilogue

THE OBITUARIES IN the British press which followed Beardsley's death were not generous. They may have served to recall Beardsley to the public's notice, but did so in grudging terms. A recurrent note was sounded: Beardsley may have been a master of 'line', but his subject matter was 'unwholesome', and this vitiated his claims to greatness.[1]

His friends did something to counter the claims: in the days and weeks that followed, Joseph Pennell, Gleeson White, Aymer Vallance, Henry Harland, John Gray and C. B. Cochran all published personal tributes.[2] Beerbohm contributed an elegant essay of appreciation to *The Idler* and Symons wrote a perceptive critique for the *Fortnightly Review*. *Past and Present* carried an obituary article by Mr Payne (April 1898), and a memorial poem by an impressionable BGS sixth-former.*

* 'Aubrey Beardsley' by C. Terrell.

> It was by night, when sleep ruled other flowers
> The pale cold moon, with weird unholy light,
> Bent down and kissed a bud which scorned the sun.
> And as I watched, methought this unknown flower
> Unfolded to the light beloved by elves.

OPPOSITE Design for the front cover of Ernest Dowson's *Pierrot of the Minute*.

353

Beardsley's international fame was attested to by the wide attention given to his death – and his achievement – in both the American and the European press. The American papers and periodicals tended to reiterate the reservations of their British counterparts, but the Europeans (and particularly the French) were more enthusiastic. There were 'flaming notices of dear Aubrey in the *Figaro* and elsewhere'.[2] *Emporium* in Italy and *Dekorative Kunst* in Germany carried obituaries.[3]

Ellen and Mabel returned to England soon after the funeral at Menton. Ellen took lodgings in Wellington Square; Mabel moved into rooms in Gloucester Place. They remained, however, united by grief. Early in May, Robbie Ross helped them to organize a memorial mass at Farm Street, when Aubrey's friends could pay their respects. Raffalovich, Gray and Mrs Gribbell were away in Rome (Gray was considering entering the priesthood; indeed Aubrey had prayed for Gray's vocation). Mabel wrote telling them of the service: 'I wish you all could have been at the requiem this morning. Fr Chew celebrated, I didn't know the other two. Everything was admirably arranged and a great many people (so it seemed to me) were there. It was an ordeal for Mother and me, but we are both the happier for it.'[4]

When it was all over, Mabel collapsed briefly, worn down by care and fatigue. Her condition can have been only a little alleviated by settlement of Aubrey's will. Probate was granted on 13 May; his estate was valued at £1015 17s 10d (£836 17s 10d net). In the emotional wake of Aubrey's death Ellen converted to Roman Catholicism. This gave her spiritual consolation and an enduring tie with

---

Its lurid petals glowed with dreadful light,
And deep within, but half discovered yet,
I could perceive its strangely formèd heart.
Yet ere it could its utmost glory gain,
The stem had drooped, though still the petals shone,
Striving through Glory yet to vanquish Death.

A gust of hot night air came sweeping by:
The blossom fell, but died without decay.

On the page opposite the poem was W. T. Horton's drawing of an angel in glory.

her son's memory. She was much heartened by Fr Bampton's assurance that Aubrey was in heaven.[5]*

In the sublunary sphere his artistic reputation flickered briefly. Twenty-three of his pictures were included in the International Exhibition at Knightsbridge in May 1898. The show was selected by Whistler and marked the aged painter's belated tribute to Beardsley's genius. Smithers set about issuing the last drawings: a portfolio of the *Mademoiselle de Maupin* designs was put together; the *Volpone* illustrations appeared in an edition enhanced by a 'Eulogy' by Robbie Ross, and early in 1899 Smithers brought out a *Second Book of Fifty Drawings*. John Lane also recognized the possibilities of the moment and published *The Early Work of Aubrey Beardsley*. Lane's reassertion of an interest was not unwelcome to Mabel, who had come to doubt Smithers' good faith. Her disillusionment began when she discovered that he had not destroyed the *Lysistrata* drawings, but had sold them to Jerome Pollitt. In her distressed state she called on the young collector and begged him to destroy them; when he tactfully refused, she offered to buy them so that she might do it herself. This, too, he declined to do.[6]

Mabel had not seen the drawings before that time, and later revised her attitude to them. After the intense religious atmosphere of Aubrey's death chamber had diffused, she acquired her own set (of Smithers' edition) and became quite blasé about their frankness. She even lent them to a young and innocent actress-friend who was convalescing and wanted something to amuse her.

Any rivalry between Lane and Smithers was short-lived. Smithers overextended himself again, and on this occasion there was no recovery. He was declared bankrupt early in 1900. All his Beardsley copyrights were bought up by Lane, who was then able to issue *The Later Work of Aubrey Beardsley* as a companion to the earlier volume. Despite the setback, Smithers continued to bring out illicit editions

---

* Raffalovich, in a letter to Gray, facetiously wondered how Father Bampton knew that Aubrey was 'in glory': 'I did not like to ask but he advanced it as fact. Perhaps Fr Bearne of Bournemouth has had some interior intimation. I hope so.' Mabel seemed to lack full confidence in the 'fact': she wondered who would introduce her in heaven when she died. 'It should be my brother,' she told Yeats, 'but then they might not appreciate the introduction. They might not have good taste.'

and even forgeries of Beardsley's work. The bulk of his collection of letters from the artist he sold to a Viennese collector, and, although he had undertaken to dispose of Aubrey's library for Mabel, she saw none of the proceeds. He lurched from crisis to crisis, and from address to address. Drink and chloral offered only the illusion of relief, and he continued on his downward course until his death – naked and alone in a bare Fulham lodging house – in 1907.

Mabel resumed her unremarkable acting career, and also returned to journalism, contributing to both *The Idler* and *Saturday Review*. She wrote an appreciative critique of Conder's show at the Carfax Gallery for *The Rambler*. She continued to exert an influence over her brother's circle of friends. Many of them – Symons, Yeats, Ricketts, MacColl – found in her an approachability and warmth they had not known in Aubrey. She kept up the tradition of her Thursday teas. In 1903 she married a young actor and Old Etonian, George Bealby-Wright, six years her junior. Vincent Beardsley was a witness at the wedding, one of the first to be held at Westminster Cathedral. He had returned to the family fold, and joined his wife and daughter in their faith. He died, nursed by Ellen, in 1909.

Ellen's bedside vigils were not over. Mabel, whose erratic health had been a cause of concern for some time, fell seriously ill in 1912. Cancer of the uterus was diagnosed, and Ellen nursed her for the four years of her illness. Mabel's bravery and cheerfulness were recorded by W. B. Yeats in a haunting series of poems 'Upon a Dying Lady'. Ellen lived on until 1932, impoverished and increasingly fretful, a relic of a past age. She was supported by a small Civil List pension and the generosity of friends.[7]

Beardsley's posthumous reputation has endured vicissitudes. In the brief flare of interest that followed his death, there was recognition that his impact had been considerable but general doubt of what its effect would be. His influence was felt most strongly overseas. With almost all his work having been produced for mass distribution in books and periodicals, his fame had spread quickly across Europe and America, and the distinctive tropes of his style had been much imitated. Although he had always insisted on being characterized as a realist, the decorative element of his work was most readily taken up. His observation that the realist art of one generation becomes the decorative art of the next was fulfilled almost as it was uttered.

Gleeson White, in an article written in 1898 on the rapid evolution of Art Nouveau, cited Beardsley as the key influence upon the movement. Beardsley, he suggested, had taken the native British tradition of 'decorative illustration' pioneered by Walter Crane and William Morris and freed it from 'the trammels of Medieval and Renaissance draughtsmen' so that it might 'embody some of the spirit of the work of both periods with other and newer influences drawn from Japan, the French poster, and other sources'. Within this eclectic mix, 'the one factor . . . that has in a way effected a revolution is undoubtedly his dexterous use of solid blacks, knit together with fantastic, nervous lines, almost or quite unrelated to nature.'[7] The pages of all the advanced art periodicals, White suggested, showed an influence that could be 'traced to Mr Beardsley'. His impact was not always happy, his imitators were often 'merely absurd', but the new energy that he had lent to decorative art could not be discounted. He 'gave other illustrators the courage to break away from realism and academic convention.'[8]

Although White, eager to assert Beardsley's importance, ignored the contributions of Toulouse-Lautrec, Mucha and others to the development of Art Nouveau, there was truth in his assessment – and truth too in his conclusion: the 'chief lesson' to be drawn from the 'orgie [sic] of riotous experiment' then in progress was that 'the only style which lasts is the one a painter evolves for himself. It is not a Beardsley who will be forgotten, but his followers; although for a time the imitators succeed in bringing ridicule on their leaders.'

There were few who were able to transmute the influence of Beardsley's intensely personal vision into their own. In England many young illustrators tried to assume his mantle. Sidney Sime, Austin Osman Spare, John Austen and Harry Clarke all caught something of his style without letting it dominate their own. The American Will Bradley, as has been mentioned, perfected the same balancing act. In Glasgow Charles Rennie Mackintosh and the Macdonald sisters achieved a synthesis derived in part from Beardsley's example. (On both the occasions that Beardsley had exhibited at the Glasgow Institute Mackintosh's work was hung nearby.) The German illustrators Franz von Bayros, 'Alastair' and Thomas Theodore Heine all acknowledged a debt to Beardsley. In Brussels, Vienna and Barcelona he had his acknowledged disciples.

Serge Diaghilev's meetings with Beardsley in Dieppe during the summer of 1897 established an enduring interest, and when, in 1898, the would-be impresario founded his cultural review *Mir Iskustva* (*The World of Art*) to 'liberate' Russian art from its moribund condition, one of his earliest acts was to commission an article on Beardsley from D. S. MacColl. His influence percolated Diaghilev's activities and flavoured some of Leon Bakst's early designs for the Ballets Russes, a telling link between Beardsley and the emerging modernist tradition. His work, with its daring refinement of form, was certainly known to Kandinsky, Klee, Matisse and Picasso during their student days, and it is not too fanciful to see in their moves towards abstraction and simplification a continuation of Beardsley's stylistic innovation.*

For the most part, however, his immediate influence evaporated quickly. A new century brought a new mood. In Britain the death of Queen Victoria, and the deaths of so many of the personalities of the nineties – Wilde, Dowson, Johnson, Harland – contributed to his relegation to what seemed a distant and irrecoverable past. The vitality of Art Nouveau dwindled quickly, and the First World War obliterated the last vestiges of his world and his memory. But, although he went into eclipse, he was not wholly forgotten. He could still surprise and even shock. The journalist Sidney Horler, writing in the 1930s, recalled the effect of being shown a copy of Beardsley's *Under the Hill*: 'I had only read three lines before I felt the urge to be violently sick.' Others were less queasy. Beardsley always had an appeal for egregious spirits who sought in the defiant individuality of his style support for their own heretical attitudes. His enduring legacy was one of manner. He offered a glimpse into a proscribed world – erotic, aesthetic, intense and unsentimental.[9]

Ronald Firbank, trying to persuade Grant Richards to take on his novel *Vainglory*, invoked the spirit of Beardsley: 'What was the matter with his story? Surely it was better than most stories. He had

---

* Some of Beardsley's drawings were published in the Barcelona art journal *Joventut*, which also reproduced early illustrations by Picasso.

attempted to do something like Beardsley had done in the illustrations to *The Rape of the Lock*. Was I an admirer of Beardsley? . . . So I knew Beardsley! Surely I would bring his child into the world. I could not be so unkind as to turn it from my door.' In the face of such imprecations (and on the understanding that Firbank would pay the production costs) Richards relented. Perhaps more surprisingly, D. H. Lawrence proclaimed a debt to Beardsley. In his autobiographical first novel, *The White Peacock*, the hero's discovery of a book of Beardsley drawings serves almost as the key to his awakening sexual feelings. The same equation between Beardsley's art and the hidden currents of sex was made by William Faulkner. Allusions to the artist's charged creations recur throughout Faulkner's work.[10]

He was, however, a vestigial figure to subsequent generations. Although in 1904 John Gray had brought out a heavily edited edition of Beardsley's letters to Raffalovich as a record of gathering religious conviction, and Ross had extended his *Volpone* 'Eulogy' into a short book, no biography had followed. It had been hoped that Mabel might attempt the task; she did compose a short biographical entry for a German art encyclopedia, but a more sustained effort seemed beyond her. John Lane planned to write in his retirement of his great discovery, but had only just begun to compile material at his death in 1925. The dealer and bibliophile R. A. Walker, who was gathering memorials of Beardsley at the same time as (and often in competition with) Lane, issued some interesting biographical material in a series of limited edition collections, but never synthesized his feelings into a biography.

It fell to Haldane MacFall to produce the first extended account of Beardsley's life. Published in 1928, his book is a combination of conceit and excruciating prose. Even though he had access to many of Beardsley's surviving friends, the factual content of the book is tantalizingly slight, and – where it is possible to check – often faulty. It was not until the 1960s that Beardsley's fortunes revived. The swinging decade of post-war liberation found an echo in his flouting of Victorian convention. A major Beardsley exhibition attracted crowds at the Victoria & Albert Museum in London. Although the *Lysistrata* drawings were on view at the museum, reproductions offered for sale in London and Edinburgh were seized by the police as indecent. The resulting furore stimulated interest, and all the offending drawings were reproduced, the following year, in Reade's magisterial illustrated collection, *Beardsley*.

Its publication coincided with the appearance of Stanley Weintraub's biography, the first attempt at providing a fuller and more scholarly account of the artist's life. His profile rose yet higher, and Beardsley images proliferated: shoe stores, public houses, dress shops adopted and adapted his distinctive style. Even the psychedelic swirls of the Beatles' film *Yellow Submarine* carried his stamp. The V&A exhibition set off to tour America and Europe. His reputation has continued to grow in subsequent decades. A collection of his letters was published in 1970; his works are frequently reproduced; there have been further studies and much exegesis; he has been embraced by Japan. Given Beardsley's desire to be considered a 'man of letters', it is an intriguing irony that academic interest in his art, particularly in America, is now concentrated in the English Literature departments of the universities. Ian Fletcher has published a study of his work in 'Twayne's English Authors Series'.

Beardsley remains difficult to categorize neatly: a recent television history of British art could find no place for him. For artists, however, his example (if not his art) still offers an inspiration and a reference point: Robert Mapplethorpe, another puckish spirit who delighted in producing shocking images in black and white, claimed kinship with him. Even more recently, Damien Hirst, the current *enfant terrible* of the British art world, has been likened to a Beardsley of the fin de millennium.[11] A hundred years after his death Beardsley still compels attention. His work, endorsed by time, retains its clarity and originality of vision; his personality burns with vivid brightness.

AB

Bibliographical Note

ALL BOOKS, articles and letters referred to in the text are credited in the notes, but it is perhaps desirable to give a brief account of my principal sources. Recently two magisterial works of reference have appeared to aid Beardsley scholars: Mark Samuels Lasner's *A Selective Checklist of the Published Work of Aubrey Beardsley* (Boston, 1995) and Nicholas A. Salerno's 'Aubrey Beardsley: An Annotated Secondary Bibliography', in Robert Langenfeld (ed.) *Reconsidering Aubrey Beardsley* (Ann Arbor/London, 1989). They have been invaluable aids to me.

I have, of course, also drawn upon the existing Beardsley biographies: the two early works – Robert Ross's brief account, *Aubrey Beardsley* (London, 1909), and Haldane MacFall's *Aubrey Beardsley: The Man and His Work* (London, 1928); and the more recent studies – Stanley Weintraub's *Aubrey Beardsley: A Biography* (London, 1967), reissued as *Aubrey Beardsley – Imp of the Perverse* (University Park, 1976), Malcolm Easton's eccentric but valuable *Aubrey and the Dying Lady* (London, 1972), Brigid Brophy's *Beardsley and his world* (London, 1976) and Miriam Benkovitz's *Aubrey Beardsley: An Account of His Life* (New York, 1981).

Like all others interested in Beardsley I have been grateful for

OPPOSITE 'A Footnote', 1896.

363

R. A. Walker's pioneering works and compilations, especially *A Beardsley Miscellany* (London, 1949), *Some Unknown Drawings of Aubrey Beardsley* (London, 1923), his edition of A. W. King's *An Aubrey Beardsley Lecture*, his introduction to his own translation of Wilde's *Salome* (London, 1957), *Nineteen Early Drawings by Aubrey Beardsley* (London, 1919) (produced under the pseudonym George Derry) and *Le Morte Darthur with Beardsley Illustrations: A Bibliographical Essay* (Bedford, 1945).

The great majority of Beardsley's letters (very sparse prior to 1896, very voluminous thereafter) were published in Henry Maas, J. L. Duncan and W. G. Good's edition of *The Letters of Aubrey Beardsley* (London, 1970); this superseded three separate collections – John Gray (ed.), *The Last Letters of Aubrey Beardsley* (London, 1904), Fritz Waerndorfer (ed.), *Briefe Kalendernotizen* (Munich, 1908); R. A. Walker (ed.), *Letters From Aubrey Beardsley To Leonard Smithers* (London, 1937). Through patient trawling in libraries and sale catalogues, and through the generosity of private collectors and fellow scholars, I have discovered a handful of overlooked and unpublished letters. Alas, almost none of Beardlsey's 'in-mail' survives.

Beardsley's early celebrity ensured him a place in the letters and memoirs of his contemporaries. Full references will be found in the notes, but – deserving of special mention – are: *The Letters of Max Beerbohm, 1892–1956* (Oxford, 1988), *Max Beerbohm's letters to Reggie Turner* (London, 1964), both ed. Rupert Hart-Davis; *Max & Will* [the correspondence of Max Beerbohm and William Rothenstein] (London, 1975) ed. Mary M. Lago and Karl Beckson; *The Letters of Ernest Dowson* (London, 1967), ed. Desmond Flower and Henry Maas; *The Letters of Oscar Wilde* (London, 1962) and *More Letters of Oscar Wilde* (London, 1985), both ed. Rupert Hart-Davis; *Arthur Symons: Selected Letters, 1880–1935* (London, 1989), ed. Karl Beckson and John M. Munro.

Beardsley figures prominently in many of the published memoirs of the period: Jacques-Emile Blanche, *Portraits of a Lifetime* (London, 1937); Charles Cochran, *The Secrets of a Showman* (London, 1925); C. Lewis Hind, *Naphtali* (London, 1926); Edgar Jepson, *Memories of a Victorian* (London, 1933); Elizabeth Robins Pennell, *Nights* (Philadelphia, 1916); Joseph Pennell, *The Adventures of an Illustrator* (Boston,

1925); Grant Richards, *Memories of a Misspent Youth* (London, 1932); William Rothenstein, *Men and Memories: Recollections 1872–1900* (London, 1931); Evelyn Sharp, *Unfinished Adventure* (London, 1933); Netta Syrett, *The Sheltering Tree* (London, 1939); and Alfred Thornton, *The Diary of an Art Student in the Nineties* (London, 1938). Amongst the unpublished memoirs the most important are G. F. Scotson-Clark's 'Aubrey Beardsley prior to 1893' at Princeton University Library, D. S. MacColl's 'The Beardsleys' at Glasgow University Library, and John Lane's 'The Yellow Book: Some Recollections', a copy of which is in the British Library.

A vivid record of Beardsley's character and career is also preserved in the contemporary interviews, reviews, memorials and press reports (including the wonderfully detailed pages of the Brighton Grammar School magazine, *Past and Present*). These are all credited fully in the notes.

For Beardsley's drawings, although I have consulted many in the original, I have also relied much on the published collections: *A Book of Fifty Drawings* (1897), *A Second Book of Fifty Drawings* (1899), *The Early Work of Aubrey Beardsley* (1899), *The Later Work of Aubrey Beardsley* (1901), *The Uncollected Work of Aubrey Beardsley* (1925), Brian Reade's *Beardsley* (1967), Simon Wilson's *Beardsley* (Oxford, 1976) (which also contains an excellent introduction). Aymer Vallance's 'Iconography' first appeared in *A Book of Fifty Drawings*; it was substantially revised and expanded for Robert Ross's 1909 study.

Exhibition catalogues have also proved a fruitful source, most especially Brian Reade and Frank Dickenson's *Aubrey Beardsley: Exhibition at the Victoria and Albert Museum 1966. Exhibition Catalogue of the Original Drawings, Letters, Manuscripts, Paintings, Books, Posters, Photographs, Documents, etc.* (London, 1966) and *National Gallery, Millbank: Catalogue of Loan Exhibition of Drawings by Aubrey Beardsley* (London, 1923).

There has been much interesting Beardsley exegesis since the time of Arthur Symons's *Aubrey Beardsley* (London, 1905 edition). Of particular note have been – in recent years – Brigid Brophy, *Black and White: A Portrait of Aubrey Beardsley* (New York, 1968); the essays in R. Langenfeld (ed.), *Reconsidering Aubrey Beardsley*, Chris Snodgrass, *Aubrey Beardsley, Dandy of the Grotesque* (New York/Oxford, 1995),

Linda Zatlin, *Aubrey Beardsley and Victorian Sexual Politics* (Oxford, 1990), In Fletcher, *Aubrey Beardsley* (Boston, 1987), Catherine Slessor, *The Art of Aubrey Beardsley* (Secaucus, N. J., 1989); and in so far as they illuminate Beardsley's life I have drawn upon them.

Of the general works of reference upon which I have relied special mention should be made of James Thorpe, *English Illustration: The Nineties* (London, 1935), John Rothenstein, *The Artists of the 1890's* (London, 1928) and Holbrook Jackson's perennially rewarding *The Eighteen Nineties* (London, 1913).

Notes

ABBREVIATIONS

AB	Aubrey Beardsley
ALS	autograph letter, signed
B. Misc.	R. A. Walker (ed.), *A Beardsley Miscellany*, (London, 1949)
cc	carbon copy
EW	*The Early Work of Aubrey Beardsley* (London, 1899)
GRO	General Registry Office, London
Iconography	Aymer Vallance, 'List of Drawings by Aubrey Beardsley' in Robert Ross, *Aubrey Beardsley* (London, 1909)
LW	*The Later Work of Aubrey Beardsley* (London, 1901)
m	microfilm
MD	Sir Thomas Malory, *Morte Darthur*, illustrated by AB (London, 1893–4)
MDG	Henry Maas, J. L. Duncan, W. G. Good (eds), *The Letters of Aubrey Beardsley* (London, 1970)
MS	manuscript
p	photocopy
P&P	*Past and Present – The Magazine of the Brighton Grammar School*
PRO	Public Record Office
RAB	Robert Langenfeld (ed.), *Reconsidering Aubrey Beardsley* (Ann Arbor/London, 1989)
TLS	typed letter, signed
TS	typescript
UW	*The Uncollected Work of Aubrey Beardsley* (London, 1925)

367

CHAPTER I · 'A DELICATE CHILD'

1. Birth announcements, *The Times* 24.8.1872; *Brighton Gazette* 29.8.1872; unattributed newspaper review of *Under the Hill* (London, 1904), H. A. Payne's cuttings-file, BGS archive (Sussex County Record Office, Lewes); R. A. Walker, 'Notes on the Family of A.B.' in *B. Misc.*, p. 102.

2. Census return, 1871, PRO, RG 10/ 1082 ff.83.

3. R. A. Walker, in *B. Misc.*, p. 100.

4. D. G. Crawford, *Roll of the Indian Medical Service 1615−1930*; record of marriage, India Office microfilms N/I/ 61/f75 and N/I/51/f14; R. A. Walker, *B. Misc.*, p. 99.

5. William Pitt's service record [MS], India Office L/MIL/10/74; Florence Pitt's birth certificate, issued by British Consulate, Boulogne-sur-Mer, 31 December 1850; GRO, London; R. A. Walker *B. Misc.*, p. 99n.

6. T. F. Wilson, *The Defence of Lucknow* (London, 1858), p. 219; W. Pitt's service record; Bengal, Madras, Bombay retired ledger 1859−60, India Office L/AG/21/15/8/f185; census return 1861 (PRO); Jersey and Brighton handbooks.

7. R. A. Walker, *B. Misc.*, pp. 101−2. F. Hamilton Maugham, *Some Brighton Churches* (London, 1922), pp. 22−32; Malcolm Easton, *Aubrey and the Dying Lady* (London, 1972), p. 159.

8. Record of baptism, India Office microfilm N/I/13/f453.

9. Last Will and Testament of George Lamb, proved at London, 11 March 1862, Somerset House, London; Death Duty Register; Bengal, Madras, Bombay Retired Ledger [MS], India Office L/AG/21/15/8/f185.

10. Marriage certificate of William Lait and Sarah Ann Beardsley, 1.6.1846, GRO, London. Walker (pp. 95−6) incorrectly gives 'Tait' for 'Lait'; R. A. Walker, *B.Misc.*, p. 101.

11. ALS, John Gray to André Raffalovich, 10.10.1904 (National Library of Scotland, Edinburgh); R. A. Walker, *B. Misc.*, p. 101.

12. R. A. Walker, *BMisc.*, pp. 101−2.

13. Birth announcement, *The Times*, 27.8.1871; *Brighton Gazette*, 8.2.1872, pp. 4−5; M. Easton, *op. cit.*, p. 92; R. A. Walker, *B. Misc.*, p. 102.

14. *ibid.* p. 105; 'Mrs Ellen A. Beardsley', *Colour* 12, 1925, p. 20; George Derry, *An Aubrey Beardsley Scrapbook* (London, 1920); the scrapbook is at Princeton University; Ellen Agnus Beardsley, 'Aubrey Beardsley' in *B. Misc.*, pp. 75, 78−9; the MS is at Princeton.

15. R. A. Walker, *B. Misc.*, p. 102; ALS, Ellen Beardsley to John Lane, 10.9.[1923?], (Princeton); Ellen Beardsley, MS notes for John Lane [1923?], (Princeton); R. A. Walker *B.Misc.*, p. 103.

16. Census returns 1871, PRO; marriage certificate of Florence Pitt and Moritz Schenkel, 6.3.1876, GRO; announcement, *The Times* 8.3.1876; R. A. Walker, *B. Misc.*, p. 102.

17. Henry Russell, *Cheer, Boys, Cheer* (London, 1895); Landon Ronald, *Variations on a Personal Theme* (London, 1922); *Myself and Others* (London, 1931), (none makes mention of the Beardsley connection); E. A. Beardsley, *B. Misc.*, pp. 75, 79−80; A. W. King, 'The Art of Aubrey Beardsley' in R. A. Walker, *A Beardsley Lecture* (London, 1924), p. 23; E. A. Beardsley, *B. Misc.*, p. 79; a marginal note on the MS indicates that AB was six at the time.

18. D. S. MacColl, 'The Beardsleys', [MS], Glasgow University Library; *John Thain Davidson by His Daughter* (London, 1906); E. A. Beardsley, *B. Misc.*, p. 75;

Walker, 'Notes on the Family of AB' in *B. Misc.*, p. 102; mALS, E. A. Beardsley to J. Lane [1924?] (British Library, London).

19. E. A. Beardsley, *B. Misc.*, p. 75; Walker, *B. Misc.*, p. 103; MDG, pp. 11, 14.

20. Walker, *B. Misc.*, p. 102; MDG, pp. 6–13; census return 1881, PRO; MDG, pp. 6–13; ALS, E. A. Beardsley to Mabel Beardsley, 10.12.[1904] (Princeton). E. A. Beardsley, *B. Misc.*, p. 75; Mabel Beardsley-Wright, 'Aubrey Beardsley' in *Allgemeines Lexikon der bilenden Künsler von der Atike bis zur Gegenwart*, U. Thieme and F. Becker (eds) (Leipzig, 1909), Vol. III, p. 111; Robert Ross, *Aubrey Beardsley* (London, 1909), p. 11.

21. E. A. Beardsley, *B. Misc.*, pp. 75, 80; *Iconography*, item 1; mALS, E. A. Beardsley to J. Lane [1924] (British Library, London); census return 1881, PRO.

22. Ben Weinreb and Christopher Hibbert, *The London Encyclopedia* (London, 1983), p. 599.

23. E. A. Beardsley to J. Lane [1924]; ALS, E. A. Beardsley to J. Lane, 10.9.[1923?] (Princeton); mALS, E. A. Beardsley to J. Lane [1924] (British Library, London); E. A Beardslay, *B.Misc.* p. 83.

24. E. A. Beardsley, *B. Misc.*, p. 83; MDG, pp. 13–14; mALS E. A Beardsley to J. Lane, 14.3.1923 (British Library, London); E. A. Beardsley, *B. Misc.*, pp. 75, 79.

25. mALS, E. A. Beardsley to J. Lane, [1924]; E. A. Beardsley, *B. Misc.*, p. 75; A. W. King, in *An Aubrey Beardsley Lecture*, p. 24; ALS, R. Ross to William Rothenstein, 23.1.1899 (Harvard University).

26. ALS, E. A. Beardsley to J. Lane, 10.9.[1923]; E. A. Beardsley, *B. Misc.*, pp. 79–80; Last Will and Testament of Sarah Pitt, proved 2.1.1892; Somerset House, London; Brighton Handbooks, 1883–5.

CHAPTER II · 'A GOOD SCHOOL TIME'

1. E. A. Beardsley, *B. Misc.*, pp. 75, 79–80; The Last Will and Testament of Sarah Pitt, Somerset House, London; E. A. Beardsley, *B. Misc.*, p. 79; MDG, p. 32.

2. E. A. Beardsley, *B. Misc.*, p. 75; W. W. Hind-Smith, 'Old Boy Jottings', *P&P*, vol. XXIII [1898], pp. 93–4; *Iconography*, item 2; E. A. Beardsley, *B. Misc.*, p. 75.

3. Arthur Symons, *Aubrey Beardsley* (London, 1905), p. 21; W. B. Yeats, *Autobiographies* (London, 1955), p. 329; H. Hamilton Maugham, *Some Brighton Churches* (London, 1922), pp. 44–5; *Some Brief Recollections of the Late Rev. George Chapman M.A., by one of his own people* (Oxford, 1892); R.S., *George Chapman* (preface by Alfred Gurney) (London, 1893); Malcolm Easton, *op. cit.* (London, 1972), p. 161; R.S., *op. cit.*

4. AB's 'Form of Application', 22.11.1884: 'Name of payor' is Miss Sarah Pitt; BGS archive (Sussex County Record Office, Lewes); D. B. Friend, *Brighton Handbook for 1886*, p. 150; *P&P*, E. J. Marshall memorial number, 1900; conversation with John Smithies, former English teacher at BGS; John Smithies, 'A. V. Beardsley and H. A. Payne' in *P&P*, June 1964; 'Rules and Regulations' [BGS Prospectus, *c.*1886]; BGS Archive (Lewes).

5. 'Aubrey Beardsley in Memoriam', *Westminster Budget*, 25.3.1898, p. 10; R. Thurston Hopkins 'Aubrey Beardsley's Schooldays', *The Bookman*, March, 1927, p. 305 (Weintraub, and others, mistook Hopkins for AB's school-fellow, but Hopkins was quoting 'one

of [AB's] contemporaries'); Hind-
Smith, *P&P*, 1898, pp. 93–4; M.
Easton, *op. cit.*, p. 3; A. W. King, *An
Aubrey Beardsley Lecture*, p. 24.

6. *P&P*, XLVII, 1922, pp. 215–17;
Hind-Smith, 'Aubrey Beardsley at
School', *John O'London's Weekly*,
22.12.1928; R. T. Hopkins, *The
Bookman*, 1927, p. 307; *P&P*, February
1887, pp. 155–6.

7. Hopkins, *The Bookman*, 1927, p. 305;
King, in *An Aubrey Beardsley Lecture*,
p. 26; Hopkins, *The Bookman*, 1927,
p. 305; G. F. Scotson-Clark,
'Beardsley's Schooldays or Early Days
Prior to 1893' [TS] (Princeton); C. B.
Cochran, *Secrets of a Showman*
(London, 1925), p. 4; H. A. Payne,
P&P, XXIII, 1898, p. 53; *Westminster
Budget*, 25.3.1898, p. 9.

8. Hopkins, *The Bookman*, 1927,
p. 305 *Westminster Budget*, 25.3.1898,
p. 9; Hopkins, *The Bookman*, 1898,
p. 305; King, in *An Aubrey Beardsley
Lecture*, pp. 23, 26; *P&P*, May 1885,
p. 8; ibid., June 1885, pp. 45–6; King,
in *An Aubrey Beardsley Lecture*, p. 23;
mALS, E. A. Beardsley to J. Lane
[1924]; G. F. Scotson-Clark, *op. cit.*
C. B. Cochran, *op. cit.*, p. 7; 'Art and
the Music Halls', *Unwin's Chapbook
1889–1900* (London, 1899), pp. 40–2.

9. Scotson-Clark, *op. cit.*; ALS, A. W.
King to H. A. Payne, 4.12.1920, BGS
Archive (Lewes); Scotson-Clark,
op. cit.; A. W. King, in *An Aubrey
Beardsley Lecture*, p. 26; UW, p. 80.

10. Hopkins, *The Bookman*, 1927, p. 307;
AB's sketchbook (Princeton); AB to
E. J. Marshall, September 1893, quoted
in *P&P*, November 1893; E. A.
Beardsley, *B. Misc.*, p. 76; UW, p. 157;
George Derry, *Nineteen Early Drawings
by Aubrey Beardsley* (London, 1919).

11. AB's copy of *Prose Writings of Swift* (ed.
Walter Lewin) (London, 1886)
(Princeton); Dulau & Co., Catalogue

165, *Books from the Library of John Lane
and Other Books of the Eighteen Nineties*
(1930), pp. 8–9; Gekoski Booksellers,
Catalogue 18, *Sale from the Collection of
Giles Gordon* (1994), p. 1; W. W.
Hind-Smith, 'Old Boy Jottings', *P&P*,
May 1898, p. 94; The drawing of
Egham church is at Princeton;
Westminster Budget, 25.3.1898, p. 10.

12. King, 'The Dome', *P&P*, 1900,
pp. 61–5; King, in *An Aubrey Beardsley
Lecture*, p. 27; 'Programme and Words
to Brighton Grammar School
Christmas Entertainment at the Dome,
Monday 20 December [1886]', *P&P*,
February 1887.

13. Scotson-Clark, *op. cit.*; Hopkins,
op. cit., p. 307; C. B. Cochran, *op. cit.*,
p. 4; C. B. Cochran, 'Aubrey
Beardsley at School', *Poster and Art
Collector*, 8.9.1898, p. 103; O. H.
Leeney, 'Recollections of Aubrey
Beardsley', *P&P*, June 1925,
pp. 169–74; C. B. Cochran, *Secrets of a
Showman*, p. 4, *Cock-a-Doodle-Do*
(London, 1941), p. 74; Cochran, *Poster
and Art Collector*, 8.9.1898, p. 103;
James Harding, *Cochran* (London,
1988), p. 6.

14. G. F. Scotson-Clark, *op. cit.*;
Programme for 'Annual Entertainment
at The Dome, 20 December, 1887',
BGS archive (Lewes); *P&P*, February
1888, pp. 167–8; *P&P*, June 1887,
p. 48; Cochran, *Poster and Art Collector*,
8.9.1898, p. 103; *Brighton Society*,
11.6.1887 and 9.7.1887, p. 11.

15. Bernard Muddiman, 'Aubrey
Beardsley: Some Reminiscences and an
Appreciation', *Brighton and Hove
Society*, 7.9.1907, p. 1037; Payne,
'Aubrey Beardsley', *P&P*, April 1898,
pp. 53–5; G. C. Williamson, 'Aubrey
Beardsley: A Few Memories', *Carmina*
9 (1931), p. 278; King, in *An Aubrey
Beardsley Lecture*, pp. 27, 44.

16. *Westminster Budget*, 25.3.1898, p. 10;

Hind-Smith, *John O'London's Weekly*, 22.12.1928; Unsigned MS reminiscence, BGS archive (Lewes); O. H. Leeney, *P&P*, June 1925, pp. 169–74; C. B. Cochran, *Poster and Art Collector*, 8.9.1898, p. 103; *Westminster Budget*, 25.3.1898, p. 10; Scotson-Clark, *op. cit.*

17. *Westminster Budget*, 25.3.1898, p. 10; B. Muddiman, *Brighton and Hove Society*, 7.9.1907, p. 1037; Scotson-Clark, *op. cit.*; MDG, pp. 14–15; the letter is illustrated in MDG, facing p. 224; quoted in Miriam J. Benkovitz, *Aubrey Beardsley* (London, 1981), p. 32.

18. M. Easton, *op. cit.*, p. 161; *Westminster Budget*, 25.3.1898, p. 10; Haldane MacFall, *Aubrey Beardsley* (London, 1928), p. 16; M. Easton, *op. cit.*, p. 264; Scotson-Clark, *op. cit.*

19. Montague Summers, *The Galanty Show* (London, 1980), p. 56; mALS, E. A. Beardsley to J. Lane, 11.9.1924 (British Library, London); Quoted in M. Easton, *op. cit.*, p. 154; M. Summers, *op. cit.*, pp. 56–7; UW, pp. 106–27; AB collection at Brighton Museum and Art Gallery.

20. UW, pp. 102–5; Scotson-Clark, *op. cit.*; UW, pp. 50, 101; George Derry, *An Aubrey Beardsley Scrap Book* (London, 1920), p. 22; the original 'Pied Piper' pictures are at Harvard; Walter Puttick, 'An Old Boy's Appreciation of Aubrey Beardsley', *P&P*, April 1898, p. 66; Scotson-Clark, *op. cit.*;' Programme and Words for . . . The Dome, on Wednesday, 19 December, 1888', BGS Archive (Lewes); *P&P*, February 1889, pp. 15–17; O. H. Leeney, *P&P*, June 1925; MDG, p. 23.

CHAPTER III · 'AN ART TRAINING'

1. UW, pp. 110–13; R. A. Walker, 'Notes on the Family of Aubrey Beardsley', *B. Misc.*, pp. 102–3; ccTLS R. A. Walker to Oliver Lodge, 22.7.1935 (Princeton); UW, p. 71; AB's entries, *Hazell's Annual, 1895, Who's Who, 1898*; MDG, pp. 15–16; John Davidson, 'Thirty Bob A Week' [poem]; MDG, pp. 15–16.

2. AB's copy of *Shakespeare's Poems* (Princeton); MDG, p. 15; M. Benkovitz, *Aubrey Beardsley* (London, 1981), p. 32; C. B. Cochran, *Poster and Art Collector*, 8.9.1898, p. 104 (Cochran dates the drawing 1888, but early 1889 seems more likely); M. Easton, *op. cit.*, p. 5; J. Harding, *Cochran*, p. 6; Scotson-Clark, *op. cit.*

3. M. Easton, 'Aubrey Beardsley and Julian Sampson: An Unrecorded Friendship', *Apollo* (1967), pp. 66–8; M. Easton, *Aubrey and the Dying Lady*, p. 164ff.; Alan Godfrey, *Pimlico, Sloane Square and Nine Elms, 1894*, Old Ordnance Survey Maps (Gateshead, n.d.); M. Easton, *Aubrey and the Dying Lady*, p. 164ff.; *Crockford's Clerical Directory, 1889*; M. Easton, *Aubrey and the Dying Lady*, p. 164ff.

4. King, *A Beardsley Lecture*, p. 31; MDG, p. 18; *Memories of Edmund Symes-Thompson MD, FRCP, A Follower of St Luke, by his wife* (London, 1908); MDG, p. 18.

5. EW, pp. 4–13; Max Beerbohm, 'Aubrey Beardsley', *A Variety of Things* (London, 1928), p. 223; MDG, p. 18; H. MacFall, *Aubrey Beardsley* (London, 1928), p. 10; AB's album (Princeton); 'The Story of a Confession Album', *Tit-Bits*, 4.1.1890, p. 203.

6. MDG, p. 18; ibid., p. 23; AB's album – flyleaf (Princeton); C. B. Cochran, *Poster and Art Collector*, 8.9.1898, p. 104.

7. C. B. Cochran, *Showman Looks On* (London, 1945), p. 164; Cochran quoted in Margery Ross (ed.), *Robert Ross, Friend of Friends* (London, 1952), p. 51; *Court Minutes of the Guardian*

Fire & Life Assurance Office, 1888–1891
[MS], (Guildhall Library, London),
p. 232; King, in *An Aubrey Beardsley
Lecture*, p. 30; A. W. Tarn & C. E.
Byles, *A Record of the Guardian
Assurance Company Ltd, 1821–1921*
(Privately Printed, 1921), p. 69; G. C.
Williamson, 'Aubrey Beardsley: A Few
Memories', *Carmina* (1931), p. 279.

8. R. A. Walker, *Some Unknown Drawings
of Aubrey Beardsley* (London, 1923),
p. 18*n*; A. W. Tarn & C. E. Byles,
op. cit.; Scotson-Clark, *op. cit.*;
MacFall, *op. cit.*, p. 10; Anne
Hammond (ed.), *Frederick H. Evans –
Selected Texts and a Bibliography*
(Oxford, 1992).

9. G. F. Scotson-Clark, 'The Artist of the
Yellow Book', *Bookman*, vol. I, No. 3
(1895), p. 161; Scotson-Clark, 'Aubrey
Beardsley – Prior to 1893'; M. Easton,
Aubrey and the Dying Lady, p. 164;
Scotson-Clark, 'Aubrey Beardsley –
Prior to 1893'; MDG, p. 23; R. A.
Walker, *Some Unknown Drawings of
Aubrey Beardsley*, p. 15; EW, p. 20.

10. EW, p. 16; Peter Ackroyd, *Blake*
(London, 1996), p. 67; *Iconography*,
item 20; *P&P*, December 1890, p. 203;
the programme is reproduced in Brigid
Brophy, *Beardsley and His World*
(London, 1976), p. 38; Scotson-Clark,
'Aubrey Beardsley – Prior to 1893';
Brighton and Sussex Telegraph,
8.11.1890, p. 5; *P&P*, December 1890,
p. 203.

11. Alfred Gurney, 'Preface' to R.S. *George
Chapman*, p. vi; *Iconography*, item 17;
*Court Minutes of the Guardian Fire and
Life Assurance Office, 1888–1891*,
pp. 268–72; census return, 1891, PRO.

12. R. Ross, *Aubrey Beardsley* (London,
1909), p. 17; ALS, A. H. Pargeter to
R. A. Walker, 1.1.1936 (Princeton).
D. S. MacColl, 'Aubrey Beardsley', *B.
Misc.*, pp. 17–32; W. P. Frith, 'Crazes
in Art', *Magazine of Art*, 1888,

pp. 190–1; D. S. MacColl, *B. Misc.*,
pp. 17–32; Graham Hough, *The Last
Romantics* (London, 1949), pp. 1–32; E.
Burne-Jones quoted in Christopher
Wood, *Olympian Dreamers* (London,
1983); J. M. Whistler, 'Ten O'Clock
Lecture', reprinted in *The Gentle Art of
Making Enemies* (London, 1890),
pp. 135–59; Walter Sickert, Preface to
*A Collection of Paintings by London
Impressionists* (London, 1889)
[exhibition catalogue].

13. G. F. Scotson-Clark, 'Aubrey
Beardsley – Prior to 1893'; MDG,
p. 19; Scotson-Clark, 'Aubrey
Beardsley – Prior to 1893'; MDG,
pp. 19–20; MacFall, *op. cit.*, p. 11; M.
Easton, *Apollo*, 1967, pp. 66–8;
Scotson-Clark, 'Aubrey Beardsley –
Prior to 1893'.

14. Lionel Lambourne, *The Aesthetic
Movement* (London, 1996), pp. 50–60;
MDG, p. 19; ALS, AB to [G. F.
Scotson-]Clark, 1891 (Library of
Congress, Washington DC); R. Ross,
op. cit., p. 45; ALS, AB to Scotson-
Clark, 1891.

15. Katherine Lyon Mix, *A Study in Yellow*
(Kansas/London, 1960), p. 44; MDG,
pp. 21–3; E. A. Beardsley, *B. Misc.*,
p. 76; W. Graham Robertson, *Time
Was* (London, 1931), p. 73ff; Angela
Thirkell, *Three Houses* (London, 1931),
pp. 15–28; MDG, pp. 21–3; E. A.
Beardsley, *B. Misc.*; MDG, pp. 22–4.
G. F. Scotson-Clark, 'Aubrey
Beardsley – Prior to 1893'; MDG,
pp. 21–3.

16. MDG, p. 23; AB to Scotson-Clark,
July 1891 (printed in Linda Zatlin,
'Beardsley and Biography', *biography*,
vol. 15, No. 2, pp. 132–3; MDG,
pp. 24–5, 27.

17. MDG, pp. 28–9 (the illustrated
original is at Princeton); EW,
pp. 30–32; UW, p. 70; MDG, p. 25;
AB to G. F. Scotson-Clark, in

biography, vol. 15, no. 2; Scotson-Clark, 'Aubrey Beardsley – Prior to 1893'; King, in *An Aubrey Beardsley Lecture*, p. 31; Alfred Gurney to AB, 23.8.[1891] (British Library, London); AB to G. F. Scotson-Clark, in *biography*, vol. 15, no. 2; MDG, p. 27.

18. G. F. Scotson-Clark, 'Aubrey Beardsley – Prior to 1893'; Hopkins, *The Bookman* (1927), p. 307; H. MacFall, *op. cit.*, p. 12.

19. Oscar Wilde, *Intentions* (London, 1891); Matthew Sturgis, *Passionate Attitudes* (London, 1995), pp. 19–55; Richard Ellman, *Oscar Wilde* (London, 1987), p. 201ff.; Oscar Wilde, 'The Decay of Lying', in *Intentions*; AB to Scotson-Clark, in *biography*, vol. 15, no. 2; Vincent O'Sullivan, 'Literature in France' [MS], p. 6 (Princeton); G. F. Scotson-Clark, 'Aubrey Beardsley – Prior to 1893'.

20. *The Times*, 1.4.1891, p. 4; *Athenaeum*, 4.4.1891, pp. 451–2; *L'Enfant prodigue* closed 29.10.1891; C. B. Cochran, *Poster and Art Collector*, 8.9.1898, p. 104; A. G. Lehmann, 'Pierrot and Fin de Siècle' in Ian Fletcher (ed.), *Romantic Mythologies* (London, 1967); MDG, p. 27.

21. R. Ross, *op. cit.*, pp. 17–18; AB to G. F. Scotson-Clark, in *biography*, vol. 15, no. 2; A. W. King, in *An Aubrey Beardsley Lecture*, p. 31; G. F. Scotson-Clark, 'Aubrey Beardsley – Prior to 1893'; MDG, pp. 29–30; G. F. Scotson-Clark, 'Aubrey Beardsley – Prior to 1893'; For Fred Brown see *DNB* (1941–50); D. S. MacColl, 'Professor Fred Brown', *Magazine of Art*, 1894, pp. 403–9; Charles W. Furse, *Illustrated Memoir* (London, 1908), p. 52; J. M. Hone, *The Life of Henry Tonks* (London, 1939), pp. 53–4.

22. D. S. MacColl, 'The Beardsleys' [MS] (University of Glasgow); D. S.

MacColl, 'Professor Fred Brown', p. 403; *DNB*; Isobel Watson, *Westminster and Pimlico Past* (London, 1993); D. S. MacColl, 'The Beardsleys'; *DNB*; C. W. Furse, *op. cit.*; J. M. Hone, *op. cit.*; C. W. Furse, *op. cit.*; D. S. MacColl, 'Professor Fred Brown,' p. 404; C. W. Furse, *op. cit.*; G. F. Scotson-Clark, 'The Artist of the Yellow Book', *Bookman*, 1895, p. 160.

23. G. F. Scotson-Clark, 'Aubrey Beardsley – Prior to 1893'; D. S. MacColl, 'The Beardsleys'; MDG, pp. 29–30; G. F. Scotson-Clark, 'Aubrey Beardsley – Prior to 1893'.

24. MDG, pp. 29–30; EW, pp. 26, 29. 'Mr Aubrey Beardsley', *Leslie's Weekly*, 6.8.1894, p. 90; William Lawler, 'Aubrey Beardsley', *London Year Book* (London, 1898), p. 49; MDG, pp. 29–30; C. B. Cochran, *Secrets of a Showman*, p. 7.

25. The Last Will and Testament of Sarah Pitt, Somerset House, London; MDG, p. 32; King, in *An Aubrey Beardsley Lecture*, p. 32; Alfred Gurney to E. A. Beardsley, 14.11.[1891] (British Library, London); EW, pp. 36–7; *Atalanta*, vol. V, no. 51, December 1891, p. 143ff.; A. W. King, 'Our Illustrator', *The Bee*, 2 November 1891, pp. 21–2; MDG, pp. 31–2.

CHAPTER IV · 'A NEW STYLE'

1. *Court Minutes of the Guardian Fire & Life Assurance Office Co., 1891–1895* [MS] (Guildhall Library, London), p. 28; MDG, pp. 31–2; the article is almost certainly Walter Crane's 'The Language of Line – Part I: Outline', *Magazine of Art*, 1888, pp. 145–9; MDG, p. 32.

2. W. Crane, 'Language of Line – Part I'; *Magazine of Art*, 1888, p. 325ff.; p. 415ff.; W. Crane, 'The Language of

Line – Part II: Design'; EW, pp. 25, 26.

3. MDG, p. 37; Aymer Vallance, 'The Furnishing and Decoration of the House' (six parts), *Art Journal*, 1892; *Crockford's Clerical Directory, 1886–8*; *Catholic Who's Who* (London, 1910); A. Vallance, 'The Invention of Aubrey Beardsley', *Magazine of Art*, 1898, pp. 362–8; H. MacFall, *Aubrey Beardsley*, p. 16; A. Vallance, *Magazine of Art*, 1898 pp. 362–3.

4. R. Ross, *Aubrey Beardsley*, pp. 15–17; MDG, p. 20; R. Ross, *op. cit.*, p. 16; *Iconography*, items 32, 34; R. Ross, *op. cit.*, p. 17; John Adlard, *Stenbock, Yeats and the Nineties* (London, 1969); Derek Hudson, *Norman O'Neill, A Life of Music* (London, 1945), pp. 18, 21.

5. A. J. L. Busst, 'The Image of the Androgyne in the Nineteenth Century' in I. Fletcher (ed.), *Romantic Mythologies* (London, 1967); MDG, p. 282; ALS, Julian Sampson to R. A. Walker, 30.10.1935 (Princeton); Charles Baudelaire, 'The Painter of Modern Life', *My Heart Laid Bare, and other prose writings* [trans. Norman Cameron] (London, 1950), pp. 21–73; Helen Thorp [nee Syrett] to Elspeth Grahame, 1933, quoted in Alison Prince, *Kenneth Grahame* (London, 1994), p. 109; M. Easton, *Aubrey and the Dying Lady*, p. 218; A. Vallance, *Magazine of Art*, 1898, p. 363.

6. Fiona MacCarthy, *William Morris* (London, 1994); A. Vallance, *Magazine of Art*, 1898, p. 363; *Iconography*, item 40.

7. Elizabeth Aslin, *The Aesthetic Movement* (London, 1981); *Westminster Budget*, 25.3.1898, p. 10; 'The Sound of Architecture', in Anne Hammond (ed.), *Frederick H. Evans – Selected Texts and a Bibliography*, pp. 11–13.

8. MDG, pp. 33–5, 37–8, 43–5; 'Mr Aubrey Beardsley', *Leslie's Weekly*,

6.8.1894, p. 90; MDG, pp. 33–5; R. Ross, *op. cit.*, p. 44.

9. MDG, p. 37; B. Brophy, *Beardsley and His World* (London, 1976), pp. 55; A. Vallance, *Magazine of Art*, 1898, p. 367.

10. *Court Minutes of the Guardian Fire and Life Assurance Office*; MDG, p. 33; *Art Journal*, 1892, pp. 243ff; 274ff.; H. MacFall, *op. cit.*, p. 20; D. S. MacColl, *B. Misc.*, p. 22; MDG, pp. 34, 37; *Iconography*, item 36; MDG, pp. 34, 37.

11. MDG, p. 44; Catherine Slessor, *The Art of Aubrey Beardsley* (New Jersey, 1989), p. 23; UW, pp. 10, 11 [misdated as 1894]; EW, pp. 22, 24; MDG, p. 44.

12. James Thorpe, *English Illustrators of the Nineties* (London, 1935); MDG, p. 44; A. S. Hartrick, *A Painter's Pilgrimage* (Cambridge, 1939), pp. 96–7; Elizabeth Robins Pennell, *Nights* (London, 1916), pp. 138–9; MDG, p. 34.

13. J. M. Dent, *Memoirs* (London, 1928), p. 68; this account is derived from: H. MacFall, *op. cit.*, pp. 25–6; J. M. Dent, *op. cit.*, pp. 68–9; and C. Lewis Hind, 'Introduction' to UW, pp. XV–XVI; Brian Reade, *Beardsley* (London, 1967), p. 313; J. M. Dent, *op. cit.*, p. 69; ALS, AB to J. M. Dent, 3.10.1892 (Private Collection).

14. R. Ross, *op. cit.*, p. 23; MDG, p. 38; *Court Minutes of the Guardian Fire & Life Assurance Office 1891–1895*, p. 118; MDG, p. 38; H. MacFall, *op. cit.*, pp. 26, 28–9; AB's copy of Anton Springer, *Albrecht Dürer* (Berlin, 1892), inscribed 'A. Beardsley, 1892' (Princeton); cf. MD Book I, chapters vi, vii, xiv; A. Vallance, 'Aubrey Beardsley' in R. A. Walker (ed.), *Morte Darthur Portfolio* (London, 1927), p. 12; Walter Pater, 'Pico della Mirandola', in *Studies in the History of the Renaissance* (London, 1873).

15. H. MacFall, *op. cit.*, p. 27; ALS, AB to

J. M. Dent, [October, 1892] (Private
Collection); A. Vallance, in *Morte
Darthur Portfolio*, p. 12; A. Vallance,
Magazine of Art, 1898, p. 365; MDG,
p. 34.

16. MDG, p. 38; MDG, p. 34; A.
Vallance, *Magazine of Art*, 1898, p. 263;
D. S. MacColl, 'The Beardsleys';
MDG, pp. 34–8.

17. MDG, p. 38; R. Ross, *op. cit.*, p. 20;
A. Vallance, *Magazine of Art*, 1898,
pp. 364–5; James G. Nelson, *The Early
Nineties, a View from the Bodley Head*
(Cambridge, Mass., 1971); A. Vallance,
Magazine of Art, 1898, pp. 364–5;
MDG, p. 47.

18. C. L. Hind, *op. cit.*, pp. xvi–xviii; For
Alice Meynell, see Richard Le
Gallienne, *The Romantic Nineties*
(London, 1926), pp. 74–7; Gertrude
Atherton, *Adventures of a Novelist*
(London, 1932), p. 286; William
Rothenstein, *Men and Memories*
(London, 1931), p. 282; K. L. Mix, *A
Study in Yellow* (Kansas/London, 1960),
p. 137; C. L. Hind, *op. cit.*,
pp. xvi–xix; Clive Ashwin, 'The
Founding of *The Studio*', *Studio
International – Centenary Number*, 1993,
p. 4; C. L. Hind, *op. cit.*, p. xix;
Iconography, items 28–iv, v.

19. C. L. Hind, *op. cit.*, p. xix; Joseph
Pennell, *Pen Drawing and Pen
Draughtsmen* (London/NY, 1889), p. 1;
J. Pennell, *Aubrey Beardsley and Other
Men of the Nineties* (Privately printed,
Philadelphia, 1924), pp. 19–20; J.
Pennell, *The Adventures of an Illustrator*
(Boston, 1925), p. 216 (these provide
very similar accounts); ALS, E. R.
Pennell to Mr Kennerly, 3.3.1929
(Library of Congress, Washington,
DC).

20. D. S. MacColl, *Confessions of a Keeper*
(London, 1931), p. 89; D. S. MacColl,
B. Misc., pp. 22, 25. J. Pennell,
Adventures of an Illustrator, p. 168; E. R.

Pennell, *Nights*, p. 179; MDG, p. 38;
ibid., p. 44; ibid., p. 38.

21. W. B. Yeats, *Autobiographies*, p. 332;
Mabel Beardsley-Wright, 'Aubrey
Beardsley' in *Allgemeines Lexikon . . .*,
vol. III, p. 111; R. Ross, *op. cit.*, p. 39;
ibid., p. 22.

22. A. Vallance, *Magazine of Art*, 1898,
pp. 363–4; MDG, pp. 35, 44.

CHAPTER V · 'OOF AND FAME'

1. C. Lewis Hind, 'Introduction' to UW,
p. xix; Clive Ashwin, 'Gleeson White
– Aesthete and Editor', *Apollo*, vol.
CVIII (1978), pp. 251–61; Gleeson
White, 'Aubrey Beardsley In
Memoriam', *Studio*, 1898, p. 260;
A. W. King, 'The Art of Aubrey
Beardsley', in R. A. Walker, *An Aubrey
Beardsley Lecture*, p. 36; C. L. Hind,
Naphtali (London, 1926), p. 74; *Studio*,
I, 1893, p. 36.

2. cf. Mark Samuels Lasner, *A Selective
Checklist of the Published Work of Aubrey
Beardsley* (Boston, 1995), pp. 10–13;
MDG, pp. 43–5; W.L. [William
Lawler], 'Aubrey Beardsley', *The
London Yearbook* (London, 1898), p. 46;
MDG, p. 44.

3. EW, p. 45; C. L. Hind, *Naphtali*,
p. 74; Q.R. [C. L. Hind], 'A
Bookman's Memories – Aubrey
Beardsley', *Christian Science Monitor*,
17.5.1921, p. 3; MDG, p. 44; Joseph
Pennell, 'A New Illustrator: Aubrey
Beardsley', *Studio* I, 1893, p. 18; G.
White, *Studio*, 1898, p. 256; *Artist*,
April 1893, p. 115; *Studio*, 3, 1893.

4. James G. Nelson, *The Early Nineties, A
View from the Bodley Head* (Cambridge,
Mass., 1971); *Pall Mall Budget*,
2.3.1893, p. 239; J. Walter Smith, 'A
Chat with Beardsley', *Boston Evening
Transcript*, 16.2.1895, p. 16; C. L.
Hind, 'Introduction' to UW, p. xx.

5. For best account of Degas débâcle, cf.

Alfred Thornton, *The Diary of an Art Student of the Nineties* (London, 1938), pp. 22–32; quoted in ibid., pp. 23, 33n; Walter Jerrold (ed.), *Bon-Mots of Charles Lamb and Douglas Jerrold* (London, 1893), p. 7.

6. Rupert Hart-Davis (ed.), *The Letters of Oscar Wilde* (London, 1962), p. 348; MDG, p. 46; A. Thornton, *op. cit.*, p. 37; 'Chronicles of Art', *Magazine of Art*, May 1893, p. xxx; *Artist*, May 1893, p. 151; *Spectator*, 22.4.1893, pp. 523–4.

7. M. S. Lasner, *op. cit.*, p. 17; J. Pennell, *Studio*, I, 1893, pp. 14–19; *Academy*, 5.4.1893, p. 331; *Artist*, May 1893, p. 141 – the cover is described as 'extremely handsome and decorative'; *London Figaro*, 20.4.1893, quoted in Stanley Weintraub, *Aubrey Beardsley – Imp of the Perverse* (Pennsylvania/ London, 1976), p. 81; *Art Student* [NY], 8–12.1893; *Le Livre et L'Image*, September 1893, p. 249; D. S. MacColl, 'The Beardsleys'.

8. MDG, p. 47; Richard Ellman, *Oscar Wilde*; 'Salome Contract', in R. A. Walker, 'Introduction', Oscar Wilde, *Salome* (London, 1957), p. 14; *Le Livre et L'Image*, August 1893, p. 57; A. Vallance, in *Morte Darthur Portfolio*, p. 12; MDG, p. 48.

9. J. Pennell, *Adventures of an Illustrator*, p. 216; J. Pennell, *Aubrey Beardsley and Some Other Men of the Nineties*, pp. 25–7; Elizabeth Robins Pennell, *Nights* (Philadelphia, 1916), p. 260; for Harland, cf. Katherine Lyon Mix, *op. cit.*, pp. 55–7; and G. Glastonbury [Aline Harland], 'The Life and Writings of Henry Harland', *Redwood*, vol. 10, no. 1 (1910), pp. 2–10; E. A. Beardsley, *B. Misc.*, p. 77; E. R. Pennell, *op. cit.*, p. 260; Margaret Stetz and Mark Samuels Lasner, *The Yellow Book – A Centenary Exhibition* (Cambridge, Mass., 1994), pp. 14–15.

10. E. R. Pennell, *op. cit.*; J. Pennell, *Adventures of an Illustrator, Aubrey Beardsley and Some Other Men of the Nineties*; *Art Journal* (1893), pp. 216–20; *Fortnightly Review*, 1.6.1893, p. 774; MDG, pp. 48–9; J. Pennell, *Adventures of an Illustrator*, p. 219; William Rothenstein, *Men and Memories* (London, 1931), pp. 134–5, 187.

11. D. S. MacColl, *B. Misc.*, p. 23; J. Pennell, *Adventures of an Illustrator*, pp. 217, 220; J. Pennell, *Aubrey Beardsley and Some Other Men*, pp. 28–30; E. R. Pennell, *op. cit.*, pp. 262–4; D. S. MacColl, 'The Beardsleys'; E. R. Pennell, 'The Two Salons', *Fortnightly Review*, 1.6.1893, p. 782; D. S. MacColl, 'The Beardsleys'.

12. ibid.; E. R. Pennell, *Nights*, pp. 262–4; J. Pennell, *Aubrey Beardsley and Some Other Men*, p. 32; J. Pennell, *Adventures of an Illustrator*, pp. 217–20; E. R. and J. Pennell, *The Life of James McNeill Whistler* (London, 1908), p. 311; J. Pennell, *Adventures of an Illustrator*, p. 220; *Iconography*, item 52; *Leonard Smithers Catalogue No. 7* (1896), item 979: 'These designs were executed at the commencement of [AB's] career.'; J. Pennell, *Adventures of an Illustrator*, p. 220; A. Stodart-Walker, 'Some Celebrities I Have Known', *Chambers Journal*, 3.4.1909, p. 283.

13. *Studio*, 1894, p. 167; A. Vallance, *Magazine of Art*, p. 365; A. Vallance, *Morte Darthur Portfolio*, p. 12; MDG, p. 50; R. Ross, *op. cit.*, p. 45; T. Wratislaw, 'The Salome of Aubrey Beardsley', *Artist*, 2.4.1894, pp. 100–1; MDG, p. 51.

14. For AB's décor cf. Herbert Small, 'Aubrey Beardsley', *Book Buyer*, February 1895, pp. 26–9; J. W. Smith, *Boston Evening Transcript*, 16.2.1895, p. 16; Penrhyn Stanlaws, 'Some

Personal Recollections of Aubrey Beardsley', *Book Buyer*, October 1898, pp. 212–14; Netta Syrett, *Sheltering Tree* (London, 1939), pp. 78–9; *Leslie's Weekly*, 6.8.1894, p. 90; and information from Stephen Calloway; R. Ross, *op. cit.*, pp. 22, 44; J.-K. Huysmans (trans. Robert Baldick), *Against Nature* (London, 1959), p. 30; N. Syrett, *op. cit.*.

15. A. Thornton, *op. cit.*, pp. 38–40; D. S. MacColl, 'The Beardsleys'; MDG, pp. 49–51.

16. W. Rothenstein, *op. cit.*, pp. 135, 185; AB holograph (Harvard); Rothenstein, p. 185; David Cecil, *Max* (London, 1964); M. Beerbohm, *A Variety of Things*, p. 222; W. Jerrold (ed.), *Bon-Mots of Samuel Foote and Theodore Hook* (London, 1894), p. 15; Desmond Flower and Henry Maas (eds), *The Letters of Ernest Dowson* (London, 1967), p. 260; Rothenstein, *op. cit.* pp. 134, 176; S. Calloway, *Charles Ricketts* (London, 1979).

17. Robert Emmons, *The Life and Opinions of Richard Sickert* (London, 1941), p. 96; Frank Harris, *Oscar Wilde* (London, 1997, edition), p. 75; Rothenstein, *op. cit.*, p. 213; Julie Speedie, *Wonderful Sphinx* (London, 1993); R. Hart-Davis (ed.), *Max Beerbohm letters to Reggie Turner* (London, 1964), pp. 67–8; Mary M. Lago and Karl Beckson, *Max & Will* (London, 1975), p. 17; Karl Beckson, *Arthur Symons – A Life* (Oxford, 1987), p. 92.

18. MDG, pp. 51–2; Pastel [T. Wratislaw], 'Some Drawings of Aubrey Beardsley', *Artist*, 1.9.1893, pp. 259–60.

19. Evelyn Sharp, *Unfinished Adventure* (London, 1933), pp. 57–8; N. Syrett, *op. cit.*, p. 79; M. Beerbohm, *op. cit.*, p. 226; N. Syrett, *op cit.*, p. 79; H. MacFall, *op. cit.*, p. 1; M. Birnbaum, 'Aubrey Beardsley', *Jacouleff and Other Artists* (NY, 1946), p. 127; N. Syrett, *op. cit.*, p. 71.

20. MDG, p. 53; 'An illustration to the Gospel of To-Day' by 'Baudrey Weirdsley', *To-Day*, 22.9.1894; 'Frontispiece to Juvenile Poems' by 'Daubaway Weirdsley' [Linley Sambourne], *Punch*, 2.2.1895, p. 58; Baby Beaumont in 'Letters from a Debutante', *Punch*, 20.10.1894, p. 180; *B. Misc.*, p. 11; *Westminster Gazette*, quoted in *P&P*, April 1894, p. 66; Henry Harland, 'Aubrey Beardsley', *Academy*, 10.12.1898, p. 437.

21. Quoted in Margery Ross (ed.), *op. cit.*, pp. 27–8; A. Vallance, *Magazine of Art*, 1898, p. 365; H. Macfall, *op. cit.*, p. 41; R. Ross, *op. cit.*, p. 21; A. Vallance, *Morte Darthur Portfolio*, pp. 14, 12; A. Vallance, *Magazine of Art*, 1898, p. 366; Mary Lago (ed.), *Burne-Jones Talking* (London, 1981), pp. 174–5.

22. UW, p. 48; MDG, p. 65; *Max Beerbohm letters to Reggie Turner*, p. 53; Frances Winwar, *Oscar Wilde and the Yellow Nineties* (London, 1940), p. 214; F. Harris, *op. cit.*, p. 75; Ada Leverson, 'The Last First Night' in Violet Wyndham, *The Sphinx and her Circle* (London, 1963), p. 107; G. B. Shaw, in Weintraub (ed.), *Shaw: An Autobiography* (NY, 1969), p. 252; quoted in Weintraub, *Aubrey Beardsley – Imp of the Perverse*, pp. 62, 65; MDG, pp. 52, 54.

23. MDG, p. 38; Lord Alfred Douglas holograph notes for Autobiography (photocopy) (British Library, London); N. Syrett, *op. cit.*, p. 95; MDG, p. 58; *The Letters of Oscar Wilde*, p. 384; *Max Beerbohm letters to Reggie Turner*, p. 84.

24. Rothenstein, *op. cit.*, pp. 134–5; *Spectator*, 23.12.1893, p. 913; *Public Opinion*, 1893, pp. 659–60; MDG, p. 58; *Spectator*, 23.12.1893, p. 912.

25. MDG, p. 58; *Public Opinion*, 1893,
    p. 700; MDG, pp. 51, 58; *Catalogue of
    Loan Exhibition of Drawings by Aubrey
    Beardsley, National Gallery, Millbank
    1923–1924*, p. 5; MDG, pp. 57 *Harper's
    New Monthly Magazine*, November
    1893, pp. 858–67; W. B. Yeats, 'The
    Autumn of the Flesh' in R. Ellman,
    Yeats – The Man and his Masks
    (London, 1979 edition) p. 214; J.-K.
    Huysmans, *op. cit.*, p. 180; MDG,
    pp. 60.

6. MDG, p. 230; D. S. MacColl, 'The
    Beardsleys', p. 3; M. Easton, *Aubrey and
    the Dying Lady*, pp. 86–7.

CHAPTER VI · 'THE BEARDSLEY
BOOM'

1. Interview with Mabel Beardsley, *Bon
    Accord*, 2.2.1900, in M. Easton, *Aubrey
    and the Dying Lady*, pp. 183–4; Henry
    Harland in Katherine Lyon Mix, *A
    Study in Yellow* (Kansas/London, 1960)
    p. 68; G. Glastonbury [Aline Harland],
    Redwood (1910), p. 5; MDG, p. 61;
    John Lane, 'The Yellow Book – Some
    Recollections' [cTS], c.1922 (British
    Library, London); K. L. Mix, *op. cit.*,
    p. 69; John Lane, 'The Yellow Book';
    MDG, p. 61.

2. J. Lewis May, *John Lane and the
    Nineties* (London, 1935), p. 72; R.
    Hart-Davis (ed.), *Letters of Max
    Beerbohm* (London, 1988), pp. 76–7;
    M. Easton, *Aubrey and the Dying Lady*,
    p. 44; Margaret D. Stetz and Mark
    Samuels Lasner, *The Yellow Book – A
    Centenary Exhibition* (Cambridge,
    Mass., 1994), p. 24; *Letters of Max
    Beerbohm*, p. 176; *Max Beerbohm letters
    to Reggie Turner*, p. 88; D. S. MacColl,
    'The Beardsleys', Laurence Housman,
    The Unexpected Years (London, 1936),
    p. 103, mALS Charles Shannon to
    John Lane, n.d. [March 1894] (British
    Library, London).

3. Joseph Pennell, *Adventures of an
    Illustrator*, p. 213; *Critic*, 7.4.1894,
    p. 240; Ernest Rhys, *Everyman
    Remembers* (London, 1931), p. 512;
    Publisher's Note, *Under the Hill*
    (London, 1904), p. 21; ALS Haldane
    MacFall to H. A. Payne, 31.3.1898
    (British Library, London); Arthur
    Waugh, *One Man's Road* (London,
    1931), p. 252; *Critic*, 21, 1894,
    pp. 42–3; quoted in M. D. Stetz and
    M. S. Lasner, *op. cit.*, p. 21; MDG,
    p. 62; *Letters of Max Beerbohm*, p. 94.

4. 'What the Yellow Book is to be',
    Sketch, 11.4.1894, p. 558; M. D. Stetz
    and M. S. Lasner, *op. cit.*, p. 7; H.
    Harland quoted in ibid., p. 21;
    'Contract for the Yellow Book', in
    Sotheby's Catalogue, 18.12.1985, item
    214; A. S. Hartrick, *op. cit.*, p. 115;
    M. D. Stetz and M. S. Lasner, *op. cit.*,
    p. 18; MDG, p. 62; M. S. Lasner, *A
    Selective Checklist of the Published Work
    of Aubrey Beardsley* (Boston, 1995),
    p. 31; *Studio* 2, 1894, pp. 183–5.

5. *Saturday Review*, 24.3.1894,
    pp. 317–18; *The Times*, 8.3.1894,
    p. 12; *Star*, 8.3.1894; *Art Journal*, 1894,
    p. 139; *Artist*, 2.4.1894, pp. 100–1; *Art
    Journal*, 1894, p. 139; *Studio*, 1894,
    pp. 183–5; *Artist*, 2.4.1894, pp. 100–1;
    Saturday Review, 24.3.1894,
    pp. 317–18; *Artist*, 2.4.1894,
    pp. 100–1; *Studio*, 1894, pp. 183–5;
    Jane Block, 'Les XX and La Libre
    Esthétique' in M. A. Stevens and R.
    Hoozee, *Impressionism to Symbolism*
    (London, 1994), p. 50; Estelle Jussim,
    *Slave to Beauty: the eccentric and
    controversial life of F. Holland Day*
    (Boston, 1981), pp. 84–5.

6. *The Letters of Oscar Wilde*, p. 353;
    Punch, 10.3.1894, p. 106; 17.3.1894,
    p. 129.

7. Ian Fletcher, 'Bedford Park: Aesthetes'
    Elysium', in I. Fletcher (ed.), *Romantic
    Mythologies* (London, 1967), p. 169ff.;

MDG, p. 63; *Studio*, 1894, pp. 183–5;
Gleeson White, *Studio*, 1898, p. 259;
Punch, 21.4.1894, p. 189; quoted in
Weintraub, *Aubrey Beardsley – Imp of
the Perverse*, p. 92; *Pelican*, 21.4.1894,
p. 3; *Artist*, 2.4.1894, p. 176; *Critic*,
21.4.1894, p. 275.

7. *Theatrical World*, 4.4.1894, p. 92, in
Bridget J. Elliot, 'Beardsley's Images of
Actresses', RAB, p. 88; *Punch*,
25.9.1894, p. 85.

8. Brian Reade, *Beardsley* (London, 1967),
p. 344; Prospectus for *Yellow Book*;
Max Beerbohm, *A Peep into the Past
and Other Prose Pieces* (Vermont, 1972);
Max Beerbohm letters to Reggie Turner,
p. 87; MDG, pp. 65–6; Chris
Snodgrass, *Aubrey Beardsley, Dandy of
the Grotesque* (NY/Oxford, 1995),
pp. 267–9; *Max Beerbohm letters to
Reggie Turner*, p. 92; cf. Bridget J.
Elliot, in *RAB*.

9. *Leslie's Weekly*, 6.8.1894, p. 90; J. W.
Smith, *Boston Evening Transcript*,
16.2.1895, p. 16; Rodney Engen,
Laurence Houseman (London, 1983),
p. 54; M. D. Stetz and M. S. Lasner,
op. cit., p. 25; AB to John Lane n.d.,
in *Dulau Catalogue 165*, item 946.

10. *Sketch*, 11.4.1894, pp. 557–8; J. Lane,
op. cit.; K. L. Mix, *op. cit.*, p. 80; J. L.
May, *op. cit.*; K. L. Mix, pp. 81–3;
Critic, 3.5.1894; A. Waugh to E. Gosse
in John Harwood, *Olivia Shakespeare &
W. B. Yeats* (London, 1989), pp. 31–2;
E. R. Pennell, *Nights*, pp. 185–7; A.
Thornton, *op. cit.*, p. 43; A. Waugh,
One Man's Road, p. 255; J. Harwood,
op. cit.; E. R. Pennell, *op. cit.*, p. 187.

11. *The Times*, 20.4.1894, p. 3; *National
Observer*, 21.4.1894, pp. 588–9;
Speaker, 28.4.1894, pp. 468–9;
Spectator, 19.5.1894, pp. 695–6; *Punch*,
28.4.1894, p. 207; *Granta*, 28.4.1894,
p. 285; *Isis*, 5.5.1894, p. 261; *Star*,
19.4.1894; *Weekly Irish Times*,
28.4.1894, p. 4; Barry Pain in *Black and

White*, 28.4.1894, quoted in *Max
Beerbohm letters to Reggie Turner*,
p. 135n; *Isis*, 5.5.1894, p. 261; 'The
Philistine' in *Westminster Gazette*,
quoted in A. Thornton, *op. cit.*; MDG,
pp. 68–9; *Westminster Gazette*,
18.4.1894, p. 3; *Whitehall Review*,
25.4.1894, pp. 13–14; *Sketch*, 2.5.1894,
p. 16; *Westminster Gazette*, 18.4.1894,
p. 3; *Academy*, 1894, p. 349; *Punch*,
18.4.1894, p. 207; *National Observer*,
21.4.1894, pp. 588–9; *Artist*, 1894,
p. 171; *Vanity Fair*, 19.4.1894, p. 240;
Athenaeum, 21.4.1894, p. 509; *Granta*,
28.4.1894, p. 278; *Punch*, 5.5.1894,
p. 208; *Daily Chronicle*, 16.4.1894, p. 3;
MDG, p. 67; *Daily Chronicle*,
17.4.1894; property of Thomas G.
Boss, Boston; Vyvyan Holland, *Oscar
Wilde* (London, 1988 edition), p. 55;
MDG, p. 68.

12. *Dial 16*, p. 335; *Chap Book*, 1,
pp. 41–2; *Book Buyer*, 11, pp. 256,
261–2; *Critic*, 21, p. 360; *Modern Art*,
2; E. Jussim, *op. cit.*, p. 78; F. Winwar,
op. cit., p. 240; *The Letters of Oscar
Wilde*, p. 354; MDG, p. 68; *P&P*,
1894, p. 87; K. L. Mix, *op. cit.*, p. 90;
M. D. Stetz and M. S. Lasner, *op. cit.*,
p. 11; J. Lane, 'The Yellow Book';
K. L. Mix, *op. cit.*, p. 95; M.
Benkovitz, *op. cit.*, p. 98; K. L. Mix,
op. cit., p. 86; J. Lane, 'The Yellow
Book'; MDG, pp. 68–9; Percy
Lubbock (ed.), *The Letters of Henry
James* (London, 1920), vol. I, p. 222,
vol. II, p. 355; MDG, p. 69; Walter
Crane, *An Artist's Reminiscences*
(London, 1907), pp. 415–16;
Rothenstein, *op. cit.*, p. 292; W. Crane,
Decorative Illustration of Books (London,
1896), pp. 218ff.; MDG, p. 72; A. S.
Hartrick, *op. cit.*, p. 97.

13. mALS H. Harland to J. Lane, n.d.
(British Library, London); MDG,
p. 67; Prince's Ladies Golf Club
opened 16.6.1894, cf. *Sketch*, 20.6.1894,

p. 406; ALS J. Lane to [Florence Farr] Mrs Emery, 19.6.1894 (University of London), *To-Day*, 12.5.1894, pp. 28–9.

14. Alexander Michaelson [André Raffalovich], 'Aubrey Beardsley', *Blackfriars* (1928), p. 610; E. A. Beardsley, *B. Misc.*, p. 77; Osbert Sitwell, *Noble Essences* (London, 1950), p. 137; *Sketch*, 10.4.1895, p. 561; O. Sitwell, *op. cit.*, p. 132; N. Syrett, *op. cit.*, pp. 68, 73; W. B. Yeats quoted in M. Easton, *op. cit.*, p. 233; Grant Richards, *Memoirs of a Misspent Youth* (London, 1932), p. 276; R. Ross, *op. cit.*, p. 19; M. Beerbohm, *A Variety of Things*, p. 230; Jevan Brandon Thomas, *Charley's Aunt's Father* (London, 1955), p. 166.

15. MDG, pp. 64–5, 70; Grant Richards, *op. cit.*, p. 275; Douglas Sladen, *Twenty Years of My Life* (London, 1915), p. 352; J. Brandon Thomas, *op. cit.*; Ann Thwaite, *Edmund Gosse* (Oxford, 1984), p. 337; Gertrude Atherton, *Adventures of a Novelist* (London, 1932), p. 244; M. Beerbohm, *op. cit.*, p. 222; Rothenstein, *op. cit.*, pp. 180, 259; E. R. Pennell, *op. cit.*, p. 205; Weintraub, *Aubrey Beardsley – Imp of the Perverse*, p. 91; Rothenstein, p. 179; G. Richards, *op. cit.*, pp. 275–6; M. Beerbohm, p. 232; Osbert Burdett, *The Beardsley Period* (London, 1925), p. 98; *To-Day*, 12.5.1894, p. 28.

16. MDG, p. 72; James Milne, *Memoirs of a Bookman* (London, 1934), p. 90; mALS H. Harland to J. Lane, 'Mon. night' [re *Yellow Book* II] (British Library, London); M. Beerbohm, *op. cit.*, p. 224; Maud Ffoulkes, *My Own Past* (London, 1915) quoted in B. Read, *Beardsley Re-Mounted* (London, 1989); R. Ross, *op. cit.*, p. 18.

17. MDG, p. 71; E. A. Beardsley, *B. Misc.*, p. 77; G. White, *Studio*, 1898, p. 256; J. Brandon Thomas, *op. cit.*, p. 132; Ian Fletcher, 'Beardsley in Verse and

Prose', in RAB, pp. 230–2; *Sketch*, 10.4.1895, p. 561; MDG, p. 72; cALS F. Leighton to AB, 16.9.1894 (British Library, London); *Leslie's Weekly*, 6.8.1894, p. 90; J. W. Smith, *Boston Evening Transcript*, 16.2.1895, p. 16; *Sketch*, 10.4.1895, p. 561; W. L. [Lawler], *London Year Book*, 1898, p. 49; ALS, AB to J. M. Dent [May 1894] (Private Collection).

18. K. L. Mix, *op. cit.*, p. 106; *Nation*, 59, 1894, p. 143, *The Times*, 20.7.1894, p. 4, *Yellow Book* II, July 1894, pp. 179–90; *Critic*, 18.9.1894, p. 109; K. L. Mix, p. 113; quoted in *Critic*, 22, 1894, p. 108; Thomas Beer, *The Mauve Decade* (NY, 1926), p. 247; A. Hammond, *op. cit.*, p. 146; MDG, p. 65; *Sketch*, 10.4.1895, p. 561; *Iconography*, item 79; AB, 'The Art of Hoarding', *B. Misc.*, pp. 93–4; the MS is at Princeton; mALS H. Harland to J. Lane, 'Saturday' [1894] (British Library, London); AB, in *B. Misc.*, pp. 93–4; Penrhyn Stanlaws, 'Some Personal Recollections of Aubrey Beardsley', *Book Buyer*, October 1898, p. 212; R. A. Walker, *Some Unknown Drawings of Aubrey Beardsley*, p. 1; *Iconography*, item 72.

19. P. Stanlaws, 'Some Personal Recollections'; E. Jussim, *op. cit.*, p. 80; P. Stanlaws, 'Some Personal Recollections'; H. MacFall, *op. cit.*, p. xiii; A. Hammon, *op. cit.*, p. 150; M. Beerbohm, *op. cit.*, p. 223; ALS AB to Mrs Williams, [n.d.] (Princeton); MDG, p. 73; quoted in Margery Ross, *op. cit.*, pp. 27–8.

20. Robert Hichens, *The Green Carnation* (London, 1894; reprinted 1949), p. 71; R. Ross, *op. cit.*, p. 24; J. L. May, *op. cit.*, p. 50; W. B. Yeats, *Autobiographies*, pp. 331–2; Frank Harris, *My Life and Loves* [1925], vol. 1, p. 15; Brian Read and Frank Dickinson, *Aubrey Beardsley Exhibition*

at the Victoria and Albert Museum 1966,
Catalogue (London, 1966), item 587.

21. M. Benkovitz, *op. cit.*, p. 106; W. B.
Yeats, *Memoirs*, p. 92; MDG, p. 115;
John Russell, 'Why Beardsley is Back',
New York Times Magazine, 5.2.1967,
p. 55; J. L. May, *op. cit.*, p. 50; *Critic*,
22, 1894, p. 108; *Sun*, 28.3.1895, p. 1,
in Linda Zatlin, *Aubrey Beardsley*
and Victorian Sexual Politics (Oxford,
1990).

22. J. W. Smith, *Boston Evening Transcript*,
16.2.1895, p. 16; *Book Buyer*, February
1895; G. White, *Studio*, 1898,
pp. 252–63; W. B. Yeats,
Autobiographies, p. 331; J. W. Smith,
Boston Evening Transcript, 16.2.1895,
p. 16; *Leslie's Weekly*, 6.8.1894, p. 90;
mALS E. A. Beardsley to J. Lane,
'Sunday' [1924] (British Library,
London); Allen Wade (ed.), *The Letters*
of W. B. Yeats (London, 1954), p. 575;
mALS E. A. Beardsley to J. Lane,
'Sunday' [1924]; J. W. Smith, *Boston*
Evening Transcript, 16.2.1895, p. 16;
Sketch, 10.4.1895.

23. J. G. Nelson, *op. cit.*, pp. 267–79;
Artist, December 1894, p. 440; *Studio*,
November 1894, p. ix; MDG, p. 76;
ALS AB to 'Billy' [Rothenstein], '3
o'clock a.m., Tuesday' [September,
1894] (Boston Public Library); *Artist*,
December 1894, pp. 439–40; *Punch*,
3.11.1894, pp. 204–5.

24. M. Beerbohm, *op. cit.*; *Saturday Review*,
27.10.1894, p. 469; *National Observer*,
17.11.1894, p. 23; K. L. Mix, *op. cit.*,
p. 127; P. Stanlaws, 'Some Personal
Recollections'; *Magazine of Art*, January
1895, p. 38; *Studio*, 1894, p. 98; M. S.
Lasner, *op. cit.*, p. 47; Jules Roques,
'Les Artistes Anglais: M. Beardsley',
Courrier Français, 23.12.1894, pp. 6–8;
Rothenstein, *op. cit.*; ALS Oliver Lodge
to R. A. Walker, 19.9.1935
(Princeton); Michael Holroyd, *Augustus*
John (London, 1974), p. 42; Charles

Hiatt, 'Designs by Will H. Bradley',
Studio, 4, 1894, p. 168.

25. *Punch*, *Sketch*, 24.10.1894, p. 72;
28.7.1894; cf. *Punch*, 107, p. 89.

26. M. Easton, *Aubrey and the Dying Lady*,
pp. 93–4; AB to J. Lane, in *Dulau*
Catalogue, 165, item 953; MDG,
pp. 78–9; ALS AB to J. M. Dent,
21.12.[1894] (Private Collection); ALS
E. Gosse to A. E. Gallatin, 19.6.1902
(Princeton); ALS F. P. Barnard to J.
Lane, 7.11.1920 (Princeton); F. P.
Barnard, 'Constantine Guys, Twelve
Unknown Drawings', *Artwork* (1930),
p. 88; *Yellow Book*, vol. VIII; mALS
M. Harland to J. Lane [December
1894] (British Library, London); MDG,
p. 79; J. Lane, 'The Yellow Book'
[Lane misspells the Canon's name,
'Crewsden']; M. Benkovitz, *op. cit.*,
p. 118; *Punch's Almanack for 1895*,
issued December 1894.

CHAPTER VII · 'A DECLARATION OF
WAR'

1. Rupert Hart-Davis (ed.), *Letters of Max*
Beerbohm, p. 8; *Sketch*, 10.4.1895,
pp. 561–2; *Punch*, 2.2.1895.

2. Alexander Michaelson [Andre
Raffalovich], 'Aubrey Beardsley',
Blackfriars, October 1928, p. 609; cf.
Nicholas Salerno, 'An Annotated
Secondary Bibliography', RAB, p. 447;
Emporiums, [1895] pp. 193–204; M. A.
Stevens and R. Hoozee, *Impressionism*
to Symbolism (London, 1994), p. 281;
Glasgow Institute of Fine Arts, 24th
Exhibition of Works of Modern Art
(4.2.1895–4.5.1895), exhibit 247,
'Madame Réjane – £15.5s'; J. W.
Smith, *Boston Evening Transcript*,
16.2.1895, p. 16; Walter Crane, *An*
Artist's Reminiscences, p. 416; G. F.
Scotson-Clark, 'The Artist of The
Yellow Book', *Bookman*, April 1895,
pp. 158–61; *The Times* [NY],

24.2.1895, p. 4; *Herald* [Boston], 21.4.1895, p. 30.

3. *Record*, 23.1.1895, p. 4; M. Easton, *Aubrey and the Dying Lady*, p. 195; Ada Leverson, in *The Sphinx and Her Circle*, pp. 109–15.

4. J. L. May, *op. cit.*, p. 208; J. Brandon Thomas, *op. cit.*, p. 166; AB to Mrs Brandon Thomas [n.d. 1895], Sotheby's [London] Catalogue, 21–22.7.1975, item 522; *Limner*, no. 3, 1895, p. 13; cALS AB to Brandon Thomas [May 1895] (British Library, London).

5. MDG, p. 22; AB to [?], Christopher Millard catalogue (from Linda Zatlin); John Stokes, *In the Nineties* (Hemel Hampstead, 1989), ch. 1.

6. John Lane, *op. cit.*; Telegram, F. Chapman to J. Lane, 6.4.1895 (Princeton); J. Lane to F. Chapman 9.4.1895, quoted in J. Lewis May, *John Lane and the Nineties*, p. 83; Telegram, F. Chapman to J. Lane, 8.4.1895 (Princeton); Jean Moorcroft Wilson, *I Was an English Poet* (London, 1981), p. 125; Vincent O'Sullivan, *Aspects of Wilde* (London, 1936), p. 118; A.M. [Alice Meynell], 'Exhibitions', *Pall Mall Gazette*, 2.11.1904, p. 10; F. Chapman to J. Lane, 8.4.1895; Ella D'Arcy to J. Lane, 20.4.1895, in Karl Beckson, 'Ella D'Arcy, Aubrey Beardsley and the Crisis at "The Yellow Book": A New Letter', *Notes & Queries*, September 1979, pp. 331–3; Telegram, William Watson to J. Lane [2.15 pm] 8.4.1895, (Princeton); J. Lane to F. Chapman, 9.4.1895; F. Chapman to J. Lane, 8.4.1895; E. D'Arcy to J. Lane, 20.4.1895; Telegram, F. Chapman to J. Lane, 17.4.1895 (Princeton); J. Lane to F. Chapman, 9.4.1895; Telegram, F. Chapman to J. Lane, 16.4.1895 (Princeton).

7. MDG, p. 82; NEAC Spring Exhibition, 1895 Catalogue, '14th Exhibition of Modern Pictures' – hanging day was 1.4.1895; MDG, p. 81.

8. E. D'Arcy to J. Lane, 20.4.1895; Telegram, F. Chapman to J. Lane, 17.4.1895 (Princeton); E. D'Arcy to J. Lane, 20.4.1895; Telegram, F. Chapman to J. Lane, 19.4.1895 (Princeton); H. Harland to E. Gosse, 5.5.1895, in Paul F. Matthieson and Michael Millgate (eds), *Transatlantic Dialogue* (Texas, 1965), p. 23; AB to F. Chapman [May 1895] from Paris, in *J. Stephen Lawrence Catalogue No. 44*; MDG, p. 83, n. 4; W. B. Yeats, *Autobiographies*, p. 323.

9. A. Michaelson, *Blackfriars*, October 1928, pp. 609–10; Brocard Sewell, *Footnote to the Nineties* (London, 1968), pp. 18ff.

10. A. Michaelson, *Blackfriars*, October 1928; Philip Healey, 'Mentor and Télémaque: A Beardsley Friendship', *Journal of Eighteen Nineties Society*, 1992; Evelyn Sharp, *Unfinished Adventure* (London, 1933), p. 57; W. B. Yeats, *op. cit.*, p. 323; A. Vallance to R. Ross, 23.5.1895 in Margery Ross, *op. cit.*, p. 38; A. Michaelson, *Blackfriars*, October 1928, p. 609; H. Harland to E. Gosse, 5.5.1895; mALS H. Harland to F. Chapman [2.5.1895] (British Library, London); J. Brandon Thomas, *op. cit.*, p. 166; Julie Speedie, *op. cit.*, p. 91; Baptismal Register of Brompton Oratory; F. Burnand to A. Leverson, 16.5.1895, in J. Speedie, *op. cit.*, p. 95.

11. MDG, pp. 84ff.; A. Michaelson, *Blackfriars*, October 1928, p. 609; MDG, pp. 84–6; David Nutt in *Studio International, Special Centenary Number* (1993), p. 117; A. Vallance to R. Ross, 23.5.1895 in M. Ross, *op. cit.*, p. 38.

12. B. Sewell, *op. cit.*, p. 43; A. Michaelson, 'Oscar Wilde', *Blackfriars*, November 1927, pp. 697–700; MDG,

p. 88; Mary Lago (ed.), *Burne-Jones Talking* (London, 1981), p. 42; MDG, p. 90.

13. mALS Arthur Machen to J. Lane, 28.9.1895 (British Library, London); *Punch*, 25.5.1895; A. Vallance to R. Ross, in Margery Ross, *op. cit.*, p. 38; J. Lane, 'The Yellow Book'; A. Vallance to R. Ross, in Margery Ross, *op. cit.*, p. 38; Weintraub, *Aubrey Beardsley – Imp of the Perverse*, p. 142n; MDG, p. 93; Rothenstein, *op. cit.*, p. 186; ibid., pp. 245–6; MDG, p. 118; MDG, p. 92; H. MacFall, *Aubrey Beardsley*, pp. 67–8 [MacFall served with the West India Regiment, receiving his commission in 1885]; A. Michaelson, *Blackfriars*, October 1928, p. 610.

14. For Leonard Smithers, cf. George F. Sims, 'Leonard Smithers', *London Magazine*, September 1956, pp. 33–4, 40; Malcolm Pinhorn, 'The Career and Ancestry of Leonard Smithers', *Blackmansbury*, August 1964, p. 5; and *Leonard Smithers and the 1890s*, the catalogue of the Booth Collection of Books published by Leonard Smithers, Phillips, 13.6.1996; *Leonard Smithers Rare Book Catalogue No. 3*, September 1895, item 391; R. Hart-Davis (ed.), *The Letters of Oscar Wilde*, pp. 630–1; 'A European Critic', *Literary Review* [NY], 5.3.1921, p. 5, in Weintraub, *Aubrey Beardsley – Imp of the Perverse*, p. 141; K. Beckson, *Arthur Symons – A Life*, pp. 112ff.; V. O'Sullivan, *op. cit.*, pp. 110–12.

15. Arthur Symons, *Aubrey Beardsley* (London, 1905), p. 13; MDG, p. 97; A. Symons to Mabel [Beardsley] Wright, 21.7.1912, in K. Beckson (ed.), *Selected Letters of Arthur Symons* (London, 1989), p. 225; A. Symons, *op. cit.*, p. 13; Edgar Jepson, *Memoirs of a Victorian* (London, 1933), pp. 279–85.

16. J. Pollitt, cf. Steven Hobbs, 'Mr Pollitt's Bookplate', *Book Collector*, Winter 1987, pp. 518–31; the photo, by Hollyer, was reproduced in the *Sketch*, 7.11.1894, p. 83; cf. also *Sketch*, 20.6.1894, p. 399; ALS AB to 'Dear Sir', 1.8.[1895] (Princeton); MDG, p. 102; AB's German trip is uncertain, but cf. M. Benkovitz, *op. cit.*, p. 141; MDG, p. 102; 'Ballad of the Barber' [MS] (Princeton); A. Symons, *op. cit.*, p. 14; MDG, pp. 97–8; *Selected Letters of Arthur Symons*, p. 111.

17. For Dieppe cf. Evelyn Sharpe, *op. cit.*, p. 65; A. Symons, 'Dieppe 1895', *Savoy* 1, January 1896; John Rothenstein, *The Life and Death of Conder* (London, 1983), pp. 104ff.; and Jacques-Emile Blanche, *Portraits of a Lifetime* (London, 1937), pp. 91ff.; Rothenstein, *op. cit.*, pp. 106–13; J.-E. Blanche, *op. cit.*, p. 94; J.-E. Blanche, 'Preface' to *Sous la Colline*, reprinted in *Propos de peintre* (Paris, 1919), p. 114; ALS J.-E. Blanche to Mrs Wright [Mabel Beardsley], 17.8.1912 (Princeton); J.-E. Blanche, 'Preface', p. 117; *Portraits of a Lifetime*, p. 95.

18. E. A. Beardsley, *B. Misc.*, p. 77; M. Easton, *Aubrey and the Dying Lady*, p. 196; but see A. Symons, *Aubrey Beardsley*, p. 13; ALS Charles Conder to W. Rothenstein, 14.8.1895 (Harvard); C. Conder to W. Rothenstein, 5.9.1895 (Harvard); Vincent O'Sullivan, 'Literature in France' [MS] (Princeton), p. 10; A. Symons, *op. cit.*, p. 14; *Savoy*, 1, January 1896, p. 5.

19. J.-E. Blanche, 'Preface', p. 114; A. Symons, *op. cit.*, p. 15; *The Story of Venus and Tannhäuser* [MS] p. 60 verso (Rosenbach Museum and Library, Philadelphia); MDG, pp. 97–8. Brigid Brophy, *Beardsley and His World*, p. 99.

20. ALS C. Conder to W. Rothenstein, 14.8.1895; A. Symons, *op. cit.*, p. 15;

MDG, p. 127; J.-E. Blanche, 'Preface',
p. 124; Herbert Small, 'Aubrey
Beardsley', *Book Buyer*, February 1895,
pp. 26–9; J.-E. Blanche, 'Preface',
p. 117; R. A. Walker, *Some Unknown
Drawings of Aubrey Beardsley*, p. 25; J.-
E. Blanche, 'Preface', p. 115; A.
Symons, *op. cit.*, p. 21.

21. MDG, pp. 98–9 [dated 'late August',
late September seems more probable];
W. B. Yeats, *Memoirs*, p. 92; W. B.
Yeats, *Autobiographies*, pp. 329–30
Under The Hill (London, 1904) p. 46.

22. ALS AB to Mrs Gosse, [8.10.95]
(Cambridge University Library); AB to
J. Lane, in *Dulau Catalogue 165*, p. 100;
Elkin Mathews note, quoted in *Boston
Evening Transcript*, 17.11.1920, p. 4;
MDG, p. 104; R. A. Walker, *op. cit.*,
p. 22.

23. G. B. Shaw, quoted in Grant Richards,
Author Hunting (London, 1936), p. 19;
E. Jepson, *op. cit.*, pp. 286–7;
Desmond Flower and Henry Maas,
The Letters of Ernest Dowson (NJ, 1967),
p. 331 [The story was not used]; Brian
Reade, *Beardsley* (London, 1967),
p. 354; Owen Seaman, 'The New
Quarterly Blue Book', *National
Observer*, 9.11.1895.

24. MDG, pp. 107ff, 109; ALS Mrs William
O'Brien [née Raffalovich] to R. A.
Walker, 24.11.1935 (Princeton); ALS E.
Gosse to A. E. Gallatin, 19.6.1902
(Princeton); *Athanaeum*, 16.3.1895,
p. 354; AB to L. Smithers, 16.12.[1895]
Warrack & Perkins Catalogue 60, item 68;
MDG, pp. 109–11; cf. MDG, p. 174*n*;
M. Beerbohm, 'Be It Cosiness', *Pageant*,
1895, pp. 230–5.

CHAPTER VIII · 'THE HARDWORKING
SOLITAIRE'

1. For *Savoy* dinner, cf. M. Beerbohm,
'First Meetings with W. B. Yeats',
Listener, 6.6.1955, pp. 15–16; W. B.

Yeats, *Autobiographies*, pp. 328–9; and
Memoirs, p. 91; Richard Ellam, *Yeats,
the Man and the Masks*, pp. 89–101;
AB to [A. Leverson] [February 1896],
Goodspeed Catalogue, No. 225, item 16;
M. Beerbohm, *Listener*, 6.6.1955,
pp. 15–16; W. B. Yeats,
Autobiographies, pp. 328–9.

2. 'Editorial Note', *Savoy*, 2; *Sunday
Times*, 26.1.1896, p. 6; *Academy*,
18.1.1896, p. 56; *Athenaeum*, 25.1.1896,
p. 117; *The Times*, 30.1.1896, p. 8;
Star, 20.1.1896, p. 1; MDG, p. 112;
Sunday Times, 26.1.1896, p. 6; *Sketch*,
quoted in Weintraub, *Savoy, a Nineties
Experiment* (London, 1966), p. xxiv;
Courrier Français, 2.2.1896, pp. 8–9;
Athenaeum, 25.1.1896, p. 117; *Academy*,
18.1.1896, p. 56; *Star*, 20.1.1896, p. 1;
World, 16.2.1896, p. 18; *Sunday Times-
Herald*, May 1896, p. 33.

3. Quoted in Julie Speedie, *op. cit.*, p. 99;
Punch, 1.2.1896, p. 49; AB to [Ada
Leverson] [February, 1896]; A.
Symons, *op. cit.*, p. 16; A. Symons to
Mabel, [Beardsley] Wright, 21.7.1912,
in K. Beckson and J. M. Munro (eds),
Arthur Symons, Selected Letters,
pp. 224–5; MDG, p. 118; the title-
page reads, 'An heroi-comic poem in
five cantos. Embroidered with nine
drawings by Aubrey Beardsley'; E. R.
and J. Pennell, *The Life of James
McNeill Whistler*, pp. 310–11.

4. D. Flower and H. Maas, *The Letters of
Ernest Dowson*, pp. 350–1; *Courrier
Français*, 2.2.1896, pp. 8–9; *Letters of
Ernest Dowson*, p. 344; Vincent
O'Sullivan, *Aspects of Wilde*, p. 127;
Letters of Ernest Dowson, p. 347; Ratif
de la Bretonne [Jean Lorrain] quoted
in Jacques Lethève, 'Aubrey Beardsley
et la France', *Gazette de Beaux Arts*,
December 1966; MDG, pp. 115–16,
119.

5. Prelim. page, *Savoy*, 2; MDG, p. 115;
cALS A. Symons to John Gray [n.d.]

(Blackfriars, Edinburgh); *Letters of
Ernest Dowson*, p. 355; MDG,
pp. 119–22 *passim*.

6. MDG, p. 123; E. A. Beardsley to R.
Ross, quoted in M. Easton, *Aubrey and
the Dying Lady*, p. 95; V. O'Sullivan,
Aspects of Wilde, pp. 123, 115; W.
Crane, *Magazine of Art*, 1888, p. 415.

7. MDG, pp. 126–9; *The Times* [NY],
7.5.1896, p. 5; *Times Herald* [Chicago],
16.5.1896; J. Gray, 'André Raffalovich',
Blackfriars, 1934, p. 405; Brocard
Sewell, *Footnote to the Nineties*, pp. 38,
112; A. Michaelson [A. Raffalovich],
'Oscar Wilde', *Blackfriars*, 1927,
pp. 697–701; E. A. Beardsley to R.
Ross, quoted in M. Easton, *Aubrey and
the Dying Lady*, p. 97; MDG,
pp. 130–1; E. A. Beardsley, *B. Misc.*,
pp. 177–8.

8. MDG, p. 131; ALS E. Gosse to AB,
16.5.1896 (Princeton); MDG, p. 146;
Manchester Guardian, 23.7.1896, p. 3;
Saturday Review, 83, p. 426; *The Times*,
19.6.1896, p. 18; *Manchester Guardian*,
23.7.1896; *Studio*, VIII, 1896, p. 250;
Metropolitan Magazine 4, [1896]
pp. 49–53; M. S. Lasner, *op. cit.*,
p. 65; ibid., p. 66; although the title-
page date of the edition is 1897, it was
first issued on 4.8.1896.

9. E. A. Beardsley to R. Ross, in M.
Easton, *Aubrey and the Dying Lady*,
p. 113; MDG, pp. 136–7, 145, 133;
AB to L. Smithers, 9.6.1896, *Warrack
& Perkins Catalogue 60*, item 133;
MDG, p. 133.

10. E. A. Beardsley to R. Ross, in M.
Easton, *Aubrey and the Dying Lady*,
p. 113; MDG, pp. 137, 138–41; Linda
Zatlin, *Aubrey Beardsley and Victorian
Sexual Politics* (Oxford, 1990),
pp. 141ff; MDG, pp. 141–4; AB's
'Last Will and Testament' (Somerset
House, London); the other witness was
Henry C. Keeble of the Spread Eagle
Hotel; MDG, p. 143; W. B. Yeats,

Autobiographies, p. 323; J. G. Nelson,
'Leonard Smithers and the Chiswick
Press', *Journal of the Eighteen Nineties
Society*, 1994.

11. MDG, pp. 147–53 *passim*; Captain Sir
Richard Burton and Leonard Smithers,
The Carmina of Catullus (Privately
Printed, 1894), p. xvi; MDG, p. 152;
Jean Lorrain, 'Bathylle', *Le Chat
noir*, 1.7.1882; W. H. Mallock
quotedin Cobham-Brewer, *Dictionary
of Phrase and Fable* (London,
1896 ed.).

12. cTLS R. A. Walker to O. W. Lodge,
13.8.1935 (Princeton); MDG, p. 151;
A. H. Lawrence, 'Mr Aubrey
Beardsley and His Work', *Idler*, 1897,
pp. 189–202; MDG, pp. 151, 153; M.
Easton, *Aubrey and the Dying Lady*,
p. 100; MDG, pp. 152, 153, 169; W.L.
[William Lawler], *London Year Book*,
p. 49; MDG, p. 169.

13. R. Ross, *op. cit.*, p. 25; MDG, pp. 154,
157, 159, 168; MDG, p. 186; MDG,
pp. 162-3, 166; J. M. Dent to E. A.
Beardsley, 9.9.1896, *Sothebys (London)
Catalogue*, 23/24.7.1987; J. M. Dent to
AB, quoted MDG, p. 181*n*.; MDG,
p. 230; *Iconography*, items 138, 139; L.
Smithers to F. Evans [n.d.] *Christies
(London) Catalogue*, 13.5.1970;
MDG, pp. 183, 185, 187; MDG,
p. 167.

14. J. G. Nelson, *Journal of the Eighteen
Nineties Society*, 1994; V. O'Sullivan,
Aspects of Wilde, p. 116; MDG, p. 176;
quoted in G. Richards, *Author Hunting*
(London, 1936), p. 18; W. B. Yeats,
Autobiographies, pp. 323–4; MDG,
p. 167; R. Burton and L. Smithers,
op. cit., p. 285; MDG, pp. 179, 173,
203.

15. MDG, pp. 171–2, MDG, p. 177;
MDG, p. 173; P. Hanks and F.
Hodges, *Dictionary of First Names*
(Oxford, 1990), p. 30; E. A. Beardsley
to R. Ross, quoted in M. Easton,

Aubrey and the Dying Lady, p. 102; MDG, pp. 204, 207.

16. E. A. Beardsley to R. Ross, in Easton, *Aubrey and the Dying Lady*; MDG, pp. 178ff.; MDG, pp. 186–200 *passim*; V. O'Sullivan, *Aspects of Wilde*, p. 127; Victor Plarr, *Ernest Dowson 1888–1897: Reminiscences* (London, 1914), p. 66.

17. MDG, pp. 201–16 *passim*.

18. MDG, p. 212; E. A. Beardsley to R. Ross, in Easton, *Aubrey and the Dying Lady*, p. 103; MDG, pp. 219, 222–6; E. A. Beardsley to R. Ross, in Easton, *Aubrey and the Dying Lady*, p. 103; ibid.; to Smithers AB refers to his conveyance as a 'donkey chair'; MDG, pp. 225–9; E. R. Pennell, *Nights*; MDG, p. 229; *Magazine of Art*, November 1896, pp. 9–12; *Academy*, 26.12.1896, p. 590; M. Beerbohm, 'Ex Cathedra: Mr Beardsley's Fifty Drawings', *Tomorrow*, 1897, pp. 28–35.

19. MDG, p. 208; V. O'Sullivan, 'Literature in France' [MS] (Princeton); A. Lawrence, *Idler*, 1897, pp. 189–202; MDG, pp. 230–2*n*, 214; E. A. Beardsley, 'Aubrey Beardsley' [MS] (Princeton), Marginal addition indicates this incident took place at Pier View; MDG, p. 323; ALS E. Gosse to AB (Princeton); MDG, pp. 233, 235, 236.

CHAPTER IX · 'AN INVALID'S DELAY'

1. MDG, p. 238; *Murray's Hampshire* (London, 1898), p. 176; MDG, pp. 244*n*, 246; MDG, pp. 265*n*, 262.

2. E. A. Beardsley to R. Ross 1.2.1897, in M. Easton, *Aubrey and the Dying Lady*, p. 113; MDG, pp. 252ff, 249ff; E. A. Beardsley to R. Ross, 1.2.1897; cf. M. Sturgis, *op. cit.*, pp. 19ff, 44; *The Letters of Oscar Wilde*, p. 122; MDG, pp. 246, 249–50; M. S. Lasner, *op. cit.*, p. 70; M. Beerbohm, 'Ex Cathedra: Mr Beardsley's Fifty Drawings', *Tomorrow*, January 1897, pp. 28–35;

Hal Dane [MacFall], *St Pauls*, 17.4.1897, pp. 97–9; *Athenaeum*, 11.9.1897, p. 360; *Daily Telegraph*, 17.2.1897, p. 9.

3. MDG, pp. 256, 260–1; *Baedeker – Great Britain* (1890), p. 46; MDG, pp. 255, 264; *Catholic Who's Who – 1910*; MDG, pp. 257, 259; E. F. Benson, *The Babe, B.A.* (London, 1897), pp. 33, 107; MDG, p. 252; Steven Hobbs, 'Mr Pollitt's Bookplate', *Book Collector*, vol. 36, No. 4 (1987), pp. 518–32.

4. MDG, pp. 263, 267; Margery Ross (ed.), *op. cit.*, pp. 46–7; MDG, p. 263; MDG, pp. 273, 269; MDG, p. 278; M. Easton, *Aubrey and the Dying Lady*, p. 107; MDG, p. 269; MDG, pp. 274–85 *passim*; A. Beardsley, 'The Celestial Lover' [MS] notes (Princeton); E. A. Beardsley to R. Ross, 1.2.1897; MDG, pp. 285–90.

5. MDG, pp. 285–8; MDG, pp. 293, 290; E. A. Beardsley to R. Ross, 1.2.1897; H. Harland, *Academy*, 10.12.1898, pp. 437–8; R. Ross, *op. cit.*, p. 26; L. Johnson to Imogen Guiney, 30.10.1898 (Private Collection); Hugh F. Blunt, 'Aubrey Beardsley – A Study in Conversion', *Catholic World*, March 1932, pp. 641–50; MDG, p. 289.

6. MDG, p. 297, 294; A. Vallance, *Magazine of Art*, 1898, p. 368.

7. MDG, pp. 297–8; E. A. Beardsley to R. Ross, 22.3.[1897], in Margery Ross, *op. cit.*, p. 47; MDG, p. 298; E. A. Beardsley to R. Ross, 22.3.[1897]; MDG, pp. 299–311 *passim*.

8. MDG, p. 308; H. Davray, 'L'Art d'Aubrey Beardsley', *L'Ermitage*, March 1897, pp. 253–61; Alexander Michaelson, *Blackfriars*, October 1928, p. 613; *Saturday Review*, 19.12.1896, pp. 645–6, reprinted in A. Symons, *Studies in Two Literatures* (London,

1897); John Stokes, 'Beardsley/Jarry: The Art of Deformation', *RAB*, pp. 55–70; A. Jarry, 'Exploits and Opinions of Dr Faustroll', in Roger Shattuck and Simon Watson-Taylor (eds/trans.), *Selected Works of Alfred Jarry* (London, 1965), pp. 186, 201–2.

9. MDG, pp. 305–9; MDG, p. 279, MDG, p. 315; Weintraub, *Aubrey Beardsley – Imp of the Perverse*, p. 235; MDG, p. 314; Claude Dauphiné, *Rachilde* (Paris, 1991); Weintraub, *Aubrey Beardsley – Imp of the Perverse*, p. 235; MDG, pp. 313–20 *passim*; Weintraub, p. 237; Rothenstein, *Men and Memories*, pp. 317–18; MDG, p. 320.

10. MDG, pp. 315–26 *passim*; ALS E. A. Beardsley to Mabel Beardsley, 10.12.[1904] (Princeton); MDG, p. 325.

11. *Letters of Ernest Dowson*, p. 388; AB to L. Smithers, in *Boston Evening Transcript*, 17.11.1920, p. 4; MDG, pp. 326–37 *passim*.

12. MDG, p. 323; MDG, pp. 335–51 *passim*; J.-E. Blanche, *Portraits of a Lifetime*, pp. 91–2.

13. R. Ellman, *Oscar Wilde*, pp. 502ff.; *The Letters of Oscar Wilde*, p. 635; Norman Page, *The Oscar Wilde Chronology* (Boston, 1991), p. 77; *The Letters of Oscar Wilde*, p. 627; MDG, p. 351; R. Hart-Davis (ed.), *More Letters of Oscar Wilde* (Oxford, 1985), p. 151; V. O'Sullivan, *Aspects of Wilde*, pp. 86–7; *The Letters of Oscar Wilde*, p. 635; L. Smithers to O. Wilde, 2.9.1897 in ibid., p. 635 *n*.2.

14. Weintraub, *Aubrey Beardsley – Imp of the Perverse*, p. 245; Rothenstein, *The Life and Death of Conder*, p. 136; MDG, pp. 355, 357–8; L. Smithers to O. Wilde, 2.9.1897; M. Beardsley to J.-E. Blanche in J.-E. Blanche, *Portraits of a Lifetime*, pp. 95–6; MDG, pp. 361–2.

15. MDG, pp. 365, 367; S. Diaghilev to

D. S. MacColl, 21.9.1898, in A. Haskell and W. Nouvel, *Diaghileff* (NY, 1935), pp. 72–3; MDG, p. 364; Douglas Ainslie, *Adventures Social and Literary* (London, 1922), p. 258; ALS E. A. Beardsley to D. Ainslie, 11.9.[1897] (Princeton).

16. MDG, pp. 368–70; for Olive Custance, cf. Brocard Sewell, *Olive Custance: Her Life and Work* (London, 1975); M. Benkovitz, *Aubrey Beardsley*, pp. 170–1; *Yellow Book*, VII; MDG, pp. 250, 267; ALS O. Custance to J. Lane [n.d.] (Private Collection); MDG, pp. 378–86 *passim*; *Letters of Ernest Dowson*, p. 397; MDG, pp. 373, 376; V. O'Sullivan, 'Literature in France' [MS] (Princeton), p. 10; MDG, pp. 382–92 *passim*.

CHAPTER X · 'THE DEATH OF PIERROT'

1. MDG, p. 396; Eustace Reynolds-Ball, *Mediterranean Winter Resorts* (London, 1899, ed.), pp. 91, 93; MDG, p. 395; last photograph of AB, reproduced in *Academy*, 10.12.1898, p. 437; MDG, p. 397, MDG, p. 426; MDG, pp. 397–407 *passim*.

2. AB, 'Volpone, by Ben Johnson, 7 January, 1898' [MS] (Princeton); MDG, pp. 404–18 *passim*; Thomas Beer, *The Mauve Decade* (NY, 1926), p. 249; H. Harland, 'Aubrey Beardsley', *Academy*, 10.12.1898, p. 437; MDG, pp. 412–27 *passim*; *Rocket*, 20.2.1898, in M. Easton, *Aubrey and the Dying Lady*, p. 202; MDG, pp. 428, 440, 436; R. Ross, *op. cit.*, p. 27; MDG, pp. 430–6; Weintraub, *op. cit.*, p. 252; MDG, p. 439; E. A. Beardsley to M. Beardsley, 10.12.[1904]; *B. Misc.*, pp. 107, 116; the MS is at Princeton; M. Easton, p. 115; MDG, p. 437; AB to Tristan Klingsor, 28.2.[1898] in *Revue Illustré*, 15.6.1898, p. 435.

3. MDG, pp. 440–1; John Gray, 'Introduction', *Last Letters of Aubrey Beardsley* (London, 1904); MDG, p. 413; Alexander Michaelson, *Blackfriars*, October 1928, p. 613; MDG, p. 439; J. Gray, *op. cit.*; MDG, p. 441; A. Michaelson, *Blackfriars*, October 1928, p. 615n; ALS A. Raffalovich to J. Gray, 9.10.1904 (National Library of Scotland, Edinburgh); MDG, pp. 404, 441; A. Michaelson, *Blackfriars*, October 1928, p. 615n; R. Ross, *op. cit.*, p. 27; Ross states that AB received the last rites two days before he died; MDG, p. 440; Mabel Beardsley to A. Raffalovich in A. Michaelson, *Blackfriars*, October 1928, p. 614; J.-E. Blanche, *Portraits of a Lifetime*, p. 94; M. Beardsley to A. Raffalovich, *Blackfriars*, October 1928, p. 614; unlabelled newspaper cutting [March, 1898], BGS Archive (Lewes); MDG, p. 441.

EPILOGUE

1. *The Times*, 18.3.1898, *St James's Budget*, 25.3.1898; *Sketch*, 23.3.1898, *Black and White*, 26.3.1898, *St Paul's*, 2.4.1898.
2. *Daily Chronicle*, 17.3.1898; *Studio*, 13,

1898; *Magazine of Art*, 22, 1898; *Academy*, 55, 1898; *Revue Blanche*, 16, 1898; *Poster and Art Collector*, 1, 1898.
3. Ross to Smithers, in *The Letters of Oscar Wilde*, pp. 729–30. *Emporium*, 7, 1898, pp. 352–5; *Dekorative Kunst*, 2, 1898, pp. 18–21.
4. cALS Mabel Beardsley to Raffalovich, 20.5.1898; Blackfriars, Edinburgh.
5. *Times* (New York), 28.5.1898 p. 358; ALS Gray to Raffalovich, 20.2.1899; National Library of Scotland.
6. TLS R. A. Walker to J. Harlin O'Connell, 5.7.1949, Princeton.
7. cf. Easton, *Aubrey and the Dying Lady*; Jack Smithers, *The Early Life and Vicissitudes of Jack Smithers* (London, 1939)
8. Gleeson White, 'The Art Movement. "Jugend": some decorations and a moral', *Magazine of Art*, 21, 1898, pp. 40–44.
9. Sidney Horler, *Strictly Personal* (London, 1950), pp. 227–8.
10. G. Richards, *Author Hunting*, p. 200; Weintraub, *Aubrey Beardsley – Imp of the Perverse*, p. 265.
11. Patricia Morrisroe, *Mapplethorpe* (London, 1995), pp. 181, 297.
12. Philip Hensher, 'Waiting for a Hundred Years', *Spectator*, 3.8.1996, pp. 8–10.

Index

Academy 134, 195, 197, 276, 277, 308

Adamson, Sydney 199

Adey, More 95, 259

Ainslie, Douglas 336, 338

Alastair (Hans Henning Voight) 358

Ali Baba and the Forty Thieves 292, 294, 326

Alston, Lady 167, 287–8

Alvary, Max 105, 208

Archer, William 211

Archives d'Anthropologie Criminelle 244

Aristophanes: *Lysistrata* 270
   see under Beardsley, Aubrey

Armour, Margaret: 'Aubrey Beardsley and
   the Decadents' 307–308

Art Amateur 125, 126*n*

Art Journal 66, 93, 118, 180

Artist, The (journal) 66, 125, 132, 134,
   180–81, 184, 194, 195, 221, 222

Artist and Journal of Home Culture, The 151

Astor, Lord 125, 128

Atalanta (journal) 66, 87

Athenaeum (journal) 195, 276, 277, 316

Austen, John 357

Avenue Theatre, Chiswick, London
   183–4, 204

Bakst, Leon 358

Ballantyne Press 176

Ballets Russes 358

Balzac, Honoré de 59, 80, 95, 255, 309
   Le Comédie humaine 59, 255
   La Fille aux Yeux d'Or 304
   Scènes de la Vie Parisienne 319

Bampton, Father J. M. 286, 322, 355

Barnard, Fred 36

Barnard, Professor 228, 229

Barnett, Miss (headmistress) 16, 17, 18

Baudelaire, Charles 79, 210, 315, 336
   'Eulogy on Cosmetics' 187
   'The Painter of Modern Life' 96–7, 229

Bayros, Franz von 357–8

Bealby-Wright, George 356

Beardsley, Aubrey: birth 3, 10; and his
   father 13, 16, 60, 75, 77, 120, 145, 153,
   296*n*; musical education 11, 13, 15, 16,
   17, 18, 21; develops tuberculosis
   15–16; sent to boarding school 16–18;
   early drawings 18, 20–21; in Epsom 19,
   21; in Brighton 22, 25–6; churchgoing
   26–8; at Brighton Grammar School
   28–50; reading interests 13–14, 33–4;
   first appearance in print 35; abandons
   music 35; friendship with Scotson-
   Clark 35–6; drawings and caricatures
   36–8; school theatricals 38–40; first
   appearance in print as an artist 40, 42;
   reputation and personality 43–4;
   romance 44, 46; home theatricals 47–8;
   artistic and theatrical triumphs at school
   48–50; Christmas Entertainment 53;
   temporary clerical job 54; reads
   voraciously 54–5; and the Gurneys
   56–7; illness 57–60; turns to French
   literature 58–9; short story published
   59–61; writes play for Cochran 61,
   64–5; at Guardian Assurance 61–3;
   caricatures his companions 62; meets
   Frederick Evans 63; 'discovers' Rossetti
   63–4; returns to drawing 64; his artistic
   education 66, 68, 70; 'castles in the air'
   with Scotson-Clark 68–9; sees
   Whistler's 'Peacock Room' 70–1; meets

Beardsley, Aubrey – *cont.*

Burne-Jones 71–4, and 'the Oscar Wildes' 73, 74–5; a summer of experiment and development 75–7; interest in Mantegna and Botticelli 76, and Whistler 77–8, and Wilde's views on art 78–80, and Moore's *Impressions and Opinions* 80, and the 'pierrot' image 80–81; at Westminster School of Art 82, 85–7; and King's continuing support 87–8; illness and sick-leave 91; preoccupied with 'lines' 91–3; meets Vallance 93–4; at Vallance's reception 94–5; makes influential friends 95–6; his dandyish pose 96–7; 'repulsed' by Morris 97–8; his 'japonesque' style 98–100, 102, 105; in Paris 102–103; 'besieges the publishers' 105–107; starts *Morte Darthur* 107–109 (*see Works, below*); resigns from Guardian Assurance 110; starts *Bon-Mot* series (*see Works*) 112; leaves Westminster School of Art 114; meets John Lane 116, Lewis Hind 116–17, Charles Holme 117–18, and Joseph Pennell 118–20; illustrates Lucian's *Comic Voyage* 120–1; his four styles 121; his working method 121; a second rebuttal from Morris 121–2; continued support from Burne-Jones 122; his *Studio* illustrations 125–6, 132–4; joins *Pall Mall Budget* 126–8; meets Crane 128*n*; his first *Salome* drawing (*see Works*) 129; and Degas's 'L'Absinthe' 131; his friendship with Wilde 131–2, 134; exhibits at NEAC 114–15, 132; second trip to Paris 134, 135–7, 139–42; meets Harland 136, Rothenstein 137, 139, and Whistler 141–2; temperamentally unsuited to deadlines 143; decorates Pimlico house 144–5; with Rothenstein in London 146–7; rapport with Beerbohm 148; a charmed circle of friends 147–50; as a decadent 151–2, 165–7; at Ellen's 'Thursday afternoons' 152–3; and cross-dressing 153–4; tries to abandon *Morte Darthur* 154–6; breaks with Burne-Jones 156–7, and Wilde 157–8, 160–62; an intellectual interest in sex 162–3; exhibits at NEAC 163–4; interest in posters 164; and *The Yellow Book* 169–79, 186–91, 194–9, 200, 201; and the publication of *Salome* 179–82; and Mrs Patrick Campbell 182, 188–9, 196; and Avenue Theatre set 183; designs theatre poster 183–4, 186; at *Yellow Book* celebratory dinner 191, 192, 193; interview in *To-Day* 200–1; a 'Realist' 201; fame 201, 202–203; his affectations 201, 203; a flirtation with Rome 201–202; and the second *Yellow Book* 204–205, 210–11; decline in health 205, 207; conceives *Tannhäuser* project 207–10, 249; further poster work 211–13; and Keats 213–14; and Evans's 'gargoyle' photograph 214; illness 214–15; and sex and the 'Beardsley woman' 216–20; and third *Yellow Book* 221–3; exhibits at International Poster Exhibition 225–7; further illness 227–9; and fourth *Yellow Book* 233–4; plans American lecture tour 234–5; and Wilde's downfall 235–9, 241–3, 245, 247–8; friendship with Raffalovich 243–5, 246–8, and Gray 247; a dissolute life 249–50, 252–3; meets Smithers 250–2, and Pollitt 253; visits Germany 253–4, and Dieppe 254–7, 259–61; plans *The Savoy* with Symons 256–7, 260–1; an unknown mistress 264; connections with Wilde 263, 264; commissions from Lane 164–5; his cover for *The Savoy* 265–6, 268; renews friendship with Raffalovich 268–9; begins *Lysistrata* and *The Rape of the Lock* 269–70; at the launch of *The Savoy* 273, 274, 275–6; and Yeats' interest in the occult 274–5; and *The Savoy*'s reception 276–7; tension with Symons 277; his 'Rape' drawings praised by Whistler 278; in Paris with (Smithers 278, 280–2; at *Salome* premiere 280; ill in Brussels 282–7; and O'Sullivan 283–4; and Raffalovich 286; further Catholic links 286, 287; 'depressed and frightened' 287; and the publication of *The Rape of the Lock*

287–9; recuperates at Crowborough
289–90; health declines in Epsom
290–95; completes *Lysistrata*
illustrations 290, 293; draws 'The Death
of Pierrot' 292; illustrates Juvenal
294–5, 298; in Boscombe 295–313;
plans the *Book of Fifty Drawings* 296–7;
and the last numbers of *The Savoy*
298–300, 301; translates Catullus
300–301; Rheingold drawings 301–302,
308; his condition deteriorates 302; and
local Jesuits 304; illustrates Dowson's
Pierrot of the Minute 305; further projects
305–306; a near ' "Al fresco" croak'
306–307; and the publication of *Fifty
Drawings* 307–308, 316; interviewed by
The Idler 308–309; 'collapses in all
directions' 310, 313; in Bournemouth
313–21; finishes 'Mademoiselle de
Maupin' 315, 320; conversion to
Catholicism 315, 316, 317, 320–21;
given an allowance by Raffalovich
316–17; and Pollitt's visit 317–18;
unfinished projects 319–20; his farewell
to London 322; in Paris 322–7; helped
by Raffalovich 323, 324, 325; produces
cover design for *Ali Baba* 326; 'all artifice
gone' 327; health improves in
St Germain-en-Laye 327–31; and
Mabel's visit 330; in Dieppe 331–6;
rejects Wilde 333–4, and is rejected by
Whistler 334; repels Conder 334–5; and
the *Mademoiselle de Maupin* illustrations
336, 337, 338–9; moves to Paris 336–9;
'utterly cast down and wretched' 338; in
Menton 339, 341–2, 346; starts *Volpone*
illustrations 342 (*see Works*); and Smithers
347–8; last months 348–50; death 350;
burial 350–1; obituaries 353–4;
posthumous reputation and influence
356–60

Works:

articles, poems and stories:

'The Art of the Hoarding' 212–13
'The Ballad of the Barber' 283, 289, 300
'Carmen CI' (Catullus translation)
300–301
'Dante in Exile' 64
'The Ivory Piece' 349

'A Ride in an Omnibus' 42
'The Story of a Confession Album'
59–60
'The Tree Musicians' 259–60
'Two-To-One' 42
Under the Hill (*The Story of Venus and
Tannhäuser*) 2, 210, 217, 220–21, 228,
239, 249, 253, 254, 257, 259, 264, 269,
277, 278, 283, 285, 289, 298, 358
'The Valiant' 34–5

drawings and paintings:

'The Achieving of the Sangreal' 109
Ali Baba and the Forty Thieves 292, 294,
326
'Ascension of Saint Rose of Lima' 282
'Balzac' 319
'The Birthday of Madama Cigale' 118,
152
'Black Coffee' 241, 265
Bon-Mot series 112, 117, 121, 131,
142–3, 146, 148, 161, 179, 216, 223
Book of Fifty Drawings (album) 296–7,
307, 316, 318
'Mrs Patrick Campbell' 188–9, 195–6
'The Comedy-Ballet of Marionettes. . .'
205, 211, 213
'The Comtesse d'Armailhacq' 281
'The Court of Love' 76, 77
'The Dame aux Camélias' 222
'Dante Designing an Angel' 73*n*
'The Death of Pierrot' 292, 299
'Le Débris d'un Poète' 105
'L'Éducation Sentimentale' 188, 195
'Et in Arcadia Ego' 302
'The Fat Woman' 187, 200
'La Femme Incomprise' 132
'From a Pastel' 223
'A Frontispiece to Juvenal' 229, 234, 294
'Les Garçons du Café [Royal]' 204–205
'Girl and a Bookshop' 163, 164, 211
'Hail Mary' 108
'Hamlet following the ghost of his father'
75, 77, 88
'Hermaphroditus' 96
Irving portraits 36, 128, 165
'Isolde' 265
'Jubilee Cricket Analysis' 40, 42, 49
Keynotes (Egerton) 150, 182, 186,
199–200, 216

Keynotes series 200, 221, 234, 242, 248, 252
'Kiss of Judas' 135, 137, 152
'Lady at the Dressing Table' 337
'Lady Gold's Escort' 222
'The Litany of Mary Magdalen' 73*n* 76, 95
Lysistrata illustrations 269–70, 282, 290, 292, 293, 305, 318, 319, 350, 355, 359–60
Mademoiselle de Maupin illustrations 315, 320, 325, 335, 336, 338–9, 355
'Mantegna' 223
Morte Darthur illustrations 77, 107–9, 110–12, 119, 121, 122, 132, 133, 135, 142, 143, 146, 154–6, 157, 198, 199, 216, 223, 261, 319
'New Coinage' (spoofs) 127, 129
'A Night Piece' 188, 195, 218
'Les Passades' 218
'Perseus and the Monstre' 95
'Perseus' panel 93, 110
Pierrot of the Minute (Dowson) illustrations 305, 319
'Portrait of Himself' 222–3
'The Procession of Joan of Arc' 76, 95
'Puck on Pegasus' 285, 292
'Rape of the Lock' illustrations 269, 270, 278, 280, 281, 287–9, 308, 322, 325
Réjane portraits 165, 205, 211, 234
'The Repentance of Mrs. . .' 229
'A Répétition of "Tristan und Isolde"' 302
'Les Revenants de Musique' 118
Salome illustrations 129, 131, 132, 143, 144, 146, 149, 150, 152, 154, 157–8, 160–62, 163, 179–82, 198, 238, 249, 288
'A Scarlet Pastorale' 249
Second Book of Fifty Drawings 355
'Siegfried' 122, 152
'The Slippers of Cinderella' 205
'Soleil Couchant' 110
'Tannhäuser returning to the Venusberg' 297–8
'Third Tableau of the Rheingold' 283
'The Toilet' 288
'Venus between Terminal Gods' 330
'The Virgin and the Lily' 76

Volpone illustrations 269, 339, 342, 344, 345–6, 355
'The Wagnerites' 222
'Waiting' 218
'Withered Spring' 93, 110
'The Woman in White' 299
'Zola' 128
Beardsley, Ellen Agnus (*née* Pitt) (mother): birth 4; and Brighton social life 5–6; marriage 8, 9–10, 16; and AB's birth 3, 10; musical talents 6, 11; and the move to London 11, 12, 13; guides her children's reading 13–14; a 'sermon taster' 6, 14; and their 'lonely life in lodgings' 15; describes AB as a child 17, 18, 21–2; provides stimulation and instruction 19–21; illness 22; and Sarah Pitt 25, 28, 87; and the children's plays 47–8, 53; and Mabel's schooling 54; and AB's artistic career 110, 114; with Mabel in France 145–6, 152; horrified at AB's lack of principles 154–5; further illness 167; and AB's friends 167; look after AB 214–15; and AB's drawings 220; sends AB to clinic 227, 228; has AB 'prayed for' 283; brings AB back from Brussels 287; takes him to Epsom 209, and Boscome 296; buys canaries 302; alarmed at AB's haemorrhaging 306–7; and AB's interest in Catholicism 310; with AB in Bournemouth 314, 315, 318, Paris 322, 323, St Germain-en-Laye 327–8, 330, 331, and Dieppe 331, 333, 335; makes preparations 336; back in Paris 337; in Menton 342; and AB's last months and death 348, 349, 350, 351; with Mabel 354; converts to Catholicism 354–5; nurses Vincent and Mabel 356; 'a relic of a past age' 356; mentioned 75, 201, 227, 298, 305
Beardsley, Mabel (*later* Bealby-Wright): birth 10; childhood 3, 11, 12, 13, 14, 15, 18, 19; tutored in recitation 19–20; an able pianist 21; in Brighton 22, 25–6; churchgoing 26, 27; academic prowess 47, 54; theatrical performances 47–8, 53; and Reverend Gurney 56; takes up teaching 61, 65; 'discovers' the Peacock Room with AB 70; meets

Burne-Jones with AB 71–2, 73, and Watts 82; receives legacy 87, 110; encourages AB to take up art 110; moves into his exciting world 114, 120; in Paris 134, 135, 139, 140; takes lease 144; in Normandy 145–6; at her mother's 'Thursdays' 152, 153; transforms herself 202; at AB's bedside 214; takes up acting 202, 215; her relationship with AB 217; on AB's art 220; at Première of *Importance of Being Earnest* 235–6; advises AB to call on Raffalovich 243; joins Catholic Church 245–6, 286; in Dieppe with AB 254, 256; theatrical career 263, 283, 287, 305, 314, 319, 321, 332; nurses AB in Brussels 283; as AB's legatee 292; finds rooms in Boscome 293, 294, 295; stays with AB 296, 302, 304; joins AB in St Germain 330, and Dieppe 335; as AB's eyes and ears 339; and Smithers' magazine plans 347, 348; and AB's death and funeral 349, 350; organizes memorial mass 354; benefits from AB's will 354; and AB's drawings 355; marriage 356; death 356; mentioned 34, 75, 121, 162, 169, 202, 208, 236, 249, 273, 289, 307, 344, 359

Beardsley, Sarah Ann (grandmother) 8

Beardsley, Vincent (father): childhood 8; meets Ellen Pitt 8; his private income 8–9; marriage 9–10; loses his money 10; relationship with Pitt family 3–4, 10, 12, 16; finds employment 11, 19; as *paterfamilias* 12–13, 16; loses his job 22, 53–4, 66n; and the children's plays 20, 47; receives a small legacy 87; and AB's artistic career 110, 114; a figure of mystery 153, 296n; death 356

Bearne, Father David 316, 317, 320, 321

Beckett, Gilbert À: *The Comic History of England* 36

Beckson, Karl: *Arthur Symons* 288n

Bee, The 88

Beerbohm, Max: rapport with AB 148, 149; on AB 153, 204, 205, 219, 223, 233, 270n, 308; and Lane 150; and *The Yellow Book* 173, 187, 192, 193, 194, 221; and Wilde 176, 187, 247; haunted by 'L'Éducation Sentimentale' 188; caricatures published 208; with AB at Windermere 228n; paradied by Ada Leverson 234n; in America 234, 239; and *The Savoy* 256, 273, 275, 281, 282; publishes essay in *The Pageant* 270; sends AB *Caricatures of Twenty-Five Gentlemen* 307; reviews *Book of Fifty Drawings* 316; writes tribute to AB 353; mentioned 157, 202, 203, 204, 214, 246, 252, 253, 297

Beerbohm-Tree, Herbert 148

Bell (George) & Sons 119, 125

Bell, R. Anning 174, 188, 225

Bella, Edward 225

Benson, E. F.: *The Babe, B. A.* 317

Bernhardt, Sarah 49, 128, 222

Beynon, David 8–9

Birnbaum, Martin 263n

Birrell, Augustine 87

Blake, William 64, 219, 293, 299
'Piping Down the Valleys Wild' 110n

Blanche, Jacques-Émile 255, 256, 261–3, 266, 326, 332, 334, 335, 338

Blavatsky, Madame (Helena) 274

Bodley, G. F. 6

Bodley Head, The 115, 144, 171, 172, 173, 174, 175, 180, 182–3, 186, 191, 193, 194, 203, 205, 218, 221, 237, 238, 249; *see also* Lane, John

Bonnard, Pierre 164, 225

Book Buyer (periodical) 196, 235

Boscombe, 293, 294, 295–6, 304, 306–307

Bossuet, Jacques 310

Boston, Mass.: Public Library 182

Boston Evening Transcript 109n

Boston Herald 270n

Botticelli, Sandro 70, 76, 87, 190, 201, 307

Bourchier, Arthur 283, 314, 319

Bourdaloue, Louis: sermons 289

Bournemouth 313, 314, 316–17

Bowden, Father Sebastian 245

Bradley, Bill 226, 357

Bradley, Katherine 197

Brangwyn, Frank 133

Brighton 6, 36–7, 68–9
12 Buckingham Road 3, 5, 9, 11
Church of the Annunciation, Washington St 26–8, 46–7, 93

Brighton – *cont.*
  The Dome 38
  21 Lower Rock Gardens 22, 25–6
Brighton Gazette 10
Brighton Grammar School 28–50, 197,
    281, 353 *and n*
  Old Boys 61, 55, 65
Brighton Society 42
Brighton & Sussex Telegraph 65
Broadbent, Muriel (Horne's mistress) 253,
    254, 314
Brompton Oratory, London 201, 202, 241,
    243, 282n, 309
Brophy, Brigid: *Beardsley and his World* 11n
Brown, Ford Madox: 'Chaucer at Court'
    70
Brown, Frederick 82–3, 85, 86, 114, 120,
    132
Brown, R. A. 127
Burdett, Osbert 270n
Burnand, Francis 246, 277
Burne-Jones, Edward: church windows 6,
    27; and the Pre-Raphaelites 66, 67, 70,
    71; and AB's visit 71–4; advises AB 75,
    76; influence on AB 77, 81–2, 86, 108,
    109, 111, 122, 133, 134, 147, 189;
    recommends AB to Brown 86, 114;
    and Symbolists 103; hangs AB's
    'Siegfried' 122; lampooned by AB 127;
    and AB's attempted 'parricide' 156–7;
    denounces AB's drawings as 'immoral'
    219; on Wilde 248
  'King Cphetua and the Beggar Maid' 188
  'Love' study for *Chant d'Amour* 96
  'Mermaid' 137
Burne-Jones, Georgiana (*née* Macdonald)
    73
Burton, Sir Richard 251, 300

Café Royal, London 148, 149, 176, 203,
    256
Campbell, Dr 344, 349, 350
Campbell, Mrs Patrick (Stella) 182, 188–9,
    195–6
Carlyle, Thomas: *The French Revolution* 13,
    34
Carnarvon, Lord 298
Caron, Dr 335
Carr, Mr 'Fred' (schoolmaster) 43

Carroll, Lewis 34
Casanova 329
Cassell's (publishers) 107, 108
Catholic Year Book 246
Catullus: *Carmina* 294, 300
Cazotte, Jacques 320
Century Magazine, The 336, 339
Chap Book (periodical) 196
Chapman, Frederic 238, 239, 241–3
Chapman, Father George 27, 46–7, 56, 65,
    93
Chapman and Hall 115, 116
Charles, Prince of Denmark 288
Charley's Aunt, 203
Chase, Pauline 263n
Chéret, Jules 69, 102–3, 183, 212, 225
Chinnery, George 35
Chiswick Press 281
Clark, Ann (landlady) 19
Clark, Mrs Savile 249, 281, 297
Clarke, Harry, 357
Cochin, Charles-Nicolas 164, 165, 261
Cochran, Charles B. 39–40, 44, 48, 50, 55,
    61, 65, 77, 81, 87, 234, 314, 318, 353
Conder, Charles 137, 140, 146, 165, 173,
    250, 252, 254, 255, 256, 261, 304, 332,
    335–6, 356
Congreve, William 34, 200
  The Double Dealer 49
  The Way of the World 269
Constable & Co. (publishers) 115
Constant, Benjamin: *Adolphe* 305
Cooper, Edith 197
Copeland, Herbert 182
Copeland & Day (publishers) 177, 234
Corelli, Marie 203
Coubé, Father 325, 328, 338
Courrier Français 225, 234, 255, 277, 324
Crackanthorpe, Hubert 172, 191, 218, 221,
    299
Craigie, Pearl 192, 197
Crane, Walter 127, 128, 128n, 189, 198,
    205, 225, 357
  'The Birth of Venus' 198
  'The Decorative Illustration of Books'
    198
  'The Language of Line' 92–3, 110, 285
Crewdsen, Canon 229
Critic, The (periodical) 176, 196, 197

Crivelli, Carlo 102, 109
Crowley & Co., Alton (brewery) 19, 22
Crown (London pub) 150, 151
Cubitt, Thomas 18, 19
Cumberland, George 64
Custance, Olive (*later* Lady Douglas) 337

Daily Chronicle 157, 192, 195–6, 203
Daily Graphic 107
Daily Mail 212*n*, 227*n*
Daily Telegraph 316
Dante Alighieri 63, 64
  Divine Comedy 64
D'Arcy, Ella 179, 239, 241–2
Davidson, John 157, 192
  'Ballad of a Nun' 221
Davidson, Revd Thain 14–15
Davray, Henry 323, 326
Day, F. Holland 182
  see also Copeland & Day
Decadent movement 79, 145, 151–2,
  165–7, 181, 187, 202, 212, 218, 257,
  276, 326
Degas, Edgar 80, 126, 129, 132, 189, 255
  'L'Absinthe' 130–31, 187, 241
Delacroix, Eugène 254
Dent, J. M. (publisher) 107–9, 111, 112,
  114, 119, 122, 135, 143*n*, 155, 210, 225,
  229, 296, 297–8, 319
Diaghilev, Serge 336, 358
Dial, The (periodical) 149, 174, 196
Dickens, Charles 13, 19–20, 33
  Barnaby Rudge 20
  Pickwick Papers 20, 39
Dieppe, France 254–5, 257, 260, 261–4,
  331–6
Dircks, Rudolf 273
Donnay, Maurice: *Lysistrata* 293
Dorat, Claude Joseph 261
Doré (tailor) 301, 319
Doucet, Jérôme 327
Douglas, Lord Alfred ('Bosie') 134, 135,
  148, 149, 157, 158, 161–2, 197, 215,
  216, 235, 236, 237, 244, 336, 337
Dowie, Menie Muriel 192, 195
Dowson, Ernest 148, 165, 192, 202, 247,
  250, 252, 254, 257, 269, 278, 280,
  286–7, 306, 323, 329, 332, 333, 338,
  358

'Cynara' 221
The Pierrot of the Minute 305, 319
Verses 285
Doyle, Arthur Conan 203
Dublin Hermetic Society 274
Dudley Gallery, London 132
Dumas, Alexandre, *fils* 261–3
  La Dame aux Camélias 59, 261
Dupuy, Dr 335, 339, 341
Duran, Carolus 136
Dürer, Albrecht 110
Duse, Eleanora 222

Earp, Henry 36
Echo 227*n*
Edmonds, Fred 38
Egerton, George 172, 191
  Keynotes 150, 182, 186, 199–200, 216
Ellis, (Henry) Havelock 257
Emporium (art journal) 234, 354
Enfant Prodigue, L' (play) 80–81, 146
Engen, Rodney: *Kate Greenaway* 259*n*
Epsom, Surrey 19, 290
Ermitage, L' 324
Evans, Frederick 63, 64, 70, 71, 77, 99,
  105, 107–109, 110*n*, 115, 211, 219,
  229, 299; photographs of AB 214,
  223
Eyton, Revd Robert 21

Family Magazine 107
Farr, Florence 183
  The Dancing Faun 200
Faulkner, William 359
Felton, Miss (early 'love') 46
Fénelon, François: *Aventures de Télémaque*
  246
Ffoulkes, Maude 205, 207
'Field, Michael' 197
Firbank, Ronald 358–9
Fitch, Clyde 327
Flaubert, Gustave 170
  Madame Bovary 59, 105
  Trois Contes 157
Fletcher, Ian 360
Fortnightly Review 135, 140, 149, 353
Fragonard, Jean-Honoré 164, 251
Frith, William Powell 66
Fry, Roger 21*n*

Furse, Charles W. 83, 85, 132, 133, 136,
    140, 174, 176

Garnett, Richard 172, 192
Gates, Father Sebastian 315
Gautier, Théophile 67, 79, 96, 157, 336
    Mademoiselle de Maupin 315, see under
    Beardsley, Aubrey
Georget, Abbé 332
Glasgow Institute of Fine Arts 234, 357
    Exhibition (1896) 268n
Globe 184
Gluck, Christoph Willibald 196
Godfrey, 'Johnny' 35, 36
Godwin, William 99
Goncourts, the 166, 324
Goold, L. B. 173
Gosse, Edmund 172, 175, 176, 191, 203,
    264, 269, 287, 310, 339
    The Secret of Narcisse 229, 269
Goupil Gallery, London 165, 183
Grafton Gallery, London 130, 164
Grahame, Kenneth 192
    Pagan Papers 150
Granta (university magazine) 193–4, 195
Grasset, Eugène 103, 164, 183, 225
Gray, John: and Wilde 134, 247; his poetry
    (and see below) 152, 165, 299; and
    Rafalovich 244, 293; and AB 247, 289,
    301, 305, 310, 314, 315, 316, 321, 330,
    349, 353; returns to Catholicism 286,
    354; and Olive Custance 337;
    publishes AB's letters to Raffalovich
    359
    'The Forge' 281
    Spiritual Poems 292
Green, J. R.: A Short History of the English
    People 26
Greenaway, Kate 14, 49, 259n
    Under the Window 259
Greiffenhagen, Maurice 85, 183, 225
Gribbell, Florance Truscott 243, 246, 286,
    293, 324, 354
Grindrod, Dr: hydropathic clinic 227–8
Guardian Fire and Life Assurance 62–3,
    64, 65, 91, 110
Guibert, Denis: Mémoires pour servir à
    l'histoire de . . . Dieppe 332
Guilbert, Yvette 154, 288n

Gurney, Revd Alfred 56, 57, 64, 65, 70,
    77, 105, 167
Gurney, Edmund 56, 57
Gurney, Helen 57
Gurney, Mrs Russell 56
Gurney, Willie 56
Guthrie, James 136, 141
Guys, Constantin 96, 229

Halifax, Lord and Lady 56
Hamilton Lodge, Hurstpierpoint 16–18
Hardy, Dudley 85, 183, 212, 225
Harland, Aline 136, 139, 152, 169, 170,
    203, 245
Harland, Henry: friendship with AB 136,
    145, 152, 154; and The Yellow Book 146,
    169–79, 190–91, 192, 193, 197, 198,
    199, 205, 211, 229; and AB's dismissal
    239, 242; writes tribute to AB 353;
    mentioned 203, 245, 358
Harris, Frank 149, 153
    My Life and Loves 217
Harsant, Dr 314, 318, 319, 320, 322
Hartrick, A. S. 199, 241
Hassall, John 183
Hawker, W. J. 318
Hawthorne, Nathaniel: Twice Told Tales 34
    Wonder Book 34
Heine, Thomas Theodore 358
Heinemann, William (publisher) 136, 229,
    265, 270, 339
    History of Dancing 325, 335
    New Review 212–13, 270
Henley, W. E. 107, 166
Henri, Père 328–9, 331
Henry & Co. (publishers) 199
Hermetic Students of the Golden Dawn
    274
Hichens, Robert: The Green Carnation
    215–16
Hind, C. Lewis 116, 117, 118, 119, 120,
    125, 126, 127, 128, 129, 131
Hind-Smith, W. W. 30–31, 32, 38, 43
Hirst, Damien 360
Hogarth Club, London 170–71, 172, 174,
    191
Hogg, Sylvia 66n
Holme, Charles 116, 117–18, 125, 281,
    288, 297

Hope, Anthony 203
Horler, Sidney 358
Horne, Herbert 252–3, 254, 266, 314
Horniman, Annie 183
Horton, W. T. 281, 299, 354n
Housman, Laurence 174
  Echo de Paris 334n
  'The Reflected Faun' 190
Huysmans, Joris-Karl 80, 152, 166, 170,
  202, 323
  À Rebours 79, 145

Idler, The 223, 308–309, 319, 348, 353, 356
Image, Selwyn 257, 266
Impressionists, English 66, 67, 68, 79, 94,
  102, 114, 126, 189
International Artistic Pictorial Poster
  Exhibition (1894) 225, 227
Irving, Henry 47, 54; AB's portraits 36,
  128, 165
Isis 194

Jackson, Charles Kains 151
James, Henry 172, 173, 191, 193, 198
Jarry, Alfred 324–5
  Ubu Roi 324
Jepson, edgar 266–8
  Memoirs of a Victorian 250n
Johnson, Lionel 148, 193, 202, 221, 321,
  358
Johnson, Robert 336, 339
Jones & Evans (bookshop) 63, 64, 99, 191
Jonson, Ben: Volpone 269, see under
  Beardsley, Aubrey
Joventut (journal) 358n
Juvenal 221, 229
  'Against Women' 294–5
  'Sixth Satire' 298

Kandinsky, Wassily 358
Keats, John 59, 69, 213–14
Keighley, T. Dove 132, 135
Kelmscott Press 77, 97, 98, 108, 111
King, Arthur William: at Brighton
  Grammar School 30n, 31, 32, 34, 36,
  38–9, 40, 43, 48, 50n, 55; at Blackburn
  Technical Institute 57, 319; advises AB
  59, 82; on AB 62; sells AB's pictures
  77, 87; publishes The Bee 88; dines with

AB 202; AB's letters to 54, 58, 72–3,
  74, 86, 87, 88, 91, 92, 102, 110, 134
Kipling, Rudyard 239
Klafsky, Katharina 105, 208
Klee, Paul 358
Kyllmann, Otto 115

Laclos, Pierre: Les Liaisons Dangereuses 305,
  307
Lady, The 235
Lait, William 8
Lamarre, Dr Edouard 329–30, 331
Lamb, Alexander 7
Lamb, David Imlach 12
Lamb, David Wright 12
Lamb, George 47
Lamb, George Henry 4, 7, 12
Lamb, Georgiana (née Lamb) 4, 12, 47
Lamb, Henry Alexander 12
Lampson, Mr (schoolmaster) 43
Lancret, Nicholas 261, 295
Lane, John: founds The Bodley Head
  115–16; meets AB 116; and Salome
  128–9, 135, 150, 160–61, 162; and
  Rothenstein 147, 153; and The Yellow
  Book 170–72, 173, 175–6, 177, 187,
  189, 191, 192, 193, 197, 205, 211;
  wants a monopoly on AB's work
  199–200; and Venus and Tannhäuser
  210, 254, 259; 'divorces' Elkin Mathews
  221; at Windermere with AB 228; visits
  US 234, 236, 238; and Wilde furore
  238, 239, 241, 242, 265; rejects
  Symons's poems 251; a 'blaze up' with
  Mathews 265; allows illustrations for
  Book of Fifty 296, 297; and Olive
  Custance 337; and posthumous
  publication of AB's work 355; death
  359; mentioned 198n, 203, 248
Lang, Andrew 326n
Laposture, Father Charles de 304
Lautrec, Gabriel 276–7, 278, 280
Lawrence, Arthur 308n
Lawrence, D. H. The White Peacock 359
Lawrence & Bullen 120, 154
Le Gallienne, Richard 180, 191, 194, 236,
  239, 337; as 'Logroller' 276, 180
Leighton, Sir Frederick 133, 175, 176, 191,
  198, 210

Le Sage, Alain: *Gil Blas* 33, 33n
Leverson, Ada 149; and AB 149, 201, 217;
  Punch spoofs 153, 233–4, 277; at
  première of *Importance of Being Earnest*
  235–6; and Wilde 241, 245; toys with
  conversion 245; and Raffalovich 248;
  mentioned 197, 203, 233, 237, 270,
  281
  'The Scarlet Parasol' 249
Leyland, Frederick 70, 76, 98
Liberty, Lazenby 133
Libre Esthétique, Le (art-group) 181, 234
Liszt, Franz 254, 260
Livre, Le 323
Livre et l'Image Le (periodical) 151
London County Council 265
London Figaro 134
Lorrain, Jean 79, 280, 280n, 295
Louÿs, Pierre: *Aphrodite* 238
Lucian: *Comic Voyage* 120–21, 154
Lugné-Poe, Aurélien 280
Lundberg, Ada 165
Luzzani, Abbé 346, 349

McCarthy, Justin 119
MacColl, D. S. 120, 130, 132, 136, 137,
  140–41, 144, 145, 146, 163, 167, 169,
  173, 265n, 356, 358
Macdonald sisters, the 357
MacFall, Haldane 250, 316, 359
Machen, Arthur 249, 252
  The Three Imposters 249
Mackintosh, Charles Rennie 357
Maeterlinck, Maurice 166
Magazine of Art 66, 92, 107, 118, 132
  'Aubrey Beardsley and the Decadents'
  (Armour) 307–308
  'The Art Movement. "Jugend" ' (White)
  357
Mallarmé, Stéphane 80, 142, 166
Mallock, W. H.: *The New Republic* 295
Malory, Sir Thomas: *Morte Darthur* 77, *see
  under* Beardsley, Aubrey
Manchester Guardian 288
Mansfield, Richard 314
Mantegna, Andrea 73n, 76, 81, 95, 103
  'The Triumph of Caesar' 72, 76
Mapplethorpe, Robert 360
Marshall, Ebenezer J. 28–29, 32, 33, 36,

38, 43, 48, 49, 55, 61n, 69, 78, 99, 115,
  135, 319n
Marshall, 'Mr Sam' (schoolmaster) 43
Marzials, Theo 192
Mathews, Elkin 115, 128, 144, 171, 176,
  183, 186, 191, 221, 229, 265–6
Matisse, Henri 358
Mattos, Alexander Teixera de 266
Maud, Princess Charles of Denmark 288
May, Phil 126, 137, 299
Meier-Graefe, Julius, 225, 254
Mendès, Catulle 79
Menter, Sophie 260
Menton, France 341–2, 344
Meredith, George 115, 116
  The Shaving of Shagpat 115, 116
Mermaid Series, the 34, 37, 47, 54
Merry England (periodical) 116
Metropolitan Magazine (New York) 288
Meynell, Alice 116–17, 238, 239
Meynell, Wilfred 116
Millais, Sir John Everett 127
  'Eve of St Agnes' 70
Mir Iskusstva (*The World of Art*) 358
Mitford, A. B.: *Tales of Old Japan* 34
Modern Art (periodical) 196
Monet, Claude 132
Moore, George 80, 102, 119, 120, 131,
  161, 192, 193, 197, 250n, 266, 268,
  289
  Esther Waters 192
  Impressions and Opinions 78, 80
Moreau, Gustave 152, 164, 165
  'Sappho' 244
Morning Leader 152
Morning Post 210
Morris, William 6, 66, 67, 68, 93, 97, 98,
  117, 119, 121–2, 128, 189, 357;
  Kelmscott Press 77, 97, 98, 107, 111
  A Dream of John Ball 108
  Earthly Paradise 77
Mucha, Alphonse 357

Nabis School 205
National Observer 107, 193, 194, 195, 223,
  268, 338
NEAC *see* New English Art Club
Nettleship, J. T. 173
New English Art Club 66, 69, 82, 114–15,

132, 137, 149, 163, 174, 189, 195, 199, 226, 241, 256

New Lyric Club, London 273

New Review 212, 270

'The Art of the Hoarding' (Beardsley) 212–13

New Westminster Brewery 11, 12

New York Times 241n

Newlyn School of Painting 133

Nicholls, H. S. 281, 282

Norman, Henry 192, 195

Nutt, David 247, 248

O'Neill, Norman 96

Orchmans, Father 348, 351

O'Sullivan, Vincent 283, 285, 286, 297, 304, 334, 338, 347

  Aspects of Wilde 214n

  The Houses of Sin 335

Pageant, The 270, 298

Pall Mall Budget (weekly magazine) 125, 126, 127–8, 129, 131, 143, 196, 199, 208, 211

Pall Mall Gazette 128, 134, 187, 274, 338

Pall Mall Magazine 132, 135, 144

Palmer, G. H. 56, 57

Pan (periodical) 254

Parade, The 298

Pargeter, A. G. 62, 63, 73n

Parkinson, William 85

Partridge, Bernard 85

Pascal, Blaise 315–16

Past and Present (school magazine) 29, 35, 40, 65, 353

Pater, Walter 79, 165, 180, 210, 219, 295

  'Imaginary Portrait' 164

  Studies in the History of the Renaissance 111

Payne, H. A. (schoolmaster) 36, 37, 43, 50n, 55, 135, 319n, 353

Payne, E. H. 50

Pelham, Lady Henrietta 16, 20

Pelham, Hon. T. H. W. 29

Pelican (magazine) 184

Pennell, Elizabeth 120, 134, 135, 140, 192, 193, 203, 307, 334

Pennell, Joseph 118; meets AB 118–20; writes 'A New Illustrator' 120, 132–3, 134; dislikes AB's journalistic efforts 128; with AB in France 134, 135, 136, 137,

139, 260; introduces AB to Whistler 141, 142; offers AB an 'etching lesson' 165; and *The Yellow Book* 174–5, 190, 191; establishes the Society of Illustrators 179; contributes to *The Savoy* 256, 281; asks AB to contribute to LCC anthology 265; witnesses Whistler's admiration of the 'Rape' drawings 278; calls on AB in Dieppe 334; publishes tribute to AB 353; mentioned 203, 297, 307

  Pen Drawing and Pen Draughtsmen 118

Peters, Margot: *Mrs Pat* 196n

Phillips, Dr 322, 331, 335

Photographers' Salon (1894) 223, 253

photo-mechanical reproduction process 106, 107, 212

Picasso, Pablo 358n

Pick-me-up (comic paper) 146

Pierrot 80–81, 146, 186, 265–6

Pimlico, London 18–19

  32 Cambridge St 53

  114 Cambridge St 144–5, 249

  59 Charlwood St 65–6, 86

  57 Denbigh St 18n

  St Barnabas 56

Pinero, Sir Arthur Wing: *The Second Mrs Tanqueray* 182, 189

Pitt, Florence *see* Schenkel, Florence

Pitt, Mary 3, 4, 5, 11, 12

Pitt, Sarah 5, 22, 25–26, 28, 47, 68, 87

Pitt, Susan (*née* Lamb) 3, 4, 5, 6–7, 11, 12, 47, 333

Pitt, Thomas Best 4

Pitt, William, the Younger 33n, 264

Pitt, Surgeon-Major William 3, 4–5, 7, 9, 10, 11, 12, 14, 47

PMB see Pall Mall Budget

Poe, Edgar Allan 33, 167, 199, 204

Pollitt, Jerome 253, 295, 301, 304, 317–18, 319, 320, 325, 336, 339, 344, 348, 350, 355

Pope, Alexander 160

'Rape of the Lock' 269, 270, *see under* Beardsley, Aubrey poster design/designers 69, 102–103, 164, 183–4, 211–12, 225

Powell, York 229

Poynter, Sir Edward 62–3, 127

Prendergast, Dr 325, 331

Pre-Raphaelites 38, 66–7, 69, 70, 77, 79, 94, 100, 102, 112, 115, 127–8, 203, 308; *see also* Burne-Jones; Morris; Rossetti

Prince's Ladies Gold Club, Mitcham, Surrey 199

Prud'hon, Pierre Paul 305–306

Public Opinion 163

Punch 36, 78*n*, 153, 182, 184, 186, 193, 195, 223, 226, 227, 230, 233–4, 246, 249, 277

Puvis de Chavannes, Pierre 103, 136, 142

Queensberry, Marquess of 216, 236, 237

Quilp, Jocelyn (pseud.): *Baron Verdigris* 199

Quilter, Harry 131
'The Gospel of Intensity' 248

Rachilde 79, 324, 326

Raffalovich, Marc André 243; and Wilde 243–4, 247–8; and Gray 244; meeting and friendship with AB 243, 244–5, 246–8, 250, 253, 268–9; received into Catholic Church 286, 316; and AB's *Lysistrata* drawings 293; and Smithers 294; generosity to AB 302, 306, 307; concerned with his spiritual well-being 304, 316; helps AB financially 310, 316, 317, 342; helps AB in France 322, 323, 324, 325; and AB and Wilde 333; AB's letters to 308, 309, 320, 321, 326, 328, 342, 344, 347, 359; mentioned 270, 277, 305, 306, 315, 327, 335, 354
L'Affaire Oscar Wilde 246, 269
Self-Seekers 268–9, 294
The Thread and The Path 247, 248
Uranisme et Unisexualité 310
L'Uranisme: Inversion Sexuelle Congénitale 246

Rambler, The 356

Ravenhill, Leonard 85, 126, 225

Read, Brian *Beardsley* 360

Redon, Odilon 99, 152

Reed, E. T. 227
'Britannia *à la* Beardsley' 229–30

Rehan, Ada 61

Réjane (actress) 165, 198, 204, 205, 234

Renoir, Pierre Auguste 255

Revue Belge 136

Rhymers' Club 148, 150, 183, 193, 273

Rhys, Ernest 174, 192

Ribera, Jusepe 80

Richards, Grant 204, 299, 358, 359

Richardson, Samuel 72

Richmond, W. B. 131

Ricketts, Charles 149, 158, 174, 197, 244, 356

Rivière, Father Félix Philpin de 315

Robertson, Mrs Ian 323, 328

Robertson, H. R.: *Handbook on Pendrawing* 36

Roques, Jules 201*n*, 225

Rolleston, T. W. 273

Ronald, Emma 11*n*, 13

Ronald, Landon 11*n*, 13

Rops, Félicien 152, 163, 180

Ross, Robert: friendship with AB 95, 105, 107, 135–6, 148, 153, 155, 204, 215; introduces him to Pennell 118, and MacColl 120; relationship with Wilde 134, 149, 237, 247; friendship with Ellen 154–5, 167, 290; and *The Yellow Book* 173; a Catholic convert 286; helps AB 287, 302; helps organize AB's memorial service 354; his *Volpone* 'Eulogy' 355, 359; AB's letters to 109*n*, 144, 162, 163, 306; mentioned 100, 102, 146, 151, 247, 289, 323
Aubrey Beardsley 30*n*, 71, 121, 150*n*, 350*n*

Rossetti, Dante Gabriel 27, 63–4, 68, 70, 74, 98, 103, 115, 214*n*, 299

Rothenstein, William 137; friendship with AB 137, 139, 147, 149–50, 153, 249, 250*n*, 253, 327; meets Beerbohm 148; gives AB book of Japanese erotica 162–3; exhibits 'Mr Beardsley' 163; and *The Yellow Book* 174, 178*n*, 190, 194; with AB at Shaw's *Arms and the Man* 204; and AB's work 219, 225; and Wilde 247; and *The Savoy* 256, 281; and *The Pageant* 298; draws AB 327; mentioned 149, 157, 189, 256, 299

Royal Institute Galleries, London 225

Royal Portrait Society exhibition (1895) 265

Ruding, Walt 265–6
An Evil Motherhood 265

Ruskin, John 67, 78, 79, 128, 226
Russell, George (AE) 274
Russell, Henry 11, 13
Russell, Lillian 222

Saint-Aubin, Charles de 164, 261
St Germain-en-Laye, France 327–30
St James's Restaurant ('Jimmies'), London 204
St James's Gazette 223
St Paul's (magazine) 146, 222, 223, 250, 316
Salon of the Champ de Mars, Paris 103, 136
Sambourne, Linley 78*n*, 227, 234
Sampson, Gerald 57
Sampson, Julian 57, 96, 165
Sand, George 255, 260
Sandys, Frederick 203, 256
 'Circe and the Swine' 203*n*
Sargent, John Singer 132, 205
 'Henry James' 198
Saturday Journal 107
Saturday Review 129*n*, 30, 181, 223, 288, 324, 356
Savoy, The (periodical) 256, 259, 261, 264, 266, 268 269, 273–6, 278; second 281, 288*n*; third 289, 292–3; fourth 292, 293; fifth 298–9; final 300, 301, 304, 308
Schenkel, Florence (*née* Pitt) 3, 4, 5, 12
Schenkel, Moritz 12
Schmidt, Paul (publisher) 129
Schwarbe, Carlos 137, 144
Scotson-Clark, Revd Frederick 35
Scotson-Clark, George: friendship with AB 35–6, 39, 44; and school plays 39–40; his drawings outclassed by AB's 48, 49; clerical work 55; shows AB Rossetti pictures 63; in AB's Old Boys' play 65; in Brighton with AB 68–9; composes cantata 77; calls on Watts with AB 82; sails to US 87; on AB 86, 201*n*, 235; AB's letters to 70, 74, 76, 81, 126, 128*n*
Scott, Edmund 6
Seaman, Owen 184, 186, 223, 268
Shakespeare, Olivia 192
Shannon, Charles 149, 174, 244, 256, 281
Shaw, G. Bernard 63, 203, 257, 266, 276

Arms and the Man 204
Shelley, Edward 239
Shelley, Lady 305
Shields, Frederic 87
Sickert, Bernhard 199
Sickert, Walter: at *Pall Mall Budget* 126; exhibits at NEAC 132; friendship with AB 149, 153, 213, 253, and his mother 167; and *The Yellow Book* 174, 192, 194, 199, 223; paintings of models 218; never parodied 227; his genius recognized by Blanche 255; and *The Savoy* 256, 281
 'Aubrey Beardsley' 211
 'Charley's Aunt' 221
 'The Future of Engraving' (article) 222*n*
Sime, Sidney 357
Singer Sewing Machines 212
Sketch, The 190–91, 194–5, 203*n*, 210, 249, 276, 327*n*
Sladen, Douglas 203, 299
Smith, W. H. (company) 192, 292–3, 299
Smithers, Alice 273, 275, 283, 285
Smithers, Jack 221*n*
Smithers, Leonard: 251–2; and AB 251, 252, 253; and *The Savoy* 252, 256, 257, 259, 265, 266, 268, 273, 281, 289, 300; suggests *Lysistrata* to AB 269–70; sodden evenings with AB 278; and *The Rape of the Lock* 278, 281, 287, 288–9, 322; in Paris with AB 278, 280; sells AB's books 259*n*, 281, 328; with AB in Brussels, 282, 283, 285; draws up AB's will 292; puts AB to work on *Ali Baba* 292; and Raffalovich 294; 317; and AB's illustration for Juvenal 294, 295; moves to Royal Arcade 296; suggests album of *Fifty Drawings* 296; 'no return' on his cheques 297, 298; translates Catullus 300; fortunes rise 304; and Dowson's *Pierrot* 305, 306; and 'Erda' drawing 308; and AB's letters 309–10; a leg ailment 315; visits AB in Bournemouth 318; and *Mademoiselle de Maupin* 320, 325, 337, 338–9; in Paris with AB 325–6; AB begins to doubt 330; and Wilde's 'Ballad of Reading Gaol' 333, 334; despairs of getting work out of AB 335; AB has further doubts 342; and

Smithers, Leonard – *cont.*
  Volpone 342, 344; plans new quarterly
  346, 347–8; asked by AB to destroy
  Lysistrata drawings 349, 350; issues AB's
  last drawings 355; from crisis to crisis
  355–6; death 356
Society of Illustrators 179
Society of Portrait Painters 281
Southwell, Robert: 'Burning Babe' 348
Spare, Austin Osman 357
Speaker 119, 193
Spectator 130, 132, 135, 163, 193
Spencer, Walter T. 107*n*
Spirit Lamp (undergraduate periodical) 148
Springer, Anton: *Dürer* 110
Stanlaws, Penrhyn 201*n*
Star 180, 194, 276, 277
Steer, Philip Wilson 126, 132, 149, 174,
  192, 199, 205, 223, 225, 241, 257
  'Ballerina Assoluta' 69
  'Skirt Dancing' 221
Steinlen, Théophile-Alexandre 225
Stephens, Reynolds: altar frontal 81
Stevenson, R. A. M. 133, 136, 141
Stone and Kimble (publishers) 167, 199
Stride, F. J. 39
Studio, The (periodical) 116, 117, 118; first
  number 133–4, 141, 175; AB's
  drawings 120, 125, 131, 132, 133,
  133–4, 152, 265, 297; reviews of AB's
  work 142–3, 179, 180, 181, 183*n*, 184,
  221–2, 225, 288; competition entries
  226
Sullivan, Sir Arthur 54
Sullivan, E. J. 199
Sullivan, Henry 126
Sunday Times 276
Sunday Times-Herald (of Chicago) 277
Swan Electric Engraving Company 176,
  242, 339
Swift, Jonathan 33, 37
Swinburne, Algernon Charles 96, 157, 210,
  315
  Study of Ben Jonson 345
Symbolists 103, 128, 141–2, 144, 166, 326
Symes-Thompson, Dr Edmund Symes 58,
  136, 227, 287, 289, 322
Symons, Arthur: his 'decadentism' 150–1,
  152, 165–7, 172, 189, 191, 218; meets

AB 149, 151; influences Smithers
  251–2; in Dieppe 252, 254, 255; and
  The Savoy 256–7, 260, 266, 273, 275,
  281, 283, 289, 292–3, 299, 300;
  strained relations with AB 277;
  introduces AB to Yvette Guilbert 288*n*;
  writes critique of AB 353; mentioned
  263, 301, 356
  'Credo' 221
  'The Decadent Movement in Literature'
  165–7
  London Nights 251–2
  Silhouettes 150
  'A Symbolist Farce' 324
Syrett, Netta 173, 191, 202

Tannhäuser myth, the 208, 210
Taylor, Sir Henry 305
Terrell, C.: 'Aubrey Beardsley' 353–4*n*
Terry, Ellen 54
Thackeray, William: *The Rose and the Ring*
  34
Thalia, the (supper club), London 253,
  278, 294, 314
Thaulow, Fritz 255, 332, 333
Theosophy Society 274
Thomas, Brandon 203, 208, 236, 245, 299
  The Queen of Brilliants adaptation 222
Thompson, Francis 116
Thompson (Robert A.) & Co. (publishers)
  177
Thomson, George 223
Thornton, Alfred 132, 145, 173, 192, 199
Thornton, Revd C. G. 47, 93–4
Times, The 80, 180, 193, 194, 244–5, 276,
  288
Tinan, Jean de 327
Tit-bits 60
To-Day (newspaper) 208, 212, 223
  'A New Master of Art: Mr Aubrey
  Beardsley' 200–201, 261
Todhunter, Dr John 183
  A Comedy of Sighs 183, 184, 186, 204
  Sicilian Idyll 183
Tomorrow (magazine) 316
Toulouse-Lautrec, Henri de 103, 137, 183,
  189, 225, 357
Towle, Mrs 305
Townsend, F. H. 242

Toynbee Hall, London 111
Turner, Reggie: Beerbohm's letters to 149,
    188, 228n
Tynan, Katharine 194

Umbria, SS 238
Underhill, Wilhemina 259
Unwin, T. Fisher (publisher) 164, 211–12
    Pseudonym and Autonym Library 211,
    225
Uzanne, Octave 323, 327

Vacossin, Abbé 323
Vale, the, London 148–9
Vallance, Aymer: visits AB 93–4; shows
    off his new discovery 94–5, 97, 98;
    delighted with AB's Morte Darthur
    drawings 111–12; introduces AB to
    Lane 115, 116, and Hind 116–17;
    shows Morte drawings to Morris 121–2;
    on AB 143; ..elps AB with house
    decoration 144–5; disappointed in AB
    156, 219; contributes to The Yellow
    Book 199; blames Lane for AB's
    predicament 249; asked to produce
    'Iconography' of AB's drawings 296;
    last meeting with AB 322; publishes
    tribute to AB 353; mentioned 102, 105,
    114, 118, 155, 247, 286
Vallotton, Félix 205
Vanity Fair 195
Verlaine, Paul 80, 137, 150, 152, 165, 166,
    167, 202
Victoria & Albert Museum: Beardsley
    exhibition 359–60
Villiers de L'Isle-Adam, Auguste, Comte
    de 166
Virgil: Aeneid 37
Vuillard, Edouard 164

Wagner, Revd Arthur Douglas 6, 26, 27
Wagner, Richard 56, 57n, 207–208, 217,
    301–302
    Götterdämmerung 105
    Lohengrin 208
    Das Rheingold 298, 301, 308
    Tannhäuser 105, 208
    Tristan und Isolde 141, 208
    Die Walküre 208

Siegfried 208
Walker, R. A. 359
Ward, Mrs Humphry 238
Watson, William 228n, 238, 239
Watteau, Antoine 164–5, 202, 261, 295,
    310
Watts, G. F. 82, 157n
Waugh, Arthur 175, 176
Wedmore, Frederick 195, 257
Weekly Irish Times 194
Weintraub, Stanley: Aubrey Beardsley . . .
    360
'Weird', the (fortune-teller) 208
West, C. T. 38
West India & Panama Telegraph Company
    11
Westminster Aquarium: Poster Exhibition
    (1894) 225, 227
Westminster Gazette 130, 194, 195, 212n
Westminster School of Art 82, 83, 85–6,
    102, 114
Whibley, Charles 136, 338
Whistler, James McNeill: influence on AB
    66, 70–71, 77–8, 81, 98, 99, and
    Wilde 79; dandyism 96, 97; portrayed
    and lampooned by AB 112, 127; and
    Rothenstein 137; early encounters with
    AB 141–2; and AB's Yellow Book
    drawings 187, 188, 200; 'Aubrey – you
    are a very great artist' 278; avoids AB
    in Dieppe 334; a belated tribute to AB
    355; mentioned 129, 136, 226, 256
    The Gentle Art of Making Enemies 78
    'Ten O'Clock Lecture' 67–8, 78
Whistler, Trixie (Beatrice) 187, 200
White, Gleeson 57n, 119, 125–6, 128, 131,
    151, 184, 222, 298, 353
    'The Art Movement, "Jugend" ' 357
White, Mrs Gleeson: 'At Homes' 128n,
    198, 205
Whitehall Review 194
Wilde, Constance 73, 74, 348
Wilde, Cyril, 73, 74, 75n
Wilde, Lady 97
Wilde, Revd Oscar Wade 57
Wilde, Oscar: on AB 1, 214n; views on art
    78–80; dandy's pose 96, 97; and AB
    131–2, 135; homosexual relationships
    134; and Beerbohm 148; and Ricketts

Wilde, Oscar – *cont.*
　149; and AB's 'pictorial pranks' 157–8,
　160, 241*n*; chooses Douglas's *Salome*
　translation 161–2; excluded from *The*
　Yellow Book 171, 176, 197; introduces
　AB to Mrs Patrick Campbell 182; as
　subject of Beerbohm's 'Peep into the
　Past' 187; buys AB's portrait of Mrs Pat
　196; portrayed in *The Green Carnation*
　215–16; at the première of *The*
　Importance of Being Earnest 235–6; arrest
　and trials 236, 237, 245, 248; and AB's
　career 237–9, 249, 263, 264; and
　Raffalovich 243–4, 247–8, 286; arrives
　at Dieppe 333; snubbed by AB 334;
　mentioned 102, 107, 152, 153, 234,
　322, 336, 346
　'The Ballad of Reading Gaol' 333
　An Ideal Husband 235, 263
　The Importance of Being Earnest 235
　Intentions 78, 79, 80
　The Picture of Dorian Gray 78, 99
　Salome 128–9, 157, 161–2, 221, 280,
　288, *see under* Beardsley, Aubrey
　A Woman of No Importance 131, 149,
　215
Wilde, Vyvyan 73, 74, 75*n*, 348

Willette, A. L. 164, 225
Williamson, Father 241
Willis's restaurant, London 236
Winwar, Frances: *Oscar Wilde and the*
　Yellow Nineties 263*n*
Wise, Miss (schoolmistress) 16, 17
Woman's World 107
World, (New York) 277
Wratislaw, Theodore 151–2, 163, 165,
　166, 172, 180–81, 218, 252
　'Salome of St James' 221

Yeats, W. B. 121, 148, 167, 183, 192, 219,
　220, 257, 264, 273, 274–5, 299, 324
　'Blake as an Illustrator of Dante' 293
　The Land of Heart's Desire 304
　The Shadowy Waters 304, 306
　'Upon a Dying Lady' 356
Yellow Book, The: first 169–79, 186–201;
　second 204, 210–11, 212; third
　215–16, 221–3; fourth 229, 233–4;
　fifth 239, 241–3

Zimern, Helen: 'Angels in Art' 87
Zola, Emile 59, 80, 136, 170, 257;
　Beardsley's portrait 128
　Rome 307